Prehistories of the Future

# CULTURAL SITINGS

Elazar Barkan, Editor

# Prehistories of the Future

## The Primitivist Project and the
## Culture of Modernism

EDITED BY

## Elazar Barkan and Ronald Bush

STANFORD
UNIVERSITY
PRESS

Stanford,
California
1995

Stanford University Press
Stanford, California
© 1995 by the Board of Trustees of the
Leland Stanford Junior University
Printed in the United States of America

CIP data are at the end of the book

Stanford University Press publications are
distributed exclusively by Stanford University Press
within the United States, Canada, Mexico, and Central America;
they are distributed exclusively by Cambridge University Press
throughout the rest of the world

Prehistories of the future

# Cultural Sitings

*A series edited by Elazar Barkan*

CULTURAL SITINGS will present focused discussions of major contemporary and historical cultural issues by prominent and promising scholars, with a special emphasis on multidisciplinary and transnational perspectives. By bridging historical and theoretical concerns, CULTURAL SITINGS will develop and examine narratives which probe the spectrum of experiences that continuously reconfigure contemporary cultures. By rethinking chronology, agency, and especially the siting of historical transformation, the books in this series will go beyond disciplinary boundaries and notions of what is marginal and what is central to knowledge. By juxtaposing the analytical, the historical, and the visual, this challenging new series will provide a venue for the development of cultural studies and for the rewriting of the canon.

# Acknowledgments

This book would have been impossible without the generous effort of more people than can be named here. The project began as a conference jointly sponsored by the California Institute of Technology and the Claremont Graduate School Humanities Center. At Caltech, the support of David Grether, chairman of the Division of the Humanities and Social Sciences, and his administrative assistant, Susan Davis, was indispensable. Equally important were the organizational wizardry of Gina Morea and the patient follow-up of Anne Fenska and Barbara Di Palma. At the Claremont Graduate School, we thank the generosity of the history department, its chair, Robert Dawidoff, and the continuing support of the students who make such endeavors so rewarding.

We wish also to acknowledge the cooperation and help of a number of people who offered suggestions and comments but whose efforts are not represented in the volume's essays. James Clifford provided advice. John Sutherland's excellent talk on Jack London unfortunately was unavailable for publication. A sizable number of scholars from the Los Angeles area and elsewhere served as moderators, respondents, and instigators, including George Pigman, Jenijoy La Belle, Kevin Gilmartin, Cindy Weinstein, Margot Norris, Vincent Cheng, Daniel Tiffany, Lawrence Rainey, Sue Houchins, Judson Emerick, Rita Roberts, and Marc Redfield.

We especially wish to thank Stanford University Press, and in particular Muriel Bell, who encouraged the project at a very early stage and contributed to it in numerous ways. Later on, the help of Victoria Scott, Amy Klatzkin, and Peggy Berg guided the manuscript through production. Through its sponsorship of the Cultural Sitings series, launched to include this volume and others, Stanford University Press has made an invaluable contribution to interdisciplinary studies.

Finally, there are several people whose patience and encouragement make our work not only possible, but enjoyable: Marilyn and Charles Bush, Ady Barkan, and Pamela Smith. Thanks.

# Contents

Contents

# Contributors

ELAZAR BARKAN is Director of the Claremont Graduate Humanities Center and Associate Professor of History at the Claremont Graduate School. He is the author of *The Retreat of Scientific Racism*.

RONALD BUSH is Professor of Literature at the California Institute of Technology. He is the author of *The Genesis of Ezra Pound's "Cantos"* and *T. S. Eliot: A Study in Character and Style* and the editor of *T. S. Eliot: The Modernist in History*.

VINCENT CRAPANZANO is Distinguished Professor of Anthropology and Comparative Literature at the City University of New York. He is the author of *Hermes' Dilemma and Hamlet's Desire: On the Epistemology of Interpretation*; *The Hamadsha: A Study in Moroccan Ethnopsychiatry*; *Tuhami: Portrait of a Moroccan*; and *Waiting: The Whites of South Africa*.

ROBERT DAWIDOFF is Professor of History and Chair of the Graduate Faculty of History at the Claremont Graduate School. He is the author of *The Genteel Tradition and the Sacred Rage: High Culture Versus Democracy in Adams, James and Santayana* and *The Education of John Randolph*.

CHRISTOPHER HERBERT is Chair of the Department of English at Northwestern University. He is the author of *Trollope and Comic Pleasure* and *Culture and Anomie: Ethnographic Imagination in the Nineteenth Century*.

SIR FRANK KERMODE was formerly Edward VII Professor of English at Cambridge University. He is a Fellow of King's College, Cambridge, and the author of many books on modern subjects, including *The Sense of an Ending* and *History and Value*.

JULIA E. LISS is Assistant Professor of History at Scripps College.

JOSS LUTZ MARSH is Assistant Professor of English at Stanford University.

WENDY MARTIN is Professor of American Literature and American Culture and Chair of the English Department at the Claremont Graduate School. She is the Author of *An American Sisterhood*; *An American Triptych: The Lives and Work of Anne Bradstreet, Emily Dickinson, and Adrienne Rich*; and *We Are the Stories We Tell*. She is the editor of *Women's Studies: An*

*Interdisciplinary Journal* and an editor of the *Heath Anthology of American Literature*.

MICHAEL NORTH is Professor of English at the University of California, Los Angeles. He is the author of *The Final Sculpture: Public Monuments and Modern Poets; Henry Green and the Writing of His Generation;* and *The Political Aesthetic of Yeats, Eliot and Pound*.

ROBERT NYE is the Thomas Hart and Mary Jones Horning Professor in the Humanities at Oregon State University. He is the author of *The Origins of Crowd Psychology* and *Crime, Madness and Politics in Modern France*.

MARJORIE PERLOFF is Sadie Dernham Patek Professor of Humanities at Stanford University. She is the author of many books on modernism, including *The Poetics of Indeterminacy: Rimbaud to Cage; The Dance of the Intellect: Studies in the Poetry of the Pound Tradition; The Futurist Moment;* and *Radical Artifice*.

NANCY PERLOFF is Collection Development Specialist at the Getty Center for the History of Art and the Humanities.

MARIE-DENISE SHELTON is Associate Professor of French at Claremont McKenna College. Her articles on modern French, Caribbean, and African literature have appeared in critical anthologies and in such journals as *The French Review, Caribbean Review, Présence Africaine, Présence Francophone, Callaloo,* and *World Literature Today.* Her book on Haitian literature was published in 1993.

CHRISTOPHER B. STEINER is Curator of Anthropology at the Natural History Museum of Los Angeles County and on the faculty at the University of Southern California and the University of California, Los Angeles.

VIRGINIA-LEE WEBB is Archivist of the Photograph Collection in the Department of the Arts of Africa, Oceania, and the Americas at the Metropolitan Museum of Art, New York.

Prehistories of the Future

# Introduction

In the 1890's, British, French, and German imperialism ransacked West Africa, each country hurrying to grab another share of the warm part of the globe. For them Africa was the "Dark Continent" that, under the banner of Social Darwinism, it was their duty to emancipate and redeem. In fact, the darkness projected all too many European horrors. Then, in the midst of the "savagery" they expected and provoked—human sacrifices in Benin, for example, reported by the British press to have depopulated an entire city—the British encountered exquisite indigenous art, treasure which they immediately looted. The British subjugated the Edo people of Benin while they were appropriating their culture, and a new fad, "primitive art," swept Europe. Meanwhile, Istekeri neighbors of the Edo "served" the British even as they misinformed their unknowing masters and gained innumerable advantages within the sphere of local politics. Many, both Europeans and Africans, believed they were beneficiaries of what had transpired. Many more, we currently believe, were victims. Whose voices should we listen to? According to which authority can we decide? [1]

In the realm of "aesthetics," the questions the Benin expedition raised are just as difficult. The Benin bronzes looted by the British, it turned out, incorporated fifteenth- and sixteenth-century Portuguese models. But at the same time it also became clear that other figures in Western museums were not, as had been previously thought, exquisite examples of medieval Western walrus carving but African ivories. Forced to reclassify the ivories, European scholars could not deny their beauty, although they ascribed it to the influence of medieval European models. Yet their initially reluctant appreciation of Benin objects was in the end revolutionary. Not only did it provide a whole new aesthetic category for European connoisseurs but (more importantly) a new idiom for Western art. In hindsight, the looting and its aftermath underline the fundamental instability of easy distinctions between the "savage" and the "civilized" and suggest the kind of ambiguous appropriation associated with modernism: a mixture of violence and aestheticism; the difficulties

1

of placing and displacing the modern and the primordial; the conflation of the past and the future.

As for "primitives," they never existed. Only Western "primitivism" did, invented in heated arguments about human society, like the ones that swirled around Darwin's 1859 *On the Origin of Species* and Henry Maine's 1861 *Ancient Law*. We now consider "primitive" a fighting word. Like "savage," it is a racist designation. In contrast, primitivism denotes an Occidental construction, a set of representations whose "reality" is purely Western.[2]

Still a powerful fixture of contemporary Western thought, the primitivism produced by Europe in the latter half of the nineteenth century supplied the necessary "Other" against whose specter embattled Victorian society reinforced itself. This construction was the defensive expression of a specific moment of crisis — the prehistory of a future whose unsettling shadow had just crossed the horizon. Late nineteenth- and early twentieth-century social theorists were haunted by this impending cultural transition. Max Weber pondered the nature of rationality, its manifestation in bureaucracy, and the resulting disenchantment of the world. Emile Durkheim focused on the change from mechanical to organic forms of solidarity. As these and other theorists searched for the ills of modern society, their ideal types approximated the polarized ideals of the primitive and the civilized.[3] A similar shift occurred in the history of art. Previously, when art historians spoke of the "primitive," they usually had in mind the "naive" style of Pre-Raphaelite and Colonial American painting — that is, artifacts of the West's own childhood. In the late nineteenth century, however, primitive painting came increasingly to connote the geographically exotic "savage" — the violence and energy of the barbaric — even as violence was beginning to receive its "positive" modern spin. Not surprisingly, perhaps, the neo-primitivist painters in France were branded Fauves — wild beasts.

Primitivism by then had a long prehistory of its own. The more we know about it, the earlier and more diffuse its origins seem. Christopher Herbert demonstrates, in *Culture and Anomie: Ethnographic Imagination in the Nineteenth Century*,[4] that before the mid-nineteenth century its themes had colored representations of the "savage" urban poor and had decisively affected Henry Mayhew's influential *London Labour and the London Poor* (1851–62). Long before that, primitivism had been shaded by ideological themes ranging from "the barbarous" to "the noble savage" in Western art, literature, and philosophy. As Christopher Steiner demonstrates in his essay below, in paintings and in travel illustrations dating to the late Renaissance (and as far back as antiquity), certain Western constructions recur: scenes of cannibalism or human sacrifice, scenes of exaggerated piety, scenes of serpentine and seemingly mindless processions, and scenes of merriment focused on drumming and dancing. Embedded in the Occidental unconscious, these scenes were reproduced in countless verbal and visual imaginations over hundreds of years. Steiner shows, however, that when the noble savage was overshadowed in Western writing by a barbarous or simply "savage" kin, the primitive achieved new power to condition and inform such constructions as Durkheim's 1912 formulation of primordial religion in *The Elementary Forms of the Religious Life*. Orgiastic dancing and drumming of the kind that Durkheim describes had been a constant in representations of peasantry and non-Western culture from the seventeenth to the twentieth century. When the late nineteenth and early twentieth centuries reimagined a "primitive" world, this long-standing trope, with its overtones of lasciviousness, became a highly charged signal of otherness — one that came to signify modernity.

Drawing on its storehouse of cultural images, the nineteenth century also inflected primitivism toward the violent politics of imperialism. But problems arise when we try to specify which politics. Just as Benin's indigenous politics were complicated by neighboring populations scheming to direct Britain's intervention, so politics in London, Paris, Berlin, and Washington were far more conflicted than the phrase "the white man's burden" now suggests. On the one hand, the self-serving function of the ideology that joined investigating savagery and justifying imperialism must be acknowledged. "Savages" needed to be civilized, and the Europeans believed that a natural component of that civilizing was extending European markets to colonized populations. On the other hand, Europeans could not get too close to the non-Western world without exposing the contradictions of the West's own intellectual and economic practices. A case in point can be found in Ronald Bush's essay below: at the 1904 St. Louis World's Fair, over a thousand "primitive" Filipinos were assembled in a "native village" on the advice of William Howard Taft, previously governor of the Philippines and then Secretary of War. Taft thought that viewing the primitive conditions of Filipino tribes would help rally support for the U.S. intervention in the Philippines and overcome public suspicion of America's imperialist adventure. But as it happened, an overenthusiastic construction of "savagery" in the form of so many unclad "natives" threatened to suggest that the Filipinos might be *too* wild for America to civilize, and led voters to think that the U.S. had no business being in the Philippines. An order was sent from Washington that the Filipino "natives" immediately be issued silk pants. As the political cartoon re-

# ᴛ THE PHILIPPINE RESERVATION.

FIG. 1. Satiric cartoon, 1904. Reprinted from Tatsushi Narita, "T. S. Eliot's 'The Man Who Was King' and Some Cross-Cultural Documentary Evidence," *Studies in Social Sciences and Humanities*, Nagoya City University, Nagoya, Japan, 34 (March 1990): 71–87. Courtesy the Missouri Historical Society.

produced in Fig. 1 demonstrates, the order became a great joke (to all, that is, but the Filipinos, who sickened in the heat of unfamiliar garments and an unfamiliar climate). The natives' authenticity, newspapers protested, had been compromised by Western garb. At the risk of weakening the force of the American imperial argument, then, the order was finally rescinded, but not before the emperor Roosevelt's own new clothes had been displayed for all to see.

At the same exposition, meanwhile, not only did Max Weber lecture (he had just finished *The Protestant Ethic and the Spirit of Capitalism*), but a sixteen-year-old boy named Thomas Stearns Eliot, the son of the man who clipped and preserved the political cartoon just mentioned, became fascinated with the Filipinos, especially with tableaux vivants of "native dancing," and began a lifelong study of anthropology that revolutionized European poetry. Once again, though, we might question the story's real beginnings and its political point. Did Eliot's response to the dancing have to do simply with the condescending framework of the exhibition, or did it perhaps draw on ambiguous representations by then several centuries old? And did the "primitivism" of Eliot's later work replicate the repressive imperialist ideology of the St. Louis Exposition, or did it utilize the liberating freedom of non-Western rhythms inadvertently made available in the new cultural space? Most likely, Eliot's encounter opened a field of contestation in which Western cultural practices were simultaneously replicated and subverted. Nor was his pattern unique.

At the turn of the century, academic anthropology was just emerging from its own adolescence, trying at once to establish a code of professional practices and to integrate a flood of destabilizing images. Attempting to systematize massive amounts of raw data from Africa, Australia, the Pacific islands, and Southeast Asia, anthropological narratives were riven by contradictions. For example, while "mainline" anthropologists at the Smithsonian were energetically reproducing an evolutionist paradigm in which "savage" society was the forerunner of civilization, other anthropologists had already begun to explicate the Enlightenment relativism of the discipline's intellectual premises. Conventional histories of anthropology notwithstanding, this acknowledgment of cultural pluralism did not wait for a shift from armchair anthropology to fieldwork. The foundational procedures of even armchair practitioners already included the seeds of an unspoken and sometimes dizzying relativism. As Christopher Herbert shows, Sir James Frazer, who in important ways remained a quintessential Victorian writer well into the twentieth century, shared the revolutionary dislocations of Einstein despite himself. In Herbert's words,

Frazer expressed only hostility toward the new theoretical physics, and he specifically ridiculed the collapsing together of space and time by Einstein. Nonetheless, Frazerian anthropology and relativity physics can be seen to take their departures from a single interpretive problem: the differing perceptions of natural and other phenomena by observers standing in what Einstein calls different coordinate systems.... Frazer's own terrestrial and comparatist anthropology hinges on this same relativism, adopting toward it, at times, the attitude of epistemological skepticism.

This sequence illustrates the slippery ways in which early modernist texts were transmitted and the poignant frequency with which they contradicted the intentions of their authors. Both Einstein and Frazer objected to being called relativists, as did turn-of-the-century social theorists like Durkheim and Franz Boas. Yet their writing has grounded much of the modernist enterprise.

On the other hand, even after field-oriented anthropology had begun to make Frazer seem outdated, implicit belief in the gap between "savage" and "high" civilization continued. Perhaps more insidious, this was frequently translated into an admiration of "savage" energy or solidarity that did not leave the primitive any less an Other. And being Other, the savage continued to function as a projection of what was both desired and feared in the Western unconscious. Thus Lucien Lévy-Bruhl wrote in *How Natives Think* (1926; *Les Fonctions mentales dans les sociétés inférieures*, 1910) of the often remarkable distinctions between primitive and civilized mental processes, yet also showed how attractive primitive irrationality could be to a modern, alienated intellectual. Lévy-Bruhl's mentor, Emile Durkheim, along with Durkheim's nephew and follower, Marcel Mauss, feared and were spellbound by the power of this irrationality and the way it empowered social groups. Durkheim, as Vincent Crapanzano shows in his essay, posited a complex mental terrain of primitive ritual observance that functions as "an explanation of how society can create and hold illusions." Mauss explicated this by writing of mana as "pure efficacy" — something, Crapanzano points out, that "resists reference, for it operates outside of reference at that asymptotic moment, both in and out of time, that is for Mauss the climax of the magic rite, the moment of prestidigitation, the moment where wish and realization are one." The mana-like fixations of the modern group posed considerable concern "to both the dandies and the sérieux" of the fin-de-siècle, who expressed fascination and revulsion with proto-fascist crowds:

Referring to the Australian aborigines, that most primitive of societies, Durkheim is left blinded to the contemporary political implication of his analysis. Despite his overt political stance, which can hardly be called fascist, his analysis leads — or, perhaps more accurately, is a symptom of — the thought that was worked through (*verarbeitet*) during the decades of fascism that followed his death and that is still being worked through today. In combination with Mauss's theory of magic and illusion, Durkheim has offered us a picture of how the (ritual) crowd's excitement in its veneration of itself produces the effervescence, the mana, the power that converts illusion into reality.

Even Franz Boas, who, perhaps more than anyone else, demystified Western attitudes of superiority toward the primitive, was, as Julia Liss shows below, himself entwined in the modernist contradictions that grounded twentieth-century anthropology. Boas endowed first his students and then his profession with a reverence (in his words) for "the value of the anthropological method . . . [which] impresses us with the relative value of all forms of culture, and thus serves as a check to an exaggerated valuation of the standpoint of our own period, which we are only too liable to consider the ultimate goal of human evolution, thus depriving ourselves of the benefits to be gained from the teachings of other cultures and hindering an objective criticism of our own work." Yet Boas emerges in Liss's portrait as a man attracted to fieldwork as an extension of his previous efforts to be initiated into the romanticized solidarity of groups from which, as a German Jew, he had been excluded. His fieldwork was in part a search for virility. Just as, for example, he exulted in exhibiting a scar that he sometimes claimed was the result of a duel, so Boas took enormous pleasure in both partaking of and writing about his participation in a communal Eskimo meal of raw and bloody seal meat: "The Eskimo," he confided to his fiancée, "are sitting around me, their mouths filled with raw seal liver (the spot of blood on the back of the paper shows you how I joined in)."

It is "true," of course, that Boas ate the meat under all the appropriate auspices of anthropological distance, but even then he was immersing himself in the rituals and communal reinforcement of yet another close-knit group (anthropologists) and in yet another idealized affirmation of primitive solidarity. The communal meal of "raw" meat transports a quintessential modern to a sphere where civilization cannot take him — a place of exoticism, eroticism, virility, and bonding. The "magical" discourse of the primitive, as understood by the ethnographer, replicates itself in the ethnologist's discourse.

Anthropology, then, in both its juvenile and professional phases, comprehended a subtly historicized universalist theory of man and a set of practices that replicated the very values its most enlightened practitioners thought they had abandoned. What makes ethnographic discourse at the century's turn even more fascinating is that, try as it might, it never succeeded in being the culture's prime access to the primitive. From its beginnings it served as just one of several avenues for Europe's quickening intellectual interest. Europe had been conquering people for four centuries and had used representations of its subjugated peoples to mediate its repressed desires. But at the end of the nineteenth century, driven by internal impulses, this appropriation accelerated at a rate that was rivaled only by the pace of political expansionism and technological and social change. The intensity and volume of the West's curiosity, combined with the ease with which new technology brought its representations home, meant that imaginative and real spaces became enormously difficult to distinguish. The artifacts sent home to Europe from military and "scientific" expeditions, the travel engravings and photographs produced for European souvenir albums, the accounts of Europeans in the "field" — all these overwhelmed anthropological explications. Alternate and provisional accounts transformed both high cultural discourses like classical scholarship and popular formations like pulp fiction and the newly invented movies. Paradoxically, the pastoralism of these representations somehow re-inforced the mechanical power of the technology that transmitted them, so that the emerging early twentieth-century "modernist" culture they shaped was inebriated by turns with the "savage" and the high tech, the past and the future.

We can get a feeling for the heterogeneity and the problematics of this process by considering the various channels of primitivist sitings (or citings) in the West, each involved with a particular discourse and a particular kind of representation. African, Australian, and Pacific materials entered Western society through "treasure" shipped back by colonial armies, "artifacts" "re-trieved" by anthropological expeditions, "artwork" imported by Western dealers and middlemen, and, perhaps most pervasively, photographs pro-duced for a public eager to fill their drawing-room souvenir albums. More-over, although it was initially assumed that "realistic" photographs, at least, must constitute unmediated transmission, it has become clear of late that even in this field things were never that simple. As Virginia-Lee Webb dem-onstrates, a combination of retouching and studio arrangements allowed co-lonial photographers to produce thousands of images that were silently "con-structed to convey European sentiments" about non-Western cultures. This instructive analysis of the technical doctoring of images in its turn provokes the question of whether there is any such thing as an authentic photograph or artifact. In other words, can we ever have a "realistic" photograph that "actually depicts a real event"? Nor is the situation very different with travel engravings and travel accounts, which, as Christopher Steiner shows, were shaped by centuries-old European conventions.

Sometimes "primitive" people themselves, rather than their images, be-came sites for representation. Since London's 1851 Crystal Palace Exhibi-tion, European expositions had included specimen populations of colonial peoples. At the Expositions Universelles of 1878 and 1889 in Paris, "native villages" were erected in which exotic peoples were presented in what amounted to zoological exhibits or tableaux vivants. And, as Nancy Perloff observes, during the 1889 exposition a great many people, including the painter Paul Gauguin, visited Javanese, Indian, and Tonkin villages and be-came enchanted with what they thought of as distant in time or space. Long before his actual travel, what would become Gauguin's Tahitian fantasies began in the midst of a domestic representation of the primitive, as did his unshakable impression that the natives of the French colonies lived without money and without toil, spending their time "carrying baskets, chiseling wood, making curios and artifacts," and tending their huts without signs of hardship or poverty. Did his confusion stem more from the cultural typologies adumbrated by Steiner or from the contemporary dislocation of the 1889 exposition? Or, as so often with modernist discontinuities, was his singularity a recontextualized instance of long-standing cultural images?

The ideological mix of pre–World War I representations was remarkably consistent from London to Paris to the United States. The villages were meant to show off the paternal generosity of the imperialist adventure yet underline the differences between savage and civilized life. In the 1901 Pan-American Exposition in Buffalo, New York, the displays were arranged to illustrate the "shift from the low levels of humanity to higher ones." And in St. Louis in 1904, we find some of the same configurations at work. Thus, when T. S. Eliot visited the Igorot section of the Philippine exhibition, it was "only natural" that, like Gauguin, he should be struck by demonstrations of indigenous dancing that had been encouraged by consulting the anthropologists and that were later memorialized in the official history of the fair. Should we be surprised at the similarities of response among Durkheim, Eliot, Gauguin, and countless others when a whole generation had been exposed to primitivism presented in almost identical venues? Hardly. Primitivism, after all, had become a road show, a public entertainment.

Nor did these showcases of "imported primitives" recede during the period between the wars. In Marie-Denise Shelton's essay on Michel Leiris, we discover that in 1931 colonialist self-advertisement had, if anything, become more florid. In that year the French government staged an Exposition Coloniale complete with African villages, mosques, pagodas, and "natives" of all sorts, while the American government did its part by displaying in the Washington pavilion its civilizing influences over Puerto Rico, Hawaii, Samoa, and Guam. "Spectators were invited to experience," Shelton writes, "the thrill and excitement of the 'jungle'" reconstructed through the efforts of "African and New Caledonian schoolteachers and civil servants [who] were enrolled to pose as 'authentic' savages."

If the native exhibits at the great world's fairs were at heart imperialist circuses, other venues for primitive materials could still seem respectable. With these, too, though, both the objectivity of the representation and the question of who controlled the discourse turn out to be quite complex. Take the case of museum exhibitions. In the 1890's, European museums reclassified primitive artifacts from curiosities to objects of either art or ethnography.

Yet the fin-de-siècle distinguished between the two only with difficulty, a difficulty that has lasted into the present. Michael North points out below that even when the distinctions had become provisionally established — in 1907, say, by which time some African sculpture had achieved the status of high art — the art obviously functioned as part of an ideologically charged and conflicted European representation. Witness the critics' inability to agree on what it was. According to North, "African art [was] portrayed as both abstract and naturalistic, highly conventional and thrillingly crude, opaque and yet more naked than any merely unadorned face. Such contradictions have survived even the most recent developments in cultural criticism."

As photographs and artifacts caused museums to redefine themselves, the same materials became building blocks for the newly professionalized disciplines of scientific and humanistic study. Anthropology, as we have seen, was the foremost of these, but primitivism also caused major reorganizations in Western writings on subjects as diverse as classical scholarship, social theory, psychology, and medicine. Classical studies, a field that had associated antiquity with the balance and composure of the eighteenth century, now preoccupied itself with violence and passion of gothic proportions. Such certainly was the case with Cambridge classicists such as James Frazer (see Christopher Herbert's essay). Freud's *Totem and Taboo* may be said to provide an emblem for the whole story. But, as Elazar Barkan points out, invoking the names of Edward Westermarck and Havelock Ellis, Freud was hardly alone: several generations of psychological and medical writers found their worlds turned upside down (or vastly enlarged) by the inescapable comparison of Western norms of rationality, behavior, and sexuality with non-Western counterparts.

Novelists, poets, painters, and musicians, whether in the sphere of high art, that of popular culture, or somewhere in between, also imported the primitive for their own purposes, whether through expropriated images or through the inflections of mediating discourses. Consider the cultural labor of "middlebrow" art. Robert Dawidoff's essay traces the cultural and political implications of the way African-American music was reappropriated and reframed by Irving Berlin. Dawidoff calls attention to the power of liminal agency for modernist appropriations. Just after the turn of the century, a new style in American popular song — "an appropriative Creole genre in which the conflicting claims of European and African traditions are settled in songs and unsettled in interpretations" — provided songwriters with an opportunity to subvert the autonomy of black and "normal" American culture alike. "This musical appropriation was an appropriation of the 'primitive' because of its sophistication, because the African diaspora had the ingredients to shake up the American, white, European normal," Dawidoff writes. New Americanisms were created by Berlin as part of "the Jewish project of making America more sophisticated, more hospitable, and more tolerant." Berlin was able to "plunder" classical African-American music "precisely because his black contemporaries could not, since white American culture was in no way prepared to grant agency or cultural identity to African Americans." At a time when whites had to go uptown to the immigrant outsider "to find the best band in the land," it was left to Berlin, who, as a "white black," could "understand the sentimental needs of cultures in formation," to invent the new American Creole.

Another representative of the new Creole sophistication was Josephine Baker, who exported this unsettling and ironic example of American popular culture from Harlem to Paris. As Wendy Martin demonstrates, Baker deployed "conventions of the burlesque to create a *danse sauvage* that played with the paradigm of the black exotic in the context of white colonialism." Clearly, Baker was simultaneously an agent and a victim of primitivist and gender stereotyping.

The mediations of the primitive in "highbrow" productions are examined by Nancy Perloff, Michael North, and Ronald Bush. Perloff reappraises the modernist parable of Gauguin's self-reinvention on the "primitive" island of Tahiti. She shows how Gauguin's images of the South Pacific were filtered through the conventions of French decadent art, then reinforced by the European / "native" pastiches of the 1889 Parisian Exposition Universelle. Gauguin's artistic persona denies both the story of "his rejection of the West and immersion in Tahitian superstition" and "his European vantage." Rather, Perloff argues, Gauguin's painting mediated "the distinctive overlay of European themes and values" and "a distant culture increasingly entangled in the colonialist enterprise." The result? A "complex fusion of decadence and colonialism."

North and Bush approach major twentieth-century figures whose transactions with the primitive are just as legendary as Gauguin's — and just as poorly understood. North's essay approaches the ethnic and racial implications of the primitive subject in Gertrude Stein's story *Melanctha*, showing how they reach out to subjects that include Picasso's celebrated discovery of African sculpture and Stein's familiarity with the black community in Baltimore. Bush looks at the primitivism of *The Waste Land* and contextualizes it by studying Eliot's philosophical engagement with anthropology, particularly with the writings of Lucien Lévy-Bruhl and Emile Durkheim. *The Waste*

*Land* reproduces the political contradictions of contemporary ethnography—at once conditioned by imperialist evolutionism and by skeptical relativism.

Michel Leiris, whose prose preserves all the original disciplinary confusions of the anthropological and colonial projects, provides a site for alternative contextualizations by Marie-Denise Shelton and Marjorie Perloff. These two approaches invite reflections about political and epistemological privileging. Perloff, as we shall see, chooses to regard Leiris's primary cultural field as French avant-garde art. Shelton sees Leiris's writing in the imperialist context of his participation in the 1931 Dakar-Djibouti Expedition commissioned by the French government to ransack West Africa for ethnographic treasure. Both point to issues crucial to any attempt to make sense of the history of primitivism, and of "encounters" between the West and its Other.

Marie-Denise Shelton dramatically highlights the reality of appropriation, points to the cost exacted when Europeans appropriated non-Western bodies, objects, images, and histories for Western cultural work, and focuses on those who paid the price. Both Michel Leiris's participation in the Dakar-Djibouti Expedition and his transformation of that experience in *L'Afrique fantôme* are replete with incidents of the brutal assertion of power. At a certain level, the issues could not be more straightforward: "When any resistance was met from the Africans, the response of the 'missionaries' was swift, surgical. The size of the object to be 'removed' from its legitimate owners in the name of scientific knowledge did not seem to act as a deterrent. . . . [Moreover,] the data-collection techniques used by the Dakar-Djibouti mission were not unusual schemes promoted by a derelict bunch. Quite to the contrary, Leiris and his friends . . . acted in conformity with the 'scientific' norms of the time, which celebrated the image of ethnologist as militant rogue." The same can be said of Leiris's appropriation of African experience in his fictional narrative:

Leiris saw in the contemporary African "at once a 'brother' and an 'other.'" This "brother," of course, had only one raison d'être—to reconnect Western man with his mythical, prehistorical past. . . . It must be emphasized, however, that the operative language of primitivism rests on this very contradiction, which can never be eliminated. In the final analysis, primitivism recognizes only one axiomatic proposition: whatever is black all over cannot be white, and therefore equal. It is on this simple principle that colonialist Europe structured its basic argument for domination and power.

The ethnographic treasure houses of Paris, Shelton insists, should provoke every visitor to reflect on how thousands of beautiful African objects came to reside so peacefully in their glass cases. It was by the appropriation of brute force, an appropriation essential to the Western primitivist experience and bearing costs to the African that are still being paid.

Primitivist appropriation, in all its various forms, raises the issue of whether dislocation and brutality can ever be transcended. Let us consider not only Leiris's part in the Dakar-Djibouti looting, or the British looting of Benin, but also other appropriations, such as those in Leiris's subsequent narrative; in photographs and travel engravings of African "natives"; in the objects in Trocadero-like ethnographic museums that were purchased rather than looted; in anthropological accounts, either from the field or the arm-chair; in theoretical discussions derived from such anthropological accounts; and in literary artifacts such as the writings of Rimbaud or Eliot. Appropri-ating the non-Western in a Western context always underlines the subjective agency of the West and the unequal passivity of the Other. But is it nothing but exploitation, all imperialism of a comparable magnitude?

Acknowledging the questions of moral and political responsibility that Shelton raises, we are still faced with what to do with peripheral phenomena in which the Western construction of primitivism either (1) involves unequal reciprocal powers, as in the case of the Benin peoples, who sought to exploit the British invasion for their own purposes; (2) involves the deliberate adop-tion of primitivist practices in the West by members of a victimized group to increase their relative cultural visibility and significance, as in the case of the Harlem Renaissance; or (3) raises the paradox that one result of long-term exploitation seems to be an inevitable familiarity in which, given certain political circumstances, the subjugated are granted a growing recognition as fellow human beings. This last phenomenon is addressed at length by Elazar Barkan, who notes that the intensive use of "native" images in the late Vic-torian discourse of sexuality eventually led to a "diminished racism" in which both Western and non-Western sexual practices were accepted as ele-ments of the same universalist spectrum.

Recognizing the violence embedded in colonialism, we still need to ac-count for the ideologically diverse representations of the primitive within the Western cultural economy. Incontestably, public racism increased as Europe subjugated a growing number of "primitives" and "savages." At the same time, primitive images shifted into the midst of European space and pro-duced a rich discourse whose texts, from Eliot and Picasso to Freud and Westermarck, were salutary as well as pernicious. As primitivism reappeared in text after text, each new ideological mix proved unpredictable.

Take primitivism's impact on the European discourse of violence and disorder. It is a commonplace that, at the turn of the century, intellectuals associated the disorder in European metropolises with an ideology of cultural crisis. Civilization was everywhere in decay or at the point of dissolution. Nietzsche — and later Weber, Freud, Sorel, and Durkheim, among others — made this crisis their subject, and the next generation of writers and artists made it their obsession. It was then that European writers mediated the experience of the violent underside of their own culture by confrontations in the African colonies, thereby charging violence in European cities with the fascination of "primitive life." As Robert Nye recounts, European writers working in various disciplines and genres quickly associated the violence of crowds with representations of the exotic. Emile Zola, Scipio Sighele, Gabriel Tarde, and Gustave LeBon suggested that violent modern crowds embodied a savage barbarism associated with unconscious elements of human nature that had survived evolution. Yet if identifying crowds with uncivilized "savages" made it easier for the authorities brutally to suppress political activity, the identification produced unexpected twists as well. These were at the heart of what Nye calls the "modernity" of the savage: "In the setting of the fin-de-siècle, one can thus understand that the savage energy of crowds might appear in two aspects: as threat and as promise. What was most ancient in crowds, the 'residues' they manifested of savage life, was precisely what made them so 'modern' — and therefore both a symptom of an effete and decadent civilization and a potential bulwark against it."

Moreover, Nye notes, once writers like the Italian criminologist Cesare Lombroso identified the agent of urban violence with (in Lombroso's words) "an atavistic being who reproduces in his person the ferocious instincts of primitive humanity and the inferior animals," it was but a short step to identifying the savagery of the crowd with the energy of the unconscious, the unconventional, the childlike. Once again, a discursive space opened and became a site where ideologies struggled for the future. "Fin-de-siècle Europeans," Nye observes, "were obsessed with fatigue, haunted by fears that human energy was being drained off both by the excessive demands that industrial civilization makes on intellect and by the ceaseless, unnatural stimulation of the organism in contemporary urban life. Fatigue became a 'problem' to be overcome by careful study of physiology and by implementing a variety of will-therapies that taught scientists how to draw on the body's latent force."

"Primitive" anonymity in a crowd thus created a peculiarly modern bond between the political and the aesthetic. Even as conservative social critics like Max Nordau identified experimental artistic movements with the expressions of a decadent civilization, Nye suggests, "many avant-garde artists considered crowds to be an important part of their aesthetic outlook." One thinks particularly here of F. T. Marinetti, the guiding spirit of Italian Futurism. Marinetti regarded an important part of his art as "techniques for mobilizing audiences." In so doing, Nye writes, he believed he was "performing an empirical exercise in pragmatic aesthetics, the aim of which was to perfect affective, nondiscursive methods for tapping into the immense energy of crowds." Marinetti, of course, became one of the precursors of Italian fascism, but the connection he made between aesthetics and political demonstration was reflected on the "left" as well, most notably among Dadaist writers and performers. In *Memoirs of a Dada Drummer*, Richard Huelsenbeck recounts his trips to provincial cities to campaign for "Berlin" Dada. And in Paris, Nye adds, "Tristan Tzara constructed his first plays to display his belief that the frankly nondiscursive forms of Dada poetics tapped into the 'primitive structures' of affective life."

Primitivist violence went hand in hand with the other great subversive force of Victorian tradition — modern sexuality. As Elazar Barkan argues, the discourse of sexuality, no less than the discourse of violence, enabled certain Victorians to differentiate and bolster the strictures of "civilized" morality by means of a primeval and savage Other, only to discover that Victorian morality had been subverted beyond recognition. The first stage followed a familiar pattern. In the positivistic and hierarchical world, the modern European family was understood to have reached the apex of civilization. Supported by the parallel findings of anthropology, Barkan writes, "there was a scholarly consensus that moral progress accounted for the evolution of the modern, monogamous, sexual family. The more the family evolved, the less sexualized it became."

Once smuggled into respectable medical and scientific discourses to justify Victorian morality, however, representations of primitive sexuality were transformed by the energies of cultural relativism and lost their demonic charge. The mediating discourses of the primitive helped broaden the scope of European sexual representations as the irrational contradictions of Victorian sexual attitudes surfaced. Barkan notes, for example, that "debates about women's sexuality, homosexuality, and masturbation became commonplace. . . . Why women supposedly without sexual urges should avoid riding the train, let alone a horse, in order not to arouse themselves is a particular example of a Victorian logic that did not need elaboration for contemporaries" but that could not stand up to examination once the culture called on the disciplines of psychology, sexology, and sociology to support itself. Together these new professions "opened a rare egalitarian space" for speculation not only about the sexuality and morality of primordial societies but also about the sexuality and morality of Europe. By bringing the paradoxes of European sexuality into the open, the discourse facilitated reform.

Opening up such shocking and unpredicted spaces in the repressive sphere of Victorian culture, the initially imperialist discourse of primitivism became a powerful engine of radical change both in society and in the arts. The relativism always lurking in the anthropological project could explode in the most unlikely places. Take, as Joss Lutz Marsh does, the late nineteenth-century predecessors of modernist fiction: vampire tales, science fiction, and stories of time travelers. All were related to "those troubling concerns Christopher Herbert identifies with *The Golden Bough* and the theoretical writings of Einstein: issues of knowledge and evidence, anxieties about space, time, and their stability, and the 'troubled and even panicky theme of the corporeal.'" After all, Marsh reminds us, H. G. Wells's Time Machine was a tool for observing "stages in the decay of civilization and the regression of human kind." And Dracula, like Dr. Jekyll, was "a creature from the dark past of mankind" — a creature who, like the primitive in the modern city, had taken his space with him. (Dracula ships "fifty cases of common earth" to London to provide him with a variety of ceremonial graves.)

Such dislocations clearly anticipate the self-consciously modernist conflations of the primitive and the futuristic, and hence the self-conscious dislocations of time and space that we find in Picasso's *Les Demoiselles d'Avignon* or Eliot's *The Waste Land*. They inform us about the sense of cultural vertigo (of the past in the present and the exotic in the familiar) that generated such works — what Michael North, writing about a parallel condition (artistic exile), associates with the experience of feeling "oneself in two places at once, at home and abroad, [equivalent to feeling] as two persons and thus [acquiring] a skepticism about the possibility of ever having an identity." The prevalence of vampires (they also exist in *The Waste Land*) suggests the inordinate anxieties of that situation, something North locates in the ambiguities of the African mask as it enters the work of Picasso and Gertrude Stein. A quintessential artifact of Western primitivism, the African mask in Picasso's portrait of Stein and *Les Demoiselles* becomes "a radically disturbing image because of the ethnographic generalizations attached to it, because these contain contradictions so acute, and because these contradictions match so closely other contradictions of gender, nationality, and genre that modernism made it its business to explore. Modernism," North concludes, "could not escape the contradictions of European colonialism; indeed, it was only because it pushed these to extremes that it could exist as a movement at all."

How modernist contradictions transformed the procedures of Western historians, philosophers, and artists has, of course, preoccupied critics for nearly a century. Frank Kermode suggests that one crucial sign of that transformation was a shift from historical modes of explanation to narratives of synchronic connectedness. Kermode calls this a "change of aspect" and links it to the way writers like Wittgenstein and Saussure criticized the false generality of encompassing genetic explanations and argued instead for a synoptic perception of necessarily inexhaustible relations. He remarks that even Freud, like Frazer or Einstein in Christopher Herbert's account, "was, as it were, caught between aspects" — between, that is, interpreting neurosis phylogenically and locating it "in the present, in the transference." Kermode observes that, perhaps because of the accelerated influx of primitive images, Western ethnography and sociology were also disoriented from the old aspect of explanation to the new. These, after all, provided images from "the real past of the world." And yet, when Europeans tried to fathom the images in a historical way, the attempt inevitably failed: "They were the primitive, *external* foreign objects that corresponded to what Freud called the 'internal foreign territory,'" and, instead of staying in their historical places in a museum of the past, they kept asserting themselves into the vertiginous dislocations of the present.

In Kermode's view, there is also an implicit connection between the relativizing disorientation of ethnography — a change in aspect of philosophic explanation — and the characteristics of modernist narrative in literature and in painting:

A Frazer could work the primitive into a quasi-evolutionary scheme, although I think it was not his quasi-scientific explanations that won him so much fame but the materials he collected, materials from all over the place, synoptically available, that could be used by those who wanted to bypass the decadence of explanation. . . . Thus there grew up a new veneration for art . . . under a new aspect, indistinct, . . . demanding that one look, and see what is not palpably there: connections, interrelations, gaps signifying the unuttered.

This correlation of the dislocating power of primitivist discourse and the corrugations of modernist narrative emerges more concretely in Kermode's description of modern poetry (a "denial of facilitating transitions, a denial of the significance of all signs, a set of unacknowledged quotations, unmotivated ellipses") in Michael North's characterization of the procedures of Picasso and Gertrude Stein, in Ronald Bush's contextualization of *The Waste Land,* and in Marjorie Perloff's defense of Michel Leiris's *L'Afrique fantôme.* Perloff, framing Leiris's text not with the Dakar-Djibouti Expedition but with the French avant-garde, affirms a relation between modernist technique and the relativizing — and therefore disorienting — power of its primitivist provocations. For her, *L'Afrique fantôme* and its companion text, *L'Age d'homme,* pursue a "powerful self-examination and pitiless self-critique" in the process of appropriating primitivist images "to depict an especially demonic . . . world, the world *entre deux guerres,* in all its excesses and contradictions."

Moreover, Perloff uses her reappropriation to question a series of recent analyses in which Western primitivism has been read as exploitation pure and simple. Such discussions suggest that the early twentieth century might have deployed a politically neutral vocabulary to describe non-Western society. Yet what vocabulary, Perloff asks, could we have employed, or can we ever employ, to surmount the dialogical nature of the ethnographic encounter? It is the essence of modernism, in Perloff's view, that it encodes the uncertainties of that dialogism at the heart of its procedural self-consciousness. Against what she sees as political reductions of Leiris by Marianna Torgovnick and others, Perloff counters that Leiris in his fallible honesty stands in for the characteristic Westerner's negotiation with cultural ambiguity since the late nineteenth century.

Amplifying postcolonial criticism's recent anti-essentialist critique of its own earlier phases (namely, Edward Said's 1978 *Orientalism*), Perloff points to a more sophisticated understanding of textualities. The problem she addresses is this: How, in a critique of primitivism, is one to avoid the essentialist move of creating a reified "Occidentalism" that refers univocally to the West? Perloff suggests that there is no easy answer to this problem but that modernism, in the compulsive doubleness of its procedures, embodies a reflexive self-questioning that at least acknowledges the inherent difficulty of the situation. "That colonialist 'fictions of the primitive,'" Perloff maintains, "have been used for at least a century to bolster the West's own self-image is incontrovertible." But so, she declares, ought to be the manifest silliness of assuming that we can surmount the conditions of the modern world in 1995 by analyzing and transcending the colonialist era.

Acknowledging the complexities, political and otherwise, of the primitivist project, the essays in this book suggest that primitivism has always involved contested ideological forces and that the process seems to have generated a set of responses inseparable from what we have come to call modernism. As Edward Said wrote in a text subsequent to *Orientalism,* "Europe and the

West" were forced "to take the Other seriously," and this "is the fundamental historical problem of modernism." He concludes, however, that modernism can be historically understood as the "formal irony of a culture unable either to say yes, we should give up control, or no, we shall hold on regardless" — that is, with "paralyzed gestures of aestheticized powerlessness."[5] Yet such a reading not only overplays modernism as a high cultural and artistic phenomenon, it also assumes that the world has now transcended modernism and lives in a "postmodern" culture in which "the idea of a collective as well as a plural destiny for mankind, Western and non-Western alike," has created heretofore unknown possibilities. An alternative reading would emphasize that, for a hundred years, the West has used the non-Western world to contemplate the prehistories of its future, and that the contradictory results have shaped a multitude of social discourses worldwide. There seems to be no end to that dynamic, and no reason to suppose that the present has been freed from working out its complicity in it.

# PART I

"Savage" Anxieties

# The Presence of the Past

## *Ethnographic Thinking /*
## *Literary Politics*

To assess the question of literary modernism's political affiliations, vexed at least since the 1930's and rubbed raw by the resurgent ideological criticism of the last ten years, it is worth reconsidering an important phase of modernist self-definition — its interchange with the discourse of ethnography. Begin with texts that for many years were accepted as programmatic markers of Anglo-American literary modernism and that now have acquired an equal notoriety. In "Tradition and the Individual Talent," the most famous of his early essays, T. S. Eliot insisted that one of the most important requisites of a mature poet was a "historical sense," "a perception, not only of the pastness of the past, but of its presence." It is precisely "the historical sense," he insisted, that

compels a man to write not only with his own generation in his bones, but with a feeling that the whole of the literature of Europe from Homer and within it the whole of the literature of his own country has a simultaneous existence and composes a simultaneous order. This historical sense, which is a sense of the timeless as well as of the temporal and of the timeless and of the temporal together, is what makes a writer traditional.

He then added, inflecting poetics and history in the direction of ethnography, that the poet must remember that "the mind of Europe . . . does not superannuate either Shakespeare, or Homer, or the rock drawing of the Magdalenian draughtsmen." And, Eliot insisted, "this development, refinement perhaps, complication certainly, is not from the point of view of the artist, any improvement."[1]

Anyone who knows these remarks, formulated before Eliot wrote *The Waste Land* but after he had begun reading serialized chapters of *Ulysses*, also knows how Eliot elaborated them a few years later, after *Ulysses* was published and had come under attack for apparent formlessness. On that occasion, Eliot observed that, in using the Odysseus myth as the framework for his novel,

Mr. Joyce is pursuing a method which others must pursue after him. They will not be imitators, any more than the scientist who uses the discoveries of an Einstein in pursuing his own, independent, further investigations. It is simply a way of controlling, of ordering, of giving a shape and a significance to the immense panorama of futility and anarchy which is contemporary history. . . . It is a method for which the horoscope is auspicious. Psychology, . . . ethnology, and *The Golden Bough* have concurred to make possible what was impossible even a few years ago. Instead of narrative method, we may now use the mythical method. It is, I seriously believe, a step toward making the modern world possible for art, toward that order and form which [Joyce's critics] so earnestly desir[e].[2]

To condense seventy years of literary history, these statements have inspired two politically charged characterizations of Anglo-American literary modernism, each the mirror image of the other.[3] In the 1930's, the New Critics, associated with forces of religious and cultural reaction in the American South, seized on Eliot's emphases on "myth" and "order" — emphases which they thought had been translated into the architecture of *The Waste Land* — and interpreted his theoretical program in their own image. Eliot, they asserted, had consciously exploded the relativist confusions of his generation's historicism by a transhistorical method that had also "br[ought] to life again" the primitive vitality of Christian rituals and beliefs.[4] To them, Eliot's "order" meant a single eternal order, and Eliot's "myth" referred to the various reflections of truth in the benighted religions of the world.

Very recently, and despite obvious problems with reconciling the absolutist cultural program of the New Critics with the troubling skepticism of Eliot's early work in philosophy and some of his early literary criticism (see Bush, *T. S. Eliot*, 1991, p. 196), Marxist, feminist, and postcolonialist critics have taken the New Critical characterization of Eliot at face value and have used it to discount the modernist project. Thus Terry Eagleton, reflecting specifically on Eliot's recourse to ethnography, argues that *The Waste Land*'s fragmentary surface is counterfeit. The poem, in his eyes, reifies its imitation of modern life through a series of "totalizing mythological forms" appropriated from Eliot's reading in Victorian anthropology. In this way *The Waste Land* produces "an ideology of [elitist] cultural knowledge" consonant with the "authoritarian cultural ideology" of Eliot's conservative political prose.[5]

But precisely what was Eliot's recourse to anthropology? If Eagleton is correct, we should be able to trace in it a consistent affiliation with imperialist practices and discover the constellation of an essentialist, politically conservative cultural formation. In fact, although Eagleton's suspicion of Eliot's anthropology is deserved, the sources of Eliot's ethnographic representations are in interesting ways ideologically conflicted. Also, the pattern of Eliot's early intellectual development shows considerable movement away from the worst excesses of Victorian primitivism.

The seriousness and duration of Eliot's study of ethnography, intertwined with his professional training in philosophy, have long been established,[6] but Eliot's first encounter with the subject has surfaced only recently. Thanks to the discoveries of a Japanese scholar in the family scrapbooks (let us credit the cultural switchboard of the postmodern world), we can trace the beginning of Eliot's interest to his fifteenth year.[7] In 1904, Henry Ware Eliot, scion of an old Boston family, son of a prominent Unitarian minister, and president of the Hydraulic-Press Brick Company of St. Louis, Missouri, took his fifteen-year-old son Tom to the Louisiana Purchase Exposition, commonly called the St. Louis World's Fair. (Eliot's identification ticket is shown in Fig. 1.) The spectacle of non-Western societies they encountered was extraordinary and (though they recorded no protest) from our present standpoint profoundly disturbing. Ever since London's 1851 Crystal Palace, international expositions had included representations of colonial peoples. Since Paris's 1878 and 1889 Expositions Universelles at the Jardin d'Acclimatation, they had included "native villages" in which exotic peoples were presented in virtual zoological exhibits or tableaux vivants. But only in America, at the 1901 Buffalo Pan-American Exposition, had the displays become "obsessed with evolutionary theory" and the "shift from the low levels of humanity to higher ones."[8] Three years after Buffalo, the centerpiece of the St. Louis Exposition was, according to its most recent historian, Robert Rydell, "the most extensive Anthropology Department of any world's fair. The directors [published] their intent to establish 'a comprehensive anthropological exhibition, constituting a Congress of Races, and exhibiting particularly the barbarous and semi-barbarous peoples of the world, as nearly as possible in their native environments.'"[9] To head the anthropology department, the directors hired W. J. McGee, earlier of the Bureau of American Ethnology and a strong believer in the evolutionary progress of culture through four stages that he called "savagery, barbarism, civilization, and enlightenment" (Rydell, *All the World's a Fair*, pp. 160–62). McGee, quickly dubbed by a local

CONDITIONS.

This special fifty-coupon ticket is issued to stockholders of record only.

This ticket is non-transferable and will not be redeemed for any reason.

Each coupon is good for one admission on any day the Exposition is open to the general public.

Not good on Sundays.

This ticket shall be forfeited if presented by any person other than person named, whose photograph appears on inside of cover.

The person using this ticket voluntarily assumes all risk of accidents and damages.

Void if showing any evidence of alteration or erasure.

When tickets are lost, prompt notice must be given the Department of Admissions in order that same may be taken up at the gates when presented.

Tickets lost will not be replaced.

I have read the above conditions and accept the same.

FIG. 1. T. S. Eliot's "Stockholder Coupon Ticket" for the St. Louis World's Fair. The Missouri Historical Society.

newspaper "overlord of the savage world" (he is pictured with his Patagonian "wards" in Fig. 2),

converted the Western portion of the exposition grounds into a field research station for the study of nonwhite "types." Groups of pygmies from Africa, "Patagonian giants" from Argentina, Ainu aborigines from Japan, and Kwakiutl Indians from Vancouver Island, as well as groups of Native Americans gathered around prominent Indian chiefs including Geronimo [Fig. 3], Chief Joseph, and Quanah Parker, were formed into living ethnological exhibits. They were supplemented by an adjoining United States Government exhibit of nearly one thousand Filipinos (ibid., p. 163).

FIG. 2. "Chief McGee and His Wards." Reprinted from the official *History of the Louisiana Purchase Exhibit,* 1904.

FIG. 3. Geronimo. Reprinted from the official *History of the Louisiana Purchase Exhibit,* which supplies as caption: "Geronimo, the Apache Chief. He led his warriors in many campaigns against the whites, and his desperate fighting and treachery cost many lives."

In the words of William Howard Taft, in 1902 civil governor of the Philippines and by 1904 Secretary of War, as quoted in the *World's Fair Bulletin*, the "Filipino participation" was expected to have "a very great influence in completing pacification and in bringing Filipinos to improve their condition." But, as Rydell comments, the Filipino reservation by the same token "created a scientifically validated impression of Filipinos as racially inferior and incapable of national self-determination" (ibid., pp. 168, 170). This justification of the Spanish American War and American imperialism was taken as a given by the official history of the exposition, which noted that back in 1902 a Philippine contribution had been envisioned by then governor Taft as "an admirable opportunity . . . [to] impress the American people with clearer ideas of what they are doing and have to do for the Philippine Islanders." The history added:

It was a leading purpose of the Philippine Civil Government to give large and representative bodies of Filipinos the benefit of a long sojourn at the Exposition in close contact with the American people and their civilization, and at the same time to familiarize the American public with the various and incongruous tribal elements of the Philippine population, differing in race, language and religion, and representing many stages of social progress from the lowest types of head-hunting savagery to the best products of Christian civilization and culture.[10]

On the island at the fair devoted to the government's Philippine Exposition (Fig. 4), a series of ethnological villages were located that "portrayed a number of Filipino 'types,' including Visayans, 'the high and more intelligent class of natives,' Moros, 'fierce followers of Mohammed,' Bagobo 'savages,' 'monkey-like' Negritos, and 'picturesque' Igorots" (Rydell, p. 171). These exhibits became wildly popular, especially the one that displayed the appealingly simple Igorots (whose attraction is satirized by the contemporary cartoon in Fig. 5, depicting "The Adoration of the Igorrote" by fashionably dressed visitors). Yet the popularity caused the government some awkwardness. President Theodore Roosevelt, fearing in an election year that the unclothed tribes would create the impression that Filipinos were savage beyond the powers of Americans to civilize, made Taft order the Negritos and Igorots to clothe their nakedness in Western garb, only to be reprimanded by resident anthropologists and newspaper editorials. ("To put pants on [the Igorots and Negritos] would change a very interesting ethnological exhibit . . . into a suggestive sideshow." "The scientific value of the display is unquestionably great. Such value would be completely lost by dressing these people in a way unlike that to which they are accustomed.") The upshot was that by mid-July

FIG. 4. "Philippine Exposition, Moro Buildings, and Boats on Arrowhead Lake." Reprinted from the official *History of the Louisiana Purchase Exhibit*.

FIG. 5. Satirical cartoon, 1904, collected by the Eliot family. The caption from the *Manila Times* reads: "The Adoration of the Igorrote. — We may expect a repetition of the St. Louis scenes at Portland this year." The Missouri Historical Society.

FIG. 6. The Eliot family's souvenir booklet: the St. Louis "Igorot Village." The Missouri Historical Society.

FIG. 7. Satiric cartoon clipped by the Eliot family from a June 1904 newspaper. The Missouri Historical Society.

the administration "abandoned its plans to compel the Igorots and Negritos to wear bright-colored silk trousers" (ibid., pp. 172–74).

In the midst of this controversy, the Eliot family visited the Igorot village a number of times (a souvenir is reproduced in Fig. 6) and collected an extensive scrapbook of clippings, including editorial cartoons concerning the flap over silk pants (Fig. 7). Young Tom Eliot seems to have been especially impressed (Narita 1984, 1985, 1988) by what the fair's official history memorializes as the Igorots' "Strange Festival Dance" (Fig. 8). He was impressed enough, in fact, that within a year of his visit, Eliot wrote a story, "The Man Who Was King," for his prep school magazine, using the Igorot exhibit for background and leading his natives in procession "beating bhghongs (a sort of cross between tin·pan and gong)" (Narita 1988, pp. 42–43). The story shows a keen interest in primitive lives before the contamination of Western culture and focuses on the fate of a white man named Magruder who is temporarily named king of a south-sea island, then ousted when he proves incapable of performing magic at public festivals.[11]

Eliot's world's fair impressions and the story that came out of them need to be approached with judiciousness. On the one hand, the author of "The Man Who Was King" was then only an adolescent, and the story is a juvenile effort in an already hackneyed genre. On the other hand, the historical formations that conditioned Eliot's adventures at the fair were anything but trivial and would resonate for years throughout his intellectual world. It is

FIG. 8. Reprinted from the official *History of the Louisiana Purchase Exhibit.* Under the heading "Bontoc Igorrotes in Their Strange Festival Dance," the caption reads in part: "The savages went so far as to take the tom-tom and give the American dancers lessons while the entire party sat by and encouraged the efforts of the students to master the steps of the dance and the manipulation of the tom-tom."

important, for example, to realize that the fair's representations of primitive man were framed by the most respectable schools of turn-of-the-century anthropology, a discipline just emerging from its own adolescence. Manning the St. Louis physical anthropology laboratories were colleagues and students of Franz Boas, who, although he would soon explode many of the commonplaces of the exhibition, was in 1904 one of McGee's advisors (Rydell, p. 164). McGee, meanwhile, had come to the fair as one of the preeminent anthropologists of the Bureau of Ethnology at the Smithsonian Institution. And in 1904 the Smithsonians continued to adhere to the evolutionist consensus of late nineteenth-century anthropology, in which human history was envisioned as a universal progress from primitivism to civilization. As Lewis Henry Morgan, one of the intellectual fathers of the group, had famously written in *Ancient Society* (1877): "It can now be asserted upon convincing evidence that savagery preceded barbarism in all the tribes of mankind as barbarism is known to have preceded civilization. The history of the human race is one in source, one in experience, and in progress." [12]

Insofar, therefore, as the young Eliot's story presented a naive opposition between primitive and civilized life, he was doing no more than the best anthropologists of the generation before him. The technical sense of "primitive" at the time was precisely other than, because previous to, civilization, along a unified evolutionary path. Nor was Eliot exceptional when in his story he reversed the valences of civilized and primitive and lamented the civilized invasion of his imaginary island. Whether in native America, India, Japan, or the South Seas — or, more recently, in Africa, Australia, or Melanesia — encounters with non-Western cultures had for several centuries been turned into celebrations of what Europe had repressed. (This, after all, was the fundamental appeal of the unclad Igorots to hordes of American spectators.) Nor need we at this late date belabor the problematic implications of the admiration Eliot shared with his fellow citizens. Even if primitives are seen as happier than we are, as long as we think of them as in some way simpler, we always regard them as inferiors. What may be worth emphasizing, though, is that Eliot's juvenile fascination anticipated a strain of unexpected and increasingly sophisticated primitivism in his own work and in European writing just before the First World War.

Six years after writing "The Man Who Was King," and following a successful undergraduate career at Harvard, during which he earned B.A. and M.A. degrees in what we would now call English and Comparative Literature, Eliot spent the 1910–11 academic year in Paris. There he read omnivorously, faithfully attended the lectures of Henri Bergson, and sampled the intellectual wares of the "skeptics" Anatole France and Rémy de Gourmont, Maurice Barrès, Charles Péguy, Paul Claudel, Emile Durkheim, Lucien Lévy-Bruhl, and Pierre Janet. Over all, Eliot said, "swung the spider-like figure of Bergson. His metaphysic was said to throw some light upon the new ways of painting, and discussion of Bergson was apt to be involved with discussion of Matisse and Picasso."[13] Once Bergson had motivated him to return to Harvard and take up graduate studies in philosophy, however, Eliot's infatuation faded, and he eventually wrote a thesis on F. H. Bradley, one of Bergson's critics. Both as a graduate student and thereafter, Eliot continued to combine philosophy with a serious interest in academic anthropology, which had been inspired by one of the writers named in his French recollections, Lucien Lévy-Bruhl. In 1910, the year Eliot went to Paris, Lévy-Bruhl published *Les Fonctions mentales dans les sociétés inférieures*, a groundbreaking work that Eliot read in French and to which he alluded frequently throughout his career. Lévy-Bruhl, as Eliot would soon point out himself, used Durkheim's sociological methods to criticize the English school of anthropology from Edward Tylor to James Frazer for postulating an evolutionarily continuous human "uniformity of mind" rather than recognizing the social conditioning of mental categories.[14] But — a weakness that Lévy-Bruhl only recognized long after it had permanently affected Eliot's thought — even as Lévy-Bruhl recognized the cultural relativity of contemporary societies, he continued to make unwarranted distinctions between the mentalities of scientific and prescientific men, otherwise primitives. (Hence the title of his book, translated in 1925 as *How Natives Think*.)

Fired by Lévy-Bruhl's sophisticated primitivism, by 1913 Eliot had read enough in the anthropological literature to quote expertly from Tylor, Andrew Lang, Frazer, Max Müller, and others. As a London man of letters a few years later, we find him reviewing extensively on ethnography and social theory; his references came to include, to give a truncated list, Wilhelm Mannhardt, Wilhelm Wundt, J. H. King, W. Robertson Smith, J. Rendel Harris, Baldwin Spencer and F. J. Gillen, and A. W. Howitt (see Skaff, *Philosophy of T. S. Eliot*, p. 214). Eliot's ethnographic writing overlapped with studies of Western mysticism, Indian thought, and comparative religion. He yearned for a dimension of experience he sensed his own situation lacked, and in his journalism he cited and defended Lévy-Bruhl's contention that man in primitive society "is capable of a state of mind into which we cannot put ourselves, in which he *is* [his totemic animal], while being at the same time a man." "In other words," Eliot added, the prelogical or "mystical mentality, though at a low level, plays a much greater part in the daily life of the savage than in that of civilised man."[15]

In later work, Eliot, as Marc Manganaro has recently shown, sought out authorities who exceeded Lévy-Bruhl and connected primitive mysticism with modern art and poetry. In 1933 Harvard lectures on *The Use of Poetry and the Use of Criticism*, for example, Eliot noted that Emile Cailliet and Jean-Albert Bédé, "who have done field work in Madagascar, apply the theories of Lévy-Bruhl: the prelogical mentality persists in civilised man, but becomes available only to or through the poet." Long before that, Eliot had observed in the artist's sensitivity to the primary elements of rhythm and symbol the character of being "more *primitive*, as well as more civilized, than his contemporaries . . . his experience is deeper than civilization, and he only uses the phenomena of civilization in expressing it." It is not surprising, then, that however consonant with the literary practices of his Romantic and Symbolist predecessors, Eliot's habitual emphasis on the prelogical force of poetry came to associate itself with Lévy-Bruhl's ideas about the mystical "participation" of prelogical mentality. Still later, Eliot's anthropological interests provoked theories that attempted to assimilate poetry to a sociological understanding of the function of theater that had been formulated by Durkheim and adopted by the Cambridge classicists. Starting in 1917 or so, Eliot generalized the arguments of Jane Ellen Harrison, F. M. Cornford, and Gilbert Murray and argued both that Greek drama had grown out of primitive ritual and that modern drama (indeed, literature itself), if it is to survive, must reconnect with the energies of ritual poetry. By 1923 we find him arguing that poetic drama, animated by "the beating of a drum," offers a way of uniting different strata of culture within the magic circle of public ritual.[16]

There was good reason, then, that when Eliot began an ambitious long poem (*The Waste Land*) in 1919, he attempted to combine "primitive" subject matter with procedures he associated with ritual practice. Nor, given the speculations of a post-conversion Eliot several years later on specifically Christian ritual (see Crawford, *The Savage and the City*, chap. 6), is it implausible that, six years before his 1926 conversion to the Anglican Church, he might have conceptualized *The Waste Land* as a poet–medicine man's effort to rehabilitate religious truths. Certainly a call to "return to the sources" plays a prominent part in an occasional essay, "Warpaint and Feathers," that Eliot wrote in 1919 on the place of anthropology in contemporary life — the same year he began *The Waste Land* and wrote "Tradition and the

Individual Talent." Reviewing *An Anthology of Songs and Chants from the Indians of North America* in the October 1919 *Athenaeum*, Eliot observed that

aborigines of every complexion and climate . . . have arrived, each tribe pressing upon us its own claims to distinction in art and literature.

Within the time of a brief generation it has become evident that some smattering of anthropology is as essential to culture as Rollin's Universal History. Just as it is necessary to know something about Freud and something about Fabre, so it is necessary to know something about the medicine-man and his works. Not necessary, perhaps not even desirable, to know all the theories about him, to peruse all the works of Miss Harrison, Cooke, Rendel Harris, Lévy-Bruhl or Durkheim. But one ought, surely, to have read at least one book such as those of Spencer and Gillen on the Australians, or Codrington on the Melanesians. And as it is certain that some study of primitive man furthers our understanding of civilised man, so it is certain that primitive art and poetry help our understanding of civilised art and poetry. Primitive art and poetry can even, through the studies and experiments of the artist or poet, revivify the contemporary activities. The maxim, Return to the sources, is a good one. More intelligibly put, it is that the poet should . . . be aware of all the metamorphoses of poetry that illustrate the stratifications of history that cover savagery. For the artist is, in an impersonal sense, the most conscious of men; he is therefore the most and the least civilised and civilisable; he is the most competent to understand both civilised and primitive.[17]

Both envying and condescending to the primitive, this is no more than a blatant expression of Romantic primitivism. But before we decide that either *The Waste Land* or Eliot's critical program should be understood wholly in terms of its evolutionist condescension to the "savage," we should consider the interesting twist with which the essay concludes. Reiterating that the poet "is the most ready and the most able of men to learn from the savage," Eliot adds a coda in which he contradicts himself and touches on a critical point of ideological contestation in early twentieth-century anthropology. Briefly, Eliot asserts that the poet is also "the last person to see the savage in a romantic light, or to yield to the weak credulity of crediting the savage with any gifts of mystical insight or artistic feeling that he does not possess himself" ("Warpaint and Feathers," p. 1036). At a minimum he here claims that there is no evolutionary separation between the savage and civilized man, a move that in the end may be no more than a reaffirmation of the modern artist's "primitive" resources. But Eliot's claim may be stronger still — in which case it reflects a flicker of the twentieth-century anthropologist's skeptical relativism and suggests that Eliot, like his contemporary ethnographers, had begun to work through the ethnographic attitudes of the St. Louis World's Fair and their condescending binary opposition between the savage and civilized. Such a view is consistent both with the development of Eliot's philosophical writings and with what seem to be the genuinely conflicted ideological attitudes of *The Waste Land*.

To repeat: after returning from Paris, Eliot began a Ph.D. program in philosophy at Harvard. In December 1913, in the midst of a seminar conducted by Josiah Royce, Eliot decided to incorporate his growing interest in anthropology into his philosophical studies and use ethnographic materials as the basis of a long seminar paper on the topic of interpretation. The paper, which Eliot entitled "The Interpretation of Primitive Ritual," has survived in manuscript, and an account also exists of the discussion that surrounded it.[18] A great deal of the paper is concerned with technical questions of idealist philosophy — specifically, with interpreting the facts of social phenomena. As Eliot later summarized it, the paper concluded that "no interpretation of a rite could explain its origin. For the meaning of the series of acts is to the performers themselves an interpretation."[19]

What is important for our purposes, however, is that, after first using Lévy-Bruhl's sociological observations on the non-Western functioning of primitive mind to refute the contention of the British anthropologists Tylor, Andrew Lang, and Frazer that there is a uniform consistency to human mental operations, Eliot invoked Durkheim to *criticize* Lévy-Bruhl. At this time he had access only to Durkheim's 1895 book, *Les Règles de la méthode sociologique*, and his 1898 essay, "Représentations individuelles et représentations collectives," both texts that Eliot had carried back from Paris. But these were enough, it seems, to initiate doubts about Lévy-Bruhl that persisted in Eliot's writing alongside remnants of his original infatuation. For instance, in the seminar paper, Eliot argued that, compared to his colleague Durkheim, Lévy-Bruhl allowed his emphasis on the social context of mental formation to be overshadowed by drawing "the distinction between primitive and civilized mental process altogether too clearly."[20] For, if Durkheim was right in arguing that "when we undertake to explain a social phenomenon, we must seek . . . the function which it fulfils," then "all questions of intention are [invalid]"[21] and there is something suspect about Lévy-Bruhl's characterization of primitive psychology. Or, as Eliot would amplify the criticism ten years later, Lévy-Bruhl had "invent[ed] an elaborate 'prelogism' to account for the savage's identification of himself with his totem, where it is not certain that the savage, except so far as he had mental processes similar to our own, had any mental processes at all."[22] According to Durkheim, in other words, the irrational categories of the so-called savage mind cannot be seen either as due to reasoning from ignorance, as the British school thought, or as a result of the mystical simplicities of primitive thinking, as in Lévy-Bruhl; rather, they are as much an expression of cultural imperatives as our own equally illogical mental categories, and as inexplicable in terms of individual psychology.

The full impact of Durkheim's cultural relativism on Eliot came a few years after the 1913 seminar paper. In 1912, Durkheim had published the full-dress ethnographic study that was to stand as the culmination of his long career, *Les Formes élémentaires de la vie religieuse*, which was translated in 1915 by Joseph Ward Swain as *The Elementary Forms of the Religious Life*.[23] Meanwhile, Eliot had traveled to Europe to finish his Ph.D. thesis and had been stranded in England, where he was making his living as a teacher and part-time reviewer. In London he wrote two separate, substantial reviews of the Swain translation and published both anonymously, one in the 1916 *Westminster Gazette* and one in a 1918 number of the philosophical journal, *The Monist*.[24] The reviews represent a significant moment of intersection between ethnographic and literary modernism and condition the formative representations of Eliot's modernist program.

This is not the place to consider *The Elementary Forms* as a contribution to anthropology, a subject that has in any case been addressed with great competence by Steven Lukes.[25] Concentrate instead on Durkheim's conclusion, in which he applies the sum of what he discovered in individual case histories to philosophic arguments about human nature and human society. Particularly I would draw attention to two passages. In the first, Durkheim rebukes Lévy-Bruhl on primitive mental functioning. Commenting on religion as a "system of ideas whose object is to explain the world" (*Elementary Forms*, p. 476),[26] Durkheim holds that, because of the way we depend on an "impersonal," socially produced and collectively shared "world of stable ideas," our thinking must be grounded in sociohistoric categories (ibid., pp. 484–85). In this sense the substance and force of twentieth-century science cannot, any more than primitive religion, claim to be true: it depends on collective agreement or "opinion at the very moment when it seems to be making its laws; for . . . it is from opinion that it holds the force necessary to act upon opinion" (ibid., p. 487). However, Durkheim continues, primitive mentality in its social production of mental concepts is fundamentally no different than our own. "Conceptual thought," he asserts, "is coeval with humanity itself. . . . There is no period in history when men have lived in a chronic confusion and contradiction" (ibid.).

For Durkheim in this mood, then, the social development of concepts obtains in more or less the same way in every society. Thought is here treated only as an element of social cohesion, and "there can be no society which does not feel the need of upholding and reaffirming at regular intervals the collective sentiments and the collective ideas which make its unity and its personality" (ibid., pp. 474–75). There thus can be no reason for making invidious and/or nostalgic distinctions between primitive peoples and ourselves on the basis of logical mentality. "We refuse to see in [primitive mentality]," he writes, "the product of a more or less retarded culture" (ibid., p. 487). These assertions represent a translation of Enlightenment rationalism into a historical key. True, all societies are the product of historical accidents, but by the same token they develop according to universal laws and therefore should be regarded as equally human.

In a second passage, Durkheim even inflects the theme of social disintegration (which in this century, as in the last, usually accompanies a neo-traditionalist call to order) in an Enlightenment way. Sounding at first like a conservative modernist on the order of D. H. Lawrence or Max Weber, Durkheim remarks that "If we find a little difficulty to-day in imagining [viable rituals], it is because we are going through a stage of transition. . . . The great things of the past which filled our fathers with enthusiasm do not excite the same ardour in us . . . but as yet there is nothing to replace them. . . . In a word, the old gods are growing old or already dead, and others are not yet born." Yet, instead of pursuing the nostalgic implications of his premises, Durkheim plays a progressive turn on Arnoldian despair, for in the next breath he assures us that "a day will come when our societies will know again those hours of creative effervescence, in the course of which new ideas arise and new formulae are found which serve for a while as a guide to humanity." On that day, Durkheim assures us, we will once again find adequate "celebrations": "There are no gospels which are immortal, but neither is there any reason for believing that humanity is incapable of inventing new ones" (ibid., pp. 475–76).

In passages like this we see how, if (as Professor Crapanzano suggests in another essay in this book) Durkheim's ethnographic discourse could idealize representations of strong social affectivity and anticipate fascist crowds, it could also harness what a recent critic has called "the relativizing potential" of ethnographic sociology as an agent of liberal change: Durkheim, after all, was "a secular republican, wary of the political power of the Catholic church. He was also a Jew . . . a member of a newly enfranchised minority, but one very much under threat . . . [since conservatives had argued] that church and family were the sources which fed morality." But if, as Durkheim's ethnographic studies illustrate, morality developed differently in comparable societies, then, in the same critic's words, "the present institutional arrangements are not facts of nature, they are human constructs" that could be reconstituted in a more egalitarian way (Kuper, *Invention of Primitive Society*, pp. 113–14).

Durkheim's ethnography itself, in other words, was a site of considerable ideological tension, and in *The Elementary Forms* his liberal project was at least as prominent as the evolutionist discourse he shared with Lévy-Bruhl or the interest in collective ritual he shared with his nephew Marcel Mauss.

Nevertheless, the Eliot who in 1933 was to imagine a Christian society undisturbed by "any large number of free-thinking Jews"[27] at the beginning of his modernist career received Durkheim's ethnography with applause. In the more serious of his reviews, published in the *Westminster Gazette* in August 1916, he called *The Elementary Forms* "exactly the sort of book which is worth translating" and one that "ought to be read not only by specialists, but by everyone who is interested in the history and in the future of religion." It reinforced, he wrote, the influence Durkheim had already had in France on "MM. Lévy-Bruhl, Hubert, Mauss, Hemelin, and others, and in England notably [on] Miss Jane Harrison, Mr. Cornford, and Mr. A. B. Cook."

The specifics of Eliot's response are as interesting as his enthusiasm. Certainly he sympathizes, as we would expect from the man who would later write *The Idea of a Christian Society*, with Durkheim's perception of anomie and his instinctive need to celebrate forms of strong social ritual. In the review, for example, after expertly setting Durkheim's discussions of totemism and animism in the context of writing from Tylor to Frazer, Eliot emphasizes passages in which Durkheim addresses "the ultimate function and destiny of religion in our own civilisation" in the context of "the doctrine of group consciousness." It is not, Eliot asserts with Durkheim, the essence of religion to provoke a mystical participation with the godhead. Instead, the "religious instinct" "for the savage or the civilised man" has to do with "the instinct for association and community with other men."

Beyond this, though, Eliot's review includes other, more unexpected observations. For one, Eliot downplays the mystical content of primitive religion. Also, as a philosopher he is irresistibly drawn to Durkheim's historicizing redefinition of Kant's universal categories. Finally, and most surprisingly, he ends with a warm endorsement of the passage in *The Elementary Forms* that voices Durkheim's most progressive mood. The last words Eliot quotes are in fact Durkheim's prediction that, in "hours of creative effervescence

. . . new ideas arise and new formulas are found which serve for a while as a guide to humanity."

In other words, in 1916 Eliot affirmed not only the conservative underside of Durkheim's ethnography but also Durkheim's progressivist aspirations and the whole bundle of his contradictions. Nor was his appropriation inconsequential. Think for a moment about two related questions, roughly "the modernist on history" and "the history of modernism," and return to Eliot's admonition that the poet cultivates a "historical sense," "a perception, not only of the pastness of the past, but of its presence." It is impossible to read Eliot's statement, or the poetry it framed, without acknowledging how much the ethnographic discourse of primitivism had colored both his idea of the past and his notion of the present. Yet acknowledging as much doesn't simplify our reading of the politics of Eliot, or of modernism.

It is true that—no less than Durkheim's interest in magic—Eliot's pronouncements about the present and the past and his vision of himself and his contemporaries as artist–medicine men reflect the mystifications of nineteenth-century evolutionist anthropology and implicate him in its imperialism. In this sense, the presence of the past has to do with the affiliations between the mystical "savage" mentality and the sensibility of the artist, and could easily be inflected in the direction of the "order" and "myths" of the early Christian church.

But it is equally true that when Eliot speaks of "the presence of the past" he is voicing Durkheim's relativist insistence that non-Western societies are involved, no less than we are, with the creation and erosion of social forms. The presence of the past in this context has to do with our understanding that religious values have always been constructed in relation to social formations. Similarly, "order" and "myth" in this light have to do with the fact that mythmaking is as contingent as it is universal.

In other words, just as the primitivist representations of the liberal, Jewish Durkheim, heir to the Enlightenment and follower of Auguste Comte, were not entirely free of the conservative problematic of culture, so the representations of the Boston-educated, idealist Eliot were not without Enlightenment overtones. The writing of both men was caught up in the contested discourse of anthropology, a discourse that blended ideological currents from both traditions.

Moreover, Eliot's case reminds us that, when we try to sort out the ideological implications of modernism, we must remember the calendar. Although the evolutionist writings of Henry Sumner Maine, Lewis Henry Morgan, Tylor, and Frazer had influenced English and American thought for fifty years before the Great War, as had secondary events like the St. Louis World's Fair, the generation of 1914 was fashioned as much by the reaction *against* that tradition as by the tradition itself. When Eliot spoke of "Magdalenian draughtsmen" in 1919, his ethnographic coordinate was not Morgan but Durkheim, who had dramatically turned away from evolutionism toward the skeptical relativism that would more and more constitute the twentieth-century study of anthropology.

Ultimately, though, the ideology of modernist ethnography cannot be decided by dates or by precedence. Given the constant recirculation of ethnographic material throughout the period, we finally have to think about the issue in a nonlinear way. To give one last citation, even after Eliot's comments on Durkheim, he could still praise Frazer for extending "the consciousness of the human mind into as dark a backward and abysm of time as has yet been explored."[28] The moments of nineteenth- and twentieth-century ethnography, that is, were not chronological, but were present in the early years of the century as conflicting frameworks, always there to be inflected by specific historical situations in different political directions, or to color the conflicting impulses of a complex situation. We can see the latter case clearly in the equivocation of *The Waste Land*'s attitude toward myth and ritual, so dramatically different from the truly nostalgic primitivism of, for example, Hart Crane's *The Bridge*. Narrating *The Waste Land*, Eliot alternately casts doubt on the efficacy of ritual survivals in societies at all times and all places *and* yearns for a "savage" condition of mystical participation. Yet if the latter set of attitudes aligns him with Lévy-Bruhl at his most mystified, the former voices the Enlightenment skepticism of twentieth-century modernity.

Equally affiliated with traditionalist reaction and socialist aspiration, modernism, as Adam Kuper has said about nineteenth-century ethnographic primitivism, "could serve . . . many ideological purposes [and] could at times also serve none. . . . It could be used equally by right or left, reactionary or progressive, poet and politician" (*Invention of Primitive Society*, p. 9). Kuper concludes by observing that "the most powerful images of primitive society were produced by very disparate political thinkers — Maine, Engels, Durkheim and Freud" (ibid., p. 240). One could say the same about the primitivist representations of Eliot, D. H. Lawrence, and James Joyce. But it would be well to remember that, inscribed within their work, there exist the already contested representations of ethnography.

ROBERT NYE

# Savage Crowds, Modernism, and Modern Politics

In the second volume of his great autobiography, *The Torch in My Ear*, Elias Canetti describes the events of July 15, 1927, which "may have been the most crucial day of my life after my father's death."[1] On that day Canetti was a participant in a violent labor demonstration in Vienna during which the Palace of Justice was burned to the ground and 90 men died. But for Canetti that day was an epiphany: he discovered the true nature of the crowd and, especially, the instinct in him that joined him to it, despite his own shyness and·detachment. In his euphoric account of the experience, he writes·that there was "something rhythmic in the air, an evil music. You could call it music; you felt elevated by it. I did not feel as if I were moving on my own legs. I felt as if I were in a resonant wind" (*Torch*, p. 248).

This occasion indicated for Canetti his vocation for the next 35 years, culminating in the book he regards as his lifework, *Crowds and Power*. Belying the reference to "evil music," Canetti aimed to contradict in his work the negative and pejorative accounts of crowd psychology he had encountered earlier in the classical literature on crowds. In Freud's *Group Psychology and the Analysis of the Ego,* and in the work of the author on whom Freud most depended, Gustave LeBon, Canetti discerned a hostility to crowds, the need for scientific distance from them, and the belief that the crowd "was something leprous, . . . it was like a disease" (ibid., pp. 147–48). Without denying the murderous capacities of crowds, their imitative and impulsive qualities, Canetti's own reaction was more generous, something akin to the fascination of the Futurist F. T. Marinetti or that of the pioneers of Dada with the creative *potential* of crowds, their boundless energy and liability to intoxication.[2] In general, Canetti's discomfort with the "classic" writers on crowds suggests the existence of two critical traditions, one negative, hyperrationalist, and politically conservative, the other sympathetic, committed to exploring nonlogical processes, and imbued with the spirit of rebellion. The scientific outlook seeks knowledge about collective behavior to justify containing or repressing crowd phenomena; the aesthetic one sees in crowds the model and the means for destroying the foundations of bankrupt art and politics and for introducing novelty in both domains.

I have identified these two traditions to make the point that one's notion of crowd psychology might well be an important touchstone for understanding the origins of modernism, in particular for sorting out various anticipations and resistances to its doctrines. I will, in general, adhere to this point throughout this paper. However, if we examine the fin-de-siècle, when crowds were first "discovered" and classified, a picture emerges that complicates my simple distinction. In what follows I will make three points. First, fin-de-siècle crowds were "modern" crowds, enjoining reactions that were different in nature from responses to earlier collective phenomena. Second, in the minds of contemporaries, the "modernity" of fin-de-siècle crowds resided in their status as atavisms, savage phenomena in an overrefined and exhausted urban civilization. Third, what was perhaps most important about contemporaries' reactions to crowds was not the difference in their views — whether they thought crowds a source of mischief or regeneration — but the beliefs they shared in common about crowd *praxis*, the methods to be employed in arousing and manipulating the sentiments of collectivities. This conviction of the advantages of pragmatic knowledge, I will argue, is the truly modern feature in the artistic avant-garde; but it is also the principle that informed the relation between ideas and action for many other contemporaries of the fin-de-siècle, establishing the basis for a convergence of politics and aesthetics in a uniquely sectarian and radical form.

To begin with, crowds have historically played an important, even honored role in popular protest in European societies. There is now a vast historical literature on festive crowds, *carnaval* crowds, crowds engaged in bread riots and *jacqueries* (rural disorder), summary lynchings, or political and religious violence. But crowds tended to operate within limited and circumscribed boundaries, seeking to redress grievances as representatives in extremis of the rural or urban poor. Once its goals were attained, the crowd's temporary political capacity evaporated. Old Regime elites acknowledged and to a degree tolerated these forms of popular protest and activity because no one took crowds to be claiming for *le peuple* some wider kind of legitimacy or political rights.[3] This changed to some extent during the French Revolution, when particular crowds did occasionally arrogate to themselves the right to act in the name of *la nation* or *la république*. However, as Colin Lucas has pointed out, crowds still acted largely within the confines of their communities on behalf of circumscribed community goals, and were perceived as doing so by contemporaries.[4] There were efforts by radicals like Robespierre to mobilize Parisian crowds in the name of his democratic cause, but political elites were largely successful in keeping matters of popular protest and justice separate from the more explosive question of sovereignty.

One may trace the changes that eventually gave rise to the modern relationship between crowds and power in various nineteenth-century literary works, whose authors were simultaneously working out their own relations as artists with collective phenomena. A brilliant account of a typical Old Regime crowd appears in Alessandro Manzoni's great novel *I Promessi Sposi* (1827). A starving Milanese crowd invades bakeries and flour warehouses, seeking the commissioner of supply responsible for bread prices to exact a bloody vengeance on him. In his description of this episode, Manzoni employed some of the characterizations of crowds and their extremist leaders that would later be used by the "classic" writers on crowds in the 1890's — the small vocabulary of the crowd, its single-mindedness, the passion of its "gross body" — but he saw no greater political implications in the episode, despite the immediate threat the crowd posed to legitimate authority.[5]

Forty-two years later, in *L'Education sentimentale*, Gustave Flaubert's novel set during the Revolution of 1848, one finds a closer connection between the actions and declarations of revolutionary "mobs" and democratic sovereignty, together with a descriptive language that speaks of the "magnetism" of crowds and focuses on irrational states of mind.[6] Significantly, Flaubert also gives voice to his horror of the crowd's sinister hatred of art in his account of the invasion of the Tuileries Palace by common folk who deck themselves out in royal finery, smash glassware, and profane the beds of the princesses, "as consolation for having been unable to rape them" (*Sentimental Education*, pp. 281–84).

In a similar vein, François Guizot, the historian who had guided the politics of the *juste milieu* during the July monarchy, recalled in 1849 his dismay at the crowds that had earlier brought the Orleanist regime into being. They were, he wrote, "a vast flood of insensate ideas, of brutal passions, of perverse desires, of terrible fantasies."[7] Twenty years later, Guizot's characterizations of fearsome crowds were echoed by the novelist Edmond de Goncourt, who experienced the siege of Paris during the Commune. Goncourt witnessed the transformation of the anti-Prussian crowds of 1870 ("the original good fellows of the *Marseillaise*") into the paranoid collectivities of the Commune: "the immense crowd that gathers on bad days, an agitated, stormy crowd, looking for disorder and victims, from which continually arises the shout: 'Arrest him!'"[8] The power of this image of modern urban crowds was such that the critic Hippolyte Taine was compelled to see it already present in the crowds of 1789 in his monumental *Origines de la France contemporaine* (1876–93). In his words, the "vertigo" of the crowd became a "cold or furious monomania, maddened in the destruction of a past it curses, and in the establishment of the millennium it pursues, and all in the name of an imaginary contract, at once anarchical and despotic, which unfetters insurrection and justifies dictatorship; all to end in a social antagonism, resembling now a bacchanalian orgy of madmen, and now a Spartan conventual group."[9]

It remained for literary naturalism to close the circle embracing the crowd, biomedical discourse, and politics. Henrik Ibsen wrote the play *An Enemy of the People* in 1882, following the hostile reception to *Ghosts* the previous year. A loyal democrat and friend of the people until the "betrayal" in act 4, Dr. Stockmann finds himself confronted by a howling, unruly crowd whipped up by his brother Peter and Peter's lieutenants. Stockmann unleashes his rage at the crowd, calling them an "ignorant and incompetent" mob and likening them to common barnyard hens and mongrels that deserve to be ruled by "aristocratic" breeds and "exterminated like vermin."[10]

But even as he is denouncing the crowd's unfitness for self-rule, Stockmann outlines a pragmatic theory of truth that accords well with the concept of avant-garde artistic truths adumbrated later by Renato Poggioli and others. Truths, says Stockmann, are short-lived. They are adopted by the free "individuals" like himself who "stand at the outposts" of society, but are passed on to the "majority" only when they have "gone sour and green and tainted" like "last year's salt pork."[11] By having Stockmann repudiate his belief in absolute scientific truth in favor of a relativist doctrine founded on personality and circumstance, Ibsen anticipated both a later chapter in the history of epistemology in the West and the subsequent evolution of his own doctrine of literary naturalism.

Emile Zola's great crowd novel, *Germinal*, appeared three years later, in 1885. Here and in *Le Débâcle* (1892), there are a number of scenes in which Zola emphasizes the savage, hysterical qualities of crowds and explores the dynamics of the leader-crowd relationship.[12] As Naomi Schor has pointed out, Zola revealed the individuality of his characters *in relation* to crowds, in the way they exercised "their will to power over the crowd" (*Zola's Crowds*, p. 80). His focus on the leader-crowd relationship seems also to have functioned analogically for Zola as a description of the relation of the modern writer with his public. Zola's preoccupation with crowds and character, together with the growing association of crowds and democracy in his novels, puts us on the cusp of the 1890's, the so-called era of crowds.

This brief historical and literary introduction to the 1890's brings me to my first point, that the "science of crowds" which emerged in the 1890's was inspired by contemporary developments that thrust crowds into a new relationship with politics. In the 1870's and 1880's, the major Continental powers were making a momentous adjustment to democratization and mass politics. The French republican regime was seeking legitimacy for the most democratic political system in Western Europe, while the Germans and Italians were attempting to culturally reinforce the state-building process through which they had just passed. The regimes of all three states chose to ensure the allegiance of the masses by invoking old national myths and symbols or inventing new ones, exemplified in "national" festivals, anthems, monuments, and the like.[13] This "nationalization of the masses" was supplemented by the inculcation of patriotic ideals in the classroom, a fire-breathing chauvinism in the new mass press, and a new, frankly emotional style of electioneering adopted to suit the requirements of popular suffrage.

To the dismay of the old political elites, working-class electors and many still unenfranchised citizens followed the banners of the new mass-based socialist parties. As a consequence, the huge increase in the size and frequency of strikes and in labor militancy assumed a far greater *political* significance than it might otherwise have done, since it now gave weight and force to the demands of parliamentary socialism.[14] Beginning in 1890, the same supportive function was performed by celebrating international working-class solidarity in colossal May Day parades and demonstrations that annually terrorized the urban bourgeoisie (Barrows, *Distorting Mirrors*, pp. 24–31). As Enzo Collotti has put it, "May Day more than any other day represents the synchronization and therefore the amplification of countless voices everywhere in the world. May Day provides a photo-fit picture of a movement of protest and by sheer weight of numbers amplifies the sense of power of a whole class."[15]

By the 1890's, crowd phenomena had become or were becoming an integral part of the public sphere, and therefore a part of the national struggle for power that was taking place everywhere between old liberal elites (and their aristocratic allies) and leaders and spokesmen for the newly enfranchised masses. Crowds were no longer merely *representative* of local or corporate interests but dramatic *representations* of powerful social and cultural forces in the modern nation-state. Both in England and on the Continent, it became conceptually impossible for political theorists who speculated on the evolution of political democracy to overlook the impact of crowds on government and statesmanship. They were obliged to rethink utterly the out-moded assumptions of elite, liberal politics by factoring in the weight of the masses.[16]

The new science of crowd and collective behavior that was invented to fill this need was initially a French and Italian undertaking; it relied primar-ily on psychiatric knowledge and theories of hypnosis — much in vogue at the time — to explain the mechanisms by which crowds were formed and how ideas spread among individuals to unite them into a compact mass.[17] The writings of Scipio Sighele, Gabriel Tarde, and especially Gustave LeBon were exceedingly popular, exerting an influence in a number of dif-ferent fields.[18] The representative work of the genre, LeBon's *Psychologie des foules* (1895), was immediately translated into fifteen foreign languages, has never been out of print, and is certainly one of the best-selling scientific books of all time.[19]

The crowd psychologists situated their subject squarely within the politi-cal and cultural crisis of their time. As LeBon put it, the power of crowds in the modern world has increased in tandem with the decline of traditional ideals in religion and authority and of the prestige of the old governing elites. Crowds were the rootless, anomic product of urban civilization; buffetted by the tides of opinion generated by the mass press, crowds were available for mobilization by those with the knowledge and will to confront them. Left to themselves, LeBon warned, they will fall under the spell of socialist dema-gogues who will ensnare them with the utopian dream of a classless society.[20]

To their dismay, LeBon and his fellow crowd psychologists realized that the crowds of the 1890's were different from the crowds that had looted bak-eries and grain wagons during the Old Regime. Traditional crowds only gath-ered for immediate, short-term aims and had remained in awe of the tradi-tional authority of church and monarchy; in a pinch, they could be readily brought to heel by superior force or bought off with free bread. But modern crowds were a permanent feature of contemporary civilization, pullulating in streets, factories, sports arenas, and assembly places in a state of perma-nent mobilization. Crowd psychologists also paid homage in their writings to the power of modern communications networks to create vast crowds — "publics" — by simultaneously generating "mental images" and currents of opinion.[21] So great was the power of crowds, LeBon pessimistically con-cluded, that one could no longer hope to govern them; at best, a knowledge of the psychology of crowds could allow one "not to be too much governed by them" (*The Crowd*, p. 19).[22]

The paradox that underlies these rationalist and liberal anxieties is the subject of my second theme. Crowds were symptoms of an age of decline. LeBon believed that progress was led by tiny intellectual elites and that the rule of crowds "is always tantamount to a barbarian phase" in the history of civilization (ibid., p. 18). But whatever their sins with respect to progress, barbarians are bursting with energy that may allow them to serve as the source of a *ricorso* (regeneration) revitalizing the whole of culture. Thus, despite its conservative bias masquerading as science, crowd psychology presents an account of crowds and the "crowd mind" that freely acknowledges both the manic energy of crowds and the boundless, eternally renewable source of their power.

According to LeBon's classic account, in a crowd, as in hypnosis, an otherwise rational individual surrenders his consciousness, yields to the atmosphere of reciprocal suggestion, and "descends several rungs in the ladder of civilization":

Isolated, he may be a cultivated individual; in a crowd he is a barbarian — that is, a creature acting by instinct. He possesses the spontaneity, the violence, the ferocity, and also the enthusiasm and heroism of primitive beings, whom he further tends to resemble by the facility with which he allows himself to be impressed by words and images — which would be entirely without action on each of the isolated individuals composing the crowd — and to be induced to commit acts contrary to his most obvious interests and his best-known habits. An individual is a grain of sand amid other grains of sand, which the wind stirs up at will. (ibid., pp. 32–33)

The sources of the crowd's energy are the unconscious and primitive elements of human nature that have survived the course of evolution, including humankind's most ancient memories and instincts. LeBon and other crowd theorists borrowed this idea from the concept of atavism, a cornerstone of the popular evolutionary science of their day. The Italian criminologist Cesare Lombroso used the idea to account for the appearance in civilized society of the "born criminal." As he explained his "discovery," the criminal was "an atavistic being who reproduces in his person the ferocious instincts of primitive humanity and the inferior animals."[23] It was precisely this aspect of LeBon's crowd psychology that so appealed to Freud's psycho-Lamarckian notion of the nature of unconscious life, provoking his agreement that one "regressed" in crowds to the mental level of "savages or children."[24]

As Anson Rabinbach has recently demonstrated, fin-de-siècle Europeans were obsessed with fatigue, haunted by fears that human energy was being drained off both by the excessive demands that industrial civilization makes on intellect and by the ceaseless, unnatural stimulation of the organism in contemporary urban life. Fatigue became a "problem" to be overcome by careful study of physiology and by implementing a variety of will-therapies that taught scientists how to draw on the body's latent force.[25] In the setting of the fin-de-siècle, one can thus understand that the savage energy of crowds might appear in two aspects: as threat and as promise. What was most ancient in crowds, the "residues" they manifested of savage life, was precisely what made them so "modern" — and therefore both a symptom of an effete and decadent civilization and a potential bulwark against it.

Aesthetes in the 1890's and after were confronted with the same ambiguity in crowds. We know one common response was akin to Flaubert's: a horror of the crowd that provoked a "foregrounding of the violent, anarchic potential of the mob."[26] As Jennifer Birkett has shown, because Symbolist and decadent painters in the 1890's saw modern collectivities as a threat to individual autonomy, they dramatized their sense of impotence in scenes of "dream and evasion" ("*Fin-de-siècle* Painting," pp. 149–51). Richard Drake has argued that in Italy Umbertian aesthetes like Gabriele D'Annunzio were so unnerved at the aspect of the new masses that "*l'art pour l'art*" functioned "not only as an esthetic theory; it also involved an explicit political ideology" by erecting a *cordon sanitaire* against pollution from the crowd.[27]

Whatever the first reaction, there is ample testimony to a growing fascination by artists and writers with the primitive as a source of renewal in a dying culture. As Renato Poggioli has argued, "in the decadent spirit one can perceive a profound and disturbed nostalgia for a new primitiveness: the wait with mixed fear and hope for the coming of a new 'return to barbarism.'"[28] If we accept Matei Calinescu's argument, this potential for artistic engagement also characterized the acolytes of "art for art's sake," who have always been linked to more activist promoters of cultural renewal through their mutual goal of desiring the "aestheticization of the world."[29]

The last point I wish to make follows directly from the second one, namely, that the most important thing about the varied reactions of contemporaries to the savage crowds of modern life was not how they differed, but what they shared in common. The convergence of politics and art in this era, which many have commented on, had its birth in this set of commonalities and in a doctrine of social pragmatics to which it gave rise. It is ironic to find evidence for this development in the work of the era's most frenzied opponent of artistic modernism, Max Nordau. In his *Degeneration* (published in 1892 in German, 1893 in French, and 1895 in English), Nordau diagnosed the Symbolists, naturalists, and Nietzscheans — and their followers — as hysterics and degenerates, that is, as beings in whom reason and will had been weakened by a combination of the hyperstimulation of urban life and pathological heredity. They were all, he believed, excitable, impulsive, highly suggestible, and so troubled by a surfeit of imagination that they mistook their own delusions, or the images presented to them, for reality itself.[30]

But for Nordau, the great danger was not simply the existence of a handful of demented poets, who might at worst delude one another, but their recruitment of an army of converts from among "weak" and "dependent" beings inflicted with an "irresistible passion for imitation" (*Degeneration*, pp. 24–25). The mechanism used by contemporary psychiatrists to explain the transmission of madness from one lunatic to another — folie à deux — Nordau applied to the formation of pathological groups. As he put it, "The common organic basis . . . [of this process], the founding of aesthetic schools, the banding of criminals — is, with the active part, viz., those who lead and inspire, the predominance of obsessions: with the associates, the disciples, the submissive part, weakness of will and morbid susceptibility to suggestion" (ibid., pp. 30–31). It was his belief in the universality of this enthrallment that allowed Nordau to claim, for instance, that the "triumph of the Symbolists marks the victory of the gang over the individual," despite the declared aim of Symbolist poets like Mallarmé to write poems that everyone could interpret in his own manner (ibid., pp. 103–4). What Nordau did was deduce from the medical literature of the era, in which he was thoroughly steeped, the implications of degeneration, and especially hysteria, for the spread throughout fin-de-siècle society of the modernist art he despised. In doing so, he anticipated the similar explanations for the dynamics of the leader-crowd relationship offered a few years later by the crowd psychologists, inspired by the same clinical model.

It is important to note, however, that the naturalist, "decadent," and Symbolist texts of which Nordau so disapproved reflected the same fascination with pathology, with the misadventures of heredity and the power of affective mental phenomena, as Nordau's own book. Though Nordau strained to make his diagnoses more "scientific" than those of Ibsen, Zola, and Huysmans, he drew on the same medical discourse of putrescence and decline. In the manner of the rationalist crowd psychologists whose work followed and complemented his own, Nordau acknowledged the primitive emotional power of those afflicted with modern diseases of the will, but he hoped that "progress" would eventually permit the "higher centers" of the brain to extend their "authority" over the "instincts and passions" (ibid., pp. 312–13).[31]

The point I wish to emphasize is that by the turn of the century a great many people were interested in the utility of mechanisms of nondiscursive and nonrational communication. Crowd psychologists like LeBon and Sighele hoped to persuade center-right politicians to use the lessons of their science to lure the masses away from socialism and back toward nationalism and class solidarity.[32] On the other side of the political spectrum, Georges Sorel, whose *Reflections on Violence* (1906) was inspired by revolutionary syndicalism, regarded the psychological crowd as the indispensable foundation of the "myth" of the general strike.[33] The work of both Sorel and LeBon was known and valued by the founders of elite theory — Vilfredo Pareto, Gaetano Mosca, and Robert Michels — all of whom considered elite manipulation of the "sentiments" of the masses an inescapable reality of modern political life.[34] The point of agreement among this politically diverse group of theorists was their pragmatic distinction between the true and the useful in social action. They all held that most modern social ideologies were false — "nonlogical," in Pareto's sense — but that they met a pragmatic test of social truth; that is, they were capable of enjoining the enthusiastic adherence of the modern masses. Mosca's "political formula," Pareto's "derivations," Sorel's "myth," and Michels's and LeBon's "suggestion" all meet this test. As in Max Weber's concept of charisma, the political legitimacy of ideas and individuals in modern democratic societies is determined by what works, namely, which ideas and leaders the masses anoint with their loyalty.

Though they operated within a more local frame of reference, many avant-garde artists considered crowds to be an important part of their aesthetic outlook. Several commentators have drawn attention to the intensity of the "psychic" relationship between the avant-garde and, in order of ascending size and diversity, its audience, its public, and the masses in general. Renato Poggioli has been unusually eloquent on this point, indicating the close connection between avant-garde "poetics" and particular political and ideological corollaries (*Theory of the Avant-Garde*, pp. 4–5). As it was variously articulated between 1914 and the mid-1920's, the relation of artist to audience / mass was held to range between a hopeless mutual antagonism and divine correspondence. The sheer nihilism of the former position was perhaps best expressed by Georges Ribemont-Dessaignes, who wrote in 1926 that "there is no remedy" to the bankruptcy of our times except a "sheet of flaming gasoline" that would consume "the civilized and those who lay claim to civilization." However, he continued,

There is a means to remedy the absence of a remedy. It is to incite the masses to destructive fanaticism, to savagery, to incomprehension of all that is "noble." When the artist can no longer go out without having his cheek covered in spittle and losing an eye, that will be the beginning of a fresh and happy era. For men will never have had purer and more enormous pleasures. And never will our "art" have been more lively and more vigorous.[35]

Nihilism, of course, is an impossible doctrine. For most avant-garde artists, such rhetoric concealed a deeper hope that this savage uprising against traditional art would cultivate an aesthetic regeneration from the scorched earth it left behind. While still aroused, the masses — like revolutionary crowds — might prove more receptive to new doctrines and more tractable for teachers schooled in their unique psychology. Thus a great act of destruction was necessary before the new city could be built. This complex outlook was more or less inherent in the avant-gardes of the war and postwar era, when they simultaneously reflected and inspired the political experiments of sovietization and "direct action" that were unfolding — from Munich to St. Petersburg — in Central and Eastern Europe. For a fleeting historical moment, direct access to the masses seemed to be the key to disrupting routine and realizing genuine — that is to say, cataclysmic — change in both politics and in art.

Perhaps the best example of this point, and of my argument in general, is Italian Futurism, especially its guiding spirit, F. T. Marinetti. Marinetti reminds us that his intellectual "precursors" include Emile Zola, J. H. Rosny, and Paul Adam, all of whom wrote novels famous for their crowd scenes: Zola's *Germinal* and *Le Débâcle*, Rosny's novel about revolutionary syndicalism, *Le Vague rouge* (1910), and Adam's story of the Boulanger affair, *Le Mystère des foules* (1895).[36] Marjorie Perloff has written about the "manifesto fever" that the Futurists did so much to raise and has pointed out that Marinetti's 1909 *Futurist Manifesto* addressed "the 'you' of the crowd, the mass audience whom he hopes to move as well as to delight."[37] The theatricality of these early manifestos, in which Marinetti used repetition, digression, and a variety of rhetorical tactics to capture the attention of his audience, anticipated his later writings on nonsyntactical speech, "words-in-freedom," and the theory and practice of Futurist theater.[38]

In all these endeavors, Marinetti's aim was not simply to convert his "crowd-audience," though that was certainly an important motive of his "anti-neutralist" crusade in 1914–15, but to goad it into action, engage it in dialogue, and then feed off its energy. As he put it in 1912, in the "Technical Manifesto of Futurist Literature," "Syntax was a kind of abstract cipher that poets used to inform the crowd about the color, musicality, plasticity, and architecture of the universe. . . . This intermediary must be suppressed in order that literature may enter directly into the universe and become one body with it" (Flint, *Marinetti*, p. 89). In his essays "The Pleasure of Being Booed" and "The Variety Theater," Marinetti insists that Futurists break with sentimental story lines and coherent syntax designed to produce applause and superficial effects in favor of a true artistic "collaboration" with the audience, which will "symphonize" it, replace "psychology" with "body-madness," and, "through unbroken contact, create between us and the crowd a current of confidence rather than respectfulness" (ibid., pp. 118, 120, 126–28).

Though Marinetti continued to introduce new techniques for mobilizing audiences ("dynamic and synoptic" declamation and onomatopoetic devices), he was not simply engaging in aesthetic innovation for its own sake. He was also performing an empirical exercise in pragmatic aesthetics, the aim of which was to perfect affective, nondiscursive methods for tapping into the immense energy of crowds, training them in the sublime "body-madness" of Futurist exaltation, and, ultimately, teaching them to scorn the "*passéist*" traditions of a decadent, moribund Italy. As Marinetti declared in a manifesto of 1920, "Beyond Communism":

Art is revolution, improvisation, impetus, enthusiasm, record-setting, elasticity, elegance, generosity, superabundance of goodness, drowning in the Absolute, struggle against every hindrance, an aerial dance on the burning summits of passion, destruction of ruins in the face of holy speed, enclosures to open, hunger and thirst for the sky. . . .

There are shadowy, flaccid human masses, blind and without light or hope or willpower.

We will tow them after us. (ibid., p. 154)

The Italian Futurists were certainly outspoken among the avant-gardes of that era in wishing to mobilize the crowds they had angered and aroused for particular political ends; elsewhere, the aims of techniques of crowd provocation appear to have been more aesthetic than worldly. In his *Memoirs of a Dada Drummer*, Richard Huelsenbeck recounts his trips to provincial cities in 1919–20 to campaign for "Berlin" Dada. He and his little troupe never had enough sound poems or nonsense chants to fill out an evening, and it was Huelsenbeck's task to inform the audience that Dada was nothing and that they could not expect them to behave "like the people who use art as a dessert in their bourgeois existence." Inevitably, "The audience became noisier and noisier, and soon the whole auditorium was in an uproar. In

Prague, we had several thousand raging spectators. It was like the outbreak of a revolution, the mob was crying havoc. . . . It was the raucous bellow of a furious mass. Now we had them where we wanted." [39]

As he later reflected, "If we hadn't been in personal danger, we would have had a splendid opportunity of studying mass psychology. I realized that masses always consist of a troop and of a small band of fighters in the front rank" (*Memoirs*, p. 70). Huelsenbeck could not resist adding, "In our case, the front ranks began pelting us with solid objects"; but the small band of fighters of which he spoke was in fact his own little troop, an avant-garde doing battle with the philistine masses. The aim was not to gain their allegiance but to obliterate their usual expectations of art: "We were irrationalists, but we weren't content with offering people 'crazy pleasantness' that they might take home like Christmas presents. We cut through the bond between credit and debit, between one human being and the next, we asked about the necessity of the transmission of values when we removed all content from what we did" (ibid.).

Paris Dada was equally versed in the techniques of crowd arousal and manipulation, depending heavily on theatrical performance to present its message. [40] Tristan Tzara constructed his first plays to display his belief that the frankly nondiscursive forms of Dada poetics tapped into the "primitive structures" of affective life. When French Dada later evolved into surrealism, André Breton likened it to narcotics: "Like them it creates a certain state of need and can impel men to terrible revolts." [41] But the anti-rational nature of surrealism would also permit him to lure "spectators into magnetic fields where they would no longer be able to find customary bearings." [42]

The apparent disinterest in particular goals contained in the oracular utterances of Dada and post-Dada poets should not blind us to the essentially pragmatic and utilitarian nature of their aesthetic philosophy; these more politically neutral examples of crowd manipulation nonetheless share with Italian Futurism the conviction that a true revolution in the artistic conventions of the day could best be achieved by unleashing the primitive emotions of crowds, thus bringing them to the surface so that they could be manipulated by artists and dreamers. For self-described "irrationalists" like Huelsenbeck, Tzara, Breton, and many other members of the postwar avant-garde, a clear part of the appeal of these encounters with angry crowds was to bathe in an atmosphere of emotion and chaos, experiencing directly what they imagined was the domain of unconscious life, illogic, and nonsyntactical communication.

But they were not so "irrational" themselves that they were incapable of taking a supremely cynical and instrumental attitude toward the lessons of crowd psychology, feigning madness in order to provoke it. Salvador Dali once said that the only difference between himself and a madman was that he was not mad. This is a perfect example in individual psychology of the pragmatic outlook toward the "beast within" that I have tried to elucidate with respect to modernism and crowds. The disdain certain modern artists expressed for inheriting the mantle of traditional artistic authority did not, for all that, annul all their hunger for influence; that hunger was, instead, displaced onto new audiences, requiring radically new techniques of mobilization and a virtual abandonment of artistic disinterestedness.

As we have learned to our regret, this point about pragmatics applies equally well to certain twentieth-century mass movements born at the same historical moment, which, more or less self-consciously, also subordinated ideological content to efficacy, reason to unreason, absolute to pragmatic truth. As José Ortega y Gasset wrote in 1930, the taste for "direct action" based on the intervention of the masses was such that it had become "the norm which proposes the annulment of all norms, which suppresses all intermediate process between our purpose and its execution. It is the Magna Carta of barbarism."[43] Mussolini and Hitler were both familiar with LeBon's text on crowds and schooled in the lessons it taught, as were many of the smaller fry in fascist and national-socialist mass movements.[44] In those places where fascism was successful, its leaders inevitably followed the ideological line of least resistance, building popularity by exploiting local issues with powerful emotional or traditional appeal. They were, above all, pragmatists for whom theory and principle were subordinate to the more immediate advantages of influence. In matters of taste — not to mention ideals of artistic freedom — we have good reason to think that avant-garde artists and fascist politicians had little in common, but in their mutual belief in an "aesthetic politics" that depended on manipulating the sentiments of crowds, they were operating within a similar frame of reference.[45]

E L A Z A R   B A R K A N

# Victorian Promiscuity
*Greek Ethics and*
*Primitive Exemplars*

In 1867, Frederick Leighton exhibited *Venus Disrobing*, the first large nude at the Royal Academy in two decades; the last had been William Etty's paintings of the 1840's. Leighton's Venus displays enough of herself to make us more voyeurs than innocent spectators, but Leighton's spectators denied what seems to us self-evident: "Nakedness is not the leading characteristic of the figure," one commentator judged, while another admired it as "eminently chaste."[1] To Leighton's contemporaries there was nothing remarkable in this evasion. Victorian explanations of respectability dissociated nudity from nakedness, a tendency that marked art history until recently. Similarly, nude photography censored the display of contemporary white female nakedness but condoned explicit depictions of women classified as "ethnographic" and hence as exhibiting "Otherness."

How did the naturalistic nude impact Victorian prudishness? This question links the genealogy of modern sexuality with Victorian respectability. In the brave new world of Queen Victoria's reign, the discourse of sexuality represented a juncture of repression and contention that involved both high and popular culture. This discourse was shaped by a growing democratization and urbanization of culture and by rapid technological innovations, primarily in communications. Clearly, Victorian sexuality served as a vehicle for the oppression of women and non-Europeans and was directly shaped by the activity of Othering. Yet the dialectically subversive nature of the Victorian encoding of sexuality should not be underestimated. In the fervor of Victorian purity campaigners, for example, sexuality was repressed, but in the process certain "freedoms" (such as the talk about sexual vice and child prostitution) were condoned. Such subversive spaces at once demonstrated the real victimization that accompanied Victorian sexual representations[2] and anticipated the emerging modernism of the 1890's.

How is one to understand images of sexuality among the late Victorians?

Let us begin by considering the variety of encoding practices by which Victorians processed eroticism. The rhetoric and the framework of the subject matter determined its constructions, thereby setting boundaries between the highbrow and the forbidden. To the former belonged sexology, with a focus on social theories of sexuality and promiscuity as applied to "savages," the supremacy of the "classical" nude as executed in academic paintings, and, to some extent, Aubrey Beardsley's modernist subversiveness. Nude photographs of European women were not respectable except as "studies" for artists but such boundaries were murky when it came to defining pornography, other parts of Beardsley's work, and the "ethnographic" nude photographs of non-European women. One can see a persistent tension in the framing of these erotic representations. Should eroticism be associated with naturalism ("positivism" in science) — in which case its verisimilitude risks offending — or should we consider erotic images to represent the continuous quest for higher truth? These questions remain as pertinent now as they were for the Victorians. Like so much else in those hardy decades, English sexual mores evolved both in the British Empire itself and in the "collective imaginations" about that empire.[3] This process of encoding provided a continuity between High Victorianism and modernism.

Victorian audiences experienced a growing tension between social norms that were adverse to the public discussion of sexuality and an increased availability of sexual material within confined circles of specialized experts. The latter included medical doctors and scientists, writers, intellectuals, artists, photographers, and pornographers. Each utilized specialized genres that legitimized otherwise unacceptable images. As these experts busied themselves producing sexual representations, a "purity" movement concurrently strove to repress the dissemination of the experts' specific information to wider groups.[4] An increasingly intense discussion of sexuality produced both more freedom and harsher repression.[5] Driven by these dynamics, debates about women's sexuality, homosexuality, and masturbation became commonplace — part of a greater controversy over the relative social place of women and men. In this context, certain self-contradictory Victorian views were accepted as "rational." Why women supposedly without sexual urges should avoid riding the train, let alone a horse, in order not to arouse themselves is a particular example of a Victorian logic that did not need elaboration for contemporaries. The paradoxical elements of this cultural construction of women's sexuality were evident in misogynist as well as feminist writings. Women, defined by their sexuality, were denied the ability to express their "essence" in a healthy physical manner. Thus Elizabeth Blackwell, a purist and leading advocate of "Christian physiology," argued that "physical sex is a larger factor in the life of the woman, married or unmarried, than in the life of the man" but that it is manifested only through an "immense spiritual force of attraction."[6]

Michel Foucault followed Havelock Ellis in dating modern sexual repression to the late eighteenth century, and he assigned its cause to the way the culture of capitalism reconfigured the rhetoric of sexual representations.[7] Foucault's well-known position is that, although many Western representations seemed in opposition to one another, their critical force, subject to the limitations of the discourse on sexuality, did not become "a roadblock to a power mechanism that had operated unchallenged up to that point" but were, rather, a "part of the same historical network as the thing [they] denounce[d]."[8] Although cultural criticism since Foucault has been anything but univocal, many critics continue to subscribe to Foucault's judgment despite indicators that twentieth-century representations of sexuality have contributed to a rich and diverse discourse. Such changes, we are told, have occurred only to be co-opted into an increasingly repressive discourse. This is, in a way, the mirror image of the conservative position, which preferred ignorance over any kind of sexual discussion because it viewed the existence of the discourse as more significant than the substance of the discussion. But such constructions are inadequate regardless of their political affinity. Sexual repression formed only one aspect of a multivocal discourse that led to a recentered, dialectical notion of respectability and that challenged both state control and social mores. The Victorian pursuit of political and ethical "truths" about sexuality led to strange coalitions between the repressive and subversive camps. For example, purity campaigners who detested the libertines opposed control by police, experts, or the state, a stance that actually facilitated the libertines' work.[9] These multiple and contradictory configurations are the very essence of modernist sexuality.

## Sexology

I resume the story in the last third of the nineteenth century, when the purity campaign was gaining momentum and the public discussion of sexuality was at an ebb. At the same time, however, Darwin's description of sexual selection had created a spacious field for discussing forbidden fruit. Since Darwin's writing was science, produced and consumed by mature men, it raised little opposition to its sexual content. For Victorians, the more elaborate the professional discourse, the "closer to home" writers / scientists might venture: in this case from animals to savages and, finally, to Europeans. Yet such professional credentials were denied to women as too precarious an endeavor: discussing plant physiology was not inconsistent with modesty, but studying animal physiology was deemed immoral. Not surprisingly, teaching human anatomy and physiology to women presented a perplexing dilemma to "concerned" physicians and hence was adopted by certain women as a major target of political liberation.[10] For many, it simply remained out of the question.

During the 1890's, the professional discourse of sex became an important site for social theory. The vehicle was "the Other"; the subject was the self. "Pathologies" and "savages" provided a mode of justification, a trope to define the normal. Freud exemplified this approach when he conflated the normal and the abnormal in the course of attributing all human motives to sexual desires, but he was not alone in doing so. Nor was the professional medical discourse able to carry the debate very far. Despite its professional respectability, the medical construction of sexuality remained morally and culturally threatening. Thus a frequent strategy for addressing the "unspeakable" was through the Other — namely, ancient Europeans and contemporary savages — even though this meant invoking the most highly esteemed images (ancient Greeks) and the most denigrated ones (savages) within a single space. This precipitated new configurations that used savage exemplars as a trope for a wide range of social and sexual theories. The attraction of primitives was that they were viewed as closer to nature than Victorians — not quite brutes, but close enough, which gave writers license to speculate about the "nature" of sexuality. In contrast, a high regard for the ancients codified sexuality as a respectable topic even in the idealized company of ethics and aesthetics.

Inescapably, the Victorian urge to study Oriental and primitive sexuality brings us up against Occidental contradictions. The Victorians venerated hierarchies while preaching transcultural human egalitarianism. Whereas the racial distance of primitive subjects blunted otherwise offensively specific depictions of sexuality, it was the unity of Homo sapiens and the implied intimate connection between aboriginal mores and the European bedroom that made the exercise stimulating. Culturally or historically distant settings enabled erotic art to flourish unchallenged. Inadvertently, however, this implied that the norms of modern Europe were an exception in human experience. Victorians viewed this "exceptionalism" as the result of repression and decadence on the one hand and of progress and refinement on the other. Either way, Victorian attitudes toward sexuality ceased to be regarded as "natural." The prevailing view was that modern, "civilized" sexuality was an unhealthy necessity, preferably divorced from any eroticism. Paradoxically, the images that were initiated by the Victorians' intensive control over sexuality led to an expansive sexual discourse. As "sex was driven out of hiding and constrained to lead a discursive existence" (Foucault, *Sexuality*, p. 33), the unprecedented quantity of sexological texts resulted in a clamorous battle over moral conventions.

Foucault argues that sexologists concerned with the study of pathology and sexual aberration were emphasizing control, but his interpretations ignore their role in rehabilitating repressed sexual mores.[11] Sexuality, after all, was politics; for many sexologists, scientific study was a form of protesting repression and advocating social reform. In its explorations of alternative moralities, aesthetics, and sexualities, the new experimentation evolved into a political battle over public morality that was dominated by the purity party but that also included oppositional voices. Thus the purity campaign's powerful insistence on censorship and prosecution became in fact a testimony to the diminished hegemony of those moral standards that the purists were most anxious to represent.

In the 1890's, sexology strove to legitimize itself as a new scientific discipline against the background of the previous generation, whose moralists and sociologists had explored global folkways in search of normal sexuality but had been too inhibited to write about their real subject. Foremost among these was Herbert Spencer, who wrote an investigation of modesty entitled *Descriptive Sociology* (with chapters on "clothing," "moral sentiments," and "aesthetic production") but never explicated his topic.[12] Among the early writers on sexology, a few became very well known — Havelock Ellis, Magnus Hirschfeld, Iwan Bloch, Edward Carpenter, and, obviously, Sigmund Freud — and most combined their scholarly work with political reform.[13] Inexorably, their activity was directed toward the growing sexual reform movement. Historical and anthropological literature began to emphasize the particular — and perhaps historically peculiar — status of Victorian mores, thereby presenting a direct challenge to society.

Consider the late nineteenth-century repression of homosexuality, which culminated in Oscar Wilde's unfortunate response to the intentional defamation directed at him by his lover Lord Douglas's father, the Marquis of Queensberry, which led in turn to an official prosecution. The state did not instigate the proceedings but was pressured to participate by the National Vigilance Association. In fact, the state mediated between two interest groups: the purists and the reformers. Despite the apparent growing repres-

sion exemplified by Wilde's trial, the politics and scholarship of homosexuality in the 1890's suggest that homosexuality was a surging, not a diminishing,
trend.[14] Wilde's imprisonment was a response to the greater visibility of alternative beliefs and the challenges these posed to respectability. For example,
Havelock Ellis wrote his first two volumes, dealing with homosexuality and
modesty, during Wilde's trial and imprisonment, although the case data and
much of his other material for the first edition had been collected before the
trial. Ellis's aim was to redefine the normal by exploring its boundaries. His
methodology combined armchair anthropology with clinical psychology. He
presented numerous examples of "folkways" (case histories) from every
group in the world in a manner similar to that of his contemporaries James
Frazer and Edward Westermarck. His explicit rationale was to enlighten and
to inform in a field where ignorance had generated prejudice. His basic
egalitarian attitude did not mean that he rejected contemporary notions of
European superiority, but he did object to the conventional view of savages
as lacking modesty and having "gross" sexual attitudes. For the same reasons
Ellis opposed the judgment of inversions as abnormal. With time, as standards have changed, his method and views have lost their egalitarian flavor,
but his impact on contemporaries was radical — sexology was ripe to lead a
reform.[15]

Ellis's erstwhile colleague, John Addington Symonds, tried to make the
discussion of homosexuality more acceptable by invoking ethics (A *Problem
in Modern Ethics: Being an Inquiry into the Phenomenon of Sexual Inversion*,
1883) and the respectability of the ancients (A *Problem in Greek Ethics*).[16]
Another sexologist, Edward Carpenter, printed his *Homogenic Love* in 1894
and, as a response to Wilde's trial, André Raffalovich published in Paris *Ur-
anisme et Unisexualité* (1896), a comprehensive survey of the field. These
and similar writings that focused on ancient exemplars became the modus
operandi of sexologists. A few years later, Freud defined the erotic life of the
ancients and compared it to that of modern Europeans according to the
then-recent recognition of the differentiation in sexuality between "instinct"
and "object": "The ancients glorified the instinct and were prepared on its
account to honour even an inferior object; while we despise the instinctual
activity in itself, and find excuses for it only in the merits of the object." [17]

Within the evolutionary and social debate over sexuality, sexologists
searched distant and immediate prehistories for exemplars of the contemporary conundrum. Although Victorians were unhappy with the tension that
resulted from their attitudes to sexuality, solutions remained elusive. For example, advocacy of eugenics and racial hygiene remained theoretical and

abstract, whereas the spread of sexual diseases was real and personal. Libidinal energy was occasionally expressed through the arts but more often was simply repressed. In this search for new sexual spaces, attention shifted to the exotic. Orientalism and travel literature had existed earlier, but the new comparative sexology explored primitive mores as candidates for Occidental exemplars and contributed to the legitimation of diversity. Nowhere was this more evident than in tracts on the institution of the family.

Family and marriage had served the Victorian as a euphemism for sex. The institution of the family was regarded as both the most esteemed ideal and, regretfully, the main locus of sexuality. And if "marriage" was a euphemism for "sex," "anthropology" was a buzzword for pornography—as the probably small number of readers of *Untrodden Fields of Anthropology* by Jacobus X discovered, along with those privileged patrons who conducted "anthropological" research in the British Museum by accessing material from its restricted shelves.[18] The debate involving sexuality and the family included, among other issues, the need to mitigate the domination of males in the household; the growing pressure to concede more freedom to women; the explosion of demand for, and practice of, prostitution; and the rising fear of sinister sexual diseases—all of which were part of a very real change in the power relations between the sexes.[19] Exploring the family preoccupied writers and scholars, several of whom transformed the debate over the status of women in England into one about social evolution and matriarchy.[20] Following changes during the 1850's in English divorce laws and the fundamental challenge to gender relations, social theorists postulated "a natural order" of patriarchy, which was replaced in the 1870's by a new matriarchal orthodoxy.[21] Despite these two conflicting paradigms of the origin of the family, there was a scholarly consensus that moral progress accounted for the evolution of the modern, monogamous, asexual family. The more the family evolved, the less sexualized it became. And although influenced by the contemporary agenda of evolutionary discourse, theorizing about the primordial family developed according to both its own "internal" terminology and the reinterpretation of ethnological data.

Anthropological conjectures coalesced around the promiscuous family. Lewis Henry Morgan's theory of matriarchy became the most popular view of the origin of the family and was adopted by Friedrich Engels, who bequeathed it to a century of socialists, followed in turn by a generation of feminists.[22] Morgan's hierarchy began with "promiscuous intercourse," followed by siblings' cohabitation and, only in the third stage, the communal

family. This matriarchal family was broken down into several exotic formations, including "the Hawaiian custom" or "the Malayan form," which preceded the patriarchal family. Exoticized naming was central to the validation
of the theory. In Morgan's construction, the matriarchal family was promiscuous. It was only with patriarchy that the acquisition of property evolved
and progress could be achieved. And although women were believed not to
have any natural sexual drives, it was precisely in the natural state, when
women dominated society, that boundless sexual relations prevailed. Consequently, matriarchy and promiscuity were synonymous, though women
and sexuality continued to be viewed as antithetical.[23]

Anthropological studies had made it abundantly clear to the Victorians
that contemporary sexual arrangements were exceptional in human history.
Given the litany of eugenics at the time and the growing, pessimistic belief
in their own decadence, the Late Victorians were not particularly inclined
to be proud of this uniqueness. Yet they did not doubt that, whatever the
precise route from promiscuity to polyandry and polygamy, evolution was
essentially progressive and led toward a superior, patriarchal order. Still, their
ambivalence about progress and decadence was aggravated after the middle
of the century by an increased sexual apprehension.[24] Redefining kinship
classification and primitive mores as nonpromiscuous therefore provided a
potential site for contesting respectable forms of behavior. This fell to Edward Westermarck, who is largely forgotten today, but who at the turn of the
century exemplified the libertine scholarly position. Westermarck was a
strong advocate of subjective morality and relative ethics, supported the Free
Thinkers, and negotiated his own sexuality through scholarly writings.[25]

Westermarck's *The History of Human Marriage* argued against formulat-
ing promiscuity as decadence and claimed instead that prudishness and repression connoted degeneration. As an armchair anthropologist, Westermarck's methodology was to substantiate his assertions with extensive
ethnographic descriptions. These attested to the diverse sexual mores of
primitive societies — from cohabiting before marriage to lending wives —
and to social customs that privileged alternative moral values, many of
which, Westermarck implied (such as friendship and hospitality), ought
to be the envy of Western civilization. Furthermore, because sexuality
was functional in evolutionary terms, it was unnatural to repress its
manifestation.

In the process of reevaluating morality, Westermarck also rejected the
claim of racial mixture as deleterious. He challenged social, moral, and epis-

temological conventions from a professional hub. Shifting from his marginal ethnic position as a Swede in Finland to the academic and bohemian world of London, he used conventional wisdom to confront accepted etiquette. He defined marriage in functional terms, as a natural institution socially structured and aimed at benefiting the young: "Marriage is nothing else than a more or less durable connection between male and female, lasting beyond the mere act of propagation till after the birth of the offspring."[26] Such sociological relativism was rare even among Victorian agnostics, who believed, with the rest of society, that the preordained affinity of nature and society had manifested itself in the form of the British Empire. Through prodigious data collected in the British Museum and through global correspondence, Westermarck sought to prove that the family (i.e., marriage) actually originated in the monogamous family. This was fundamentally an egalitarian statement, but it was also a subtle denigration of Victorian society, whose most celebrated institution, the monogamous family, was thus identified with the most savage of unions.

Westermarck's scandalous conclusion was that "promiscuity" resulted from evolution. Westermarck reinterpreted ethnological data to conclude that promiscuity did not correspond to evolutionary stages: "In the lowest tribes chastity is more respected than in the higher ones." He also attributed "wantonness" among primitives to the "influence of civilization": "It has been sufficiently proved that contact with a higher culture, or, more properly, the dregs of it, is pernicious to the morality of peoples living in a more or less primitive condition" (*History of Human Marriage*, p. 66). Here was a direct challenge to the commonplace belief in linear moral progress, a new type of armchair imperialism. The words "human marriage" in Westermarck's title were a convenient, encoding misnomer for sexuality, meant not to hide the real issue but rather to enable a radical yet respectable critique.[27] Westermarck "apologized" to the reader who, he announced, "may find much that will outrage his feelings, and, possibly, hurt his sense of modesty." But Westermarck also excused himself. He had no choice: to "keep anything secret within its cold and passionless expanses, would be the same as to throw a cloth round a naked statue" (ibid., p. 7). This was an especially apt metaphor in light of the most prestigious paintings in the Royal Academy at the time by Frederick Leighton, Lawrence Alma-Tadema, and others (see below).

These sociological narratives and conjectural histories of the evolution of sexuality parallel the history of encoded sexuality in visual images. The Late Victorian proliferation of visual eroticism included academic paintings, modernist art, photography, ethnography, and pornography, to mention only the most indisputable. All employed images of the Other as a central trope of legitimation, and their discourses were often intertwined. For example, although photography was subject to its own aesthetic criteria, it also served as a general device for artists and became a global form of expression. But before focusing on non-European erotica, consider the reconfiguration of the classical nude among Victorians.

## The Classical Nude

The artificiality of accepted boundaries between sexuality and art can be discerned most obviously in the newly evolving domain of photography. Initially, the medium was viewed as comparable to painting, but soon the Victorians sensed that it might be too realistic to preserve the privilege of art. Hence erotic photographs were officially restricted to use by artists as *académies* and, especially in France, also became a dominant genre in the illicit pornography market. From Delacroix on, practically every major painter used photographs of models for his work. Studios specialized in the sale of these photos, and although nude photographs could be sold only within the Ecole des Beaux Arts, a prohibited trade flourished. Legal *académies* were defined as photos of "feminine nudes in natural poses either standing or reclining"; hence the distinction between *académies* and pornographic photos was presumed to be the pose of the woman. In a Peeping Tom photo the woman is supposedly unaware of the camera, whereas in the *académie* the model stares at the camera. This murky definition led to many legal disputes,[28] and was at best sanctimonious.

Art critics contended that representations of nudes in masterpieces were necessarily nonerotic and therefore legitimate,[29] yet criticism of nude art in Victorian society had always existed. Historians have tended to dismiss these critics as narrow-minded, substantiating their condescension by disputing either the eroticism of the paintings in question or the critics' right to be offended by it. Neither argument is tenable. Western nude painting had always existed, and it maintained its respectability during the Victorian period despite becoming controversial when its aristocratic patrons were supplanted by the growing middle classes. The last "pre-modern" English nude painter was William Etty (1787–1849), who painted nude studies in the Life School of the Royal Academy. His work was very "realistic," the poses natural and the colors bright. The Victorian conundrum about erotic art was exemplified by *The Spectator*'s criticism of Etty's *The Sirens and Ulysses* as "a disgusting combination of voluptuousness and loathsome putridity — glowing in colour and wonderful in execution, but conceived in the worst possible taste." This criticism displayed the prevailing attitudes toward nudes: guilt mixed with pleasure; naturalism contrasted with art as higher truth. The intensity of the rhetoric used suggests how middle-class prudishness was replacing the older aristocratic respectability.[30] Ruskin, the spokesperson for the sensibilities of the middle class at its best, assailed nudes as "most vulgar," "degraded and bestial."[31] During the 1850's only a few minor artists in England continued to paint nudes,[32] although this hiatus should not be overinterpreted, since it probably reflected a generational transition. In France, which was to provide the artistic paradigm for the next generation, these were the years when Ingres was doing his best erotic work and Courbet painting naturalistic nudes.

Meanwhile, the art market was responding to the newly affluent middle classes and their desire for imitations of the old masters. The patronage of the merchant class from the industrial regions created a new demand for "fresh" classicism. This may have been a facet of Matthew Arnold's barbarism (the newly rich found it cheaper to buy art by living artists, believing these to be similar to the old masters),[33] or possibly a manifestation of the new merchants' efforts to establish their own preferences for naturalism. In either case it had the effect of creating unprecedented opportunities for artists. The next generation of Academicians took full advantage of it and became, as a group, richer and socially more prestigious than painters had ever been before. But before turning to these Academicians, it is useful to look at the limitations placed on nude photography as art. In the 1850's, nude photography was potentially comparable to nude painting, although it failed to become a domain of high culture and respectability and was, consequently, censored in large part.

## Nude Photography

Photography's failure was not for lack of trying. For example, there was a popular 1850's photographic construction of "The Rape of the Sabines" that was used by Cézanne, Degas, Gauguin, and many others. In France a score of photographers specialized in such images, and in 1902 a new journal edited by Emile Bayard, *Le Nu Esthétique*, published ten pages of nude studies of women, children, and, infrequently, men, primarily in neoclassical and baroque style. The publication lasted three years. Hardly any comparable work was done in England. But the failure of nude photography to garner respectability was not a foregone conclusion. This uncertainty was best exemplified by the Swede Oscar Gustave Rejlander, who began working in Wolverhampton and who, by 1857, had become perhaps the most prominent artist-photographer in England.

The year 1857 shone with Old World confidence. Progress was there for the taking, and nowhere was it more evident than in the Manchester Art Treasures Exhibition, billed as the richest collection "north of the Trent" and as one that included Titians, Raphaels, and Rembrandts as well as photographs of paintings and drawings. Among its six hundred photographs, three, including *The Two Ways of Life*, were by Rejlander (Fig. 1). Although the exhibition presented photography as art rather than as technology, its status remained borderline, in part because art was transforming its own traditional meaning as skill. At the 1862 International Exhibition in England, for example, photography was classified in the artisan section while "highbrow" art was beginning to acquire its *post*industrial meaning.[34] But in 1857, oblivious to the gathering clouds of modernity, Queen Victoria, the embodiment of propriety, gazed at nude photography in public at the Treasures Exhibition: photography was, at that point, too novel to be indecent. The empress-to-be was trying on a new outfit for the arts, and photography seems to have qualified. Victoria is said to have purchased one of the reproductions of *The Two Ways of Life* for Prince Albert's studio.[35]

*The Two Ways of Life* (1857) is a composite photo presenting an allegory of life: a sage is leading two young men through the gate of life and showing them the paths of temptation and righteousness. Each path is illustrated by a group of representative characters. One leads to a religious, industrious life in which a young man with dreaming eyes wanders toward a group of praying people; elsewhere, others are working or studying diligently while three couples are shown simply as married. Meanwhile, the second youth, ignorant of his responsibilities, gaily strolls toward a bacchanalia where gambling is in progress and nude women gaze at him — and the world — in a most tantalizing manner.

Rejlander's initial difficulties in composing an idealistic tableau in a realistic genre were mundane — first, the technological constraints of a new medium, and second, obtaining models. The models who came could not relax. They did not look natural and were too stiff, inhibited, and nervous. The women who posed in the nude were said to have been "far too conscious of their semi nudity to conceal their feelings"[36] and to have remained unaware of the connoisseur's higher truth. Hence Rejlander had to resort to

professional models. However, given contemporary art connoisseurs' inclination to deny any erotic quality in allegoric paintings, this did not adversely affect the initial enthusiastic reception of the work. Many were all too eager to exalt the emperor's new clothes.

The glowing reception began at Court. Prince Albert, an eager photographer, had previewed *The Two Ways of Life* in March 1857, before it was displayed in Manchester. Rejlander had been a provincial photographer, and the invitation to the palace was a momentous turning point in his life; more importantly, it testified that photography was "aesthetically correct." *The Athenaeum* praised the work as masterly ("worthy to be painted as a fresco"), and a large number of people saw it before Queen Victoria opened the exhibition on June 30. The Queen's presence and Albert's enthusiasm absolved nude photography of its indecency, but this respectability lasted only a very short while.

FIG. 1. Oscar Gustave Rejlander,
*The Two Ways of Life* (1857). Reprinted
with permission of the International
Museum of Photography at George
Eastman House GEH #17238.

Almost immediately, ingenuous people commented that photography's
new clothes were indecent and others began to question the appropriateness
of applying art's aesthetic standards to the new medium. Ultimately, this un-
easiness led them to view Rejlander's composition as allegorically inadequate. Further, the deficiency was said to be inherent in photography rather
than in Rejlander's work itself. In the early discussions of whether *The Two
Ways of Life* offended the standards of "delicacy," many objected to the
scandalous intimation of impropriety. Rejlander had hoped the work would
celebrate the plasticity of photography: "I cannot understand how a painting upon the same subject can, except in its colouring, be more real or
truthful than a photograph," he said, and spoke of both painting and photography as "representative."[37] For Rejlander, realism was naturalism transformed into art through symbolism and was representative of higher truths;
it was not merely lifelike depictions. But others viewed photography as

too "naturalistic" and thus as incapable of transcending the limitations of respectability.[38]

A cool Scottish reception prompted further opposition. Following an 1857 refusal to exhibit *The Two Ways of Life* in Scotland, the composition was shown there in 1858 with the "dissolute half being curtained off." This was part of a growing campaign against indecent photography that came from the new middle classes, primarily from consumers who complained that photographic exhibitions were becoming too indecent to allow "a family" to view them together.[39] No longer confined to the private display of the rich, art now had to contend with middle-class moral standards. By 1863 even Rejlander's early supporters had become his adversaries. The controversy did not involve merely the intentions of the artist, but the discourse or medium itself. The photographer was regarded less as an artist than as a technician. Thomas Sutton, for example, who had received a copy of *The Two Ways of Life* from Rejlander in 1857 (for which he showed gratitude in the pages of the *Photographic News*), had by 1863 shifted his position dramatically. Sutton criticized Rejlander's realism for depicting a condition "in which degraded females were exhibited in a state of nudity, with all the uncompromising truthfulness of photography." If nude art was not ipso facto improper to begin with, it became so "in publicly exhibiting photographs of nude prostitutes, in flesh and blood truthfulness and minuteness of detail."[40] Thus, for the Victorians, the realistic nature of photography was limited to projecting life-like images and could not genuinely aspire to represent "forms more real than living man," as Shelley phrased it. Similar criticism was aimed during the same decade at Manet's *Olympia*.[41]

A wavering society, faced with a new medium, chose, after an initial surprise, to retrench. Although Victoria and Victorianism had been unprepared, standards quickly evolved. Faced with growing criticism, a new space was carved out for photography that excluded its aspirations toward art as higher truth. Rejlander may have chosen to press his claims,[42] but he was not a martyr and the time was unsuitable. It took several decades and a cultural revolution for photographic nudes of European women to be legitimized. In the meantime, the genre was limited to subjects of the empire. In Europe, the aesthetic legitimacy of nudity was permitted to Greek (and Roman) images, which enjoyed the dubious glamour of the quintessential Other. Thus the Academicians' encoded "Greek" erotic aestheticism achieved unparalleled respectability.

The material success of the Academicians was especially marked in comparison to the precarious existence of their French (Impressionist) contemporaries. But prestige had little correlation to long-term reputation, which in the case of many Academicians did not even last for their own lifetimes. While *Olympia* and early modernism were causing a tumult in Paris, the English Academicians borrowed from traditional Continental art to reinvent the classical. This was a rebuttal of Ruskin and the insular impact of the Pre-Raphaelites, which was celebrated through neoclassicism.[43] Naturalistic renditions of the noble and the pagan, the masculine and even homosexual were celebrated in the English Academy as respectful "higher truths." Among the younger Academicians who led the new movement, none was more illustrious than Frederick Leighton, who excelled in producing an endless number of classically inspired, realistic nudes.[44]

Lord Leighton (1830–1896) was amply honored. With "his noble appearance, his superhuman energy, his lofty devotion to high art, and his unique position as President of the Royal Academy and prince of the Victorian art establishment, he seemed to his contemporaries to belong to the world of gods and heroes rather than that of mere men. He saw himself as presiding over a new Periclean Athens in London." Upon being told of Leighton's expertise in music and administration, his superior knowledge, his good looks, and his social prominence, James Whistler is said to have responded: "Paints too, don't he?" (Wood, *Olympian Dreamers*, p. 33). This nineteenth-century Pericles was the most modern among the classicists and maintained his popularity into the 1890's. Leighton even contributed two drawings to *The Yellow Book* (the most celebrated avant-garde publication of the decade) and commissioned work from Aubrey Beardsley. Reputedly, he was generous toward "young and struggling artists" — one more virtue that was, no doubt, enhanced by the specific mold in which he chose to sublimate his sexual preferences.[45] Yet while Leighton shrouded his own private life, he also eroticized the bodies in his paintings. Among his early erotic depictions after *Venus Disrobing* were *Actaea, Nymph of the Shore* (1868) — a very realistic reclining frontal nude parading a large body and what might be seen as an "English" rather than "Greek" face — and a splendid *Daedalus and Icarus* (1869) in which Icarus stands in a self-consciously artistic pose, disrobed of his majestic dress. This Icarus is the very antithesis of an energetic, forceful person about to fly toward the sun (Fig. 2). Such was the way Victorians encoded the unspeakable, and it did prompt critics to pontificate about how lifeless Icarus seemed. Leighton himself seems to have wanted to portray Icarus's narcissism. Is it an exaggeration to see the canvas as a male pinup? Like Leighton's other heroes, Icarus seems pretentious, unemotional, staged. (Leighton's heroines were mostly passive, daydreaming, pensive, meditating,

FIG. 2. Frederick Leighton, *Daedalus and Icarus* (1869). Reprinted with permission of the Faringdon Collection Trust, Faringdon, Oxon.

and lacking explicit fervor or drama.) Given the controversial sense of realism at the time — true-to-life versus higher truth — Leighton's paintings may be said to have legitimated the realistic representations of nudes by displaying nakedness as sublime. Is this fundamentally alien to the cultural construction of *Playboy* or *Playgirl*? Does it anticipate gay aesthetics? All that can be said is that in 1890 no one would have formulated it this way.

A spectator in the 1990's may be inclined to suspect the aesthetic claims of such (erotic) representations and emphasize instead the potential exploitations involved. But given the stifling Victorian atmosphere, it is perhaps not insignificant to point to the Academicians' use of Greek aesthetics as a mode for sanctioning the representations of the body and for legitimizing the erotic. In a letter to G. F. (George Frederick) Watts, Leighton wrote that his whole life "seems spent trying to conquer my temper,"[46] and his paintings suggest that as he got older he became better at it. Yet Leighton's statement is too vague, his paintings too erotic, and both are too prone to being manipulated. While the Parisian avant-garde openly espoused the demimonde, certain English artists sublimated their unrespectable desires through what might be termed "Othering." For example, Leighton's melancholic heroines often had alluring, foreign-sounding names that accentuated their Otherness while simultaneously bestowing respectability. Reproductions and engravings of these paintings were widely marketed for the middle classes, "democraticizing" Leighton's erotic, aristocratic Others. The Academicians' commercial and social success prompts us to view them as rich males who exploited the female body for their own titillation, with no aesthetic or moral redeeming features. After all, as the genre became more explicit at the turn of the century, even artists who were relatively subdued thrived on paintings of female nudes that were seductive but not particularly coy or self-conscious.[47] Yet in this particular Victorian version of "The Empress's New Clothes," the Academicians legitimized a display of contemporary nudes and helped open a subversive, discursive erotic space for the body.

Not all nude representations lend themselves to such "neutral" constructions. It is tempting to ridicule paintings such as Leighton's *Perseus and Andromeda* (ca. 1891), in which a struggling, contorted, naked Andromeda is overshadowed by an immense dragon, cliffs, and rocks. In an atmosphere of horror and nightmare, Perseus may be said either to ride high above on Pegasus in an effort to save Andromeda or to gaze at the thrills below, where the pure and white Andromeda is about to be taken by evil (Fig. 3). Here Perseus's heroism is mostly evident by its absence. But other, more "benign"

FIG. 3. Frederick Leighton, *Perseus and Andromeda* (ca. 1891).
Reprinted from Wood, *Olympian Dreamers*, p. 63.

FIG. 4. Frederick Leighton, *The Bath of Psyche* (ca. 1890). Reprinted with permission of the Tate Gallery, London.

myths also seem to subvert the accepted morality as, for example, in *The Bath of Psyche* (ca. 1890), which involves a lesbian nymph (Fig. 4). Leighton's composition is arranged with classical Victorian formalism: "girlish and slight . . . self-consciously elegant . . . strictly formal, draperies and columns framing the figure on both sides . . . vertical and horizontal are carefully balanced . . . chaste, aesthetic, decorative and evocative" (Wood, *Olympian Dreamers*, p. 66). But Leighton's extensive decor only accentuates the evocative nature of Psyche, who gazes at her own image in the water. Psyche belonged, after all, to a genre of women exhibited in the tepidarium, frigidarium, apodyterium, or Oriental and Japanese baths, individually or in groups, and all defined by their radiating sexuality. Even in eras when the nude itself was not admitted to be highly sensual, the context seems to have sufficed to eroticize the painting.

Sir Lawrence Alma-Tadema (1836–1912), a native of Holland who had migrated to England, excelled more than anyone else in portraying Roman baths and depicting pretty, statuesque women, many of whom were nude. His attention to detail and his emulation of ancient sculpture led *Punch* to refer to his paintings as "marbelous" and to nominate him for KCMB— "Knight of the Cool Marble Bath." His attachment to ancient themes seems to have begun during his 1863 honeymoon in Italy. His "Pompeian works" were done primarily from 1865 to 1870, and are rich with red but not sexually explicit. Before the late 1870's he did not often paint nudes, but his 1877 *A Sculptor's Model* caused a minor stir and marked a turning point: the full-length standing nude in an "uncompromising frontality" titillated viewers a tad more than was respectable. So, even the Bishop of Carlyle had to respond. It has been suggested that Alma-Tadema was taken aback by the criticism and that his "future nudes were more chaste" (ibid., p. 115), a judgment that is especially difficult to support when looking at his *In the Tepidarium* (1881)—a demure *Playboy* centerfold (Fig. 5). As he grew older, Alma-Tadema's women became ever more beautiful and sensual. His imitators accentuated these tendencies further during the first decade of the twentieth century, but by then their claim to "higher truth" had been widely ridiculed.

Alma-Tadema enjoyed immense popularity and grew rich in wealth and honors while leading a perfectly normal, middle-class family life. How, then, is one to read his obsession with Roman baths and antique details, which manifested itself in a growing eroticism? Was it merely a trope and a fad, or was he sublimating libidinal urges by fetishizing historical accuracy? The latter interpretation may be rendered plausible if Alma-Tadema's interest in ancient sexuality is traced back to his honeymoon in Pompeii, which took place concurrently with the excavations of a major part of the pornographic paintings and sculptures there.[48] These explicit depictions of bodies and sexual acts extended beyond the conventional Victorian imagination. Little is known about which of the archaeological finds Alma-Tadema actually saw, but in the next few years the daily life of the Romans became his inspiration and obsession. After the death of his first wife, his move to England, and a

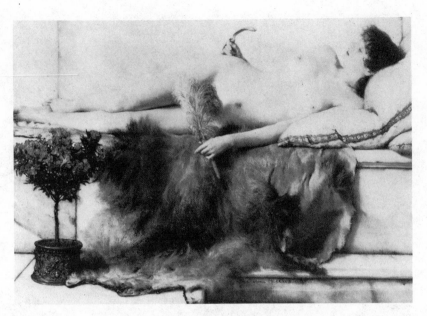

FIG. 5. Lawrence Alma-Tadema, *In the Tepidarium* (1881). Reprinted with permission of the National Museums and Galleries on Merseyside, Liverpool.

second marriage (his new wife was a painter in her own right), his libido seems to have been drawn more explicitly into Pompeii's fantasies. Older and honored, Alma-Tadema could finally release his energies on canvas, as in *A Favourite Custom*, which he painted about 1909 (Fig. 6). Nevertheless, his life-style and respectability suggest that, despite the famous sex scandals of the late Victorian period, the details of which are frequently rehearsed by historians, it is the public encoding of what was otherwise "indiscrete" that ought to occupy our attention. Notwithstanding numerous recent histories of sexuality, we know very little about even the most prominent Victorians who shaped the erotic imagination of their generation. Especially successful, but not unique, were Leighton and Alma-Tadema, who greatly enhanced their own prestige as artists by the erotic allure of the canvas. The Victorian ambivalence about classical sexuality had to do with the perceived promiscuity — in the forms of liberated goddesses, aristocratic orgies, and homosexuality — of a highly civilized society, possibly the only one more civilized than their own. Portraying antiquity through enticing nudes was therefore a double subversion — namely, that of coupling classical virtues with steamy daydreaming. Yet by the 1890's Alma-Tadema's art had turned into fashion

FIG. 6. Lawrence Alma-Tadema, *A Favourite Custom* (ca. 1909).
Reprinted with permission of the Tate Gallery, London.

and become a precursor of Hollywood and of the mass consumption of insinuated eroticism.

Victorian standards for judging these portrayals remained viable until very recently. Thus, for example, just before the 1970's, when feminist art criticism became central to the profession, one commentator could still say about the Academician's paintings: "One is often scarcely aware that the figures are nude at all, so completely are they subordinated to the central idea of the design on the rarefied plane of High Art."[49] This evaluation seems closer in certain respects to the Victorian era than to the 1990's.

## Modernism and Dirty Pictures

The precarious aesthetic position of the Academicians was underscored by the rapid decline of their prestige and their displacement by high modernism. Moreover, as Victorian respectability was challenged, its borders of propriety were reshaped by naming certain representations as high art while relegating others to the realms of "photography" or "pornography." Without dwelling long on pornography, it is significant that it was a mid nineteenth-century "invention." Notwithstanding pornography's earlier manifestations, it was only then that the new technologies of photography, printing, and intensive commercialized production created a market for middle-class sexual representations. Legislation soon accommodated the new standards.[50] Pornography became an inclusive name for depictions of "real" sex — more civilized than savagery yet below the Olympus of art. Although much of what the Victorians classified as pornography is prudish by today's standards, it must be noted that, although pornographers often shared their contemporaries' aestheticism, they chose to offend rather than to conform. It is therefore not wholly ironic to view them as "experts" who approached their subject as a professional discourse. For example, pornographic literature was expensive, mostly privately printed and circulated, and laced with literary jargon that presumably screened its readers (notice the translation of explicit language in Greek texts into Latin, and vice versa, but not into English)[51] and that certainly permitted the pretense of propriety. Not infrequently, pornographers aspired in their writings to the poetical sublime, although the quality of the genre was at best mixed and included every imaginable species of deviance and violence.[52] Their readers, to extrapolate from references and metaphors in the texts, were educated, well-read middle-class professionals.

Much of historians' emphasis on upper-middle-class Victorian pornography stems from the legacy of H. S. Ashbee, the bibliophile who donated his major pornography collection to the British Museum, thus providing the archive on which most historical writings about the period are based. Even from this limited supply of sources, it is clear that pornography included high- and lowbrow. The notoriety during the 1890's of both Oscar Wilde and Cleveland Street, where upper-class customers intermingled with working-class youth, demonstrated how rigid class boundaries were diminished by pornography. Writers, publishers, booksellers, and customers often played more than one role. In this mildly unstable social situation, there was a potential for contesting not merely the law but the line between connoisseurship and offense. This was, of course, also a characteristic of modernist writing and was anticipated above all by Aubrey Beardsley's wit.

## Beardsley the Obscure

It is almost too convenient to use Beardsley as an example of ambiguous practices that confused the status of subversive versus clandestine eroticism during the "yellow nineties." At a time when the yellow press was invented to serve jingoist politics and *The Yellow Book* displayed the latest spin on avant-garde respectability, Beardsley fused aestheticism and immorality with anti-war sentiments. As decadence proliferated, the adoration of youth flourished. This was the last gasp of Victorianism. The encoded paintings of Leighton and Alma-Tadema replicated, in their carnality, Victorian celebrations of decadence and youth, but it was the avant-garde who pushed the adoration of youth to its conclusion.[53] The year 1896 was one more annus mirabilis. It was the year when Max Beerbohm gave in to the spirit of the age and announced his retirement at the advanced age of 25, after publishing his "works" in a lilliputian volume.[54] Beardsley himself was 24 years old in 1896, but it was said that "the Beardsley Set" had to make room for the new, younger generation. Beardsley, unfortunately, embodied decadence no less than youth. Periodically ill and unable to work, he died two years later.

Partially because Beardsley had neither formal training nor ties to a specific school, it is difficult to classify him. His art shows signs of descending from older and contemporary forms, but his mixture of styles makes a precise genealogy impossible. Clearly he borrowed from popular artists of the day, yet it was his unique synthesis that transformed this very young man into an emblem of the counterculture of his age. Beardsley's work lay somewhere between that of William Morris and James Whistler, and might also be compared to that of Gilbert and Sullivan — albeit with much sharper irony and heightened sensitivity. Yet Beardsley subverted whatever evolving pattern the historian might be tempted to see in the surging "sexual anarchy" of the 1890's.[55] Moreover, his aestheticism went beyond personal or ideological disagreements with fellow members of the avant-garde. When Beardsley illustrated J. M. Dent's edition of Sir Thomas Mallory's *Morte d'Arthur* (1893), Morris was infuriated by the resemblance to his own style,[56] even though Beardsley displayed strong Japanese influences (which Morris opposed) and later challenged the avant-garde as well as the traditionalists. With Beardsley, Japanese themes served to legitimate the violation of all norms. By 1890, incorporation of Japonisms into painting was considered "old hat"; it had become banal. By then, the Impressionists were cultivating a stylized Western Japonism in a transparent effort to further several countercultural agendas: aestheticism, expressive energy, contestational morality, and sexuality.[57] For Beardsley, this called for public experimentation with explicit sexual depictions, such as *The Toilette of Salome*.

Regardless of the actual effects of their paintings, the Academicians persuaded the public (and probably believed themselves) that the allegorical nudes in their work were devoid of sensuality or sexuality. In contrast, Beardsley mingled highbrow drawing and flagrant pornography to such an extent that even his moderate representations offended people and were censored for decades. Often in the minimalist style of a caricature, Beardsley confronts his viewer with the constant possibility of ridicule, multiple meanings, and the subversiveness of pornography. Not surprisingly, this has baffled historians and critics. In a "century [that] depicted woman as vampire, as castrator, as killer so consistently, so programmatically, and so nakedly," as never before,[58] Beardsley, we are told, was one of the most misogynist among artists. Or was he? In a recent feminist work on Beardsley and Victorian sexual politics, he is said to have supported the position of women, portraying their "intelligence and . . . sexuality," though he was largely unaware that he did so.[59] The inherent difficulty of privileging any interpretation of Beardsley's work is exacerbated by the fact that he left very little information about his brief life. Despite several biographies, we have little sense of Beardsley's own point of view or of his attitude toward sexuality. His life, like his art, cloaked publicity with mystery. Even the basic information is missing: there are no good descriptions of his work habits, nor are there rough sketches of his drawings.

The difficulties of "reading" Beardsley date from one of his most famous early works—the illustrations to Wilde's *Salome* (1893). It has been argued that Beardsley's work has no clear correlation to the text, although that seems to overstate the case.[60] Yet whether we read his drawings as a parody of Wilde's *Salome* or as a unique interpretation of it, they remain undeniably erotic. His males, effeminate or not, have exposed penises. Beardsley emulated the classics, but his drawings have a rich contemporary subtext. This is certainly true of *The Man in the Moon* (1888), one of the more famous illustrations in *Salome* and one in which the caption serves as an antithesis to the visual image (Fig. 7). The erotic image is of the naked effeminate male, but the caption directs attention to the woman in a gown, creating tension between the image and the text. Here, as elsewhere, Beardsley mediated powerful taboos and created an enigma characteristic of the next phase of modernism.[61] His ironic pornography is ripe for misrepresentations. In collapsing conventional pornography and aestheticism, Beardsley ridiculed both, not least by a transformation of gender roles. Thus, for example, in an illustrated

FIG. 7. Aubrey Beardsley,
*The Man in the Moon* (1888).
Reprinted from Slessor, *The
Art of Aubrey Beardsley*, p. 41.

story penned in 1896, he depicted Tannhäuser / Teutonic manhood with Venus in a failed conjugation. Because Tannhäuser lacks the necessary "gargantuan facility" to satisfy Venus, she resorts to a third party.[62] The rebellion, the play, the parody—Beardsley's libertarian energy was searching everywhere. Was his a global fear of women, or merely scorn for pretentiousness? Sexuality and language were the vehicles for his escape from conventional mores as he secured in his text a temporary independence from cultural expectations, affecting an irrational and intimidating world that recognized its own limitations.

By 1896, Beardsley's brief career had peaked. Wilde had been arrested the year before, and the subsequent witch-hunt led to Beardsley's dismissal from *The Yellow Book*. A few of his benefactors maintained their patronage, but his public life was almost over. His health deteriorating, Beardsley continued to draw and produced, among his last works, *Lysistrata*, which he considered one of his "best."[63] *Lysistrata* was such a sensational composition that few ever saw it at the time. It transgresses respectability in such a way that, given the wrong company, it makes people uncomfortable even a century later. A generation ago, while the original drawings were being displayed at the Victoria and Albert Museum, reproductions were being seized from a London store by Scotland Yard detectives acting in compliance with the Obscene Publications Act of 1959.[64] Had *Lysistrata* not been confined primarily to the clandestine, "private" pornography market, its images of the Athenians would have bewildered even the most liberated members of the emerging middle class. Although the illustrations were stylized and contained mythical allusions, their "obscenity" was so theatrical that there can be little doubt of Beardsley's intention to offend. That he used an anti-war myth in the midst of an imperialist "scramble" combined erotic and political offensiveness. For the general public, R. A. Walker's *The Best of Beardsley* could never have included *Lysistrata* (Fig. 8).[65]

*Lysistrata* included drawings of erect penises of megalomaniac propor-

LYSISTRATA.

FIG. 8. Aubrey Beardsley, *Lysistrata* (1896). Reprinted from Slessor, *The Art of Aubrey Beardsley*, p. 97.

tions, as well as lavish female pubic hair, effeminate men, and acts of homosexuality, coitus, and masturbation—all characteristic of pornography that were, of course, forbidden in "formal" highbrow art. In this ultimate work of decadence, Beardsley created a pornographic egalitarianism, mocking both men and women, sexuality, and war. *Lysistrata* ruptured moral, aesthetic, and political standards. Whether this constituted exploitation, abuse, or liberation depended on the viewer's political disposition and attitude toward erotica (and war), but also on what he or she saw in the drawings. It is possible to indulge in an extensive analysis of the numerous representations included, and even to construct a ranking according to which one gender could perhaps be viewed as less exploited than the other. The captions *The Lacadaemonian Ambassadors* or *Lysistrata Defending the Acropolis* cannot begin to describe the drawings themselves. Others are more revealing—for example, *Cinesias Entreating Myrrhina to Coition* (Fig. 9).[66] The

FIG. 9. Aubrey Beardsley, *Cinesias Entreating Myrrhina to Coition* (1896). Reprinted with permission of the Board of Trustees of the Victoria & Albert Museum, South Kensington, London.

story of the Athenian women denying their men sex until peace was made can be read as empowering of women and therefore, by certain standards, as contradictory to pornography.[67] Nevertheless, even though the women are larger than the men and have reversed ordinary power relations, Beardsley's depictions remain pornographic in a context where such a category makes sense. Frustrated rape scenes are presumably not less pornographic than successful ones, and some of the pictures in fact leave the audience in suspense.

Whatever gender lines are drawn, *Lysistrata's* illustrations are so shocking and so fantastically done that they resist definitive interpretation, accommodating a plethora of analyses. It is this sense of uncertainty that makes Beardsley so strikingly modern. His contemporaries understood it, if only intuitively, although critics, surprisingly, are still trying to discover his "real meaning." It is perhaps more productive to note how Beardsley emphasized hate and aggression rather than enticement, affection, and sexual fantasy, given the unconsummated and uncontrolled energies characteristic of the 1890's avant-garde. Whatever Beardsley's precise formula was, he spiced it with a lot of sarcasm. A dying young man, Beardsley answered Freud by releasing rather than repressing the creative imagination. If pornography is defined as a representation that conveys "only sex," Beardsley's work does not qualify. Yet if his does not, nothing else should.

Notwithstanding the modernist impulse they exhibited, however, paintings and drawings remained largely secondary to mechanical reproductions of pornography — most notably photographs — which dramatically increased the number of producers and consumers of visual eroticism. The subjects were primarily non-European women, the photographers European men.

## The Imperialist Brow

The imperialist brow had its own high and low. Although sexuality has yet to figure prominently in the histories of imperialism, anti-colonialist and, recently, mainstream accounts have assigned it a major role in shaping the relationship between Europeans and their "subalterns."[68] The reach of the British Empire offered sexual opportunities of all types to hundreds of thousands of Europeans. Yet whatever sexual allure the East had in European minds, few actually chose foreign service as a career for that reason. Explorers and travelers were more likely to be thus drawn abroad than were imperial agents.[69] Non-Western sexual allure encompassed the vast majority of the global population and was essentially heterogeneous. Unified constructs such as "Oriental exoticism" or "savage promiscuity" are Occidental. They do not reflect indigenous mores but are, rather, the standards by which imperial attitudes have been (and still are) evaluated.[70] And yet there has, of course, never been a single "Occidental attitude."

Despite the obvious disparity in power between conqueror and conquered in the British Empire, there is conflicting evidence about the role of sexuality in aggravating this imbalance. At the microlevel, imperial agents were less than all-powerful and the indigenous peoples were not always powerless. Local rivalries often shaped imperial policies, at times unbeknownst to the Europeans. This became especially evident when the imperialists were missionaries, travelers, or ethnographers.[71] Rebels' complaints against the Empire did include British mistreatment of indigenous women,[72] but such charges were comparatively rare. The record, however, may be more misleading than helpful. European sexual exploitation of indigenous women was very unlikely to be seen as exceptional in societies in which women were ordinarily subordinated by men, and the scant testimony leaves historians with conjectures rather than information.[73]

One source for examining Occidental perspectives on primitive sexuality is photography. Anti-colonialist critique would have it that erotic representations were invariably exploitative, exceeding European norms. This is only partially true. The impression is most striking in some recent collections but is largely a consequence of the writer's selection.[74] Comparing these publications to late nineteenth-century albums, the distinction is readily apparent.[75] Sexual representations were relatively infrequent in the earlier archives, which deserve closer examination, but here I would only like to suggest that, as on the European scene, sexuality and eroticism in the Empire depended on the process of encoding.

By far the largest group of ethnographic photographs was made for the purpose of racial classification, primarily to advance anthropometry, which nineteenth-century anthropologists treated as a valid positivist science. Among these appear a number of photographs of native belles, some of which could not but conjure up eroticism (see, for example, Fig. 10 in Virginia-Lee Webb's essay in this volume). As with Academic paintings, the discourse of anthropology was supposed to make these images respectable and nonsexual, although the difference between certain photographs in the archives and those that were published shows that in most cases the Victorians had little difficulty in distinguishing between ethnographic and erotic photographs (Figs. 10 and 11, respectively).[76] But perhaps the very existence of erotic photographs in a scientific collection is as noteworthy as their limited extent.

FIG. 10. An example of an ethnographic nude. Reprinted with permission of the Pitt-Rivers Museum, Oxford, # B40.2A.

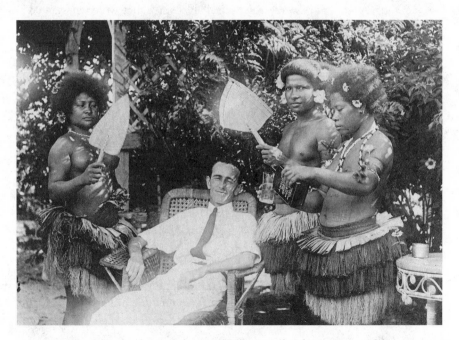

FIG. 11. An example of erotic ethnography. Reprinted with permission of the British Museum, cat. no. MM 007624.

As in the Academicians' paintings of Greek and Roman nudes, there is a tension in photographs such as Fig. 11 between the distance and the availability of non-European women. The discourse of ethnography creates respectability, which justifies nakedness even as its innocence is undermined by embedded eroticism. As objects of erotic representations, so-called primitives provided convenient bridges between several genres. Myths of an oceanic paradise or of noble savages were not, in effect, qualitatively different than myths of Olympus or the Arabian Nights: through spatial and temporal distancing, all bespoke remote and unavailable sexual fantasies. That such representations of "bodies," "bathing," and "brothels" often had real counterparts reveals how uncertain the dichotomy was between victimization and sublimation. Indeed, the confusion between the two led at times to exploitation and at other times to unequal accommodations. Which of the two is represented in Gauguin's or Loti's Tahiti — or Loti's Japan, for that matter? Popular erotic constructions often displayed young native women ornamented with theatrical jewelry to enhance their exotic allure. Such enticements were enhanced by the belief that the non-European women shown in ethnographic photos were sexually available, since they were represented as such by the medium (Fig. 12). These studio constructions were copied or changed slightly by using different models in response to a seemingly active demand for this "cottage industry" (see Virginia-Lee Webb's essay below). The photos resembled the *académies* (see section on the classical nude above), and in many pictures eroticism survived despite terribly executed photography. One such photograph shows a "Tonga woman" seated on a low bunk covered with rags, partially dressed in what is supposedly Pacific Islander attire and surrounded by Japanese accessories. The screen, the umbrella, the fan, and the tea set are explicitly meant to construct the scene of a geisha in paradise. This composition, which possesses no ethnographic merit, was nonetheless preserved in an ethnographic collection and is one of a series. The enchantment for the voyeur/collector apparently did not diminish because of the displeasure on the model's face (Fig. 13).

Yet the remoteness of the Other in erotic ethnographic images — a remoteness that legitimizes the erotic display — also dialectically lessens the Otherness. In the work of Loti, Gauguin, Malinowski, and Margaret Mead, among others, non-European images become more familiar and are, consequently, subjected to the great egalitarian forces of modernization and censorship.

Naming an entity that evokes the category of the Other, one that specifies for readers an image which has no signifier, may be seen as belonging only

FIG. 12. Oceanic paradise. Reprinted with permission of the Pitt-Rivers Museum, Oxford, #B36.22A.

in a borderline manner to nonfiction. Travel literature has always mediated between what may generally be called accurate reporting and forging perceptible images of the unknown. From medieval illustrations of distant cities that all look alike (see Christopher Steiner's essay below) to those of distant, alien civilizations in sci-fi movies, naming is often meant not to be read literally but to stand for a group, using real places and identities in order to familiarize Otherness. Ethnography stood for eroticism, but the more familiar the Other became, through myth and kitsch, the more the Occident became aware of its own acts of exploitation.

It has almost become a credo that "to photograph is to appropriate the thing photographed."[77] This is reductive, because it assumes an unequal power relationship between the parties involved and allows nothing for the specificity of the image. It is equally misleading when applied to colonial / ethnographic photography. Some non-Europeans objected to being photographed because they believed the camera was robbing them of their souls.[78] They saw their own images being appropriated in a literal sense. But other non-Europeans were fascinated and loved to be photographed.[79] Although this still involved questions of power between the subject and the photogra-

FIG. 13. Tonga Woman. Reprinted with permission of the Peabody Museum, Harvard, cat. no. H24543.

pher, plus the enigma of control, these instances force a revaluation of photographs as knowledge and power that is unidirectional. The images ipso facto tell us little about the actual power involved. But here we are back to the elusiveness of postmodernism. Photographic images are not more self-evident than other texts. As the role of sexual alienation in aggravating racial and imperial domination is further explored, we need to remember that such exploitation was not the only type of sexuality involved in imperialism, or in its representations.

One way to comprehend imperial representations of the erotic is to delineate notions of respectability. Although European and non-European women were depicted in comparable settings — in *académies* and in scientific-medical-criminal images — the display of the primitive was more permissive. When the circulation of European nudes was censored, primitive nudes were openly displayed. The *National Geographic* genre is familiar. Yet the respectability of non-European erotica was continuously questioned and its boundaries redefined. Examining private collections not mixed with obvious examples of European pornography, it becomes obvious that, when it came to primitives, Victorians allowed themselves to transgress their own accepted morality. The encoding of erotic non-European representations involved specific boundaries — most evident in the distinction between published and private images. The unpublished photos include pathetic pictures, not in great numbers but clearly very different from those that were published. Yet although collectors assembled these nude and erotic images, including them with those of real ethnographic interest, they never constituted more than a small fraction of the whole. One possible conclusion may be that, as compared, for instance, to the Victorians' markedly polarized views about race, their aesthetic and erotic encoding was not particularly different from our own.

## Conclusion

The contemporary anti-colonialist critique may very well have become possible partially as a result of the self-contradictory approach to sexuality exhibited by the late Victorians and their descendants — an approach that led at times to exploitation and at other times to a growing egalitarianism. Sexual representations — whether of the Greek or the primitive, visual or textual — first diminished the Victorians' profound ignorance about sexual relations and then led to familiarity with many of its forms. Racism enabled depictions of native eroticism that contributed dialectically to the liberation of Western sexuality and consequently to diminished racism, thus extricating the European libido, which then converged with other previously forbidden energies to recast bourgeois morality. Hence an initial negative / repressed approach to both white and black nudes was followed by a proliferation of black erotica. Paradoxically, it was the mass production of these images that led to the legitimization of white erotica and greater receptivity to black equality. Whites' recognition that their sense of superiority toward blacks constituted racism required empathy — an empathy that was achieved partially through familiarity.[80]

Victorian sexual representations challenged not only morality and etiquette but the very understanding of human nature in society. Middle-class culture invested heavily in repressing sexual representations, and the strong momentum of the purity campaign was a response to the growing legitimacy of such sexual language and images. Although the manifestations in contemporary society are greatly dissimilar, we are subject to a peculiar phase of an analogous trend. A particular contemporary cultural critique views sexuality in terms of appropriation and domination, where white males are invariably exploiters and sinister agents. First-generation feminists have presented censoring eroticism and the body favorably — that is, as leading to a subversion of the patriarchal society. Such prudishness has in turn caused feminists to subscribe to aesthetic standards similar to those of conservatives, thus replicating the purity campaign of a century ago. Historically, such attitudes failed, and the unintended happened: patriarchy, which had flourished when representations of sexuality and erotica were repressed, was reformed as a result of the dissonance between a general aspiration toward (democratic) egalitarianism and specific (sexual) domination. By bringing sexuality into the open, Victorian discord was reconfigured as a modernist reform. If familiarity encourages fragmentation, it is highly unlikely that the genie of sexuality can be shut back into the bottle.

# PART II

# Raw Anthropology

VINCENT CRAPANZANO

# The Moment of Prestidigitation
## Magic, Illusion, and Mana in the Thought of Emile Durkheim and Marcel Mauss

From top to bottom of the ladder, greed is aroused without knowing where to find ultimate foothold. Nothing can calm it, since its goal is far beyond all it can attain. Reality seems valueless by comparison with the dreams of fevered imaginations; reality is therefore abandoned, but so too is possibility abandoned when it in turn becomes reality. A thirst arises for novelties, unfamiliar pleasures [*jouissances ignorées*], nameless sensations, all of which lose their savor once known. Henceforth one has no strength to endure the least reverse. The whole fever subsides and the sterility of all the tumult is apparent, and it is seen that all these new sensations in their infinite quantity cannot form a solid foundation of happiness to support one during days of trial. . . . The man who has always pinned all his hopes on the future and lived with his eyes fixed upon it, has nothing in the past as a comfort against the present's afflictions [*amertumes*], for the past was nothing to him but stages. What blinded him to himself was his expectation always to find further on the happiness he had so far missed. Now he is stopped in his tracks; from now on nothing remains behind or ahead of him to fix his gaze upon. Weariness [*fatigue*] alone, moreover, is enough to bring disillusionment [*désenchantement*], for he cannot in the end escape the futility [*inutilité*] of an endless pursuit.[1]

Whether or not this lengthy quotation from Emile Durkheim's *Suicide*, written in 1897, gives us an accurate picture of the anomic conditions, the confused *effervescence*[2] in France at the time he was writing, it does describe a reality to which he and his nephew and collaborator, Marcel Mauss, *un peu son alter ego*,[3] respond in their subsequent studies of primitive society, magic, and religion. Sociological pretense aside, Durkheim's picture is literary. Despite his bleak moralism, his lack of irony, and his refusal to acknowledge the aesthetic, beauty, and style, his description reminds us of Baudelaire. Insatiable desire, the continual deferment of *real* satisfaction, the thirst

for novelties, unfamiliar pleasures, nameless sensations, the inability to with-
stand reversals of fortune, weariness, disillusionment—all are symptoms of
the flaneur, the dandy, who looks only for "*le plaisir fugitif de circonstance*,"[4]
the decadent and degenerate who were treated with such ambivalence at the
century's end in Paris.[5] For Durkheim, *un sérieux*, these "symptoms" are the
consequence of unconstrained industrial expansion—of the loss of moral
and religious values—which leaves desire boundless and insatiable. Ultimately, they result from what was an almost obsessive fear among social critics of late nineteenth-century France: the fear of social dissolution, of the
breakdown of those social bonds that govern the individual's goals and ideals
and regulate his desires and aspirations.[6]

"The apparent collapse of established ideals, the reaction against scientific materialism and rational explanations," Eugen Weber writes in *France:
Fin de Siècle*, "encouraged interest in mystery and the supernatural, appreciation of faith for the sake of faith—and of the sensations faith can spur"
(p. 32). It produced a fascination with the esoteric, spiritualism, mysticism,
magic, and the Satanic.[7] A loss of faith in *an* objective reality, the knowledge
that no experience is ultimate, that everything finally is deception, Weber
goes on to argue, led "to a falling back upon imagination, which alone cannot let us down; to the decision, since illusion fulfilled must end in disillu-
sion, to avoid fulfillment and concentrate on the safer realms of illusion"
(p. 143).[8] Such a conviction and the play that ensued were of course not
without their critics, who sought sociological, psychological, or physiological
explanations for the decadent—the anomic—conditions in which they
found themselves.

Whatever the conditions that were responsible for the loss of faith in objective reality, for the failure of the moral, the sustaining order, there was, it
would seem, a pervasive sense of the artifice of social and cultural life that
was threatening to the *sérieux*—a type that should be contrasted with the
dandy and the decadent. Within this context the "primitive" could—and
did—give stress to this artifice. At the time, it referred generally to non-
Europeans, their culture and style.[9] Van Gogh called the Egyptians and Aztecs "primitive" and the Japanese masters "savage." Gauguin characterized
Persian, Egyptian, Indian, Javanese, Cambodian, and Peruvian styles, as well
as Polynesian ones, as "primitive" or "savage."[10] Thus "primitive" had both
positive and negative connotations. Innocent, idealized, pure, embodied
since Rousseau by the Noble Savage, placed mythically on an island paradise, Tahiti, Bougainville's Nouvelle Cythère, the "primitive" provided, in
this eighteenth-century sense, a vantage point for criticizing civilized—that

is, European — society.[11] Pejoratively it served a definitional function, separating the civilized from the uncivilized, the European from, in the words of the *Nouveau Larousse illustré* (1897–1904), "les peuples qui sont encore au degré le moins avancé de civilisation."

Still, despite its definitional function, the primitive was framed to preclude any real challenge to the French or European cultural assumption. The incorporation of a primitive aesthetic — perception and artifact — in the arts was still to come. Picasso had yet to paint *Les Demoiselles d'Avignon* (1907).[12] For the anthropologist, the primitive was quite literally primitive, a simple folk, a leftover, perhaps, from a previous age to be studied, described, classified, and kept carefully at a distance even by the exoticist, whose exoticism has always required distance. Evolutionary theory helped at once to preserve this distance and to break it down. The primitive, however different, was ancestral — well, perhaps not quite ancestral, but lurking there, somewhere, in (our) past. He — his society and his culture, in their simplicity — could provide clues for understanding not only the past and vestiges of the past (*that* was current evolutionary thinking) but also social and cultural organization — Durkheim and Mauss's manifest goal. That their quest reflected an ambivalent interest in the primitive as both pure and innocent *and* impure and savage can be detected, at least stylistically, in their writings.[13]

Within five years of the publication of *Suicide*, Mauss, who had collaborated with his uncle on the study, published his *Outline of a General Theory of Magic* in *L'Année sociologique* (1902–3).[14] The *Outline* followed his study (with Henri Hubert) of sacrifice and numerous reviews of ethnographic monographs by, among others, Jevons, Brinton, Lang, Frazer, Rohde, and Skeat, and it was immediately followed in 1903 by *Primitive Classification*, which he wrote with Durkheim. (During these same years, Durkheim had turned to the primitive and written on the origins of the incest prohibition, totemism, and religion.) Though sociological, Durkheim and Mauss's project was also a response to current philosophical — neo-Kantian — concerns that were not yet fully developed.[15] Today, in an even less certain age, we would understand them in terms of cultural — or, more accurately, cognitive or epistemological — relativism.[16]

To simplify, philological, historical, and ethnographic study, not to mention critical studies in the Kantian tradition itself, challenged the universalist assumption of Kantian epistemology.[17] Were space and time experienced as Kant had postulated? Was Kant's list of categories complete? Was it shared by people living in very different worlds? The great German ethnographer

Adolph Bastian[18] had spent decades roaming around the world, collecting his *Elementargedanken*. Ethnographic and missionary reports suggested that primitive peoples did in fact construct their world differently, less critically perhaps, with categories that seemed alien to those of Western philosophical thought — indeed, that they thought differently, magically, and, according to Lucien Lévy-Bruhl, prelogically.[19]

In question was the psychic unity of man, a theologically derived anthropology, a mode of essentialist thought that postulated mind, modes of thinking, classification, understanding, and reason as given immutably. Differences could be accounted for, if this position were strictly held to, through essentialist classification: one form of racism or another. Primitives were different; categorically so. And yet, according to evolutionary theory, which mediated difference here, they were survivals of modern man's past. Alternatively, a more flexible view of the psychic unity of man could be taken — one which recognized that individuals were subject to environmental influences. Such an approach — one current in anthropology today — requires theories of socialization and enculturation.

Durkheim, Mauss, and their followers held society responsible for the elaboration of categories and modes of classification — indeed, for thought itself. In *Primitive Classification*, Durkheim and Mauss stress the evolution of logical classification from "the general mental confusion" that characterized (putatively, projectively, according to Bastian) the *Naturvölker*: "Here, the individual himself loses his personality. There is a complete lack of distinction between him and his exterior soul or his totem. He and his 'fellow-animal' together compose a single personality. The identification is such that the man assumes the characteristics of the thing or animal with which he is united."[20] Anxious to lay sociological claim to this alleged evolution — there was / is little enough evidence for such primordial mental confusion — Durkheim and Mauss argue uncritically that individual psychology cannot account for this evolution because it assumes that the essential features of logical thought, including the classificatory function, "have been fully formed as long as mankind has existed" (*Primitive Classification*, p. 3). Although an individual may have the innate capacity to perceive resemblances between objects, they maintain, there is no reason to suppose that the demarcation of these objects, their classification into groups, and the organization of the relations between these groups (into a hierarchy, for example) is given from birth. In contrast to James Frazer (and without recognizing that men and their relations also have to be discriminated and grouped), Durkheim and Mauss assert that it is society — the relations between men and groups—which provides the model that primitive classificatory thought follows (ibid., p. 82):[21] "The ties which unite things of the same group or different groups to each other are themselves conceived as social ties" (p. 84). Unlike logical classification, which follows "the laws of pure understanding," primitive classification is infused with emotion: its objects are products of sentiment. For the primitive, "a species of things is not a simple object of knowledge but corresponds above all to a certain sentimental attitude," and it is this sentiment which facilitates the blurring of categories that characterizes that thought (pp. 85–86). Durkheim and Mauss argue here, as Durkheim will argue a decade later in *The Elementary Forms of the Religious Life* (1912), that the history of scientific classification "is, in the last analysis, the history of the stages by which this element of social affectivity has progressively weakened" (p. 88). Their study is exemplary: "The same method could help us likewise to understand the manner in which the ideas of cause, substance, and the different modes of reasoning, etc. were formed" (ibid.).

The assumption that primitive thought is emotionally charged and that this cathexis is responsible for its lack of clarity, its seemingly bizarre associations, and its resistance to the logic of the excluded middle was characteristic of late nineteenth-century pictures of the primitive. With a tolerance at times approaching the ironic, Mauss recognizes the role of emotion and sentiment in the picture of magic he draws in the *Outline*: "We have come thus to think that at the root itself of magic there are affective states productive of illusions." Mauss suggests that these affective states are not individual but are derived from a mixture of individual and collective sentiments.[22]

Mauss's insistence on the role of the collectivity in generating the emotions and sentiments surrounding magical practices is reminiscent of Durkheim's, though he has far less vested in upholding society's foundational role. Like his uncle, his view is both logically and dramatically derived. In discussing negative rites (the precautions and prohibitions in which magic is couched), Mauss notes the apprehension, fear, and repugnance that accompany magic and argues for the collective origin of its interdictions (*Esquisse*, p. 129). Magic has a true predilection for the forbidden; it is transgressive; it exploits the violation of taboos. It is a product of the collectivity, for only the collectivity can produce interdictions that frame the magical act and thus enable both transgression and the emotions accompanying that transgression.[23]

Individual psychology, Mauss argues, cannot account for the emotional state, the mental excitability, the hyperesthesia, the errors of perception, the illusions, the hallucinations produced by magic. The magician cannot arrive at this condition alone: "Behind Moses who touched the bare rock was all of

Israel, and if Moses doubted, Israel did not doubt." This rhetorical flourish covers up the absence of any theory of the internalization of social norms. Mauss can only assert a relationship between the individual and the collectivity: "The state of the individual is, for us, always conditioned by the state of society" (ibid., p. 124). But what is this conditioning? How does it function? How does society — the law — affect the individual? We can see here the (theoretical) precipitation of a problematic space, that between objective laws, the norms and values of a society, and the subjective experience of the individual, which Freud will elaborate in dynamic terms a few years later, without, however, a well-developed theory of society.

For Mauss, the collectivity occupies an ambiguous space that is usually external to, though impinging on, the isolated individual, constraining him and producing, through authorized, dramatic behaviors (rituals and ceremonies), socially effective subjective states. He suggests (but never develops the suggestion) that the role of society in modern magic is "almost completely subconscious" (*à peu près entièrement subconsciente*). It is rare today for the remnants of traditional magic to be carried out in groups (ibid.). But in words that reveal, perhaps, a longing for more primitive conditions, Mauss cautions that one should not consider these *formes cadaverisées et pauvres* (cadaverized and poor forms), euphemistically translated as "moribund, poorly developed systems," as fundamental.[24] It is "in primitive societies where these phenomena are more complex and richer that it is necessary to search out the facts that explain their origin and are collective." There, collectively induced emotions form a *terrain mental* where false perceptions flourish, illusions immediately spread, and ensuing "miracles" are confirmed: "There forms around this [magical] act a circle of impassioned spectators whom the spectacle immobilizes, absorbs, and hypnotises. Like the chorus in ancient tragedy, they feel themselves no less actors than spectators in this magical drama. All of society is in a state of expectation and prepossession" (ibid., p. 125).

In an age fascinated by the crowd, when, in the words of Walter Benjamin, "fear, revulsion, and horror were the emotions which the big-city crowd aroused in those who first observed it,"[25] the collective observance — rite and ceremony — was the *momentum classicum* of the primitive, as projected by the lonely scholar, the academic equivalent of, to quote Mallarmé, *le promeneur solitaire et pensif* on a crowded Parisian boulevard. It was a moment in time — a movement, an impulse — during which, so it was argued, primitive society could realize itself.[26] It was also, at a discursive level, in Paris, entirely removed from that realization, "primitive society's" constitutive moment. Magical collaboration does not demand immobility and abstention, Mauss tells us. The whole group moves unanimously as it pursues its unique goal. There are no longer any individuals but just pieces in a machine, spokes in a wheel, the magical round, danced and sung, being its primitive, ideal image. Mauss gets carried away by his imagined rite:

This continuous, monotonous rhythmic movement is the immediate expression of a mental state in which the consciousness of each [participant] is taken over by one feeling, a single, hallucinatory idea, that of a common goal. All the bodies are in the same motion, all the faces have the same mask, all the voices the same cry; not to count the depth of the impression produced by the cadence, the music, and the song. To see in all their faces the image of desire, to hear in all their mouths evidence of certainty — without any possible resistance, each one is carried away by the conviction of all. Confounded by the transport of their dance, by the fever of their movement, they form a single body and a single soul. It is only then that the social body is truly realized. (ibid., p. 126)

Under these conditions, which are no longer realizable *dans nos sociétés*, not even in the overexcited crowd, universal consent can create realities. *Les lois de la psychologie collective violent ici les lois de la psychologie individuelle.* Here the laws of collective psychology violate, desecrate, transgress, rape, the laws of individual psychology. (The exaggerated rhetoric, the violence of Mauss's description of the primitive rite is itself, like magic, like crowd psychology, contagious; it is even transferred to his critical evaluation of psychological laws. "Magical belief is vital because society gesticulates, and it is because of its belief in magic that society gesticulates" (p. 127).

This circle of belief is critical to Mauss's theory of magic, because magic is self-contained. And yet sociology, his sociology, demands an explanation: a violation of the circle, the attribution of a cause, an origin. Earlier in the *Outline* (p. 114), he speaks of magic in Kantian terms, as a judgment. At first he refers to it as a play of value judgments (*un jeu de jugements de valeur*), that is, as a play of "sentimental aphorisms that attribute diverse qualities to diverse objects that enter into its system." But then, after asserting the collective origin of these sentiments, he goes on to consider the judgments in epistemological terms. Are they analytic? Whether or not *we* see them as analytic, that is, as tautological (the rite kills the spirit, by definition; the magician levitates his astral body because that body is his own), they are not understood as such by the magician. He always introduces a heterogeneous term: force, power, *phusis*, or mana. The notion of magical efficacy is always present; in a way, it plays the role of the copula in a proposition. Are the judgments then a posteriori? No, answers Mauss definitively. Sensible experience has never furnished proof of a magical judgment: "It is evident that one has never seen except with the eyes of faith an astral body" (p. 116).

Before proceeding with his catalogue of Kantian judgments, Mauss asks if magical propositions — he shifts back and forth from proposition to judgment — are simply the object of the subjective experiences of the magician and his clients. Does the magician see the propositions realized because he has entered into ecstasy and dreamed them? Does the client see them realized because he desires them so intensely? Without denying the importance of desire and dream in magic, Mauss argues that they do not offer sufficient explanation. He notes a discordance between the magician's dream — which may lead him to the beyond, to the world of souls, animals, and spirits — and the client's (prosaic) desires. They only coincide at "the moment of prestidigitation" when, for example, the magician draws a pebble out of his client's body. "There is, then, no longer at this unique moment a truly psychological experience, either on the side of the magician, who cannot delude himself at this point, or on that of the client, because the alleged experience of the latter is no more than an error of perception, beyond a state of critical resistance, and thus [beyond] being repeated if it is not supported by tradition or by an act of constant faith." (*Il n'y a donc plus, à ce moment unique, de veritable expérience psychologique, ni du côté du magicien, qui ne peut se faire illusion à ce point. . . .* I give the French here because Robert Brain's English translation, irresponsible throughout, says exactly the opposite of what Mauss is saying.) Mauss's point is that the climactic moment of a magical rite is in fact intractable, if not outside language, then outside critical regard. Magical judgments, he argues, precede magical experiences. They are ritual canons or chains of representations: "The experiences, the experiments [the French *expérience* connotes the two] are only made to confirm them, and they almost never succeed in invalidating them" (p. 117). The general belief in magic dominates particular magical beliefs and facilitates the objectification of subjective ideas and the generalization of individual illusions. It gives to the magical judgment a positive, necessary, and absolute character. Magical judgments are, Mauss asserts in a sloppy Kantianism, almost perfect synthetic a priori judgments. One relates the terms before any type of experience.

Mauss's argument is confused. He notes that one cannot ask who in fact makes such synthetic a priori judgments simply because they are given as prejudices and prescriptions; that is, they have a collective origin. As though resting his argument on a pun, he notes that when there is a magical judgment, there is a "collective synthesis" that determines the "quasi-conventions" of magic (like the sign creates the thing, the part the whole, the word the event), generalizes associations of ideas, and gives imperative aphoristic expression to these determinations and generalizations. It would seem that the synthetic a priori judgment can be crudely translated as collective or generalized prejudices and prohibitions, where the collective or generalizing is equivalent to the synthesis, and the articulated prejudices and prohibitions to the a priori.

Even if we were to ignore Mauss's confusion — he was never a rigorous thinker — and accept his argument, we would still have to account for the source of the imperative of the prejudices and prohibitions. Mauss himself holds the "felt collective needs of a group" responsible. They force the individual members of the group to perform the same synthesis at the same time (p. 118). "Magical judgment is the object of a social consensus, itself a translation of a social need, whose pressure triggers off a whole series of collective psychological phenomena" (p. 119). It is collective — or, perhaps more accurately, collectivized — desire that confirms the magical means. The synthesis of cause and effect is produced in public opinion. Elsewhere in the *Outline*, Mauss remarks that, however distinct the diverse moments of the representation of the magical rite may be, they are included in a synthetic representation, in which cause and effect are confused: "This is the idea itself of magic, of immediate and boundless efficacy, of direct creation; it is absolute illusion. . . . In magic there is no interval between the wish and its realization" (p. 56).

Whatever psychological process is responsible for the belief in the immediate and boundless efficacy of magic, this efficacy is understood in terms of some sort of force or power of peculiar linguistic status (noun, verb, adjective) that Mauss calls *mana* and finds at the basis of all magic. "It is a pure efficacy, which is, however, a localizable material substance at the same time as it is spiritual, that acts at a distance and yet through direct connection, if not by contact, mobile and moving without moving itself, impersonal and clothed in personal form, divisible and continuous" (pp. 110–11). Mana is — it creates — a force, a context, a world apart, a sort of fourth dimension, a sphere superimposed on reality in which magic operates. It legitimates magical belief. Given a priori, it is unquestioned and unquestionable. It is not a representation of magic; rather, it governs magical representations. It acts as a category, rendering possible magical ideas as categories render possible human ideas. It is an unconscious category of understanding whose origin as a category is, needless to say, social.

It is remarkable, Mauss notes, that an opaque term that resists abstract conceptualization and can barely be disengaged from waves of affect is in fact able to clarify magic for the adept. It converts the magical judgment, Mauss argues, into an analytic one. If, in the magical proposition that "the smoke from aquatic plants produces [rain] clouds," we were to insert "mana" after the subject, we would have an immediate identity: "smoke with mana = cloud." Mana also renders the a priori a posteriori, Mauss tells us, because it dominates and conditions the experience itself. Ah, so here we have the analytic a posteriori judgment that Kant thought to be impossible.

It is perhaps no accident that in the paragraph preceding this argument, Mauss asks whether or not humanity's many hasty generalizations do not have the same origin as magic. Mauss has already given us more than a theory of magic: he has offered an explanation of how society can create and hold illusions — a point of considerable concern, as I have suggested, to both the dandies and the sérieux of fin-de-siècle France. Mauss's failure to delimit the meaning of mana does not result merely from the confusions of primitive thought or of his own thinking. It reflects, I believe, the instability of those referential terms that are used to gloss such pragmatic functions of language as the performative.[27] Claude Lévi-Strauss's commitment to a purely referential understanding of language in his influential "Introduction à l'oeuvre de Marcel Mauss" (1950) led him to underplay the "power" of the ritually contextualized verbal formulae on which Mauss insisted.[28] Mana is not simply "the subjective reflection of the demand of non-perceived totality" ("Introduction," p. xvvi), nor is it simply a "floating signifier," a "zero symbolic value," a sign that marks the necessity of a supplementary symbolic content to that with which the signified is already charged (ibid., p. l). The point is that mana as "pure efficacy" (or, as we might say today, "illocutionary force") resists reference, for it operates outside of reference at that asymptotic moment, both in and out of time, that is for Mauss the climax of the magic rite, the moment of prestidigitation, the moment where wish and realization are one, where there is only timeless but effective tautology or, as Mauss might prefer, analyticity.

Put another way, implicitly developed twenty years later in Mauss's most famous essay, "The Gift," the mana — the illocutionary force — of the magical act manifests itself in the betwixt and between of an (interpersonal) exchange. Like the Maori hau, which Mauss, following Elsdon Best, glosses as the "spiritual power" that resides in an object (taonga) and motivates its exchange, mana or its equivalent appears to be the efficacy of exchange. Insofar as it is ascribed, however, to a person, object, or act (to a vehicle), it is localized, embodied, and positioned in a symbolic system, a linguistic structure, a ritual process. Technically, the referentially expressed, metapragmatic description of a pragmatic function (here magical efficacy, the force of / behind gift exchange) inserts that nonreferential "function" into a system or structure of reference — an ideology — that masks its context-casting function. Ironically, the terms "mana" and "*hau*," which *refer* to power, in fact mask the "real" plays of power that occur in magical transactions and gift exchanges.[29] We are here within language at the limit of language.

The ascription of mana or *hau* to an object, person, or act covers up that instant in any exchange, in and out of time, between giving and receiving, in which the plays of power, the stakes of the transaction, are in exquisite suspense. It is a moment of terrible risk — to be obliterated.[30] The necessity for instantaneous forgetting (*oubli*) is, I believe, rather more existential than conceptual, as Jacques Derrida[31] would have it. (Roughly, Derrida argues that the inevitable contradiction, the aporia, in any gift exchange — between the appreciation of the gift in its pure, unmotivated singularity and its recognition as a "gift" in a system that obliges reciprocation — necessitates forgetting.)[32]

It is also a moment to be repeated. For the Maori, on whose understanding of gift exchange Mauss builds his own, the gift is not inert.[33] Their understanding, at least in Mauss's terms, is animistic. The *hau*, as "partaking" of the gift-giver, motivates exchange, for it tends to gravitate back to its "*foyer d'origine*." To keep it is dangerous. It can result in death. What is not clear, however, in Mauss's account, and no doubt in the Maori's own understanding, is the degree to which the *hau* can be distinguished from the *taonga*, efficacy from its vehicle. Best's informant, whom Mauss quotes, appears to confound the two. He describes circulating, and ultimately returning, the *taonga*. He speaks of the *hau* as the spirit of the *taonga*. He reduces everything to the *hau*: "I must give [the *taonga*] to you since they are the *hau* of the *taonga* which you gave me. If I were to keep this second *taonga* for myself I might become ill or even die. Such is *hau*, the *hau* of personal property, the *hau* of the *taonga*, the *hau* of the forest" (Mauss, "Essai," p. 158). Whether we call "*hau*" or "mana" a floating signifier, give it zero symbolic value, or provide it, as do the "primitives" — and, for that matter, the "civilized," like Mauss — with multiple, contradictory representational values, mana demands always another, foundational referent.[34]

It is extraordinary that the "magical" discourse of the primitive, as understood by the ethnographer, replicates itself in the ethnologist's — Mauss's — discourse. Both attempt to locate mana referentially, and their attempts remain always unstable, skipping from representation to representation.

Mauss does resist a final referent, though (no doubt under the influence of his uncle Durkheim), he circles around one — society — not knowing exactly how or where to alight. We may refer this replication to Mauss's primitivism — that is, to his seemingly uncritical use of indigenous categories of understanding in his ethnographic descriptions and ethnological explanations.[35] But, I would suggest, a hasty attribution of this feature of Mauss's thought to his primitivism blinds us to similar replications in our use of our own categories of social understanding, and to the dangers that lie in the failure to appreciate critically that replication.

More than a decade after the publication of the *Outline,* Durkheim published *The Elementary Forms of the Religious Life,* which is deeply indebted to Mauss's study of magic. In this work Durkheim finds a primary referent for mana in the effervescent energy of the ritual crowd as its members come to realize — and venerate — their society.[36] As is well known, Durkheim sought an explanation for religion in the most primitive one he could find, that of the Australian aborigines. (With the publication of Spencer and Gillen's descriptions of the native tribes of Central Australia in 1899 and 1904, and Howitt's of the southeastern tribes in 1904, the aborigines had become an object of intense ethnographic interest — the prototypical primitive.)[37] By "the most primitive religion" (*Les Formes élémentaires,* p. 1), Durkheim meant one that occurs in a society whose social organization is simpler than any other and that has not borrowed from any earlier religion. His quest, within an evolutionary paradigm, is for the elementary, the original, the source, the *Abgrund* of the religions of "advanced" societies, and he finds totemism to be this most primitive religion.

The laying out of Durkheim's argument and his ethnographic presentation mirror at a textual level his intellectual quest, though never in a fully and self-consciously contrived fashion. They are cast as a descent into the primitive — into the most primordial rites of those most elemental people, the ab-originals, whose emotional and passional faculties are but imperfectly subject to the control of reason and will (ibid., p. 308). Durkheim is himself swept up by his description of the corroboree. To illustrate, I quote the French:

Une fois les individus assemblés il se dégage de leur rapprochement une sorte d'électricité qui les transporte vite à un degré extraordinaire d'exaltation. Chaque sentiment exprimé vient retenir, sans resistance, dans toutes ces consciences largement ouvertes aux impressions extérieures; chacune d'elles fait écho aux autres et réciproquement. L'impulsion initiale va ainsi s'amplifiant à mesure qu'elle se répercute, comme une avalanche grossit à mesure qu'elle avance. Et comme des passions aussi vives et aussi affranchies de tout contrôle ne peuvent pas ne pas se répandre au dehors, ce ne sont, de toutes parts, que gestes violents, que cris, véritables hurlements, bruits assourdissants de toutes sorte qui contribuent encore à intensifier l'état qu'ils manifestent. (ibid.)[38]

Durkheim goes on to describe the rhythm of the cries, movements, and gestures, the songs and dances, their *violence naturelle*, the insufficiency of the human voice, the clapping of boomerangs against each other, the whirling of bullroarers, the unleashing of passions. His *pudeur*, like that of his sources (Spencer and Gillen, and Howitt), permits only abstract description:

L'effervescence devient souvent telle qu'elle entraîne à des actes inouïs. Les passions déchaînées sont d'une telle impétuosité qu'elles ne se laissent contenir par rien. On est tellement en dehors des conditions ordinaires de la vie et on en a si bien conscience qu'on éprouve comme le besoin de se mettre en dehors et au-dessus de la morale ordinaire. Les sexes s'accouplent contrairement aux règles qui président au commerce sexuel. Les hommes échangent leurs femmes. Parfois même, des unions incestueuses qui, en temps normal, sont jugées abominables et sont sévèrement condamnées se contractent ostensiblement et impunément. (ibid., p. 309)[39]

Shifting his emphasis from the auditory to the visual, Durkheim adds that these ceremonies take place at night, when the light of the fires pierces the darkness, producing so violent an excitement that they cannot be sustained for long. Their principal actor falls to the ground exhausted.

Durkheim's description is composite. It appears in the middle of his treatise, in its most important theoretical chapter. It follows—and is followed by—three hundred pages of argument, critical discussions of theories of religion, and a detailed picture of aboriginal beliefs and social organization. As though he (and his reader) are coming up for breath, these pages are punctuated with reflections on modern society, "advanced" religions, and the source of contemporary cognitive categories in the primitive. After presenting the corroboree, Durkheim goes on to describe two rituals, taken from Spencer and Gillen, that are rather more specific (though no doubt themselves composites), objectively weightier, and, he attests, more violent (ibid., pp. 310–13). In all three descriptions, as elsewhere in *The Elementary Forms*, Durkheim (re-)creates the rituals, their emotional tone, and their effect on the spectators (as, indeed, on readers) from relatively dry descriptions, thereby reinforcing through exposition, rhetoric, and hypotyposis the *effervescence* on which his argument rests. Note his emphasis on violence, on unleashed passions and emotions, on the loss of control. These are familiar themes in Durkheim's work. Note also the centrality of sexual transgression and incest, less in the ritual cycle, one suspects, than in his ethnographic description.

The circularity of Durkheim's arguments, their petitio principii, has often been noted by critics (especially Steven Lukes). In *The Elementary Forms*, the circularity is also carried by style. Despite his insistence on pure sociological explanation, Durkheim's argument as well as his ritual re-creations rest on a set of psychological assumptions about the nature of primitive man that are rather closer to those of Lévy-Bruhl than his criticism of that author would warrant.[40]

It is from these effervescent social milieux, from this effervescence itself, Durkheim states, that the religious idea is born (ibid., p. 313). The Australian tribesman's life is divided, he notes, between periods of dispersion, devoid of ritual activity and characterized by a complete emotional atonia, and those of clan assembly, of intense ritual activity in which super-excitation reigns: "One can even ask whether the violence of this contrast is not necessary for the sensation of the sacred to gush forth in its first form" (ibid., pp. 313–14; my translation).[41] This effervescence is (the source of) that diffuse energy, that impersonal force, that mana which characterizes the most elementary — the totemic — religion: "Totemism is the religion, not of such and such animals or men or images, but of an anonymous and impersonal force, found in each of these beings but not to be confounded with any of them" (Durkheim, *The Elementary Forms*, p. 217). The totem is the "material form" by which this "diffuse energy," this "immaterial substance" is represented to the imagination (*Les Formes élémentaires*, p. 270). (Like Mauss, like the savage, Durkheim flits without consistency from one referential figuration to another of this impersonal force.) The totem is at once an object (plant, animal), an emblem, the members of a clan, and a conception of the universe (ibid., p. 200). It both represents the clan — its referential function — and gives to the clan, pragmatically, performatively, its sense of unity; it becomes the model, in societies less fragmented than those of Australia, for a unified notion of the universe (p. 281).[42] Yet the totemic objects themselves, and their emblems, are insignificant. They cannot inspire the sentiments — respect, fear, *crainte révérentielle*, feelings of dependency — to which they are attached (p. 293).

The force of ritual, of the crowd, is experienced as external to, though immanent in, the ritual participant. It gives him the sense of having a double nature, with part of himself outside his control.[43] A "moral imperative" (p. 271), it creates a sense of obligation that can force him to act not in his own immediate interests but in those of the collectivity. It produces a sense of "joyous confidence" in the primitive, who does not yet know terrible, jealous gods, whose society is not yet a "Leviathan" overwhelming him with the enormity of its power and subjecting him to its harsh discipline (p. 321). The force of ritual is a moral force whose referential figuration, as totem — or as spirit, demon, or god in more advanced religions (p. 284) — comes to represent, in a manner that is not altogether clear in Durkheim's argument, society itself. The totem and, more specifically, its emblems — *churinga, nurtunja, waninga* — enable society to become conscious of itself (p. 331). They participate in, condense, carry, and spread this force, this mana.

Durkheim notes that the totemic emblem is in fact more sacred than the objects (animals, plants, the clan) for which it stands (*The Elementary Forms*, pp. 188–89; *Les Formes élémentaires*, p. 315). He argues that the sentiments awakened in us by an object are communicated spontaneously, as by contagion, to another object, a symbol that comes to represent that object (*Les Formes élémentaires*, p. 314). The symbol is particularly powerful if it is simple and concrete. It is a sign that is loved, feared, respected.[44] It is for the sign that one sacrifices oneself. The soldier who surrenders his life for his flag does not see the flag as a sign of no value in itself, serving only to recall the reality it represents; rather, he treats it as though it were that reality itself. For the primitive, whose intelligence is too "rudimentary" to grasp a reality as complex as the clan, who is unable to recognize in the collectivity the source of his *transport*, his ecstasis, his being raised above himself, the tendency to respond to the symbol as though it were the symbolized is even stronger:

Now what does he see about him? On every side those things which appeal to his senses and strike his imagination are the numerous images of the totem. They are the waninga and the nurtunja, which are symbols of the sacred being. They are the churinga and the bullroarers upon which are generally carved [*gravé*, engraved] combinations of lines having the same significance. They are the decorations covering the different parts of his body, which are totemic marks. How could this image, repeated everywhere and in all sorts of forms, fail to stand out with exceptional relief in his mind? Placed thus in the centre of the scene, it becomes representative. The sentiments experienced fix themselves upon it, for it is the only concrete object upon which they can fix themselves. It continues to bring them to mind and to evoke them even after the assembly has dissolved, for it survives the assembly, being carved [*gravée*] upon the instruments of the cult, upon the sides of rocks, upon bucklers, etc. By it, the emotions experienced are perpetually sustained and revived. Everything happens just as if they inspired them directly. (*The Elementary Forms*, p. 252; see also *Les Formes élémentaires*, pp. 315–16.)

Durkheim's argument stereotypically assumes a primitive mentality, for which he offers no evidence. He does give us a theory of symbolism reminiscent of the Symbolist preoccupations of his age: the symbol as vehicle of emotion, the symbol as distinct from the symbolized and yet tied to it, the symbol as capable under certain special circumstances (here, among the primitives, in ritual; elsewhere, in France, in poetry, not to mention liturgy) of becoming one with the symbolized.

What is striking in this passage and throughout *The Elementary Forms* is what Jacques Derrida would regard as a projection (or, perhaps, a recognition) of a logocentric sensibility.[45] Durkheim (*The Elementary Forms*, p. 179; *Les Formes élémentaires*, pp. 334–35) refers to the marks on the body, the designs on the totemic emblems, as a form of writing: "If the Australian is so strongly inclined to represent [*figurer*] the totem, it is in order not to have a portrait of it before his eyes which would constantly renew the sensation of it; it is merely because he feels the need to represent [*représenter*] the idea which he forms of it by means of material and external signs, no matter what these signs may be" (*The Elementary Forms*, p. 149; *Les Formes élémentaires*, p. 179). He even speculates about the origin of writing: to translate materially thought (*Les Formes élémentaires*, p. 180, n. 1). The totem appears to be a hierarchically ordered series of displaced symbols, each external to the other, as letter is to sound, sound to meaning, each representing, indeed participating in, supplementing, as it were, the other: society, the clan, the members of the clan, the animal or plant that represents the clan, its members, the totemic emblems. To each is attributed the effervescent force, the mana, of ritual, the crowd, society. (We should take note of Durkheim's confusion of crowd and society and, at times, opinion.) Each becomes a referentially dominated vehicle of that (pragmatic) force, and thereby, in Durkheim's thought, the symbol, ultimately the source, of that force. Through attribution (read, perhaps, contagion), source, vehicle, and symbol or sign are collapsed in Durkheim's putative totemic thought. We are at the limit of referentiality or, if you prefer, figuration. Unlike Mauss, Durkheim insists on an ultimate referent, society, whose referential stability is assured by declaring it not just a symbol of that force but its source. Its position is further guaranteed by Durkheim's rhetorical and theoretical "sociolatry."

In contrast to those scholars — the majority, Durkheim (ibid., p. 322) tells us — who see in religion the superimposition on reality of an "irreal world" constructed entirely out of fantastic dream images or out of "often monstrous aberrations that the mythological imagination has given birth to under the prestigious though deceptive influence of language," Durkheim (pp. 322,

597) argues that religion is rooted in reality, that the moral force on which the Australian tribesman depends is no illusion: "*Cette puissance existe, c'est la société.*" Yet Durkheim has to admit that the Australian is wrong when he believes, for example, that the increase in vitality he experiences during a ceremony comes from the totemic animal or plant:

But this error is merely in regard to the letter of the symbol by which this being is represented to the mind and the external appearance which the imagination has given it, and not in regard to the fact of its existence [*Mais l'erreur porte uniquement sur la lettre du symbole au moyen duquel cet être est représesenté à l'esprit, sur l'aspect de son existence.*] Behind these figures and metaphors, be they gross or refined, there is a concrete and living reality. Thus religion acquires a meaning and a reasonableness that the most intransigent rationalist cannot misunderstand. (*The Elementary Forms*, p. 257; *Les Formes élémentaires*, p. 322)

It is not altogether clear what Durkheim means by the "letter of the symbol." He appears to be affirming the reality of the symbolized — here society (itself, however, in one of his understandings, a symbolic objectification of effervescent force) — and giving short shrift to the symbol (though, as we have noted, he acknowledges that the symbol, the emblem, may be even more potent than its referent). What, then, is the status of the symbolic? The aborigines respond to their totems as though they were real and not symbols of something they cannot grasp. Durkheim sidesteps the issue by arguing that "the principal object of religion is not to give to man a representation of the universe"; rather, religion is — note the grammatical shift — "before all else a system of notions by means of which individuals represent their society and the obscure but intimate relations they have with it" (*The Elementary Forms*, p. 223). Metaphoric or symbolic, this representation is nevertheless faithful to society.

Durkheim's argument is circular, confused, and, finally, dangerous. What are the consequences of attributing reality to the object of erroneous symbols, which are, as we have seen, highly effective precisely because they partake of (the power of) the reality they symbolize? Can the "reality" of a referent give *reality* to its symbol? We are back to the problem of illusion I raised in my discussion of Mauss. Has Durkheim provided us with a theory of — indeed, a justification for — illusion?

Durkheim does not discuss illusion but, more extravagantly, delirium: "If we give the name delirious [*délire*] to every state in which the mind adds to the immediate data given by the senses and projects its own sentiments and feelings unto things, then nearly every collective representation is in a sense

delirious" (*The Elementary Forms*, p. 259; *Les Formes élémentaires*, p. 325).
The French *délire* does not have the same pathological connotations as the
English delirium; it can refer to a state of dreamlike irreality. The examples
that Durkheim gives of this *délire* are of radically different ontological and
epistemological status: symbolic vehicles (the flag, blood), projected sentiments and emotions, categories and classifications (man distinct from animal), economic value (a canceled postage stamp), even perception (odors,
tastes). It would seem that the entire interpreted and evaluated world —
culture — would be a delirium in this sense! But, Durkheim insists, it is an
effective delirium, because its objects and images are endowed with power
and influence the conduct of men: "This is because social thought, owing to
the imperative authority that is in it, has an efficacy that individual thought
could never have; by the power which it has over minds, it can make us see
things in whatever light it pleases; it adds to reality or deducts from it according to circumstance" (*The Elementary Forms*, p. 260; *Les Formes élémentaires*, p. 326).

In the case of society this "formula of idealism," as Durkheim refers to it,
is especially applicable. "Here more than anywhere else, the idea [the sym-
bol] is the reality." The object that serves as a support for the idea — note the
contradiction — is reduced to a minimum within the "ideal superstructure."
There is in fact no delirium, Durkheim argues yet again in circular fashion,
"because the ideas thus objectified are well-founded, not in the nature of the
material things upon which they are grafted, but in the nature of society"
(*Les Formes élémentaires*, p. 327; my translation).

Durkheim does not consider the effectiveness of the empowered vehicles,
the sacralized symbols, in and of themselves, as part of a system or structure
(ibid., p. 625). However contingent they may be, they orient conduct. They
formulate reality.[46] It is the force of society, of the ritual crowd, that is objectified through the symbols, giving them not only power but reality. The formulation is in fact Mauss's. Totemic power functions for Durkheim as
mana does for Mauss: it gives empowered and empowering reality to objects — symbols — that have, in and of themselves, neither reality nor power.
Durkheim affirms the importance of social effervescence and predicts that
one day "our societies will know again hours of creative effervescence during
the course of which new ideals will emerge, new formulas will be released
to serve for a time as a guide to humanity" (p. 611).

Referring to the Australian aborigines, that most primitive of societies,
Durkheim is left blinded to the contemporary political implication of his
analysis. Despite his overt political stance, which can hardly be called fascist,

his analysis leads to — or, perhaps more accurately, is a symptom of — the thought that was worked through (*verarbeitet*) during the decades of fascism following his death and that is still being worked through today. In combination with Mauss's theory of magic and illusion, Durkheim has offered us a picture of how the (ritual) crowd's excitement in its veneration of itself produces the effervescence, the mana, the power that converts illusion into reality.

This Marcel Mauss came to recognize. He wrote to S. Ranulf in 1936 and 1939:

One thing that, fundamentally, we never foresaw was how many large modern societies, that have more or less emerged from the Middle Ages in other respects, could be hypnotized like the Australians are by their dances, and set in motion like a children's roundabout. We contented ourselves with several allusions to crowd situations, while it was a question of something different. We also contented ourselves with proving that it was in the collective mind [*dans l'esprit collectif*] that the individual could find the basis and sustenance for his liberty, his independence, his personality and his criticism [*critique*]. Basically, we never allowed for the extraordinary new possibilities. . . . I believe that all this is a real tragedy for us, too powerful a verification of things that we had indicated and the proof that we should have expected this verification through evil rather than a verification through goodness [*le bien*].[47]

We must, I believe, consider the notion — indeed, the location, the dislocation — of the primitive within modernist thought in terms of this verification.

JULIA E. LISS

# Patterns of Strangeness
*Franz Boas, Modernism, and
the Origins of Anthropology*

Anthropology embodies a central paradox. Ostensibly a discipline that critically analyzes the myths and narratives of alien cultures, it creates its own
myths in the process. This is the modernist dilemma embedded in anthropology: the "modern" and the "primitive" are mutually defining, intrinsi-
cally yet unstably connected. The myth of anthropology's origins, for instance, places Franz Boas at the center of academic anthropology in the
United States. Through his own career and those of his students, who were
found in almost every department of anthropology in the nation for over a
generation, Boas imposed his vision on an entire field and helped codify the
study of "primitive" peoples as a subject of academic inquiry.[1]

Yet Boas's history reveals the tensions of modernism inherent in the project and practice of anthropology. Boas's appeals to rationalism and science,
on the one hand, and the repressed, ever-shifting narrative of his own life,
on the other, exemplify the discipline of anthropology. Indeed, the triumphs
of his career obscure the more uncertain trajectory that connected his personal experience and the anthropology he began to develop in the 1880's and
1890's. A destabilized sense of self—one formed out of experiences of perpetual marginality—contributed to an anthropology that focused on connections and relatedness. Anthropology, conceived of as a science that would
transcend all particulars, addressed the experience of fluctuation and contingency. In this respect, Boasian anthropology developed squarely within the
aesthetic, epistemological, and political transformations of modernism—
especially its emphasis on the multiple and shifting realities of modernity.[2]

The importance of flux and contingency in turn challenges one of the
commonplaces of anthropology: the transformative power of fieldwork. One
of the conventions of the discipline—among its practitioners as well as its
historians—is to view anthropologists' first field experiences as turning
points, initiations into the life of another people that revolutionize how they

view themselves and their own society. Even those who have contextualized these first expeditions by considering how earlier life influenced later anthropological experience have emphasized the formative effect of fieldwork. In his introduction to Boas's Baffin Island Letter-Diary, for instance, Douglas Cole calls the trip his "ethnographic initiation." He also omits almost all the sections written on board ship, about one-third of the journal. For his part, George W. Stocking, Jr., has questioned the trip's effect and connects it with Boas's existing views, but he is more concerned with Boas's intellectual development than with the way his fieldwork related to his existing social precariousness. Boas's stay among the Eskimo of Baffin Island, in Stocking's view, was an experience that drew him to the people rather than the geography of the area and through which he observed the promise of a deeper community of human fellowship than European society provided. In the process, Boas the "physicist" became Boas the "anthropologist."[3]

If such a discrete transition did not actually take place, however, then what was the ongoing dynamic between fieldwork and more familiar experience? If that first trip into the bush (or ice) was not a threshold which, once crossed, transformed one's perspective, then how did it interact with preconceived notions and later life? How did Boas himself evaluate that process as he anticipated his confrontation with strange surroundings, struggled to understand them, and ultimately returned home? By contextualizing Boas's early field experiences as part of ongoing patterns, rather than in the relative isolation that viewing them as crucial episodes suggests, one can see more clearly how this dynamic emerges.[4]

Through the feelings of estrangement and marginality and the opposite longings they generated — for loyalty and belonging — Boas's life and work interacted in especially powerful ways. Official trips, first to the far reaches of Baffin Island in 1883–84 and later to the Northwest Coast of America in 1886, were juxtaposed with other voyages between Germany and America, which repeated the experience of transience and crystallized it in a continuing struggle of identity. As an explorer / geographer and as an immigrant, Boas hung between worlds; as an anthropologist he would normalize those experiences and make them meaningful.[5]

Boas's peculiar status was exemplary rather than idiosyncratic. In his study of the philosophy of anthropology, I. C. Jarvie makes provocative suggestions about the connection between various kinds of marginal experience and anthropology, in particular regarding the foreigners and colonials among British social anthropologists: Malinowski from Poland; Gluckman, Schaperer, and Fortes from South Africa; and Firth from New Zealand. For the socially and culturally marginal, he contends, the idea of the "unity of mankind" was essentially an argument for their own assimilation. Similarly, fieldwork activated a "fantasy of penetrating an alien society without causing significant disturbance." For both Boas and Malinowski, he suggests, the emphasis on fieldwork paralleled their own experience as immigrants.[6] In this respect, it is best to consider how Boas's conception of anthropology developed not out of a single fieldwork experience but out of the ongoing tensions between belonging and exclusion, of which fieldwork was only one part—a part that would help normalize and reconcile life's fluctuations.

In fact, because fieldwork lacked a singular, transformative power— because there was no stable moment—there were also no cultural wholes.[7] So much attention has been paid to the "culture concept" as the paradigmatic development in the history of anthropology that this central experience of transience and concern with interrelationships have been overlooked.[8] Its significance, however, cannot be overstated. Through it Boas's personal experience and intellectual development informed the anthropology he organized. Boasian anthropology was not a search for cultural wholes outside of the modern world but, rather, an exercise of modernist sensibility, a recognition of the world of contingency in which the anthropologist defined himself and his task against a series of destabilizing experiences.

In this way, cosmopolitanism underlay both Boas's growth as an anthropologist and the configuration of American anthropology. As a concern with universality and transcending particularity, cosmopolitanism provided a way of valuing and experiencing diversity by escaping the narrowness of one's own experience. Unlike pluralism, which stresses the importance of self-contained entities, cosmopolitanism stresses the multiplicity of experience as it is shared and appreciated. Cosmopolitanism implies not only the importance of these particularities but, even more significantly, the ability to transcend one's own particularities in order to understand those of others. In this respect, the cosmopolitan is neither "provincial"—bound by his or her own (narrow) experience—nor essentialist—certain of definable and authentic forms of identity.

Cosmopolitanism was, therefore, the particular and prescriptive form that modernism took in Boasian anthropology and through which it engaged the transformations of modernity. In the context of nationalism, imperialism, immigration, travel, and the expansion of capital, cosmopolitanism helped anthropologists rethink relationships in an increasingly interconnected world. For Boas, as for a more disparate group of critics and social observers, cosmopolitanism provided a language with which to create a world without particulars, where the universals of experience would be engaged and addressed. In his own experience as an immigrant and upwardly mobile anthropologist, Boas embodied and addressed these problems.[9]

Boas's Jewishness played a particular role in these dynamics of self-actualization. Unlike German Jews who alternated between assimilation and reconfirming their Judaism, Boas had no positive religious identification to mobilize either of these choices.[10] Instead, his confrontation with anti-Semitism and the forced, negative identity it generated helped motivate his ethnic sensibility. Although he claimed that his parents' liberation from "the shackles of dogma" had "spared [him] the struggle against religious dogma that besets the lives of so many young people,"[11] he still waged his own struggles against anti-Semitism and paternal authority, struggles that propelled him against social, intellectual, and political as well as personal obstacles.

Boas began working out the dynamics of this situation in the 1870's, while he was a university student. During these years he walked a tightrope between a quest for belonging and disaffection from the world around him. In answering the call to science, Boas strove to actualize his universality and transcend the boundaries imposed on him. Although he conceived of this enterprise as a liberation that would take him definitively beyond the limits of his existence, it was nevertheless rooted in a series of conflicts and tensions that would be reenacted throughout his life. When he entered Heidelberg in 1877, amidst escalating German anti-Semitism, his ambivalence about being both inside and outside local networks of intellectual life became more pressing. At the same time, especially in the study of geography, Boas addressed the problems of universality and particularity.[12] Increasingly, he looked to science as a source of authority against arbitrary power and as a way to overcome the limits of his own existence. Simultaneously, however, he demonstrated the degree to which anthropology was built out of the effort to come to terms with an unstable experience.

In each of these instances, Boas's quest for liberation was enacted through a gendered discourse. The search for a scientific career against his father's preference that he pursue a career in medicine, social activities while at the university, experiences in the field, and control over the emerging discipline of academic anthropology all furthered Boas's struggles for manhood while putatively severing relationships with existing authorities. In each of these searches — whether the goal was maturity, social status, or intellectual influence — Boas's personal and professional self-definition proceeded together. In the end, the man his students called "Papa Franz" could indeed proclaim himself the father of his discipline.

Boas's search for manhood was condensed in the stories told about his famous facial scars. According to one version, he had challenged a man to a duel after hearing an anti-Semitic insult in a café. Although the comment was not clearly directed at him, young Franz had the man thrown out of doors and, even though his opponent offered to apologize, Boas defended his honor and insisted on a confrontation. Boas apparently told his children, however, that he had been scratched by an "ice bear." In a third version, the scars were evidence of the foreign, inhumane practices that the scientists at Clark University, where Boas taught briefly in the 1890's, visited on their laboratory animals and on themselves.[13]

These various accounts, some of which Boas himself apparently perpetuated, combine a number of different incidents and conflate his scientific work and social involvements. In fact Boas participated in many duels, not only to protest anti-Semitism but, more broadly, to enter a world from which he was excluded. For Boas, however, the status of membership and the importance of defending one's standing through duels had both added urgency and questionable effectiveness. The quest for belonging in the midst of the heightened nationalism and anti-Semitism of the late nineteenth century made the enterprise an inherently problematic one, highlighting rather than reconciling the tensions between his desire to belong and his exclusion.[14] Moreover, in turning wounds that had been inflicted during a series of battles over honor and status into injuries sustained during his first field trip to the Arctic, Boas made his scientific experience stand in for social confrontations. The problems of exclusion, dueling, and scientific enterprise were connected.

At Heidelberg, Boas distanced himself from Jewish students and tried to become an integral part of the student culture. Although this was partly an effort to counter exclusion with a new sense of belonging, Boas's own sense of identity remained problematic and precarious. Especially in an actively anti-Semitic society, it was difficult to find a place between the two mutually exclusive labels of Jew and non-Jew. Over his parents' objections, in 1877 Boas joined the Allemannen, one of the *Burschenschaften* (students' associations) at Bonn, providing himself with a ready-made community that offered close companionship and an opportunity to meet those he considered to be of the better sort.[15] Like his peers, Boas engaged in ritualistic camaraderie — drinking and dueling — with the predictable outcome of a series of scars and wounds.

Boas's dueling escapades speak to the tensions inherent in the ideals of cultivation to which he aspired. As a rite of passage, an exercise of manhood through blood, comradeship, and mannered violence, the duel was a significant moment in a man's coming of age. Nonetheless, this cultivation was won only through bloody aggression — even if controlled by the rituals of the event — which often sent pieces of scalp and face flying, leaving the "victim" triumphant, with a scar as emblem of his manhood.[16] Although at least one of Boas's wounds resulted from an anti-Semitic incident, there were other duels in which he battled for his honor and manhood, thus fully engaging the doubleness of "cultivation" in "civilized" society.

By the time he finished his degree in 1881, Boas increasingly turned to science to reconcile the unfulfilled promises of his social existence. Through science he transcended the boundaries that he could not surmount within the exclusive community of the German university and the ritualistic acts it encouraged. The need for community and the desire for authority, status, manhood, and honor persisted, but he now aimed to achieve them in another way. Boas hoped that science, an activity that ostensibly rose above particulars and granted standing through the pursuit of truth and free interchange of ideas, would enable him to escape the limitations of his world. At the same time, scientific activity would fulfill his needs by working through those very problems of belonging and exclusion, expressiveness and control that preoccupied him.

More directly, Boas's emerging anthropological work constantly reenacted and addressed these tensions between belonging and exclusion, particularity and universals. Following his student days, when his developing scientific interests and social commitments struggled with his conflicts of identity and manhood, Boas transported these concerns to a new arena. As he wrote to his fiancée, Marie Krackowizer, en route to his first field trip among the Eskimo of Baffin Island in 1883–84, his newfound life of reason had replaced his earlier emotionalism. On the day of the anniversary cele- · bration of his fraternity, Boas thought

of the many acquaintances, of most of whom I have lost track completely. It is strange that I lived among them for almost 2 years and never found a real friend. . . . I wonder what you would have thought of me, Marie, if you had gotten to know me during my student years. I was an irresponsible, superficial, "brother" Studio. I had to take myself in hand to become a sensible, rational being. I still have to wonder how it was possible for me to take part in that wild and irresponsible life (and it was only four years ago). Now I would tire of it in one day. And yet I never wish for their return. Not until now have I lived honestly and true to myself, really lived, and will live more so when I shall be back with you, my Marie.[17]

Now a "rational being," his fieldwork suspended him constantly between worlds, even as it threw up memories and fantasies of belonging. The field of anthropology, as Boas came to define it, made its central focus these interconnections and relationships, and hence replaced his earlier, student activities.

In organizing his expedition, Boas exploited contemporary interest in exploration and travel to faraway places. In the second half of the nineteenth century, a combination of nationalist, imperialist, scientific, and moral aims encouraged European and American expeditions, especially to Africa, Asia, and the Arctic. At the same time, middle-class urbanites took vacations to escape the drudgery of industrial work and the dirt and disease of industrial cities, while improvements in transportation made increased mobility possible. Bourgeois fascination with the "primitive" and strange further excited interest in exotic locales, enabling geographic societies, which took an active role in funding expeditions in Germany and England as well as America, to build large followings. Meetings on special topics, such as Stanley's expeditions to Africa; publications such as *National Geographic*; and newspaper series on global travels and prominent expeditions catered to public interest.[18]

Boas's own views, however, challenged the commonplace divisions on which such expeditions were based. After he had been among "Messieurs les Esquimaux" for several months, Boas reflected on the nature of Eskimo community, the power of human fellowship, and the relativity of social values:

Is it not a beautiful custom that these "savages" ["*Wilden*"] suffer all deprivations in common, but, in happy times when some one has brought back booty from the hunt, all join in eating and drinking? I often ask myself what advantages our "good society" possesses over that of the "savages." The more I see their customs, the more I realize that we have no right to look down upon them. Where amongst our people could you find such true hospitality? Here, without the least complaint people are willing to perform *every* task demanded of them. We have no right to blame them for their forms and superstitions which may seem ridiculous to us. We "highly educated people" are much worse, relatively speaking. The fear of tradition and old customs is deeply implanted in mankind, and in the same way as it regulates life here, it halts all progress for us. I believe it is a difficult struggle for every individual and every people to give up traditions and follow the path to truth. The Eskimo are sitting around me, their mouths filled with raw seal liver (the spot of blood on the back of the paper shows you how I joined in). As a thinking person, for me the most important result of this trip lies in the strengthening of my point of view that the ideal of "cultivation" ["*Bildung*"] is merely relative and that a person's worth should be judged by his cultivation of the heart [*Herzensbildung*]. This quality is present or absent here among the Eskimo, just as among us. All that man can do for humanity is to further the *truth*, whether it be sweet or bitter. Such a man may truly say that he has not lived in vain. But now I must really get back to the cold Eskimo land.[19]

Boas betrayed a number of ambivalences in these closing comments. Pointing out the difficulty of breaking the bonds of tradition and joining the quest for truth, he then laid out just such a path by departing from one of his society's own conventions, the distinction between savage and cultured. Moreover, he based his authority on his participation in these "savage" acts, a practice that gave him intimate knowledge of this alternate world and took him outside the realm of "civilized" discourse. In the end, however, he spoke as the "thinking person," with a rational voice, who saw the value of the individual, cultivated heart as he tried to give his own life purpose by pursuing the truth himself. In this sense, the science of culture — which is how Boas came to define anthropology — objectified and challenged the European (German) ideal of cultivation. In making this argument, Boas achieved what he could not do at home: he integrated himself into a close-knit community. If dueling had embodied the conflicting demands of cultivated society and manly violence that Boas could never truly fulfill, then here he achieved a new form of bloody manhood by eating (and later hunting) seal and by sharing "how he joined in" as a challenge to the conventions of "civilized" and "savage."

In this sense, the existence of the modern derives from the *experience* of savagery and blood, of authenticity and irrationality, the "modern" and the "primitive" existing only, by definition, with each other. Tempting as it is, therefore, to suggest that Boas's life of perpetual marginality encouraged a romanticization of communal existence, and that the destabilizing results of his experience generated an alternative world of the eternal and holistic primitive, the essential dynamic was different. Boas's observations were not simply idealized but also full of contradictions, which are signaled by the abrupt ending to his enthusiastic ruminations. First, he celebrated the community and humanity of those often deemed uncivilized, even unhuman. Having once sought companionship through "eating and drinking" festivities himself, Boas both validated these expressions and used them to criticize the society that he himself represented. But after questioning Western judgments about "savages," Boas went on to play on them through the shock value of reporting his eating of raw seal meat. He then reinvigorated his moral authority "as a thinking person" and confirmed what he says he knew *before* he embarked on his trip: that cultivation is "merely relative" and the *real* standard should be not thinking but cultivation of the *heart*. Having dissolved differences, Boas laid claim to a higher purpose — the pursuit of *"truth"* — in the cause of "humanity," but then he escaped suddenly from his reader to return to the people of the North, that forbidding land. Strangely, he implied, one must cultivate one's heart but not live by it — that responsibility rested with the mind of the thinking person. While he broke down the distinctions between "savage" and "civilized" through participant observation, Boas left himself on unstable ground and asserted his alternative value system within the framework of the old.

With an ambivalent relationship to German society, both desiring to emulate its ideals and feeling excluded from it, Boas turned against social convention and the ideal of the cultivated individual that was central to it. At the same time, however, he asserted a new form of *Bildung*, a cultivation of the heart, which all people potentially share. Instead of worshiping false standards of superiority, the best effort entailed a search for transcendent "truth," outside of particularist standards of judgment. Boas thereby revealed his marginal position, both participating in this newfound world and drawing back from it as "a thinking person." From this vantage point of a truth-seeker, paradoxically, Boas sought to weigh different customs, actualize himself, and control his discipline.

Because it was ineluctably tied to his life experience, fieldwork did not instantaneously or irrevocably immerse Boas in a world of strangeness. Instead, the entire process — bounded on one side by the journey to Baffinland and, on the other, by a return to Germany — was made up of a series of critical encounters. En route to Baffinland in June and July 1883, Boas imagined the world he had left behind and anticipated a new one, feeling variously drawn to Baffinland and pulled back to Germany.[20] Once he arrived, however, there was no reconciliation of this feeling of displacement. Instead, Boas told of a continually fluctuating sense of self. Dressing like an Eskimo,[21] writing Eskimo melodies on his letters,[22] and triumphantly announcing he had caught a seal and was "now a true Eskimo . . . belong[ing] to the men of Anaritung,"[23] Boas partook of the bloody comradeship he had observed. If he had earlier engaged in acts that tore at the flesh of German youth, seeking to prove his manhood and legitimacy through dueling, now he proved himself a man of a different sort by killing seals and eating their flesh.

These moments, however, existed in tension with others, emphasizing the contradictory pulls of different homelands and marking the dilemma of cosmopolitan experience. Boas felt "at home" in his new environment but communicated with the native peoples in English (although his own tongue was German);[24] he yearned for Beethoven[25] and European food[26] while recalling his alienation from that familiar world and the falsehood of life in "society." [27] Yet Boas's attachments to Europe existed only alongside his feelings of marginality and alienation. Moreover, these conflicts were reinforced, not solved, by his return, when Boas was literally between two worlds. In March 1884 he predicted "that I will be the same as when I left. What I have seen and experienced here has not changed me, perhaps made me a little more appreciative of all the beauty and goodness that is to be found *at home*." [28] At the same time, however, he longed for Germany, using the American vernacular to say that he had "the Blues in the highest degree." [29] When he finally returned to Germany the following year, he found the experience oddly dislocating: "I must become accustomed to things here — I feel so strange, but at the same time so at home here." [30]

Significantly, there is no linear trajectory in these sentiments. By disembarking in New York — and by envisioning his immigration there — before traveling on to his hometown of Minden, Boas's return to Germany complicated even further the already intricate pattern of strangeness and familiarity. Had he gone immediately to Germany, his emotions might have been more easily directed toward adjustment and assimilation of old and new experience. Instead, Boas's adaptation was incomplete and shifting. His departure had produced in him various visions of home; when he returned, those "homes" created new dissatisfactions. According to Boas's own testimony, the "anthropological experience" of strangeness occurred not just in the field but in the context of ongoing events: just as his sense of marginality existed before he went to Baffin Island, encouraging his questions about European society and his attraction to the Eskimo, so his return to Germany was another anthropological encounter that he also perceived as alien.

Boas's dominant experience, therefore, is best seen as that of an exile. In his study of the representation of exilic experience in literature, Michael Seidel has defined an exile as "someone who inhabits one place and remembers or projects another." According to Paul Tabori, an exile may consider uprootedness as temporary, "though it lasts a lifetime." [31] In his letters from the field, Boas engaged in just such an exercise of memory and comparison, struggling with the permanence of his own transience. Instead of seeking and finding fulfillment in the alien world of the Baffinland Eskimo, or returning to Germany with a reaffirmed sense of his own identity, Boas alternated between both desires, his recurrent assertions of frustration and withdrawal challenging his periodic experiences of belonging. Boas did not, therefore, simply immerse himself in Eskimo life and idealize it, nor was he consistently repelled by it. Instead, he lived perpetually with marginality, shuttling back and forth between different worlds — his past, present, and future.

Boas's anthropology focused on these problems of migration, contact, and interrelationship, problems that paralleled the experience of migration and exile. It is significant, therefore, that when he was trying to decide whether or not to settle in America, Boas used similar language to define his personal plight and professional objectives. When he returned from Baffin Island with his own sack of booty, his quest for truth caught him in bonds tighter still than those he had felt among the Eskimo. Recently engaged to be married, Boas needed to plan his life. "I came here from the Eskimos with definite possibilities and intentions and have not changed my course one bit," he wrote his parents from Washington, D.C., in early 1885:

If I find a better field of work in Germany, then I will go back to Germany even though we have to wait longer to marry. If I find a better one here, then I shall stay here even if we must wait longer. . . . Do you believe that I would gladly cut all the thousand ties that bind me to my homeland, that these few months since my return have been a thousand times more painful than the long time with loneliness in the North?[32]

As Boas conceived of it, he was on a double journey—one a professional course, the other a literal voyage that he had undertaken to further his career as well as to conduct his research. Although both aspects proceeded in tandem, the twofold quest resulted in paradox and conflict rather than unity of purpose. Boas had traveled far to advance his career, experiencing a sense of human fellowship and questioning the normative standards of German society in the process. He now prepared to emigrate in order to pursue his goals, with the result that he felt more estranged from Europe than he had when he was thousands of miles away from it.

Even as the image of the cold, lonely North pushed aside the memory of the human fellowship he had found there, Boas connected his fieldwork with his career dilemma. With the same words he had used to plead his case with his parents, Boas wrote in his diary from British Columbia in December 1886, "The difference between American and Canadian cities is strange. The ties that bind the inhabitants of the cities to England are much stronger than I had thought. However, the influx of so great a number of foreigners must certainly influence the relation of the people."[33] Here the would-be immigrant, neophyte anthropologist, and striving son brought together the various threads of his experience. The "ties that bind," which first had connected him to his parents and to Germany, now linked diverse peoples to their homelands. Instead of envying the bonds of fellowship as he had in Baffinland, however, Boas now perceived more painful attachments directly at odds with the claims of companionship. Vacillation between fellowship and estrangement became his organizing principle of experience, affecting both Boas's perceptions of that experience and the anthropological work which emerged from it. There were two main features of this process: the first proclaimed anthropology as a science that would transcend particulars; the second focused that science on the problem of human connectedness.

As a science, anthropology had multiple roles to play in the cosmopolitan effort to overcome particularities. Science transcended national boundaries: it searched for overarching laws to explain particular evidence; its scrutiny of particulars pointed to their historicity and interrelationships; and an international community of scholars addressed shared concerns in a common language. As Boas said later in life, "as a scientist I do not feel any attachment to any particular group." [34] Through claims to this universalism, Boas could ensure his place as an interpreter of these cosmopolitan directives. He could now, "as a thinking person," claim authority to scrutinize the particulars of existence, the customs that he could admire from a distance but of which he could never truly be a part.

Anthropology's cosmopolitan posture was, in turn, defined in its project to trace the history of human migrations and to explore local or provincial manifestations that stressed human commonality and interrelatedness and the scientific examination of particularities. "The task of ethnology," Boas wrote in 1889, taking the inclusive, German definition of the term to mean, in his words, "language, customs, migrations [and] bodily characteristics . . . is the study of the history of mankind; not that of civilized nations alone, but that of the deposits of the ice age, up to modern times." [35] This work, supported by "inductive methods," would help investigations of the "history of culture of definite areas" and, through comparative study, "the laws governing the growth of human culture," especially those of the "human mind." [36]

Increasingly, however, Boas saw arguments for the psychic unity of mankind as speculative and not susceptible to "ethnological methods." In an 1896 discussion of "The Growth of Indian Mythologies," for instance, he took issue with those who assumed "that sameness of ethnical phenomena is *always* due to the sameness of the human mind." Making his argument one of anthropological legitimacy, Boas continued to "take issue clearly and expressly with the view of those modern anthropologists who go so far as to say that he who looks for acculturation as a cause of similarity of culture has not grasped the true spirit of anthropology." Although he acknowledged that some phenomena develop independently and are due to the "organization of the human *mind*," he thought the argument had become exaggerated, leading to "a priori" conclusions on "psychical causes" rather than to demands for increased methodological rigor on the part of the historical school of anthropology. The primary task of this historical reconstruction, therefore, was to trace connections, diffusion, and dissemination of linguistic, cultural, and racial forms.[37]

Boas's preoccupation with the question of contact, especially in language, began with his 1886 trip to British Columbia (after which he wrote to his parents about the ties that bound him). There Boas discovered similarities of language in geographically proximate but discontinuous areas. Using linguistic evidence, Boas "made an important discovery about the distribution of the tribes . . . namely that on the mainland the same language is always spoken as on the corresponding part of the island." Two years later, he found that Haida and Tlingit had the structure of Asiatic, not American, languages, suggesting a history of contact between the continents.[38] As Boas struggled with his own allegiances, he evaluated the transitory ways of the people of the Northwest Coast and the interconnectedness of the peoples of British Columbia.

The study of race also indicated the interconnections within human history. In a lecture at the U.S. National Museum on March 2, 1895, Boas discussed "the history of the peopling of the earth," which required an understanding of "the distribution and development of each separate type of man. . . . [N]ot withstanding the good definition of ethnical types," he said, "we find these types to merge into each other through a long series of intermediate forms. This is not surprising as we know how fluctuating the population of the earth has been[,] how waves of people swept over immense distance, how slow mixture of blood through intermarriage has taken place constantly."[39] To illustrate this point, at a lecture at the American Museum of Natural History in 1896, Boas invited his listeners on a journey through the countries of the world, to "become familiar with the various types of mankind," and schooled them in the heterogeneity of human populations. In a way that paralleled the interactive encounters of the anthropological enterprise but also incorporated the conventions of travel literature and the experience of tourism — two foundations of the modern experience of cosmopolitan possibilities so popular at the time — Boas drew his audience into a new view of the world they inhabited. Beginning with Europe, the region with which they were most familiar, he emphasized how types changed gradually across neighboring areas. Rather than each having a distinctive type, moreover, racial characteristics of neighboring areas overlapped.[40]

Similarly, the study of cultural life revealed a history of diffusion and dissemination that accompanied contact between peoples. "It is not too much to say," Boas wrote in "The Aims of Ethnology," "that there is no people whose customs have developed uninfluenced by foreign culture, that has not borrowed arts and ideas which it has developed in its own way."[41] This process suggested that tales, for instance, spoke to the group's history, particularly to their contact with neighboring tribes, rather than to their innate worldview. "A great many other important legends prove to be of foreign origin," Boas found,

being grafted upon more ancient mythologies. This being the case, I draw the conclusion that the mythologies as we find them now are not organic growths, but have gradually developed and obtained their present form by accretion of foreign material. Much of this material must have been ready-made, and has been adapted and changed in form according to the genius of the people who borrowed it. The proofs of this process are so ample that there is not reason to doubt the fact.[42]

In each of these cases, Boas's primary interest was not the internal workings of societies, nor did he consider them as holistic cultural systems, as the concept of culture later suggested. Instead, individual tribes were units in the larger, systematic investigation of the history of an area. As he wrote in an early essay, "the first aim of ethnological inquiry must be critical analysis of the characteristics of each people. This is the only way of attaining a satisfactory understanding of the cultures found in wider areas." Similarly, he criticized comparative methods because apparent likenesses could derive from different causes, and instead endorsed a more rigorous contextualism that emphasized "customs in relation to the total culture of the tribe practicing them . . . in connection with our investigation of their geographical distribution among neighboring tribes."[43] Boas studied individual tribes not as ends in themselves but as pieces of larger patterns of dissemination.

Anthropological science thus derived its cosmopolitan perspective from investigating local particularities. In studies of race this meant "local or social varieties"; in linguistics it meant "dialects" or "provincialisms." Similarly, Boas focused on the "peculiar province" of a group of tales to examine their dissemination.[44] His early anthropological work concentrated on individual societies in order to answer, in a universal way, questions about human contact and how it contributed to the development of human history.

The emphasis on interrelationships also served Boas's aims of transcending particularities in a more didactic way. In this respect the internal, subjective world of individual tribes was tied to a larger concern with showing the worth and value of others and, in turn, making Boas's audience see themselves differently. Thus the study of interrelations and dissemination furthered the understanding of dislocation, and Boas's emerging anthropological theory spoke to his own ethnographic experience. As Boas said about his stay among the Eskimo,

Without an intimate knowledge of the language, without an understanding of the thinking and feeling, of the religious concepts and traditions, all patterns of life of native peoples, who live completely beyond the pale of the manner of our thinking and living, must seem absurd and unworthy of human society. The appellation "savages" for many aboriginal peoples has found such wide acceptance only because the traveler observed the life and activity of the natives from the viewpoint of his European social background. The investigator who lives completely as a member of the tribe which he is studying learns to recognize, under the strange and foreign mode of life, the thinking and feeling human being, who resembles us in character more than we could imagine from our first superficial impression.[45]

In piecing together the larger puzzle of human history, Boas asserted a greater human commonality, transforming the revelations of his fieldwork experience into a model for scientific enterprise. This universalizing, however, also tended to deny the reality of "the Other," obliterating differences as well as softening the harshness of judgment. Racial mixture showed the folly of ideals of racial purity; linguistic studies demonstrated the complexity of so-called primitive languages; and cultural formations showed a rich and complex mental world.[46]

In this way, the "civilized" European and American were the real provincials. Anthropology allowed them to see their own particularity, to emerge from the cultural blinders that blocked their vision of the broader humanity. As he wrote in "The Aims of Ethnology," "We learn from the data of ethnology that not only our ability and knowledge but also the manner and ways of our feeling and thinking is the result of our upbringing as individuals and our history as a people. To draw conclusions about the development of mankind as a whole we must try to divest ourselves of these influences."[47]

In making his argument, Boas performed a familiar cosmopolitan dance and shifted his perspective of strangeness, exemplifying the mutually dependent poles of modernism. Although he began with the strange Other and familiar self, he familiarized the Other and made the self distant. In the process, anthropology focused not only on the contact of one culture with another but also on the communication of a familiar way of life with a foreign one. While the "data of ethnology" taught the historical and cultural embeddedness of our views, the *experience* of ethnology, the alternation between alienation and attraction, made attachments to those assumptions all the more problematic, difficulties that Boas sought to surmount through anthropology itself. The role of anthropology, therefore, was to illuminate the contingency of cultural values and to provide emancipation from them.

Here the view of the subjective world of different cultures played a crucial role. Such a declaration of freedom was "only possible," Boas continued,

by immersing ourselves in the spirit of primitive peoples whose perspectives and development have almost nothing in common with our own. If we use our feelings in an effort to establish how our ancestors behaved, we should not expect to achieve truthful results, since their feeling and thinking were different from our own. We must reject many presuppositions that seem self-evident to us because precisely such mental states were not self-evident in earlier times. It is indeed impossible to recognize a priori what in our feelings is common to all mankind and what is only the result of history — except through the teachings of ethnology. It alone opens to us the possibility of judging our own culture objectively, in that it permits us to strip off the presumably self-evident manner of thinking and feeling which determines even the fundamental part of our culture. Only in this way can our intellect, instructed and formed under the influences of our culture, attain a correct judgment of this same culture.[48]

As he had done earlier, in his letter from Baffinland, Boas shifted his emphasis from the perspective of an insider — the position of total immersion — to that of the outsider who is legitimated in his search for "truthful results." But now his were official recommendations pertaining to the practice of the discipline. At this juncture, however, his vantage point again changed; it was not "the spirit of primitive peoples" that ultimately concerned him but "the possibility of judging our own culture objectively." Thus anthropology suspended preconceptions and unjustified assumptions, turning its gaze on the society of its practitioners rather than on its putative subjects.

This final task was the most difficult. In his own "History of Anthropology," Boas acknowledged the tendency to use oneself as the standard against which to measure the accomplishments of others. But such "Kulturbrille" (cultural blinders), he said, must be set aside in the quest for liberation from cultural particulars. This, he concluded, was

the value of the anthropological method . . . its power to make us understand the roots from which our civilization has sprung, that it impresses us with the relative value of all forms of culture, and thus serves as a check to an exaggerated valuation of the standpoint of our own period, which we are only too liable to consider the ultimate goal of human evolution, thus depriving ourselves of the benefits to be gained from the teachings of other cultures and hindering an objective criticism of our own work.[49]

In this respect, Boas's relativism was based on two connected assumptions: that people were *related* (as the history of linguistic, cultural, and racial contact documented), and that values were contingent.

Scientific anthropology, therefore, served the missions of reason and progress against the conservatism of tradition and emotion, challenging ideas about both the "primitive" and "civilized." Unlike travelers, for instance, who were by definition casual observers wedded to their own preconceptions, anthropologists deployed rigorous methods and walked a tightrope between careful scrutiny and total immersion. The emancipation they promised consisted of ultimate liberation from the particulars of existence, their own even more than others'.

Boas was probably too hopeful about the possibilities for self-knowledge, just as he was too sanguine about the process of interactive encounters. In this sense the universal claims of Boas's anthropology were inextricably wedded to the particulars of his experience. The late nineteenth-century bourgeois fascination with the primitive took place in the context of new forms of contact, allegiance, and power: namely, the growth of travel and immigration, nationalism and imperialism. Boas experienced these developments in a particular way, and his solution — to seek transcendence in science — was rooted, ultimately, in this particularity. Paradoxically, the ties that bound him created both his desire to escape and his feelings of attachment. What he did not address were the systems of power over which even his science could not rise.

# PART III

Victorian Vertigo

CHRISTOPHER HERBERT

# Frazer, Einstein, and Free Play

> Thus we avoid any kind of comparison at a
> distance which is as objectionable as action at
> a distance.
>
> — Sir Arthur Eddington

James Frazer continues, in spite of everything, to find sympathetic commentators, whose efforts on behalf of his reputation typically center on tracking his far-reaching "influence" on subsequent generations of poets and novelists.[1] But Frazer's claims to serious consideration as a scientific investigator of primitive society have long fallen into disrepute, and the field of Frazer studies is dominated nowadays by a voluminous literature (produced largely by anthropologists) in which *The Golden Bough*[2] is portrayed as antiquated, reactionary, conceptually vacuous, and even, in René Girard's words, "fanatical and superstitious."[3] Marilyn Strathern sums up the current view by declaring that Frazerian anthropology has come to seem "not simply erroneous but absurd."[4] In the face of this mass of denigrating commentary and of abundant evidence that *The Golden Bough* has become next to unreadable for sophisticated present-day audiences, I wish to speculate about some of the reasons why Frazer's contemporaries were able to see his famous book not as regressive at all but as an expression of a bold literary and intellectual modernism — indeed, as a founding text of modern consciousness.

To this end, I propose considering *The Golden Bough* in the light of another great scholarly production of almost exactly its period, Einstein's special theory of relativity (published in 1905, after ten years of incubation), and, just as importantly, in the light of Einstein's philosophy of scientific method. If so apparently implausible a comparative exercise yields substantial results, it will testify to the principle that the significant texts of any era, even texts from remote technical disciplines and of very unequal "greatness" and originality, inhabit cultural matrices or epistemes that inscribe them unfailingly (though not necessarily in easily decipherable form) with the emergent mentality and the determining expressive codes of their period. The more immediate goal of this essay, however, is simply to unsettle the established image of Frazer's work by showing it to be traversed by provocative themes of indeterminacy and relativistic imagination — themes sharply at odds with the complacently conservative ideological and scholarly attitudes that he repeatedly proclaims, and with which many readers have uncritically identified him.

In seeking to bring a new angle of vision to bear on *The Golden Bough*, I suspend as irrelevancies a series of questions, chief among which is that of the worth of Frazer's theories as scientific propositions. I treat *The Golden Bough* purely as an instance of a certain configuration of modernist discourse — discourse the principal theme of which lies precisely, as it happens, in the impulse to break down the categorical distinction between factual truths, on the one hand, and the various functions of discourse and rhetoric, on the other. By the same token, I waive the question of how "conscious" Frazer could have been of the modernistic style of thought that I here attribute to him. Such a question may be of legitimate interest to an intellectual biographer, but it has little bearing on critical textual interpretation, which can only follow as rigorously as possible whatever evidence the text affords — the more rigorously, in fact, the more incongruous this evidence appears to be with what we think we know already about the intentions of an author. I offer, finally, no "explanation" for what I take to be a deeply self-contradicting pattern of skepticism and dogmatic assertion in Frazer, except to observe that this pattern is nothing other than the characteristic discursive phenomenon of periods undergoing profound shifts of sensibility. It is characteristic in particular of early modernist writers, who almost are definable, as D. H. Lawrence claimed classic American novelists to be, by the chronic disjunction in their work between professions of loyalty to received values (foremost among which may be the belief in the possibility of secure, unambiguous knowledge) and currents of increasingly radical, even nihilistic, skepticism. With the introduction of this metaphor of *disjunction*, I move into the heart of my matter.

## The Horror of the Physical

The disparities of Einsteinian and Frazerian discourse do seem initially so extreme as to render futile any attempt to find common ground between the two. First and foremost, Frazer's insistent grounding of his anthropology on dogmatic value judgments divides him from relativity theory in precisely the same way that it divides him from later, more progressive modes of anthropology.

The central and revolutionary concept of relativity physics was the principle that none of the innumerable "reference frames" or vantage points that can be defined for a given physical event can possibly be given preference over any other. No point of view is invalid: this is the cardinal proposition of relativity. Einstein thus insists, first and foremost, on the doctrine of what he calls "the equal legitimacy of all inertial systems"; according to special relativity, "there is no such thing," he declares, "as a 'specially favoured' (unique) co-ordinate system."[5] This formula is reiterated tirelessly by early philosophical interpreters of relativity theory such as Sir Arthur Eddington, Bertrand Russell, and Ernst Cassirer. We are naturally prone to imagine our own frame of reference to be the true one, says Eddington, "but this egocentric outlook should now be abandoned, and all frames treated as on the same footing."[6] However differently the motion of a railway train would be measured by a flea in one of the carriages and by an inhabitant of the sun, says Russell, neither point of view is scientifically preferable to the other: "each is equally justified."[7]

This fundamental axiom of interpretation (which, with its language of legitimacy, justification, and anti-egocentrism, hovers tantalizingly between the realms of physical science and ethics) is what bonds Einsteinian physics and post-Frazerian anthropology inseparably together as two cognate branches of a single revolutionary modernist discourse. It is invoked just as insistently in the latter as in the former, forming not just the motto of the discipline of enlightened anthropology but the guarantee of its claim to rigorous and impartial scientific method. Anthropological research depends on rejecting the prejudice "that our society with its customs and norms enjoys a privileged position," says Lévi-Strauss, because human societies "are all equally valid"; "the comparison of cultures" in a scientific fashion requires the recognition of them "as equally significant," says James A. Boon; and any number of similar declarations by anthropological writers could be adduced.[8] Such statements mark the point at which Frazer seems to estrange himself beyond recall from reputable science, given what Mary Douglas speaks of as "his complacency and undisguised contempt of primitive society."[9] Frazer, indeed, is unequivocal in describing primitive culture as debased and repugnant in comparison to the modern culture he calls "civilized" and, in particular, in declaring the frame of reference of modern scientific thought to be manifestly superior to that of prescientific magic and religion. Primitive mythology, he thus makes a point of declaring (in language that Strathern's comments on Frazer's own science echo strikingly), he regards "not merely as false but as preposterous and absurd" (abridged *Golden Bough*, p. vii). Here there can be no question of equal legitimacy. Whatever forms of relativity thinking may be discoverable in *The Golden Bough*, "cultural relativism" is not one of them.

The seemingly vast unlikeness between Einstein and Frazer expresses itself in another form in the sharply diverging connotations of the "physical" in the two writers' works. For Einstein, this term functions purely as the adjectival form of "physics," a science, in the modern age, of ever-more-rarefied theoretical entities or pseudoentities like the "luminiferous ether" and of undetectable phenomena like the FitzGerald Contraction. "Physical" in this context does not refer to any world of tangible material bodies, and especially not to any relation of such a world to one's own body of flesh and blood. Einstein's analysis of the "physical" universe transpires, accordingly, on a plane of very high conceptual abstraction, connecting itself to the domain of objects and of sensory experience only by means of increasingly lengthy chains of increasingly abstruse mathematical equations.[10] Here, on the level of "purely mathematical constructions" (Einstein, *Essays in Science*, p. 17), is the plane on which physicists can seek indications of that "mysterious harmony of nature" (ibid., p. 27) which is the essential principle of Einsteinian subjectivity and which dictates that high-level scientific theories are likely to be verifiable more decisively by their possession of "beauty" and "simplicity" than by their reference to empirical data.[11] In contrast, the relation of Frazer's anthropology to the order of experiential realities, and to that of human bodies in particular, is acutely registered — and deeply equivocal.

Like his student Bronislaw Malinowski, who argues that all human culture derives from "the fact that man has a body subject to various organic needs,"[12] Frazer insists on the primacy of the flesh in all his speculation about primitive culture. In his account, urgent biological need drives the investing of agricultural processes with divine attributes, particularly that of possessing "life-giving and fertilising influence" (abridged *Golden Bough*, p. 543), and generates in turn the magical practices to which primitive people resort systematically, he claims, to ensure the food supply.[13] But whereas in Malinowski bodily drives give rise smoothly and efficiently to that constellation of value-laden symbolism which properly constitutes culture, Frazer, in his study of sacrifice in primitive culture, depicts a process laden with pathological-seeming violence. Sacrifice is portrayed in *The Golden*

*Bough* as a compulsive, sadistic assault on the human body, an assault which, in the course of this text, takes on an almost endless array of different forms. Under Frazer's calm gaze, bodies are decapitated, dismembered, burned, pierced with swords and pointed sticks, torn with ceremonial knives, hacked with sickles, buried alive, scourged, flayed.[14] The dominance of such themes in *The Golden Bough*, complicit as it undoubtedly is with the Victorian fantasy of primitive people as "savages" defined first and foremost by a propensity for violence and cruelty,[15] projects an image of the human body as a site of incessant torment and incipient panic.[16] It would be hard to decipher the cultural and libidinal dynamics that impel Frazer's seemingly obsessive fixation on physical abuse, which it is tempting to interpret as an outpouring of morbid Swiftian or puritanical vindictiveness toward the human body. At another interpretive level, this aspect of Frazer's text seems to foreshadow Freud's *Civilization and Its Discontents* by implying that the institution of sacrifice may ultimately rest on some unconscious collective impulse to exact revenge on the physical body, to the imperative nutritional and other needs of which human society is so thoroughly indentured. I stress this complex of themes simply to acknowledge the obvious: that, in its profound engagement with problems of carnal and passional experience, Frazerian scientific discourse seems incalculably remote from the abstract world of "purely mathematical constructions" posited by Einsteinian physics.

## Indeterminacy

Considering the gulf of sensibility that separates them and renders their respective scientific idioms so dissimilar, it comes as a surprise to discover that Einstein and Frazer hold certain epistemological ideas — unorthodox and paradoxical ones — in common. The possibility that these ideas might bear significantly upon their scientific work in general has hitherto gone unexplored, as far as I can tell. One might almost speak of a scholarly conspiracy to overlook or explain away this factor in their careers, though the conspiracy (if there is one) functions in opposite ways in the two cases. In Einstein's, it works to protect relativity theory from the danger of itself being relativized, and in Frazer's, to protect the legend (vital to the tendentious founding myth of latter-day anthropology) of his intellectual backwardness.

Einstein's interpreters thus have often stridently insisted that relativity theory yields so-called absolute, not just relative, knowledge of nature, and Einstein himself vigorously opposed the influx of indeterminacy theory and of merely probabilistic, as opposed to determinate, causal relations into modern physics. At the same time, however, diverging from his youthful infatuation with the radical empiricism of Ernst Mach, he ever more forcefully proclaimed his belief in what he spoke of, invoking a metaphor that we shall trace at length in the remainder of this essay, as "the gulf—logically unbridgeable—which separates the world of sensory experiences from the world of concepts and propositions."[17] If the world of sense experience and that of concepts are in fact sundered from each other by an unbridgeable gulf, then *theories cannot possibly be derived from the study of empirical data.* This was exactly Einstein's conclusion. Scientific theories, he repeatedly declared, are "free inventions of the human mind" and have, fundamentally, what he called a "purely fictitious character."[18] They involve, according to Einstein, "a free play with symbols according to . . . arbitrarily given rules of the game" ("Remarks on Bertrand Russell's Theory of Knowledge," p. 289). "All our thinking," he asserts elsewhere, "is of this nature of a free play with concepts"; "all concepts, even those which are closest to experience, are . . . freely chosen conventions."[19]

Thus "the axiomatic basis of theoretical physics cannot be extracted from experience but must be freely invented" (*Essays in Science*, p. 17). Scientific theories are imaginary productions, pure and simple. We are bedeviled by a "prejudice," says Einstein, summing up this line of his mature thinking, "that facts by themselves can and should yield scientific knowledge without free conceptual construction. Such a misconception is possible only because one does not easily become aware of the free choice of such concepts, which, through verification and long usage, appear to be immediately connected with the empirical material" ("Autobiographical Notes," p. 49). The veiled allusion here is evidently to Nietzsche's declaration that "what passes for truth in every age" is nothing in reality but a "mobile army of metaphors, metonyms, and anthropomorphisms: in short a sum of human relations which . . . after long usage seem to a nation fixed, canonic and binding."[20] Scientific genius, for Albert Einstein, consists of precisely the mode of playful free imaginativeness that can liberate us from the mystified regime of this kind of "truth."[21]

To hold the doctrine that "there is no logical bridge between phenomena and their theoretical principles" (*Essays in Science*, p. 4), and to hold at the same time the belief "that pure thought can grasp reality, as the ancients dreamed" (ibid., p. 18)—that "free play" with such intellectual toys as the equations of higher mathematics can yield determinate, experimentally verifiable knowledge of nature—this is a mighty conundrum indeed, and one that lends an acutely problematic aspect to scientific rationality. It would seem to involve nothing less than a sheer leap of faith or, rather, a leap of a kind of ludic speculative impulse over the gap between reality and theory—the gap that Einstein declares, categorically, to be an infrangible one. He was keenly aware, in fact, of the logical incoherence of his account of scientific knowledge. He did not draw from it the pessimistic conclusion that Adam Smith had come to, that even the most successful scientific theories are nothing but "imaginary machines," "mere inventions of the imagination" sundered utterly from the world of external nature.[22] But Einstein evaded such an outcome only by describing his "conviction . . . of the rationality or intelligibility of the world" as "akin to religious feeling," which is to say, unjustifiable by the norms of reason.[23] Hence his assertion that "the fact that the totality of our sense experiences is such that by means of thinking . . . it can be put in order . . . is one which leaves us in awe, but which we shall never understand. One may say 'the eternal mystery of the world is its comprehensibility.' . . . The fact that [experience] is comprehensible is a miracle."[24]

Frazer's anthropology directs sharp, surprising attention to exactly this philosophical predicament recklessly defined by Einstein and Adam Smith, and even perhaps grows out of it to some degree, though Frazer's commentators, in their eagerness to annex him to every Victorian commonplace, seem to have attended to this factor in his work only in order to suppress it forcibly from consideration.

In the opening chapter of *The Golden Bough*, Frazer declares that the goal of his gigantic project of research into the world of primitive society and belief is to assemble enough evidence, which necessarily will consist for the most part of cross-cultural analogies, to make possible a credible inference regarding the origin and character of the homicidal priesthood at Nemi. In comparing a well-documented society to a poorly documented one by means of the rule of analogy invoked by Frazer, a seeming congruence between a couple of cultural features in the two societies enables us to fill in the gaps in our knowledge of the latter by guessing that similar congruences must have obtained for other features as well; thus we can hypothesize the existence of institutions about which no other testimony exists. "Direct evidence . . . there is none," Frazer says, for example, in reference to his theory of annual wedding rites at Nemi, "but analogy pleads in favour of the view" (abridged *Golden Bough*, p. 162). Yet he stresses in the same breath, and again and again, that the original character of the Nemi priesthood *can never be determined conclusively*, given the epistemological defects of the scholarly procedures available to him—procedures, that is to say, dependent at every step on inferential reasoning by analogy: "Such an inference, in default of direct evidence as to how the priesthood did actually arise, can never amount to demonstration. But it will be more or less probable according to the degree of completeness with which it fulfills the [evidentiary] conditions I have indicated. The object of this book is, by meeting these conditions, to offer a fairly probable explanation of the priesthood of Nemi" (ibid., pp. 2–3).

In thus disclaiming any conclusions other than "fairly probable" ones, Frazer, like Einstein a professed Humean,[25] perhaps had in mind, if only subconsciously, Hume's declaration that "knowledge and probability are of such contrary and disagreeing natures, that they cannot well run insensibly into each other."[26] The analysis of themes in cultural evolution by the method that he himself employs is bound in any case to "fall far short of certainty," Frazer later declares, in another of several noteworthy passages on this theme (ibid., p. 823); the whole project of data-gathering and interpretation will be governed by a kind of Heisenberg Uncertainty Principle of anthropology. "A full and satisfactory solution of so profound a problem [as that of the displacement of magic by religion] is hardly to be hoped for," he announces elsewhere. "The most we can do . . . is to hazard a more or less plausible conjecture" (ibid., p. 65).

Frazer does partly veil the iconoclastic import of such passages by presenting the inconclusiveness and provisionality of his research results as nothing but a technical failure, the consequence of a shortage of corroborative data — as simply the best he can do "in default of direct evidence." These statements of Frazer's have duly been read as expressions of "outstanding intellectual humility,"[27] as testimony to their author's uncompromising code of scholarly integrity — and, implicitly, as an apologia for the rationalistic ideal of perfectly interlocking facts and theory (in other words, of conclusively verifiable knowledge) in scientific inquiry.[28] But there is every reason to understand them differently, as positing (for the time being, at least) a *necessary*, incurable disjunction between empirical data and the explanatory hypotheses that we profess to extract from them, or, alternately, between any factual datum and any other. "Hypotheses are necessary but often temporary bridges built to connect isolated facts," Frazer says in the preface to the second edition, looking ahead to the time when his own "light bridges" of theory will "sooner or later break down or be superseded" (*Magic Art*, 1: xix–xx).

He goes on to express the hope that, even when its theories are outmoded, his book "may still have its utility and its interest as a repertory of facts" (ibid.,

1: xx), but *The Golden Bough* ends with a passage that undermines even this residual faith in "facts." Comparing science to magic, Frazer begins by praising the former in the conventional way, for its rigorous attention to natural fact and for "the abundance, the solidity, and the splendour" of the results it has achieved. But the passage swerves suddenly into another register:

> Yet the history of thought should warn us against concluding that because the scientific theory of the world is the best that has yet been formulated, it is necessarily complete and final. We must remember that at bottom the generalizations of science or, in common parlance, the laws of nature are merely hypotheses devised to explain that ever-shifting phantasmagoria of thought which we dignify with the high-sounding names of the world and the universe. In the last analysis, magic, religion, and science are nothing but theories of thought. . . . The advance of knowledge is an infinite progression towards a goal that for ever recedes. (abridged *Golden Bough*, pp. 825–26)

Giving the Einsteinian figure of the epistemological gap or disconnection its most drastic possible form, Frazer here makes explicit the trend of disenchanted modernist theory that inhabits his book from the outset. Determinate conclusions elude scientific research not, after all, because data are meager, not because analogies are dubious logical instruments, but because there is *no such thing* as a world of solid reality outside of thought—none, at any rate, with which thought is able to come into direct contact.[29] Elsewhere in the same passage, he speaks of certain laws of modern science as being "only parts of that unsubstantial world which thought has conjured up out of the void."

Scientific reasoning under such a regime, one that sees the world not as a solid fabric external to our minds but as an "ever-shifting phantasmagoria of thought," could scarcely take any other form than some version of conjuring, or, in Einstein's phrase, intellectual "free play," the results of which are likely to bear telltale marks of their "purely fictitious character." It is an essential part of the rhetoric of Einstein's discourse in his scientific papers (as it is of the discourse of modern science at large) to efface all such marks as far as may be possible, representing all conclusions as the necessary outcomes of rigorously analytical logic. Einstein thus carefully quarantines his skeptical epistemology in essays that are distinct from scientific papers as such. Frazer, we have seen, proceeds differently, taking his own skepticism as a main theme of his scientific text itself, as though to sharpen our attentiveness to signs of his addiction to what Einstein called "the freely constructive element" of scientific reasoning.[30] We will discuss below in greater detail how this element of free constructiveness manifests itself in *The Golden*

*Bough,* simply noting for now its general symptoms: the vast disproportion of Frazer's scholarly machinery to the relatively trivial question that he purports to address (i.e., the likely character of the Nemi priesthood), and the maddening elusiveness of his train of scholarly logic amid ever-proliferating skeins of anthropological lore. He makes a point of stressing these features of his work in the preface to the third edition. Originally having meant to treat his topic in a single "small volume," says Frazer, "step by step I was lured on into far-spreading fields of primitive thought. . . . Soon the projected essay became in fact a . . . series of separate dissertations loosely linked together by a slender thread of connexion with my original subject" (*Magic Art,* 1: vii). Uncontrollable textual expansiveness and the logical incoherency which results are the stylistic signs that Frazer invokes the "problem" of Nemi heuristically: not really in order to solve it (since this, he states, is not possible), but rather as a pretext for displaying the wonderful conjuring powers of a certain investigative method.

Frazer's apologies for the deficiencies of his data and (thus) the impossibility of definitive proofs are to this extent crucially disingenuous. Rather than constituting an impediment to his work, its inherent indeterminacy — its self-exoneration from the burden of producing decisive evidence — forms in practice its enabling condition and its very principle of operation. It is not so much that Frazer's method of building his vast and complicated architecture of ethnographic analogies turns out to fall short of proving his theory about the Nemi priesthood; rather, it is the disavowal of proof that frees him to employ the analogical method in the first place, and thus to gratify his longing to venture unconstrainedly across "far-spreading fields of primitive thought." The indeterminacy principle so insistently promulgated by Frazer functions in *The Golden Bough* expressly to guarantee the prevalence of "the freely constructive element" in this text.

Frazer's repeated stress on the logical disjunctiveness of his scholarly work and on "the hypothetical nature of much that is advanced in it" (ibid., 1: xix) seems therefore best read not as a modest apology at all but as announcing an experiment with a new mode of scholarly discourse that *takes as its very first principle the indeterminacy of factual truth* — a mode in fact like Einstein's, which begins with the indeterminacy of simultaneity for spatially separate events, and with the central tenet of the indeterminacy of any privileged frame of reference, and then, taking as a point of doctrine the radical disconnection of fact from theory, rationalizes itself as "free play." Logical incoherence and the arrival at merely "tentative and provisional" conclusions (ibid., 1: xx) are not the marks of scholarly error (so runs Frazer's implicit or subliminal argument) but the signs under which philosophically knowing research of a modern style inescapably is placed.[31] The point of emergence of this style, Frazer tells us plainly, is the unhealable breach between data and scientific theory, both components now being understood as "conjured up out of the void": ungrounded, inherently provisional and unstable, freely produced by scientific thinking. *The Golden Bough* appears, therefore, to be governed by a central irony or aporia, the axis of which is the discrepancy between two incompatible principles. On the one hand, the book is marked by its assertion of a would-be rigorous and logically deterministic method — "the comparative method" of E. B. Tylor and of Herbert Spencer, which supposedly permits scientific reconstruction of ancient practices on a basis of analogical evidence. On the other hand are Frazer's insistent disavowals of belief in secure knowledge and their methodological corollary — namely, his commitment to a professedly futile program of a kind of pseudologic, each link of which is constituted by no evidence more conclusive than the beguiling rhetorical figure of analogy. We can take this ambivalence, once we recognize its centrality in *The Golden Bough*, as evidence of a disabling logical failure, but we will make more interesting sense of it as a signal of an emerging, potentially transformative modernist critique of the category of scientific knowledge itself.

## Magic and Myth

One of the most distinct signs of the essential lacunary structure of *The Golden Bough* is the stress that Frazer insistently places on the figure of an uncrossable gap between things and symbolic representations. This figure is invoked prominently by Einstein and Frazer alike in disquisitions on scientific method, as we have seen; it emerges further as the paramount principle of Frazer's theories of both magic and myth. One result of this pattern is that the two lines of thought tend to fuse together in *The Golden Bough*, making Frazer's analysis of primitive superstition seem to turn back on itself and implicate the whole scheme of scientific rationality that he professes to deploy.

This analysis hinges on Frazer's theory of Sympathetic Magic, which, in its two modes, Homeopathic and Contagious, is said to work by drawing connections among things and events through "a mistaken conception of the association of ideas" (abridged *Golden Bough*, p. 22). In homeopathic magic, the more significant of the two modes for a theory of collective representations, mere resemblance or symbolic affiliation is taken as exerting between distant objects a real physical connection — one along which causal force can move. Hence Frazer's explanation of the practice of putting divine kings to death: since they are imagined to embody the natural fertility on which the life of their people depends, they must be killed at the first sign of approaching old age, lest their withering bodily vigor transmit itself to the fields and flocks that they symbolically represent. Magical reasoning has a surprising affinity with modern science, Frazer argues, since both magic and science presume an invariant system of natural processes; at the same time, he indicts primitive magical thought for the "great disastrous fallacy" (ibid.) of failing to recognize the insuperable distinctions, gaps both in logic and in physical space, between things and ideas or symbolic images of them.

One science especially is brought at this point into an invidious alliance with primitive superstition: physics. "The physical basis of Homeopathic Magic," says Frazer, "is a material medium of some sort which, like the ether of modern physics [the ether abolished in Einstein's 1905 paper], is assumed to unite distant objects and to convey impressions from one to the other" (ibid., p. 43); such an assumption explains "how things can physically affect each other through a space which appears to be empty" (p. 14). With evident malicious intent, Frazer repeatedly stresses that the essence of magical thinking lies in its postulation of the possibility of physical action "at a distance" (p. 25) on the basis of a purely mental association. The suggestion seems to be that modern physical science, in its continuing reliance on a concept such as that of action at a distance, remains in thrall to the fantasies of magical thinking.[32] I would argue, however, that the salient linkage brought forth in this area of *The Golden Bough* is the one not explicitly named by Frazer: not the one between sympathetic magic and physics, but the one between magic and his own occult anthropological science.

The whole method of this science lies in asserting apparently fantastic connections among the most remote-seeming cultural entities — Maypole dances in the modern English countryside and Aztec human sacrifice, for instance — through a sheer association of ideas based on no theory of causal relations at all, but merely, as it were, on the sovereignty of analogical reasoning. The "magical" character of such reasoning is plainly enough insinuated in Frazer's text. The "spurious science" of homeopathic magic bases itself, he explains, on what he names "the Law of Similarity," which superstitiously assumes "that things which resemble each other are the same" (pp. 12–13); in just the same way, his own modernistic science of anthropological analogies founds itself, he explains, on the doctrine of "the essential similarity" of seemingly unconnected cultural formations "specifically different but generically alike" (p. 2). Comparatist anthropology takes as its declared first principle its own magical Law of Similarity, in other words.

Frazer's audacious irony points to the scandalous character of comparatist reasoning by analogy, though at the same time it implies that, in a field of inquiry where the data are known from the outset to be insufficient to yield anything but "more or less plausible" results, magical reasoning may in fact be our only means of grasping at knowledge. Einstein, as we saw, suggests that *all* fields of inquiry are of this kind, that data never can suffice to generate theoretical knowledge in the absence of "miracle" and intellectual "free play," though his response to this intuition was the possibly paradoxical one of constructing a new, relativistic science relentlessly purged of every metaphysical or magical element. The Law of Similarity formed one especially significant such element, indeed. When Frazer had Eddington's *The Nature of the Physical World* read aloud to him around 1936,[33] he must have been struck, for example, by the passage on scientific "world-building" that appears as the epigraph of this paper, a passage that almost seems to have *The Golden Bough* and the affinities of the "comparative method" to relativity physics specifically in mind. The theoretical scientist constructs a world by connecting data together on the basis of "the criterion of likeness," says Eddington, but this procedure is valid — untainted by magic, as we may say — only when the data linked by "this one-to-one correspondence of 'likeness'" are found in close proximity to one another. "Thus we avoid any kind of comparison at a distance which is as objectionable as action at a distance" (Eddington, *Nature of the Physical World*, p. 232). The one is as fantastic as the other, says Eddington.

Frazer's comparatist argument in *The Golden Bough* is a magical one precisely because its linkages of geographically and temporally distant cultural phenomena on the grounds of their alleged "essential similarity" imply an idea of unaccountable causal force flowing from one cultural locale to another. Hence the impressiveness of, for example, Frazer's revelation that professional burglars in such remote areas as South Slavonia, Java, India, Peru, and the Ukraine all employ similar magic spells using dead men's bones or ashes, or earth from their graves, to put their intended victims to sleep (abridged *Golden Bough*, pp. 34–35), or that in New Zealand, the Tyrol, ancient Rome, the Highlands of Scotland, and among the Thlinkeet Indians, it was or is believed that "cut or combed-out hair may disturb the weather by producing rain and hail, thunder and lightning" (ibid., p. 273). If these are significant and not just amazingly fortuitous "comparisons at a distance," not just figments of "a mistaken conception of the association of ideas" on the anthropologist's part, it must be that these different societies are actually connected in some fashion by an occult ether of cultural transmission — although what its character might be it is impossible to say. Frazer finesses this question altogether, simply invoking by way of "explanation" the great postulate that primitive thinking "remains everywhere and at all times substantially alike" (p. 64).

Frazer's reliance on this method of long-distance comparative analysis goes a long way to explain Girard's view of *The Golden Bough* as "fanatical and superstitious." The book can be said to yield little in the way of defensible anthropological results, but it retains a claim on the attention of scholars of modern thinking, if only for the insidious deconstructive pressure that it exerts on its own profession of scientific rationality by alluding so plainly to its own magical or "hypothetical" character — and to its inevitable falling short of definite results. No wonder subsequent generations of anthropological writers have shown such a desperate eagerness to expel Frazer from the canon of reputable scientific literature: branding him "not simply erroneous but absurd" signals the anxiety of later writers that the philosophical scandal of Victorian comparatism, if not firmly suppressed, might eventually compromise the claims of scientific rigor put forward by various subsequent anthropologies. (The newer master concept of "culture," for instance, might turn out to be subject to the same critique of superstition and logical incoherence as the comparatist Law of Similarity.)[34]

Like magic, myth in Frazer's theory also appears under the allegorical sign of disjunction: specifically, the disjunction between traditional rituals and customs and the beliefs that originally formed a rationale for them. Mythic narrative, he declares, typically "has all the air of a fiction devised to explain an old custom, of which the real meaning and origin [have] been forgotten" (p. 334).[35] By this presumptive definition mythic symbolism is always, like the fictional constructs of Frazerian comparatist anthropology itself, a product of *a rupture of the chain of knowledge*, and always situates itself in what Susan Stewart calls "the gap between signifier and signified that is the place of generation for the symbolic."[36] Interpreting the Persephone myth, for instance, Frazer offers a typical formulation: "The story is obviously a forced and awkward attempt to bridge over the gulf between the old conception of the corn-spirit as a pig and the new conception of her as an anthropomorphic goddess" (p. 544). Given Frazer's analysis of cultural phenomena like magic and myth in terms of this insistent symbology of gulfs, gaps, disjunctions, misapprehensions — "rents and fissures and yawning crevasses" in various systems of thought (p. 64) — and given his theoretical pronouncements on the inevitable incoherency of his own mode of research, epistemological failure can be said without much exaggeration to form the prevailing motif of *The Golden Bough*.

Yet the lesson of Frazer's text is in this respect congruent with the most profound lesson of the relativity revolution in physics: that the failure of the logic of mechanical models of reasoning (in which, among other things, facts and theories mesh like gears) — the failure, indeed, of the whole structure of scientific common sense — is simply the precondition of sophisticated scientific inquiry in the twentieth century. To dismantle the ether hypothesis as Einstein does makes it impossible to imagine, according to the old causal model, how light defined as electromagnetic waves could cross utterly empty space: how can a wave propagate itself without a medium through which to move? In relativity thinking, such questions may simply be set aside, in defiance of what heretofore passed as the basis of scientific rationality, in order to preserve such an amazing finding as (say) the precise agreement of Maxwell's predictions of the velocity of electromagnetic waves and the empirically measured velocity of light in vacuo. *The Golden Bough* exerts the same destabilizing force on received systems of logic — or would, were we willing to entertain its stated epistemology seriously. Since there is probably no satisfactory way to explain in causal terms a phenomenon such as the multiplication of identical burglars' magic spells among remote primitive peoples, a would-be rigorous scientific anthropology treats such a finding (and a thousand others like it) as mere Frazerian associationism pitifully masquerading as science, "absurd" and "superstitious" like all his arguments. But there is another option: to treat such a finding, and networks of similar ones in *The Golden Bough*, as so beautiful, so irresistible to the intellect, that we insist on them and seek to elaborate their implications for the theory of great, global structures of thought in "early society" *in the absence of rationally satisfying explanation*. From a scientific point of view, this would be no more — and no less — outlandish than Einstein's insisting on the electromagnetic character of light even when its logically necessary medium of transmission, the "luminiferous" or light-bearing ether, could not be found.

To essay the thought experiment of adopting a skeptical attitude toward the assumptions of prerelativity logic is to enter into the analytical realm evoked (with a lot of ambivalence) by Frazer in his preamble and elsewhere — the realm where theoretical knowledge and empirical reality are fatally disconnected from each other, where factual truth no longer enjoys the illusion of an absolute, categorical existence, and where scientific problems can as a result be "solved" only on the relativistic plane of "probability" and varying degrees of rhetorical efficacy. In this disconcerting realm, where, as Frazer says at one point in *The Golden Bough*, "what we call truth is only the hypothesis which is found to work best" (p. 307), the notion of physical or cultural causality and that of mental associationism do not seem unambiguously distinct from each other. It is obvious that Frazer was full of anxiety about this trend in his thinking, given its potential for seeming to reduce scholarly investigation to a kind of conjuring or ever-inconclusive free play. But it is perhaps possible to read a veiled self-reference in his paean to the liberating effect of magic in the history of thought: "The public profession of magic," he declares, "has contributed to emancipate mankind from the thraldom of tradition and to elevate them into a larger, freer life, with a broader outlook on the world." Magic has been "the mother of freedom and truth" (p. 55). In his own practice of a quasi-magical mode of argument by "comparison at a distance," he had little hope of reaching a convincing solution to the riddle of the Nemi priesthood, but he evidently did hope to have an emancipating effect on his readers, not only (as is well known) from the superstition of Christian religion but, more generally, from the thraldom of a mechanical rationality unsuited to a relativistic world in which truth itself has come to seem an imaginary production.

## Anarchy

Operating within the indeterminate cognitive field where Frazer expressly situates his research, the comparative method generates a billowing anomic text in which the ruling aesthetic law is not the Einsteinian one of parsimony and elegance but, rather, one of nearly boundless proliferation. No cultural formation can be cited in *The Golden Bough* without immediately generating networks of analogical citations through which organizing motifs wind and ramify. This is because the only method available to Frazer to support his crucial claim that the primitive thought-world is everywhere identical is the accumulation of so many analogous instances of each primitive idea that their sheer numbers alone silence all doubt. The vastness of Frazer's catalogues of ethnographic evidence, in other words, is the sign of the equivocal logic of his demonstrations, which in every case necessarily omit thousands of negative instances (societies where the formation in question is *not* found) and which have no explanation to offer as to why a particular formation appears here and not there.

As an illustration of the allegedly fundamental cultural theme of "eating the god," to cite just one example, Frazer initially reports a Swedish custom of using the grain of the last sheaf of wheat in a year's harvest to bake a cake in the shape of a little girl (abridged *Golden Bough*, p. 556). From this original instance springs an amazing multitude of variations. In Scotland the corn-spirit is represented by "the last sheaf made up in the form of a woman and bearing the name of the Maiden" (ibid.). In the French town of La Palisse, "a man made of dough is hung upon the fir-tree which is carried on the last harvest-waggon," after which the mayor breaks up the dough-man and distributes the pieces to the townspeople for consumption (ibid.). In cases where there is no explicit representation of human shape in the form of cakes or loaves, "still the solemn ceremonies with which [the corn] is eaten suffice to indicate that it is partaken of sacramentally, that is, as the body of the corn-spirit" (ibid.). A long account follows of a harvest festival formerly observed in Lithuania, in which the previously delineated pattern appears to undergo rich expansion and elaboration: "[Each farmer] took nine good handfuls of each kind of crop — wheat, barley, oats, flax, beans, lentils, and the rest; and each handful he divided into three parts. The twenty-seven portions of each grain were then thrown on a heap and all mixed up together." Then there unfolds an exquisitely complicated sequence of rites involving the baking of loaves and brewing of beer, the sacrifice by special methods of "a black or white or speckled (not a red) cock and a hen of the same colour and of the same brood, which must have been hatched within the year," prayers, ceremonial eating and drinking, and ritual disposal of leftovers (ibid., p. 557).

Frazer ventures no interpretation at all of the densely coded semiology of these practices; as far as his text tells us, it is as though they occur less in obedience to any determinable symbolic function than in obedience to some imperative cultural motive of free elaboration, expansion, and imaginative whimsy. This impression is greatly amplified in the following pages, which catalogue a galaxy of other "first-fruits" customs from Japan, various regions of India, the Celebes, numerous regions in Africa, among Brazilian and North American Indian tribes, and among the Aztecs. As constructed within *The Golden Bough* according to the laws of Frazerian anthropology, this chain of references demonstrates one thing above all: a seemingly endless capacity for creative extrapolation of cultural themes. A cultural form seems never to attain definitive statement in any ritual, however vivid and extravagant, but to improvise itself anew again and again, in one society after another, perpetually unsatisfied. Of course, this impulse of extrapolation and dissatisfaction is an attribute not of primitive society at all but of the fiction-

alizing process of Frazer's text itself, which, in its own virtually uncontrollable expansiveness (from the original two to twelve volumes), seems to dis-
own the rules of disciplined scientific exposition in favor of a potentially
anarchic regime of analogical "free construction."

Frazer comments on this tendency of his text not only directly, in the
preface already quoted, but also indirectly, by taking as one of his principal
themes various saturnalian festivals that, in their glorification of "general
license, during which the ordinary restraints of society are thrown aside"
(ibid., p. 666), in effect bring the principle of free play to its supreme, virtually anarchic, expression. "At Axim, on the Gold Coast, this annual expulsion
[of the devil] is preceded by a feast of eight days, during which mirth and
jollity, skipping, dancing, and singing prevail, and 'a perfect lampooning liberty is allowed, and scandal so highly exalted, that they may freely sing of all
the faults, villainies, and frauds of their superiors as well as inferiors, without
punishment, or so much as the least interruption'" (p. 642). Frazer is quick
to register alarm at such outbreaks of licentious free play and "utmost freedom of speech," during which "servants forget their duty to their masters,
children their reverence for parents, men their respect for women, and
women all notions of modesty" (p. 645); but he foregrounds them in his
conjectural history of culture as though in testimony to that subversion of
rational order and decorum which is implicit (and sometimes explicit, as we
have seen) in his own mode of scholarly research. Perhaps, too, he foresees
in these episodes of his text the logic of his own subsequent expulsion from
the society of respectable anthropology, as the designated scapegoat for all
the methodological "faults . . . and frauds" of which this vexed discipline has
never been able to purge itself to its own satisfaction.

Readers performing the ritual expulsion of Frazer have remarked again
and again on the culpable tendency toward anarchic free invention in his
anthropology. Some, like Margaret Hodgen, have complained of its hope-
lessly circular logic,[37] while others have protested the distortion of ethnographic data caused by its reliance on conjectural "comparisons at a distance." The weaknesses of Frazer's account, said one early reviewer, raise for
anthropologists the question of "whether the time has not come to study
more deeply special ethnic areas, rather than to make continual free excursions round the globe."[38] The "free invention" of theory and the fantasy of
free excursion, of free movement in space, are exactly equivalent in Frazer's
deployment of the so-called Comparative Method, the reviewer's comment
implies. Ruth Benedict makes the same point in a heightened polemical
register, suggesting that Frazer's method of adducing cultural material in-

volves nothing less than a method of perverted intellectual violence — one implicitly continuous with his obsessive connoisseurship of ritual mutilations of the human body. She denounces Frazerian comparatism in this spirit for "[building] up a kind of mechanical Frankenstein's monster with a right eye from Fiji, a left from Europe, one leg from Tierra del Fuego, and one from Tahiti, and all the fingers and toes from still different regions." Such a monstrous figure, she significantly observes, "corresponds to no reality in the past or present"; it is a pure fabrication, grossly unscientific, intellectual free construction so reckless and anarchic as to arouse a kind of horror.[39]

Benedict thus throws into high relief the scandalous, anomic quality of Frazer's imagination (specifically, the sense in which his text seems to become contaminated with the "primitive" magical thinking and "primitive" sadism that it professes to study from a comfortable analytical distance), and suggests its relation to other modernist experiments, notably Einstein's physics, which aroused similar terms of panicky revulsion.[40] Benedict's figures of dismemberment and grotesquely creative recombination also refer in a more oblique fashion to Frazer's intimations that his work has led him into a field where traditional modes of argument have fallen under the sway of indeterminacy and thus, implicitly, that scholarly procedures appropriate to this field — procedures frankly accepting of "the freely constructive element" of scientific theory — will be *bound* to scandalize normal codes of rationality, to seem perverse and indecent. In venting such powerful detestation on the "purely fictitious character" of Frazer's anthropology, Benedict exhibits — and focuses on Frazer — that very dread of rampant fictionality that Foucault claims is central to modern sensibility, a dread of "the cancerous and dangerous proliferation of significations," which fills us with the need to prohibit or impede "the free circulation, the free manipulation, the free composition, decomposition, and recomposition of fiction."[41] Exacting just such a prohibition, one might say, forms the primary cultural imperative embodied in modern science. Moreover, it explains why Frazer (his incipient skepticism and strong tendency toward "cancerous and dangerous proliferation" in scholarship notwithstanding) could scarcely do otherwise than to present his work as at least striving earnestly toward the goal of rigorous logical argument based on objective fact — and why Einstein himself, though idealizing the principle of sheer free play in scientific thinking, insisted no less strongly on the sanctity of experimental "verification" of theory (ignoring, however, what appeared in the years after 1905 to be unambiguous experimental disproofs of special relativity).[42]

## Space, Time, and Simultaneity

Frazer's always ambivalent experiment with Einsteinian principles of indeterminacy and scholarly free play leads to a more tangible conjunction with relativity theory in physics than we have traced thus far. *The Golden Bough* can be described as a monument to the logical incoherence of Victorian comparatism in anthropology and as an instance of the perversion of sound scholarly method by magical associationism. But it can equally well be described as an attempt to imagine the history of human thought and social life in a radically modern form, in fact *in specifically Einsteinian form*, as a gigantic space / time construction in which the mechanistic relations ordinarily linking orders of data together undergo fantastical transformation.

In his persona of orthodox intellectual conservative, Frazer expressed only hostility toward the new theoretical physics, and he specifically ridiculed the collapsing together of space and time by Einstein.[43] Nonetheless, Frazerian anthropology and relativity physics can be seen to take their departures from a single interpretive problem: the differing perceptions of natural and other phenomena by observers standing in what Einstein calls different coordinate systems. He and his early interpreters express this principle in terms of thought experiments centering on the different perceptions of a given event by observers on Earth and, in Eddington's example, observers in a distant nebula rocketing away from Earth at great velocity, causing their measurements of time and space, compared with earthly measurements, to dilate and to contract, respectively (see Eddington, *Nature of the Physical World*, p. 14). Differently situated groups of people interpret the world differently, assigning different values to the same things: Frazer's own terrestrial and comparatist anthropology hinges on this same relativism, adopting toward it, at times, the attitude of epistemological skepticism evident in various passages I have cited from *The Golden Bough*. "We can never completely replace ourselves at the standpoint of primitive man, see things with his eyes, and feel our hearts beat with the emotions that stirred his," says Frazer, for example, highlighting again his idée fixe of uncrossable, quasi-physical gaps of knowledge. "All our theories concerning him and his ways must therefore fall far short of certainty; the utmost we can aspire to in such matters is a reasonable degree of certainty" (abridged *Golden Bough*, p. 823).

Special relativity theory claims more than this reasonable degree, of course: it claims to make possible definite, exact corrections of physical measurements from one point of observation to another, enabling us truly to "see things with [the] eyes" of someone inhabiting a different reference system.

This it does by means of the series of equations called the "Lorentz transformations," which Einstein in his 1905 relativity paper derives independently. Frazer's anthropology proposes, in effect, a similar conversion mechanism, by which ideas held by observers in one place are in theory transposable into ideas of observers at another place, though the phenomena and indeed the very concept of "place" to which Frazer's calculus applies are cultural rather than physical and though its analysis transpires along the diachronic rather than the synchronic axis. Frazer's anthropology posits, first, a set of laws of cultural evolution (such as the fundamental law that magic always precedes religion); it then claims to be able, by a series of equations systematic enough almost to be representable mathematically, to transpose a given cultural entity — the idea of a mythic personification of agricultural fertility, for example — into the signifier that corresponds to it at any given level of cultural evolution (a human sacrifice, a cake in the form of a maiden, a sacramental sheaf of corn).

One Frazerian law based on the assumption of a kind of inescapable, progressive deterioration of cultural practices declares, for example, that symbolic representations of the killing of a victim in popular holiday celebrations are bound to indicate that at earlier periods actual blood sacrifices were ritually performed on the same occasions. Further, by a secondary equation based on the axiom that every nation passes through an originary stage of magic, we can show (so Frazer claims) that such blood sacrifice began by centering on a magical symbolism which was thought to produce, by homeopathic agency, practical results in the real world of nature. Given, then, a datum such as a modern peasant custom of seizing a stranger at harvest-time, binding him in wheat-sheaves, and pantomiming menacing gestures at him with scythes and flails, the equations of the "Frazer transformations" enable us to declare confidently that the same event, transposed to the cultural system of the peasants' ancestors, would appear as a full-fledged rite in which "human beings have been . . . killed as an agricultural ceremony to promote the fertility of the fields" via "a sacrifice which resembles the effect that it is designed to bring about" (ibid., pp. 500, 515). The Lorentz-Einstein transformations have their counterpart, therefore, in the transformations of symbolic orders computed by what Frazer calls the Comparative Method.

As soon as special relativity theory began to gain attention, it was realized that its core lies in the problematizing and unifying of the concepts of time and of space, which, in Newtonian mechanics as in Kantian philosophy and common sense, figure as absolute and distinct categories. The Newtonian view was placed in jeopardy from the moment Einstein enunciated his almost unbelievably homely definition of "time" at the opening of his 1905 relativity paper, a definition that turned out to entail far-reaching consequences. "We first have to clarify what is to be understood here by 'time,'" says Einstein in this epochal text. "We have to bear in mind that all our propositions involving time are always propositions about simultaneous events." His example is an analysis of the meaning of the phrase "the train arrives here at 7 o'clock," which has no meaning, he declares, beyond that of asserting that the train pulls in at the same time one's watch reads 7:00.[44] In the field of Einsteinian time (as in the linguistic field of Ferdinand de Saussure, which was being elaborated simultaneously), there are thus no absolute values, "no positive terms," only terms constituted by binary schemes of similarity and difference; hence special relativity theory is, in this essential sense, as much an instance of "the comparative method" as is Frazerian anthropology. Einstein goes on to show that clocks are affected by motion. To use one of his favorite illustrations of this principle, a clock in a passing train would seem to an observer seated on the embankment to tick more slowly than the one he holds in his hand. This means that we no longer can think scientifically of space and time as independent factors, but only of their compound form, space / time. "Unless we are told the reference-body to which the statement of time refers, there is no meaning in a statement of the time of an event"; "every reference-body (co-ordinate system) has its own particular time" (Einstein, *Relativity*, p. 26).

In the special theory of relativity, time thus becomes a manifold, a multiplex phenomenon. This line of reasoning crystallizes in the startling conception that Einstein called "the relativity of simultaneity." The idea of the simultaneity of two events is easy to grasp intuitively when the two events occur in one place, but it is impossible to conceive, Einstein insisted, when they are spatially remote from one another ("comparison at a distance" being sheer metaphysics, as Eddington said). This fundamental problem is resolved in relativity theory by abandoning the idea of time as an absolute and unified structure of relations. Events A and B may thus, according to the special theory, be simultaneous from one point of view, A may precede B from a second point of view, and B may precede A from a third.

This mode of fantastic-seeming reasoning (which in relativity physics becomes the norm of scientific rationality) runs throughout Frazer's demonstrations in *The Golden Bough*. The intensely spatialized character of his anthropological world is dramatized in the famous passage at the beginning where, having outlined the problem of the priesthood at Nemi, he portrays his scholarly enterprise in the figure of "a voyage of discovery, in which we shall visit many strange foreign lands" the world over. "The wind is in the shrouds: we shake out our sails to it, and leave the coast of Italy behind us for a time" (abridged *Golden Bough*, p. 10). Seeing the centrality of the voyage metaphor to this text, one critic of Frazer's speaks of *The Golden Bough* as scholarly "tourism."[45] However, Frazer in his far-flung researches is not visiting mundanely picturesque locales; rather, like Wordsworth's Newton, he is sailing strange seas of thought—four-dimensional and, in fact, post-Newtonian ones. His chief principle of navigation in this conceptual environment is that time, at least in the domain of culture, is not uniform and absolute but radically differential, and thus subject to scientific reorderings by means of the comparatist Law of Similarity. Time passes much more quickly in some geographical areas (Europe, for example) than in others, where it may seem, culturally speaking, virtually to stand still (Tierra del Fuego, for example). Frazer thus takes up, relative to his ethnographic materials, the position of the Einsteinian observer on an embankment studying life as it unfolds, according to fixed laws of nature, in railway carriages passing before him at greatly differing velocities. In other words, references to time in *The Golden Bough* are always radically spatialized, and spatial locations are radically temporalized, for the purposes of the comparative method: in Frazerian analysis, as in special relativity, the key proposition is that "time is robbed of its independence" (Einstein, *Relativity*, p. 56). An "early mode of thought" can therefore be fully as characteristic of certain backward twentieth-century peoples as of peoples of centuries ago, since simultaneity in the field of cultural phenomena has nothing to do with a fixed scale of chronology. The midsummer pageantry of contemporary peasants in remote areas of Scotland is, in this sense, the only one that matters to Frazer, *simultaneous* with similar practices documented (or hypothesized) in classical antiquity. The characteristic effect of Frazer's constellations of ethnographic data, constructed as they thus are under the aegis of a thoroughgoing principle of "the relativity of simultaneity," is this vertiginous one of entering a thought-world where fixed hierarchies of time and place are abruptly dissolved.

The play of simultaneities in Frazerian analysis involves further complexities, as we can see in a typical instance from *The Golden Bough*. In Chapter 12, "The Sacred Marriage," Frazer's immediate goal is to argue the possibility that the union of the priest of Nemi and the goddess of the grove, Diana, may have been celebrated in an annual ceremony coordinated with the season and the agricultural cycle. He thus begins by imagining a series of ritual observances that are, from the perspective of the ceremonial calendar, absolutely simultaneous from one year to the next: that is, they occupy the same moment in time frames whose defining principle is that they are permanently, sacramentally identical to one another. Yet Frazer's argument insists also on the primary fact of evolutionary progress in culture; two enactments of the rite in successive years are simultaneous when viewed from the reference frame of the ceremonial calendar, but when viewed from the external reference frame of cultural evolution, they are found to be slightly desynchronized, the imperceptibly minute gap between them being the space of historical change. A similar ambiguity affects any single performance of the (suppositious) magical rite of divine marriage: on the one hand, the moment of performance situates itself within a sequence of time frames stretching to the fertile harvest it later produces by homeopathic magic; on the other, for the magic consciousness, the rite in some sense is identical to the event that it symbolically enacts. The gap between temporally distant events, performed rite and anticipated harvest, is magically suspended or collapsed: this is precisely what makes ritual representation "magical." These complicated gyrations of time frames are fundamental to all Frazer's analyses. Their effect, and perhaps the most inclusive imaginative and intellectual motive of *The Golden Bough*, is to fill the reader with a dizzying awareness of the convoluted nature of the temporal field, governed as it so powerfully is by the relativity of cultural simultaneity.

Frazerian interpretation of cultural space / time thus entails another mode of "free play," yet for all its aspect of scholarly "tourism," *The Golden Bough* is remote from the model of even the most carefree travelogue. In Frazer's rapid sequences of analogizing allusions to primitive and ancient societies around the globe, transition from one to the next is as instantaneous as the transition from one thought to another. In one survey of modified versions of ceremonial regicide, we leap in a few pages from Cambodia to Siam to Egypt to Uganda to Morocco to Cornwall to Sumatra, and to many further locales besides (abridged *Golden Bough*, pp. 330–34): such is the breathtaking efficacy of the Frazerian Law of Similarity. Unlike what happens in a true anthropological travelogue, such as *Tristes tropiques*, however, there is no lapse of time and no experience of a physical journey in going from one cultural place to another in *The Golden Bough*. This is not merely a device of scholarly exposition, as one might be tempted to assume, but a significant textual structure closely bound up with the relativizing trends that I have been trying to highlight in Frazer's work. For Lévi-Strauss, travel in the anthropological field is arduous and dramatized; time must be painfully spent in traversing space, in *Tristes tropiques* at least:

We had gone from Ultiarity to Juruena, then on to Juina, Campos Novos and Uil-hena; we were now advancing towards the last outposts on the plateau: Tres Buritis, and Barao de Melgaço, which, in fact, lies at the foot of the plateau. At almost every halt, we had lost one or two oxen: through thirst, exhaustion or *hervado*, that is, killed by grazing on poisonous plants. Several fell into a river with the baggage while cross-ing a rotten wooden bridge, and only with great difficulty did we manage to salvage our precious anthropological collections. (*Tristes tropiques*, p. 321)

Even in so solidly factual an environment, anthropological knowledge appears to be subject to its perpetual hazard of falling at last into some scarcely bridgeable gulf. (One recalls Frazer's prediction that his various hy-potheses, "necessary but often temporary bridges built to connect isolated facts," will "sooner or later break down," leaving the whole work of scientific analysis to be begun again from scratch; see *Magic Art*, 1: xix–xx.) But in *The Golden Bough*, as we have seen, time is eclipsed in the observer's co-ordinate frame, and space, in the sense of physical distance between two points, collapses together as a result. We can pass from ancient Mexico to modern rural England in an instant. Given the virtually uncrossable hiatus between factual reality and scholarly proof that Frazer begins by positing, this amazing transcendence of space / time intervals via a form of science fiction or scholarly free play possesses, after all, a compelling rationale. It offers a method of analysis enabling him in effect to leap weightlessly across the gap separating reality from knowledge without having to encounter the perils of laboriously constructed scholarly bridges built of planks and ropes infested by epistemological termites.

Frazer's effortless excursions in cultural space / time evidently correspond to a further impulse of his text. Einstein's childhood fantasy of riding on a beam of light, at which speed time would stand still, is prohibited by the statutes of special relativity, since, as Eddington significantly remarks, "we ourselves are attached to material bodies" (*Nature of the Physical World*, p. 50) and thus are bound inescapably by the law limiting all physical nature to velocities less than the speed of light. The Frazerian observer is effectively enabled to transcend this restriction, thanks to the transformational vehicle of the Law of Similarity and to the special version of the relativity of simul-taneity that forms its essential principle, as we have seen. Eddington's phrase, however, points back to the anxiety-laden theme of the corporeal in *The Golden Bough*, and hints at the implication of this theme, too, in Frazer's deployment of the comparatist analogical method. Given the depiction of the human body in *The Golden Bough* as the anguished object of ever-renewed, ever-varied sadistic inflictions, the physics of "comparison at a distance" amounts, among other things, to an imaginary deliverance from the potentially atrocious burden of physical existence. (Practically speaking, of course, it has exactly this function: it permits the anthropologist who uses this method to carry out his research from the comfort of his armchair in Cambridge or elsewhere, exempt from the need to expose himself to the bodily perils of fieldwork.) To a reader attuned to the Einsteinian valences of Frazer's text, *The Golden Bough* offers, at what may be its deepest level of metaphor, a euphoric release from the ordeal of the "physical" into the dimension toward which all its discourse powerfully gravitates: the dimension of intellectual free play.

JOSS LUTZ MARSH

# In a Glass Darkly
## Photography, the Premodern, and Victorian Horror

One of the little-sung minor classics of Victorian fiction, at once a belated descendant of the late eighteenth-century Gothic "tale of terror" and a precursor of the horror/science-fiction genre of the fin-de-siècle and thereafter, is Sheridan Le Fanu's "Carmilla" (1872). An allegory of lesbian sexuality, it is cast in the guise of a vampire story: the languorous, sharp-toothed vamp of the title seduces Laura, the innocent daughter of her host, in a castle nestled in the remote forests of Styria.

Le Fanu's story is a treasure trove for cultural archaeologists digging at the history of sexuality, and it has been treated as such in the few commentaries published. In "Carmilla," masculine Law, Science, and Medicine act out in stylized but literal-minded ritual the containment of feminine Nature — a Nature that exhibits a disturbing post-Darwin capacity for mutation and autonomous female self-creation. "Girls are caterpillars when they live in the world," Carmilla tells her lover-victim, "to be finally butterflies when the summer comes."[1] The containing rituals ultimately include the stalking to her grave-lair of the vampire, who is found "immersed . . . to a depth of seven inches" in blood (Le Fanu, *In a Glass Darkly*, p. 378), and who must be stabbed through the heart with a sharp stake and decapitated. This pre-Freudian symbolic scene of rape and castration is replayed in the more famous *Dracula* (1897), by Le Fanu's admirer, Bram Stoker, in which narrative attention is very largely shifted from the masculine "monster of the nether world" who lends the book his name to the two Englishwomen who become his vassals and on whom he feasts.[2] "Horror" in both tales springs from their apparent contradiction of the Victorian association of womanliness with civilization: but Le Fanu and Stoker knew better, at bottom, than to be taken in by such sham. "Woman," they apprehended, like the misogynist anti-hero of George Meredith's *The Ordeal of Richard Feverel* (1859), "will be the last thing civilized by Man."[3]

Our interest on this occasion centers on what seems at first sight to be a moment of inexplicable excess or superfluity in the text of "Carmilla" (there is also another, of which more below). At the opening of the story, a disconsolate Laura is rudely startled from her disappointed reverie upon the canceled visit of a girlfriend by a dramatic accident immediately outside the castle gates: a carriage and four are overturned, and Carmilla taken out, in a faint, from the wreckage. Carmilla's mother (or such she seems) entreats Laura's father to care for her daughter, for she is herself embarked upon "a journey of life and death" (ibid., p. 305) and cannot bide the time of Carmilla's recovery. Laura enthusiastically supports the request (thus supplying for herself a changeling guest, in traditional faery-fashion) and, with her carriage righted and the horses calmed, the mother hastens away. Later, Laura's two governess-tutors discuss the incident:

"Did you remark a woman in the carriage, after it was set up again, who did not get out," inquired Mademoiselle, "but only looked from the window?"

No, we had not seen her.

Then she described a hideous black woman, with a sort of coloured turban on her head, who was gazing all the time from the carriage window, nodding and grinning derisively towards the ladies, with gleaming eyes and large white eye-balls, and her teeth set as if in fury. (ibid., p. 309)

The "hideous black woman" never reappears and is never again mentioned, but she has nevertheless a necessary function. More than simply a double for Carmilla herself, she is the text's horror-principle incarnate: the savage female; the black African woman, complete with "coloured turban" and "gleaming" white eyeballs; the primitive of Victorian fantasy who is "defined first and foremost," as Christopher Herbert remarks (see his essay in this volume), by her pleasure in cruelty and lack of self-control (a cliché of racialist anthropology, nowhere imagined so influentially as in Conrad's portrait of the tribal woman lamenting Kurtz's incipient departure in *Heart of Darkness*).[4] She is also the originating point of the matrilineage that spawns Le Fanu's womanly monsters: Laura, we discover, is directly descended on the maternal side from Carmilla herself. In her combine two necessary principles and prerequisites to the production of horror and the creation of the primitive: the female and the black.

Blackness must be of a specific sort, however — not merely the vague blackness of Erebus and evil. Given that the Gothic and its literary descendants depend — at the microlinguistic as well as the narrative level, as Tzvetan Todorov makes clear in *The Fantastic*[5] — on ambiguous slippages from the figurative to the literal, it matters that one of the metaphors repeatedly reliteralized and reanimated by the genre (for example, in Matthew Lewis's 1796 *The Monk*) recurs again and again in "Carmilla" (and *Dracula*): "his / her face darkened." So, as we "peep through the small crevice" at the door of another of Carmilla's victim's bedrooms, we see "a large black object, very ill-defined, crawl . . . over the foot of the bed, and swiftly spread itself up to the poor girl's throat, where it swelled, in a moment, into a great, palpitating mass" (ibid., p. 372). Likewise, as we watch Stevenson's Dr. Jekyll undergoing the horrible transformation that will turn him into apelike, libidinous Mr. Hyde, "he seemed to swell — his face became suddenly black, the features seemed to melt and alter."[6]

Blackness is a mediating condition between the human and the not human. It is a condition shared by Count Dracula, repeatedly figured as "something long and black," bending over a "half-reclining white figure" (Stoker, *Dracula*, p. 90) — who on this particular occasion turns out to be a girl, Lucy Westenra, fresh from meditating on the impossibility of not sympathizing with "poor Desdemona when she had such a dangerous stream" of adventure stories "poured in her ear" by a suitor, "even by a black man" (ibid., p. 57). Blackness is also a condition illogically but necessarily invoked by H. G. Wells's more open-minded intellectual tale of an effete civilization and the cannibalistic underworld that serves and battens upon it, "The Time Machine" (1897). "Conceive the tale of London which a negro, fresh from Central Africa, would take back to his tribe!" exclaims the Time Traveller.[7] The Negro's travel through space would parallel the Traveller's through time, which has taken him to a lotusland presided over, suggestively, by a "colossal" statue of a "White Sphinx" (Wells, *Complete Short Stories*, pp. 26, 45). Here, although their subterranean existence has made of them, over time, a race of larva-pale, stooped and hairy creatures, the Morlocks are nevertheless — with the logic of a nightmare of primitivism — "dreaded" as "black things" (ibid., p. 47).

"The Time Machine" — the ultimate Einsteinian "fantasy of free excursion," as Herbert puts it (just as he notes that James Frazer's *The Golden Bough* reads like "a form of science fiction") — is not, of course, a text normally classified under the same heading as *Dracula*. The reasons why I should like here to suggest some rethinking of categories have a very great deal to do with moving beyond observation of the common inheritance I have just outlined (i.e., the racial phobia, sexism, and terror of the primitive encoded in all these texts) and toward a theory of a certain kind of pre- or proto-modern fiction.

One proposition I wish to make is simply this: if we alter our angle of focus, we will find in some of the best-sellers of late Victorian England an alternative perspective on the modern and the primitive, and a writing-in of precisely those concerns Christopher Herbert has traced through Einstein and Frazer. But it is to a different genre than the adventure story that we must turn, one in which ideas are not explicitly articulated but inhere in narrative shape and structural possibility — namely, the horror-fictions and science-fiction fantasies of precursor Le Fanu, inheritor Stoker, Robert Louis Stevenson, and realist-fantasist H. G. Wells. (We might add to the list, among others, George Du Maurier, Marie Corelli, and, especially, Rider Haggard.)[8] In these stories, a popular mythology materialized that gave fictional expression to precisely those troubling concerns which Professor Herbert has identified with both *The Golden Bough* and the theoretical writings of Einstein: (1) issues of knowledge and evidence (of which more later); (2) anxieties about space, time, and their instability; and (3) in Herbert's words, the "troubled and even panicky theme of the corporeal." These stories initiated a mythology by which we still unconsciously, casually live: Francis Ford Coppolla's major new film adaptation of *Dracula*, released in 1992, was greeted both as a return (in luscious opera mode) to Stoker's text and as a commentary on the age of AIDS; Stevenson's *Dr. Jekyll and Mr. Hyde* (1887), the most-filmed literary text in world cinema history (nudging ahead of *Dracula*), shows no sign, even after more than sixty screen versions, of what John Sutherland has appropriately termed cultural "exhaustion."[9] Of course these stories offer filmmakers extraordinary opportunities for opening wide their bags of technological tricks, from games with mirrors and "fade-outs" that kill to climactic transformation scenes. But there are also more profound reasons why stories like these live long and prosper, and why, as we shall see, they may be said to be not merely the most filmed but even the founding (literary) texts of cinema.

To take first the anxieties of space and time that pervade the modern mind, what else is Wells's Time Machine but a construction that enables the "experimental verification" (ibid., p. 13) of the Time Traveller's contention that "There is no difference between Time and any of the three dimensions of Space except that our consciousness moves along it" (p. 10)? Thus the Time Machine enables, in effect, the empirical proof of Einstein's special theory of relativity before Einstein himself articulated it. Moreover, the machine that collapses time into space explodes the cherished Victorian myth of progress: as the Time Traveller moves forward in time, he witnesses the

decay of civilization and regression of humankind into the ineffectual, vege-
tarian Eloi and their subterranean servant-cannibals, the Morlocks (the upper and lower social classes of Wells's Britain, explicitly developed along
separate evolutionary lines). According to this view, then, the future end of
life is not to be a Tennysonian "crowning race" but simple "green slime"
(p. 84), strongly reminiscent of the primitive "protoplasm" Ernst Haeckel
posits as the beginning of life in *The Riddle of the Universe*.[10] It is unsettling
that the Traveller does not even know whether the small-scale model of his
machine, which dematerializes into time before the witnessing narrator's
eyes, has traveled "into the future or the past — I don't, for certain, know
which" (p. 16).

Similarly, Dr. Jekyll's scientific knowledge releases into modern urban life
(indeed, into a London stifled under a "chocolate-colored pall" of smog
[Stevenson, *Dr. Jekyll and Mr. Hyde*, p. 48] — the urban environment that
Dracula, also, all too easily invades) a creature from the dark past of mankind: a small, stooped, Neanderthal with something of the troglodyte about
him. The creature is the founding type both for Wells's Morlocks and for his
contention, in *The Outline of History* (1919–20), that Homo sapiens's ancestral memories of the primitive Neanderthaler were the seeds of his legends
of goblins and trolls.[11]

Count Dracula, too, is a creature who has, on the one hand, achieved
spatial ubiquity through the simple device of taking his space with him.
"Fifty cases of common earth," as a carrier's invoice puts it, "to be used for
experimental purposes" are shipped from Transylvania to London (*Dracula*,
p. 226); these provide the Count with a variety of graves filled with hallowed
earth (or a chain of "earths" in which to go to ground, like a fox, as the novel's
rather poor jokester-hunters put it). On the other hand, Dracula is a creature
who can "spread" his revenge "over centuries," because "time is on [his]
side" (ibid., p. 306); he "grow[s] young" (an effectively simple phrase; p. 172),
sleek-faced, and dark haired whilst the youthful husband of his latest victim,
saintly "Madame Mina," is transformed overnight into a "drawn, haggard old
man, whose white hair matches well with the hollow burning eyes and grief-
written lines of his face" (p. 301). "How shall we find his where?" asks Professor Van Helsing (p. 237), in his unidiomatic but erratically effective English; and how can the hunters oppose the Count's powers of extension in
time with their own diurnal ability to function between noon and sunset,
"when he is at his most weak" (p. 242)? When space and time become relative, they become horrible. And horror demands relativity — sometimes,

even, the ethical relativity that results from sharing, momentarily, the perspective of the monster who is struggling (like Frankenstein's creature) for survival.

Through what Christopher Herbert calls "the occult ether of cultural transmission," the horror / science-fiction genre's message of anxiety about the body also resonates. Stevenson's narrator, the lawyer Utterson, repeatedly goes to the door of his friend's townhouse to inquire of his servant: "Is Dr. Jekyll at home, Poole?" (*Dr. Jekyll and Mr. Hyde*, p. 41). This is the disturbed cliché of the Gothic opened out to its fullest extent, Freud's uncanny-*unheimlich* reliteralized, for two distinct personalities or creatures are indeed "at home" in Dr. Jekyll's body (or is it Mr. Hyde's?). The tensions of that physical convergence are also mapped out, for good measure, in the layout of Jekyll's dwelling—the main house fronting onto a respectable square, while the rear, with its separate laboratory enclosing a small private cabinet and the back door through which Hyde slips away to his nocturnal adventures, backs on to a nondescript commercial street. "I began to perceive," Dr. Jekyll finally recounts in his "Full Confession," near the end of Stevenson's tale, "more deeply than it has ever yet been stated, the trembling immateriality, the mist-like transience, of this seemingly so solid body in which we walk attired. Certain agents I found to have the power to shake and pluck back that fleshly vestment, even as a wind might toss the curtains of a pavilion" (ibid., p. 82).

Likewise, a wind accompanies the rush through time that Wells's Traveller accomplishes in his Machine. In Stevenson's tale, drugs, and in Wells's story, time-travel instantly accomplish the disturbing dematerialization of the body. As the Traveller's little experimental machine "swung round," set in motion on a table, it "became indistinct, was seen as a ghost for a second perhaps, as an eddy of faintly glittering brass and ivory; and it was gone—vanished!" (*Complete Short Stories*, p. 15). In Stoker's seemingly very different narrative, the case is the same: *Dracula* obsessively recounts (to use the tale's own terminology) the materializations and dematerializations of its Count in a demotic, post-Christian universe of ubiquitous bodies that refuse to lie down and die. "I suppose you do not believe in corporeal transference," Van Helsing asks his friend and coworker Dr. Seward. "No? Nor in materialization. No? Nor in astral bodies. No?" (*Dracula*, p. 191). "We all looked on in horrified amazement," reports Dr. Seward in his diary, "as we saw [Lucy Westenra, Dracula's other English victim], with a corporeal body as real at the moment as our own, pass in through the interstice [of her tomb-door] where scarce a knife-blade could have gone" (ibid., p. 212).

How powerful is the urge in the post-Christian world still to cling to the powers of embodiment and spiritual dematerialization (transcendence, or ascension, perhaps) that the Christian revelation claims. How conveniently, in both *Dracula* and *Dr. Jekyll and Mr. Hyde*, do those powers allow the solution of locked-room mysteries that might have baffled Edgar Allan Poe. How easy is the transition from Count to bat to wolf to rat. And how the narrative of *Dracula* insists that body and no-body (like Jekyll and Hyde, sharing an identity) can be one and the same! As Van Helsing recounts: "Then they began to materialize, till — if God have not take away my reason, for I saw it through my own eyes — there were before me in actual flesh the same three women that Jonathan [Harker] saw. . . . I knew the swaying round forms, the bright hard eyes, the white teeth, the ruddy colour, the voluptuous lips" (p. 366).

The enemies of Dracula fight him with every technological trick available — many only a few years off the drawing board: typewriters and carbon paper for gathering evidence; phonographic wax cylinders (on which Dr. Seward records his diary); telegrams (which arrive faster than Dracula's body can move through space); even "these so small electric lamps, which you can fasten to your breast" so as to penetrate the darkness of the Count's London mansion (p. 249). The Traveller of Wells's tale also obviously has the most advanced of technological instruments at his disposal. "A year ago," Mina Harker records Van Helsing saying, in her journal, "which of us would have received [the] possibility [of belief in vampires], in the midst of our scientific, sceptical, matter-of-fact nineteenth century?" (p. 238). What underpins these best-sellers' willed convergences of the primitive and the technologically ultramodern? Something powerful and ubiquitous in culture must.

For answer, it is perhaps best to disassemble the question and return first to the crucial materialization scenes of Stoker's overstated yet still curiously underread fantasy. Jonathan Harker records that, as Count Dracula's driver (who, it turns out, is Dracula himself) gets down from the box of the carriage to investigate what seem to be *ignes fatui* burning at the roadside, "there appeared a strange optical effect: when he stood between me and the flame he did not obstruct it, for I could see its ghostly flicker all the same" (p. 13). The body that seems so material is translucent, after all; it throws no reflections in mirrors (p. 25). And the text, which supposedly strives to recount nothing but facts, seems excessively interested in other optical phenomena as well, such as a "diorama" of cloud-play (p. 90), the quasi-magical dark-lantern whose "slide" can be drawn to throw a transfixing light on vampire

Lucy (p. 211), and "the figures of my late companions crossing themselves" that Harker sees "projected against . . . the steam from the horses of the coach by the light of the lamps" (p. 10).

Likewise, somewhat to our surprise, we discover that the Time Traveller's numerous academic publications — all, as he perceives it, chaff in the wind of winnowing time — have focused on the subject of "physical optics" (*Complete Short Stories*, p. 69). And Utterson has extraordinary dreams about the peculiar will and testament of Harry Jekyll, which allows for inheritance by Edward Hyde solely on the grounds of the testator's disappearance: "Once more," we read, at the end of a sleepless night of worry, "he saw before his mind's eye, as clear as a transparency, the strange clauses of the will" (*Dr. Jekyll and Mr. Hyde*, p. 42).

All this strange evidence of imagistic superfluity brings us to the second excessive element in Sheridan Le Fanu's "Carmilla." A curious mountebank joins the cast of unnecessary characters, toting into the story a giant pack of curiosities and trivia that includes, prominently, a magic lantern (*In a Glass Darkly*, p. 322). "With my sharp and long sight," he claims, he can see that Carmilla has a tooth "long, thin, and pointed, . . . like a needle" (ibid., p. 324). His "piercing" eye is a match for her "piercing" tooth. "Carmilla" and its descendants are not simply extraordinarily visual texts, I believe, but texts that depend for their inspiration on, and are culturally grounded in, a very specific modern invention, perhaps the founding modern technology: photography.

For its first early-Victorian practitioners and admirers, photography seemed to (and, indeed, logically did) abolish and manipulate time as it was measured by the movement of the sun: in pioneer Fox Talbot's phrase, the principle of photography was chemically and permanently to "fix the shadow" of images thrown by the sun itself — the "fairy pictures, creatures of a moment" that one might view through the camera obscura.[12] Oliver Wendell Holmes dubbed the new daguerrotype of the 1840's "the mirror with a memory";[13] a rhyme of the period urged prospective consumers, in view of their limited time on earth, to:

Secure the shadow 'ere the substance fade,
Let Nature imitate what Nature made.[14]

In an uncanny play on notions of presence and absence, each development of the new technology profoundly queried the Victorians' sense of time, especially in the last quarter of the nineteenth century, when photography achieved a deeper and more widespread cultural impact than ever before or since. Dry gelatin plates superseded the cumbersome, expensive, and complex wet collodion process in the 1870's, eliminating at a stroke the world-roving photographer's need for what one of them called "a little army [of] forty-two coolies."[15] At the same time, accelerated split-second shutter speeds enabled the production of images such as no human eye could apprehend (most famously, Eadweard Muybridge's studies of *Animal Locomotion*). George Eastman's introduction of the cheap "Kodak" in 1888 bred a "curious contagion of the camera"[16] that led four million people — one in ten of the population of England — to purchase a box of their own by 1900, and that ushered in the era of the candid "snapshot" (after the hunting term, tellingly, for a hurried shot at a moving target).[17] Thus in *Dracula* we see Jonathan Harker, who will soon become the hunted, take realtor's snaps of Carfax Abbey with his own Kodak to show to the Count (*Dracula*, p. 23).

Meanwhile, between 1880 and 1900, development of the halftone printing process ensured that people not only could take photographs for and of themselves but would live everywhere surrounded by them: thirteen photojournals were published in London by 1899; photojournalism took shape; the picture postcard was born. From promising fixity beyond the ravages of time (a promise best exemplified by the common earlier practice of taking funeral portraits), photography had flip-flopped, in one generation, to proffering the ephemeral, the transitory, the momentary. In sum, exactly at the historical moment when Stevenson, Stoker, and Wells began to write, the "witch machine," as the papers called it,[18] had become, as Terry Castle puts it, "the ultimate ghost-producing technology of the nineteenth century."[19] Photography was the inheritor — and more — of the techniques and the cultural niche of the eighteenth-century magic lantern that haunts Le Fanu's "Carmilla."

Photography assuredly grounds and provokes the disturbingly material ghost-production of a text like *Dracula*. Jonathan Harker, alone in an untrodden wing of the Castle Dracula, falls into a hypnotic trance and seems to see "floating motes of dust . . . take new shapes . . . as they danced in the moonlight"; "more and more [the moonbeams] gathered till they seemed to take dim phantom shapes . . . which were becoming gradually materialized" (ibid., pp. 44–45). The "three ghostly women" who result are the products of a perverse and profoundly physical kind of photographic development — the gradual emergence, under correct chemical conditions, of an image that creates a profound illusion of presence, a "transcript" of reality (to use film theorist André Bazin's term). To the same photographic world belongs Wells's narrator's final description of the Time Traveller, seen, as it were, in double exposure: "I seemed to see a ghostly, indistinct figure sitting in a whirling mass of black and brass for a moment — a figure so transparent that the bench behind, with its sheets of drawings, was absolutely distinct; but this phantasm vanished as I rubbed my eyes."[20] And to the same world belongs the term repeatedly applied to Stoker's Lucy Westenra as she sinks into bloodless acquiescence in death, namely, "fading away" (ibid., pp. 95, 147). Indeed, *Fading Away* is the title of a famous composite 1858 "art-photograph" of a dying girl by Henry Peach Robinson, whose photographs so impressed Prince Albert that he gave him a standing order for a copy of every print he made.[21] Others, like some of *Dracula's* first readers, accused Robinson of "tasteless exploitation and 'morbid sentiment,'"[22] but for our purposes it is his technique that most merits attention: the assembling of different negatives, like the editing together of disparate shots in cinema, made possible the photographic manipulation not only of time but of space.[23]

The third anxiety that Christopher Herbert identifies in Frazer and Einstein concerns evidence (see preceding essay in this volume). Though all fantasies must make claims to empirical truth in order to suspend disbelief and secure their effects, the late nineteenth-century Victorian horror tale does so to excess, displaying its proofs no less elaborately and obsessively than does Frazer in *The Golden Bough*. The narrator of "Carmilla" recounts, in neutral legalese, witnessing the processes of execution and decapitation, referring us for corroboration to the documents of an "Imperial Commission." Similarly, Stevenson pieces together a series of sources — Utterson's, Dr. Lanyon's, Jekyll's "Confession," testaments, letters, marginalia, and laboratory notes. Not to be outdone, Stoker orchestrates a cacophony of diaries, letters, newspaper items, telegrams, and reports, making climactic narrative use of his battery of evidence-producing machines, and of the very processes of reconciling various pieces of evidence (only when Madame Mina types up the accounts together does a true pattern emerge). What is more, textual evidence is supported by the witness of one's eyes: Utterson glimpses Jekyll at his window, struck with terror at the onset of another transformation (full sight of the same horror kills Dr. Lanyon); the anonymous narrator of "The Time Machine" witnesses the Traveller's flight into space / time; and Madame Mina, under Van Helsing's hypnotic spell, "sees" and can spy on the movements of their vampiric enemy.[24]

So intense an obsession with evidence has multiple causes: one, at least, again relates directly, though less obviously, to the new technology of photography. As Emile Zola, an enthusiastic amateur photographer, remarked:

"You cannot say you have thoroughly seen anything until you have got a photograph of it."[25] "Prints, sketches, travellers' tales, *objets d'art* — not one of these earlier forms of evidence," writes Alan Thomas in *Time in a Frame: Photography and the Nineteenth-Century Mind*, "could match the power of witness" of the supposedly anonymous, objective, and transparent photograph:[26] it gave, as expedition photographer John Thomson put it, "incontestable pictorial evidence of my *bona fides*."[27] Thus, between 1883 and 1893, Alphonse Bertillon photographically documented a hundred thousand criminals for the Paris police (by no means the earliest but certainly one of the most systematic criminological uses of the new technology), and Englishman Francis Galton's *Inquiries into Human Faculty* (1883) used "composite photographs made by precisely aligned multiple exposures" to construct and classify abnormal physiognomic types, such as consumptives and maniacs.[28]

One of the new technology's first tasks (as the potential of Galton's work for exploiting racial and cultural stereotypes would suggest) was the visual classification of the races and cultures the British Empire encountered in its expansion into Africa, Asia, and the Pacific; this photographic taxonomy of native "types" was (often explicitly) intended to provide evidence of their inferiority. The Army and the Imperial Civil Service numbered thousands of amateur photographers among their ranks. In India alone, a Photographic Society founded in Bombay in 1854 had 250 members within a year, publishing a journal and fostering publication of members' work; a single military photographer, Linnaeus Tripe, published ten books between 1857 and 1858. The first major ethnographic-classificatory study produced by the camera, the hundred thousand prints collected and eight volumes published of *The People of India* (1868–75),[29] grew out of retiring Governor-General and photography enthusiast Lord Canning's desire for a collection of photographs that might "recall to [his] memory the peculiarities of Indian life"[30] and express "the various divisions in the great Asiatic family."[31]

Often a naked appropriation of its "subjects" (since the images were destined for the mass market as well as for the museums), the ethnographic photographic record, like the funerary portrait, froze societies and worlds (the Tasmanians, the Maoris, the Zulus) at the precise moment when they were being swept into the dustbin of history:[32] as Thomson put it, the camera was indeed the "forerunner of death."[33] Through photography, the Empire both imposed order and bore witness to primitive chaos: one thinks, for example, of Captain Willoughby Wallace Hooper's dispassionate and macabre 1877 group portrait of emaciated victims of the Madras famine, in which six

million people died, posed in studio style.[34] And through the camera the two
principals of Victorian horror, the female and the black, could be brought
together in compositions that contained their threat: in one 1870's portrait of
three Zulu women, posed to the taste of an unknown photographer, one
offers her rump and one her bared breasts to the camera, while a third re-
clines in classic odalisque pose.[35]

The history of photography is paralleled, duplicated, revisited by the history of moving pictures; and cinema history provides a direct link between
visual ethnography and the production of celluloid horror ("optical glut-
tons," as O. Henry said, "feast on the misfortunes of others").[36] Merian
Cooper and Ernest Schoedsack, the two adventurers who made some of the
most famous anthropological films of the silent era, notably *Grass* (1925),
went on to make *King Kong* (1933), a virtual parable of the principle that,
regardless of the increasing relativization of the discipline of anthropology
from which it sprang, horror must think in black and white.[37] If there are no
absolutes, there can be no transgression of boundaries ("neither man nor
beast," Kong is "something monstrous"): we never assume anything but that
Conrad's Kurtz, at the heart of darkness, has absolute knowledge of the horror of which he whispers.

There is something profoundly appropriate in the prolonged cinematic
afterlife of the classics of the late-Victorian fantastic, especially *Dracula* and
*Dr. Jekyll and Mr. Hyde*. The fading away of the Count in Stoker's text, under
gaslight, in the sparkle of a match, or in the glare of the sun, anticipates his
fate in the most famous, though least literal, of the cinematic adap-
tations — F. W. Murnau's classic *Nosferatu*, made in 1922. Here the filmic /
photographic trickery of the overlapping dissolve creates the vampire's death
by sunlight, and cinema itself is explicitly imaged as the vampiric hypnotizer
of its audience in designer Albin Grau's sketches for the production, in which
"monstrous dreams, projected outward, transfix the spectator / victim."[38] In
Carl Dreyer's 1932 *Vampyr* (inspired by Le Fanu's "Carmilla"), a veritable
shadow play of a film, hero David Gray's shadow-self at one point disengages
from his body (courtesy of double exposure), while "lights and shadows,
voices and faces" (to quote the film's intertitles) indeed "possess a hidden
significance" for the protagonist — and the audience. *Dr. Jekyll*, meanwhile,
spells out the terms of its own cultural transmission: "One may," in the case
of Stevenson's "crawler," "say, not too fancifully," as Stanley Kaufmann says
of D. W. Griffith's *Way Down East*, "that cultural dynamics foretold the arrival of the film, that the nineteenth-century audience *demanded* that film
be invented."[39]

In one of the most extraordinary presaging passages in fiction, penned several years before the invention of the flexible celluloid film stock that made cinema possible, we read that the images of the day's events go by before narrator Utterson's mind "in the gross darkness of the night and the curtained room," in "a scroll of lighted pictures" (*Dr. Jekyll and Mr. Hyde*, p. 37). Premodern horror and science-fiction stories turn out to be coterminous with the film medium that has immortalized and cannibalized them. Fiction here comes full circle: inspired — among other things — by the photography of the new-modern world, it reaches fruition in that same world's cinematography, imaging the supposed primitive in the lens of the supposed new.

# PART IV

# (Ethno)graphic Images

# Manipulated Images
## European Photographs of Pacific Peoples

The manipulation of the photographic image to suit the needs of the photographer or audience is not new: it is as old as photography itself. Technical tricks, verbal instructions to the model, printed captions, and visual props drastically change the content of the image. The revolutionary medium of photography, which reproduces aspects of the surrounding world on metal, glass, and paper supports, does not always correspond to reality and never has, despite what some of its early nineteenth-century practitioners claimed. On the contrary, "In spite of every precaution on the part of the operator, the photographic negative, as well as the positive proof, are often imperfect."[1]

Early retouching techniques, initially developed to remove the flaws on photographic plates or emulsions, could hide imperfections and correct the consequences of slow exposure times. These simple techniques included etching and using India ink with brush or pen. Portraits were especially problematic and often required some alteration: "The sitter often moves his eyes, which prevents their appearing sufficiently distinct and sharp in the photograph. A few delicate touches with the brush easily repair these and similar imperfections."[2] It was soon discovered that slight changes or additions to the image could enhance or soften facial expressions, eyes could be intensified, and even skimpy landscapes could be made lush and full by the skillful hand of the photographer or engraver.[3]

The content of the photograph could also be controlled by manipulating the setting or pose of the human model. Both interior studios and exterior locations were commonly used for picture taking in the nineteenth century. In both settings people and scenery could be arranged to create a composition and construct an image favorable to client and photographer alike. In elaborate interior studios, scenes were created using foliage, rocks, architectural elements, furniture, and backdrops. Tableaux recreating daily life, occupation, or social status were constructed from scratch in these theatrical spaces, where the photographer had total control.

Although exterior photography was cumbersome, the composition of outdoor scenes was equally controlled. Having to transport bulky supplies neither hindered nor inhibited photographers from using a multitude of props and costumes to modify the world outside their studios. Glass plates, chemicals, large cameras, tripods, and even portable darkrooms were also transported to all manner of terrain and climate. Initially, photographic plates had to be processed directly after exposure. The wet-plate process, which used glass plates prepared with collodion and other chemicals, needed to take place before the collodion dried (*Encyclopedia of Photography*, pp. 554–56). Environmental irritants such as dust were attracted to these damp, sticky plates, thereby exacerbating the need for later retouching. The 1870's brought the perfection of the dry-plate process, which did not require immediate processing, so that multiple plates could be exposed and later processed and printed (ibid., p. 156). Although these techniques now seem restrictive, expedition photographers obtained fantastic and technically exquisite results.

The use of retouching techniques and controlled settings by and for nineteenth-century Europeans was generally well suited to their canons of portraiture and representation. But these two practices had serious implications when Europeans used them to photograph cultures other than their own. Nineteenth- and early twentieth-century colonial photographers produced thousands of images constructed to convey European sentiments about non-Western cultures that European expansionism had interrupted and dominated. Now, because colonial intervention and the passage of time have irrevocably changed these local cultures, historians turn to such photographs as sources of information. Although these images can in fact be "documentary," representing cultural traditions now changed, or supply other historical information, the researcher must be cautious before accepting their content as true and using it as evidence of an occurrence or event.[4] For example, many images were used to help construct pejorative myths that served colonial interests in the Pacific Islands. Thus colonial-period photographs representing an aspect of or person from a non-European culture vary in authenticity and must be examined on a case-by-case basis. Even scientists who deal with tangible evidence have altered photographs and used them to "prove" their scientific theories.[5]

Oddly, exterior photographs often seem to escape rigorous scrutiny by historians who are looking to an image for proof of a particular event. Exterior scenes are assumed to be more reliable or authentic in content, despite the fact that they can be (and were) just as easily manipulated as a studio interior — especially in the context of anthropology.[6]

This essay discusses the work of several European photographers and the problems that can occur when photographs are accepted as evidence of particular events without examining the contexts in and purposes for which they were made.[7] Some startling and obvious information often reveals that a given event was staged entirely at the suggestion of the photographer. This essay explores some European pictorial conventions from 1870 to 1920 — conventions that were slightly twisted and adapted when used to "picture" Pacific Island peoples. It was during this fifty-year period that photography made many seminal technical advances and spread rapidly around the world. This was also a time when organized missionary and colonial activity was highly concentrated in parts of Melanesia and Polynesia; photography proved particularly useful in establishing mission stations and providing memorabilia of a life spent in the colonies. Photographs played an important role in industrial expansion as well, and were useful in promoting further colonial intervention, since they documented so-called European progress and could be used to justify any aspect of the colonial enterprise.

The work of John W. Lindt, Charles Kerry, Allan Hughan, G. B. Nething, and Reverend George Brown illustrates the types of direct alteration of images and subtle manipulation of subjects used in the pictorial record of Pacific Islanders. The work of these men[8] includes images that could be entirely misinterpreted if taken at face value. The examples considered here are from different Pacific countries and cultures, including Australia, Melanesia, and Polynesia. They were deliberately chosen to reflect the various colonial situations and objectives that prompted the picture taking in the first place — and hence to demonstrate the widespread and routine manipulation of photographic subjects throughout the area.

The photographs discussed here fall into two categories: studio and exterior.[9] Studio photographs were the perfect vehicle for constructing misinformation and stereotypes about Pacific peoples.[10] They were generally made or marketed by commercial photographers and are defined as photos taken within a theatrical space designated by the photographer. The studio was usually an interior room with access to natural light controlled by shades or shutters. Painted backdrops, textiles, furniture, architectural elements, and even animals were used with the human model to create a scene that was felt to be appropriate for the client. Studios ranged from simple "lean-to" structures with partial glass roofs on a 45-degree angle to elaborate "tunnel studios," in which a combination of direct and reflected natural light was bounced off white walls or filtered through white glass. The photographer operated in the surrounding darkness.[11]

Exterior photographs came to have several names when non-Europeans were the subject—the terms field, ethnographic, anthropometric, and anthropological were all applied. These various labels derived from the fact that ethnologists, anthropologists, scientists, and missionaries used cameras in their work. Commercial photographers also made exterior photographs, so technical proficiency varies a great deal in this category.

In both interior and exterior settings, photographers attempted to picture people in their local surroundings or to recreate actual events as they supposedly took place. But both genres typically present people in stiff, uncharacteristic arrangements that show only how the photographer perceived the event to have occurred. Compositions were also informed by the technical limitations of the medium, which could not stop action. Walking, performing, throwing, and other body movements of any kind had to be held for the duration of the exposure.

The types of image manipulation were also twofold: direct physical alteration of the negative support or resulting positive image (Fig. 1), and manipulation of the subject or model. Direct alterations ranged from simple retouching to elaborate multiple exposures and printing techniques. All these techniques became more proficient as the negative support changed from glass to celluloid in 1888 (Encyclopedia of Photography, p. 101).

The most common types of manipulation were written about by Major-General Horatio Gordon Robley (1840–1930), an Englishman who fought in New Zealand with the Imperial Forces in 1864–66. Robley was also an amateur artist who drew and collected objects of Maori art and material culture.[12] He was particularly fascinated with *moko* (traditional facial tattoos) and reproduced many drawings of *moko* patterns in his book on the subject.[13] Robley observed that "Photography came into use just in time for the recorder of *moko*. . . . One often notices that a photographer has inked in the lines, a magnifying glass shows where he has failed to follow them accurately; or one sees the native just touched up with the brush to give the requisite strength and make the pattern come out well" (*Moko*, pp. 126–27). Both drawing on the plate and using makeup or paint directly on the model's face can commonly be seen in portraits of Maori men and women.

Extreme examples of plate retouching can be seen in the work of Pulman & Company of Auckland, New Zealand (Figs. 2 and 3), who produced a series of portraits in which extensive retouching was drawn onto the plate,

FIGS. 1 & 2. *Left:* Exterior photograph by Josiah Martin and William Partington, Auckland, New Zealand, 1880–90. Martin and Partington operated a studio together in Auckland and Wanganui during the 1880's. This photograph shows an unidentified Maori woman with *moko* or facial tattoos drawn or etched on the negative. Traditional facial tattooing had declined among the Maori by the time this photograph was taken. When *moko* was absent, the photographers often drew it directly onto the glass plate. On male subjects, photographers even removed facial hair, in order to visualize the patterns (see King, *Maori: A Photographic History*, p. 14). Reprinted courtesy of the Department of Library Services, American Museum of Natural History, New York, Neg. #33120.

*Right:* Studio photograph by Pulman & Company, Auckland, New Zealand, late nineteenth century. In this albumen print, the *moko* of a man identified as "Patara" has been entirely drawn onto the negative. Reprinted courtesy of the Photograph Study Collection, Department of the Arts of Africa, Oceania, and the Americas, the Metropolitan Museum of Art, New York.

just as Robley described, to replicate the faded *moko* of the models. The Iles Brothers of Rotorua, New Zealand, were also famous for their Maori portraits, especially of women. Both George and Arthur are reported to have used paint to touch up the face of a model before making a photograph,[14] which is readily seen in many of their portraits (Fig. 4).

FIGS. 3 & 4. *Left:* Studio photograph by Pulman & Company, Auckland, and J. Spiller, City Photo Rooms, Oxford Terrace, Christchurch, New Zealand, late nineteenth century. This image, an albumen print in *carte-de-visite* format, was taken by Pulman & Company around 1870 and published or distributed by J. Spiller at a later date. This may be John Spiller (1833–1921). The *moko* has been drawn onto the photograph of this unidentified man's face. Over his left shoulder, a chevron pattern seems to indicate that he is wearing a *taaniko* type garment, whose lower border has been draped over his shoulder for the photograph. Reprinted courtesy of the Photograph Study Collection, Department of the Arts of Africa, Oceania, and the Americas, the Metropolitan Museum of Art, New York.

*Right:* Studio photograph by the Iles Brothers, Rotorua, New Zealand, late nineteenth-century. In this albumen print *moko* has been enhanced directly on the face of the model. Iles identifies this man as "Tuterei Karewa Ngatimaru Chief." Reprinted courtesy of the Photograph Study Collection, Department of the Arts of Africa, Oceania, and the Americas, the Metropolitan Museum of Art, New York.

The second type of manipulation, that of the subject or model, is subtler and more difficult to detect. It is often not visible either to the eye alone or with the aid of optical magnification and is revealed only through investigating the context in which the image was made. It was common for commercial photographers to pose models or arrange props, but these stiff, uncharacteristic, or inaccurate poses were also assembled by missionaries and explorers. After their makers retired or died, missionary photographs often found their way into the commercial sector. Industrious photographers added captions to these images and then marketed them to the public as exotic travel photographs.[15]

Manipulation of the subject also took place in a group of well-known images produced by a German-born immigrant to Australia, John William Lindt (1845–1926). Lindt's biographer states that he was born in Frankfurt, Germany, and arrived in Melbourne in 1862, at the age of seventeen. Lindt made his home among other German settlers in the town of Grafton, near the Clarence River. He was taught photography by a man named Conrad Wagner, who had established a photography business in this growing agricultural settlement.[16]

With the skills and equipment of his new profession, Lindt traveled to photograph Aboriginal people in their communities. In these early exterior photographs, he often took the liberty of manipulating the people into static poses, thus forming generic arrangements.[17]

Lindt's studio business expanded, offering a variety of images for sale, such as portraits of fellow colonists and floral arrangements (Jones, *J. W. Lindt*, p. 4), and the studio series he made during 1870–72, entitled an *Album of Australian Aboriginals*, brought him world renown. It also resulted in his being appointed the official photographer for the 1885 expedition to British New Guinea led by Sir Peter Scratchley.

The photographs in the *Album* are arresting. They are technically proficient albumen prints that were carefully arranged and staged in Lindt's studio, according to his memory of the settlements on the Clarence River and to his notions of "ideal" Aboriginal life. These photographs are truly nineteenth-century, European tableaux (Figs. 5 and 6). His biographer recounts that "Lindt placed Aborigines, carefully selected to show a range of age, sex and status, with stuffed animals posed as if freshly killed, in settings showing typical vegetation. Usually the figures were positioned with their artefacts and weapons alongside a native shelter which in turn stood in front of a painted scenic background, possibly the work of Lindt's father-in-law, Conrad Wagner" (ibid.).

When producing this series, Lindt engaged in a curious practice quite common among European photographers of the period. In an effort to recreate or capture what were thought to be vanishing indigenous cultures for the very camera that was, ironically, changing them, nineteenth-century pictorial conventions were appropriated. These included painted backdrops and

FIG. 5. Studio photograph by John W. Lindt, 1870–72, *carte-de-visite* format, albumen print. This photograph of an unidentified Aboriginal man shows one of the studio tableaux that Lindt created for his *Album of Australian Aboriginals*. Reprinted courtesy of the Photograph Study Collection, Department of the Arts of Africa, Oceania, and the Americas, the Metropolitan Museum of Art, New York.

FIG. 6. Studio photograph by John W. Lindt, 1870–72, *carte-de-visite* format, albumen print. This image of unidentified women and children is characteristic of Lindt's studio compositions for his *Album of Australian Aboriginals*, in which the models are portrayed near shelters or out in the open landscape. The compositions form a narrative of what Lindt felt constituted ideal Aboriginal life. Reprinted courtesy of the Photograph Study Collection, Department of the Arts of Africa, Oceania, and the Americas, the Metropolitan Museum of Art, New York.

FIG. 7. Exterior photograph by John W. Lindt, 1885. This Autotype is published in Lindt's *Picturesque New Guinea* (1887), where it is captioned "Tree House, Koiari Village" (p. 36, plate XIV). In the lower right corner of the photograph, on the ground, is the name card that Lindt placed in his compositions. Lindt recounted this particular picture-taking event in the book itself: "When Hunter, at my request, asked the men to mount to one of the tree houses, and to group themselves in war-like array on the platform, they ran up the ladders . . . donned their war coronets and masks, and in full war-paint, armed with shields and spears, went through all the evolutions of Papuan defensive fighting" (p. 44). Reprinted courtesy of the Robert Goldwater Library, the Metropolitan Museum of Art, New York.

depictions of fictitious exterior locations; normally used as settings for portraits of European colonists, they were reinterpreted when used to photograph indigenous peoples,[18] while props and other objects were changed to alter the message that the scene would normally convey. Backdrops of landscapes and gardens used as signifiers of prestige for European models suddenly became indicators of forest or shoreline settings when local people were the subject. Props were also changed slightly by adding weapons, re-creations of local shelters, and / or clothing specific to indigenous cultures to signify and perpetuate myths of so-called primitive life.[19] It was common for studio photographers to own examples of indigenous art and material culture that could be readily used as props, just as European furniture and decorative arts were incorporated into photographs of Europeans.[20]

Piracy of images was common among Lindt's contemporaries. When a photographer died or went out of business, his stock would often be purchased by another individual or firm. The new owner would obliterate the former name, then etch or paint his own directly onto the plate.[21] This practice led to multiple photographer attributions and confusing dates. Lindt, however, had an interesting way to get his name onto the image and make it hard to obliterate by unscrupulous colleagues: when working in New Guinea and Australia, he inserted his name into the scene on a placard that was usually placed on the ground somewhere in the composition (Fig. 7).

The widespread pictorial conventions Lindt employed in the studio were associated with the popularity of photography at the time. People rushed to studios like Lindt's to have their portraits taken in an appropriate thematic setting (Fig. 8). The practice of posing in a studio with props that conveyed proper social standing and morality was at its height during the later part of the nineteenth century. Even the occupation of the sitter was indicated: soldiers were pictured in uniform; children were often seen with toys or pets; men were seated at tables or positioned in front of rows of books; women had sewing baskets in their laps or gazed at their husbands; and manual laborers, farmers, and miners were pictured with the tools of their trade. These images have now been classified as occupational *cartes-de-visite*.[22]

The search for new, saleable subjects also produced numerous depictions of so-called folk culture. Lindt and other photographers from European countries where *cartes-de-visite* were produced naturally chose the indigenous cultures around them as a subject for their photographs. Lindt even bought his supplies from Europe (Jones, *J. W. Lindt*, pp. 5–6), so he would have been able to purchase visual aids (such as backdrops) to enhance the similarity of pictorial conventions. But the new subjects depicted on these

FIG. 8. Studio photograph by G. B. Coggan, 1870–90, *carte-de-visite* format, albumen print. This unidentified Englishman is posed in a studio situation that was typical of the time. A painted backdrop with a landscape or a body of water in the distance serves to frame the model. The man leans his left hand (also to steady himself for the exposure) against an architectural element. Coggan's inscription on the reverse of this mount reads, "Photograph by G. B. Coggan, Artist, Dentist," attesting to his multiple occupations. Reprinted courtesy of a private collection, New York.

cards soon included indigenous people from colonized nations, in presentations that were stereotypical and often derogatory in tone. In studio arrangements, animal skins were substituted for lush embroidered textiles, tree stumps replaced European chairs, and shields, spears, and dead stuffed animals stood where library books and sewing baskets would otherwise have been. The signifiers of prestige, social position, and morality thus gave way to objects that represented Eurocentric notions of the so-called exotic, tribal, or primitive life.

Photographers produced thousands of these studio creations in Africa, Melanesia, Asia, and Polynesia. What is remarkable is that these images remained in public circulation, with only slight changes in form, for a very long period of time. With the rise of the picture postcard, nineteenth-century photographs endured into the twentieth century by being appropriated, repainted, recaptioned, and reproduced for sale as souvenirs. Often the original photographer was not given credit for the photograph on which the painted reinterpretation was based.

Lindt's studio photographs of Aborigines were widely distributed and sold in many formats. He presented copies to many prominent Australians and Europeans in the fields of government, science, and exploration. These images survive in many museums and photographic archives worldwide; today, however, their significance lies in the fact that Lindt had the ability and commercial opportunity to disseminate misinformation and false notions of primitivism via the photographic image.[23]

Lindt's studio work informed his later exterior photography in British New Guinea. The Autotypes[24] published in *Picturesque New Guinea* (1887), made during his travels with the Scratchley Expedition, are similar in composition to the "ideal" studio tableaux of daily life that he constructed in interior locations.[25] Lindt's exterior views were greatly influenced by his studio compositions. When working outdoors, Lindt arranged his subjects within the spatial restrictions that a studio then imposed. For example, people from Papua New Guinea were arranged in ensembles. His image *Young Cocoa-nut Trees on Stacey Island; Farm Peak in the Distance* (Fig. 9) shows that he sought exterior landscapes that mirrored the studio. Lindt composed this image with the trees to the left, two unidentified men seated on rocks just left of center, and a distant view of a mountain to the right, directly behind several large rocks. One need only consult the studio photographs in his *Album of Australian Aboriginals* to find similar compositions. The lack of depth of field made *Farm Peak* and the horizon come forward, just like a painted backdrop with trees and shoreline seen in the studio. Although people were photographed in the actual villages in which they lived, with objects that belonged to them, they were posed in an idyllic manner. Lindt describes making this image: "Early next morning I went ashore to attempt some photographs. . . . I was able to get some very characteristic pictures, both of scenery and houses, with native groups. The people were most obliging, and did everything in their power to please us" (*Picturesque New Guinea*, p. 81).

Many photographers went to extremes in their various manipulations: indeed, the nineteenth-century studio was where the photographic stylist was born. Unfortunately, where Pacific peoples were concerned, much exploitation took place. Photographs were vehicles for sexist and racist attitudes. The commodification of women, already prominent in photography, was exacerbated by posing non-European women as though they were sexually available beings who existed solely for the pleasure of European males. Captions describing them as maidens, belles, or beautés added to the sexual innuendo. A photographer named Charles Kerry (1858–1928), working primarily in and

F I G . 9. Exterior photograph by John W. Lindt, 1885. This Autotype is one of the many that illustrate his work for the 1885 Sir Peter Scratchley Expedition to British New Guinea. See Lindt, *Picturesque New Guinea*, p. 104, plate XL, where it is captioned "Young Cocoa-nut Trees on Stacey Island; Farm Peak in the Distance." In this image, Lindt used a composition similar to his studio creations — people sitting on boulders and rocks in the foreground and a landscape or seascape in the distance. Foliage or trees were usually positioned on either side of the models. Reprinted courtesy of the Robert Goldwater Library, the Metropolitan Museum of Art, New York.

FIG. 10. Studio photograph published by Charles Kerry, Sydney, Australia, 1880–90. Kerry and his contemporaries often added captions directly onto the negative, identifying the scene and subject meant to be conveyed. Here, his "Samoan Fruit Seller (1403)" is an example of how studio images were staged and the negatives retouched to appear as exterior views. The lower portion of the photograph has been retouched to suggest water. We are to assume that Kerry wanted the woman to appear to be lying on the shoreline of an island or river. Reprinted courtesy of the Peabody Museum, Harvard University, and the President and Fellows of Harvard College.

around Sydney, used studio settings and direct retouching to construct images that are particularly characteristic of this genre (Fig. 10).[26]

Men were not exempt from Kerry's gaze and are often depicted as warriors in stereotypical scenes, such as the heavily retouched image of an unidentified man from the Solomon Islands (Fig. 11), which may in fact be a photograph marketed by the Kerry firm but not taken by him. Although it is formally very similar to Kerry's photograph of an unidentified Samoan woman (see Fig. 10), it seems to have been taken by the Melanesian missionary Bishop H. H. Montgomery.[27] But regardless of their original attribution, re-

FIG. 11. Photograph by Bishop H. H. Montgomery, ca. 1890, and Charles Kerry, Sydney, Australia. Men of the Pacific Islands were often pictured engaged in battle or hunting. This retouched photograph presents an unidentified man from the Solomon Islands posing as if to throw his spear at a distant target. At the lower edge "grass" has been drawn into the photograph. Reprinted courtesy of the Trustees of the British Museum, MM034.178/89.

touched images by Kerry & Company were aggressively distributed. Kerry's photographs dominated the picture-postcard market in parts of Australia, and his photos can be seen in publications well into the twentieth century.[28]

During the time Kerry and Lindt worked, Allan Hughan (1834–83) was operating a studio in New Caledonia. From the mid to late 1870's, Hughan traveled on the main island and smaller surrounding ones photographing a variety of subjects, including mission stations, colonial buildings, landscapes, mining sites, and, of course, people.[29] Hughan made many portraits of indigenous people both in their own villages and in his Noumea studio (Fig. 12).[30] His studio photographs follow a formula similar to those of Kerry and Lindt. Hughan used his own props,[31] which he obtained locally, to convey his own version of local life and thus present certain themes in his

FIGS. 12 & 13. *Left:* Studio photograph by Allan Hughan, Noumea, New Caledonia, 1870's. This is one of several *carte-de-visite* format, albumen prints made by Hughan in his Noumea studio. The scenery and studio props among which an unidentified woman is seated are carefully arranged. Reprinted courtesy of the Haddon Photograph Collection, MEL.NC.46, Cambridge University Museum of Archaeology and Anthropology, Cambridge, England.

*Right:* Studio photograph by G. B. Nething, New Caledonia, 1870–90, albumen print. Many of Nething's photographs were retouched and published in early-twentieth-century travel books about world cultures. This one can be seen, with the backdrop painted out, in T. Athol Joyce and N. W. Thomas, *Women of All Nations* (New York: Metro Publications, 1942), p. 99. A French photographer named Charles Nething (1866–1947) was active in New Caledonia in 1889 (Patrick O'Reilly, *La Nouvelle-Calédonie au temps des cartes postales* [Paris: Nouvelles Éditions Latines, 1973], p. 14). Although this photo is attributed to G. B. Nething, there is a possibility it was made by Charles. Reprinted courtesy of the Haddon Photograph Collection, MEL.NC.14, Cambridge University Museum of Archaeology and Anthropology, Cambridge, England.

*Rabu Banaky, Son of Koapena, a*

FIG. 14. Studio photograph by G. H. Woodelton, late nineteenth century, albumen print. Near the top and right of this cabinet card, the edges of the painted backdrop depicting a shoreline, a body of water, and cliffs are visible. The caption, handwritten on the card mount (which may or may not be by Woodelton), reads: "Rabu Banaky, Son of Koapena, a powerful Aroma chief, New Guinea." During the Scratchley Expedition, J. W. Lindt met Rabu Banaky's father, Koapena, but under the circumstances of the meeting, he was unable to secure a photograph of him (see Lindt, *Picturesque New Guinea*, pp. 71–79). A cabinet card is a larger and later version of the *carte-de-visite*, the cardstock mount usually being 6 1/4″ × 4 1/4″. See Darrah, *Cartes de Visite*, pp. 4–11, for a discussion of both formats. Reprinted courtesy of the Trustees of the British Museum, MMO34.179/2.

FIG. 15. Studio photograph published by Charles Kerry, Sydney, Australia, late nineteenth century, albumen print, captioned "N. G. Water Carrier.806, Kerry Photo. Sydney." The illusion of an exterior location is broken with the edge of the backdrop seen on the left of the image. Reprinted courtesy of the Photograph Study Collection, Department of the Arts of Africa, Oceania, and the Americas, the Metropolitan Museum of Art, New York.

photographs. He arranged people in generic groups, such as married couples and mothers with children, and showed them eating or sitting among a clutter of objects. These were typical tableaux that all photographers from this period used, as a selection of studio portraits of the time clearly shows. Compare, for example, the composition of photographs by G. B. Nething, working in New Caledonia (Fig. 13); G. H. Woodelton, working in New Guinea (Fig. 14); and Charles Kerry (Fig. 15), whose field operators also worked in New Guinea.

An entirely different and, in a way, invisible kind of manipulation of the photographic subject can be seen in some of the work of Reverend George Brown (1835–1917). The photographs discussed here are part of a series made in the Solomon Islands, Melanesia.[32] Brown was a prominent member of the Wesleyan Methodists, who were very organized in their pursuit of converts and mission territory in the Pacific Islands. He began his mission career in 1860, and was General Secretary for Foreign Missions of the Australasian Board of Missions from 1887 to 1908.[33] Brown spent the majority of his time in the Pacific on the islands of New Britain, Tonga, Fiji, and Samoa, with frequent visits to New Ireland, New Guinea. He was instrumental in founding mission stations and training local preachers. He traveled extensively throughout Melanesia, making visits to the Solomon Islands in 1879, 1899, and 1902.

Brown was an avid photographer who used his own images to illustrate publications about his missionary activities in the Pacific.[34] He mentions having a camera in his possession as early as September 8, 1875, in the Duke of York Islands.[35] Brown also used photography extensively in his day-to-day mission work. When he preached the gospel to the people of Melanesia, he often presented "lantern entertainment,"[36] for he took photographs of people in the Pacific who had been converted to Christianity and used them to convince prospective converts to join his fold: "I gave a lantern lecture in the evening and showed the people what the Gospel had done for other people like themselves. The views showed what the people of Fiji, New Guinea, and other places were before the introduction of Christianity, and what they were afterwards."[37]

Brown, like many of his colleagues, wrote about the art and customs of the people he was trying to convert. It was quite common for missionaries to describe and photograph those practices they found most abhorrent. Numerous images were made of body ornamentation and cicatrization processes to illustrate what missionaries felt were inappropriate modes of dress and behavior. A series of photographs taken by Brown in 1902 in Ruviana Lagoon, on the Solomon island of New Georgia, falls into this category. These images were made when Brown and his party arrived in the Solomons to establish a mission station, and some of them were published in a Sydney newspaper soon after they were made.[38] Several people were posed outside for the photographs. One of the unidentified men is in profile to show the ear ornament he is wearing (Fig. 16). This image is published in Brown's autobiography with the caption, "Man with clock placed in the lobe of his ear to show the size of the orifice. Circumference of clock, thirteen inches" (Brown,

F I G . 1 6. Exterior photograph by George Brown, 1902, New Georgia, Solomon Islands. This photograph of a young man with a clock inserted into his ear is published in Brown's autobiography, *George D. D. Brown*, p. 518. A copy photograph was made from the book with permission of the Mitchell Library, State Library of New South Wales, Sydney.

*George D. D. Brown*, plate facing p. 518). An image of another young man appears two pages later. As in an almost identical photograph (Fig. 17), this man is seated facing the camera on what appears to be a wooden crate, his head turned slightly to his right to reveal an ornament in his left ear. The caption Brown supplied reads, "Man with box of sparklet cartridges placed in the lobe of the ear, to show size of the orifice." [39] This same man was posed similarly for another photo (Fig. 18), but this time he has the clock that was used in Fig. 16 in his left lobe. [40]

This is a rare situation, in that Brown's captions tell the reader exactly what he has done to construct the photograph — namely, that a clock and an ammunition canister were deliberately placed in the earlobes of the two young men for photographic purposes. No references have been found in Brown's journals, diaries, or letterbooks indicating that he came upon the men of Ruviana wearing appropriated European objects as personal ornamentation. On the contrary, Brown describes at length the traditional methods of ear piercing and the practice of extending the earlobe, as well as the

195

FIG. 17. Exterior photograph by George Brown, New Georgia, Solomon Islands, 1902. The man seen in this photo is one of two used by Brown to show the ear lobe distention practiced by the residents of New Georgia. A related photograph appears in Brown's autobiography (facing p. 520). Reprinted courtesy of the Photograph Archive, Rautenstrauch-Joest-Museum, Cologne, and George Brown Photographs, Mitchell Library, State Library of New South Wales, Sydney.

type of ornaments worn. He also made photographs of unidentified men from the Solomon Islands wearing traditional ear ornaments (Brown, *George D. D. Brown*, pp. 380, 388, and idem, *Melanesians and Polynesians*, pp. 8, 58).

What is fascinating is that these photographs could so easily be misinterpreted as documenting a scene of cultural appropriation that Brown "discovered" during his travels. According to Brown's captions this was not at all the case, yet without inquiring into the specific photographic event, one could

F I G . 1 8 . Exterior photograph by George Brown, New Georgia, Solomon Islands, 1902. The man in Fig. 17 with the ammunition cannister in his left ear is now seen with a clock in his ear. The pose is almost identical, seated frontally on a wooden crate. Here we can see his right ear with a traditional ear ornament, which forms a loop, inserted in the lobe. Reprinted courtesy of the Trustees of the British Museum, MM034.104/6, and George Brown Photographs, Mitchell Library, State Library of New South Wales, Sydney.

innocently interpret them as such. This is not to say that the people of the Pacific did not appropriate European objects: they definitely did, particularly when it came to body ornamentation.[41]

Whether the unidentified men whom Brown photographed continued to use the clock and ammunition canister as ear ornaments is, in a way, irrelevant to this discussion. The important point is that Brown did not come upon the scene and quickly photograph it for posterity. All European contact had an effect on the cultures of the Pacific; the cross-cultural appropriation in both directions was, and is, significant to both cultures. As for Brown, he

FIG. 19. Exterior photograph by George Brown, New Georgia, Solomon Islands, 1902. The man in the photograph wears a chest ornament called a *tarkola* (Waite, *Art of the Solomon Islands*, p. 32–33). In this full frontal standing pose a clock inserted by Brown is visible in the man's left ear. In his right earlobe is the traditional ornament. Reprinted courtesy of the Photograph Archive, Rautenstrauch-Joest-Museum, Cologne.

meant his photographs to display size and explicate a form of adornment—hence the scenes he constructed to illustrate what he perceived as an extreme size and manner of body ornamentation.

Note, too, that Brown was establishing a mission station in Ruviana when these images were made. To validate his project, he had to offer proof that his services were needed. The logical way to do so was to show what he felt to be the excessive nature of the local practice of adornment. Thus he merely replaced the traditional ebony ear ornament with a European object of known use and familiar dimensions. Brown also manipulated the type of information provided when he gave the circumference of the clock rather than the diameter of its face, the circumference being much the greater of the two dimensions (Fig. 19).

The clock and ammunition canister were direct metaphors for Brown's photographic scenario of contact, not only filling the voids in the men's ear-lobes perfectly but altering the meaning of the images themselves and thus becoming signifiers of time, change, and European contact. The use of the clock marked the moment of Brown's contact, signifying his arrival and, with it, the imposition of European structure and timekeeping. Brown obviously took photographs intended for public consumption, since he wrote articles at his mission stations that were regularly mailed to Australia for publication, and wrote frequently to the editor of *The Sydney Morning Herald* throughout his career. He also knew that photographs recording his visit to the Solomon Islands had a great chance of being published because his mission voyages to the Pacific were very well known.[42]

Personal adornment intrigued other Europeans who visited the Solomon Islands during this period. Charles M. Woodford (1852–1927) also photographed and discussed how males decorated themselves in New Georgia (Fig. 20).[43] Woodford visited the Solomon Islands in 1886–88, but makes no reference to the appropriation of European objects for personal ornamentation. He does describe the traditional type of ear decoration, which can be seen in his photographs (Woodford, A *Naturalist Among the Headhunters*, p. 159).

Another European account of the Solomons, this one by Henry B. Guppy, does state that "singular uses are made of these holes in the lobes of the ear, pipes and matchboxes being sometimes placed in them,"[44] while Lieutenant Henry B. T. Somerville (1863–1932) wrote about men with slightly different ear ornamentation in New Georgia: "Eventually a circle of wood occupies the hole; or, as I have seen, a disc of ebony inlaid with mother-of-pearl, sometimes even a circular trade looking glass. The largest that I measured was 4 inches in diameter" (Fig. 21).[45] Somerville's account is the only one among those mentioned that documents the use of trade items as personal ornamentation by local people during the time when he, Brown, Woodford, Guppy, and a host of other European visitors passed through that part of Melanesia.

FIG. 20. Exterior photograph by Charles M. Woodford, Sólomon Islands, 1886–88. Published in Woodford's 1890 account of his travels, *A Naturalist Among the Headhunters*, opposite p. 152, this image carries the caption "Man of Rubiana Lagoon, ears pierced and distended." It shows an unidentified man wearing traditional ear ornaments that fit into his distended earlobes. Reprinted courtesy of the Trustees of the British Museum, MM034.179/3.

In closing, it bears repeating that photographs made by Europeans often represent their visions of non-European societies. They were usually made for a specific agenda or commercial market in order to achieve various colonial objectives and produce a body of evidence to support European endeavors. The types of photographic manipulation discussed here were typical and familiar modes of representation at the time. As we look at these images more than a century later, we can clearly see that indigenous people were often depicted via the Eurocentric memory and imagination, which was, in turn, greatly influenced by myths of primitivism and Orientalism.

FIG. 21. Exterior photograph by Lt. Henry B. T. Somerville, 1893–94, New Georgia, Solomon Islands. This photograph shows different types of ear ornamentation worn by unidentified men in New Georgia. Reprinted courtesy of the Royal Anthropological Institute of Great Britain and Ireland Photographic Collection, #1783.

Thus we must be vigilant now to ensure that photographic manipulations of past eras do not trick us into finding evidence for situations that may well have been created by colonial contact but that did not exist at the time of the photographic encounter. If these images are interpreted without investigating the specific circumstances under which they were made, only parallel manipulated histories will result.

CHRISTOPHER B. STEINER

# Travel Engravings and the
# Construction of the Primitive

From the Age of Discovery through the mid-nineteenth century, explorers, missionaries, and amateur ethnographers compiled an immense record of life among the so-called primitive races. In the latter part of the nineteenth century, when anthropology was slowly coming into existence as a professional and academic discipline, the European anthropologists who inherited this record began to try to interpret it and, in particular, to explain what seemed to them its most striking and puzzling feature: namely, the impressive number of similarities in the myths, rituals, and cultural practices of geographically separated societies. How, they asked themselves, could populations at opposite ends of the globe have what appeared to be nearly identical ceremonies, folktales, and forms of material culture?

The search for the origins of these cultural affinities grew into a formal debate between two competing schools of thought in early anthropology. The first, represented by the writings of such figures as W. H. R. Rivers, Grafton Elliot Smith, and Friedrich Ratzel, maintained that worldwide similarities of customs and beliefs were the result of specific historical encounters among peoples moving from one settlement to another. According to these authors, all cultural resemblances were the product of transhuman migration, direct contact or exchange, and the diffusion of both cultural institutions and material artifacts from a common center or generative core. In its most extreme manifestation, the diffusionist school argued that the entire inventory of human culture could be traced to the early civilization of ancient Egypt.[1]

The alternate view, which was espoused by Adolf Bastian and Edward Tylor, among others, attributed the striking resemblances among different cultures to the shared proclivities of the human mind. Bastian called these universal tendencies the *Elementargedanken* (elementary ideas), while Tylor referred to them collectively as the "psychic unity of mankind."[2] Both Bastian and Tylor believed that cross-cultural similarities arose not from direct contact between different societies but rather from the natural tendency of human beings everywhere to think in parallel and largely predictable ways.

The debate was never settled. In the early decades of this century, anthropologists turned away from these seemingly unresolvable global enigmas to focus instead on what appeared to be a more controlled "scientific" topic — namely, the structure and function of the single tribe in a putatively fragmented and unconnected world.[3] In this essay, I return for a brief moment to the fin-de-siècle puzzle of transcultural similarities. This time, however, rather than look for solutions within the ethnographic record itself, I redirect the gaze of analysis inward so as to offer a phenomenology of the West's own representations of other cultures.

The alternative perspective that emerges from this method leads us to view the basic elements of transcultural similarity not as a product of the diffusion of ethnographic traits but as a consequence of the diffusion of ethnographic fictions. That is to say, perceived cultural similarities result not from the homogeneity of other cultures but from the reductionism inherent in *our own representations* of other cultures. Displacing the positivist ideology of Victorian anthropology, this alternative approach draws on the reflexive and self-critical strain in postmodernist social theory, as well as on a critical reading of the history of science. From this new vantage point, one could say that the perceived similarities in the customs and institutions of diverse non-Western peoples are not linked necessarily by an objective affinity among the purported facts but are, rather, bound through their common ancestry, which is deeply rooted in the prejudiced assumptions of Western thought. Apparent shared attributes would thus arise not from the collective unconscious of the primitive mind but from the collective arrogance of the Western gaze.[4] As Howard Eilberg-Schwartz recently put it, "The savage . . . was a creation of . . . a generation that was not only confident of the difference between its own culture and the ones it was discovering, but certain also of its own superiority."[5]

Primitives in the Age of Discovery appeared to be identical throughout the globe because, wherever they were encountered, they were portrayed and represented by the same people — European observers who reduced them to a metaphor of Otherness that served only to confirm European expectations of the exotic rather than to challenge those assumptions. In this essay, I examine the putative similarities among various non-Western cultures as an example of the construction and dissemination of Western knowledge about these societies. To accomplish this, I focus on the printed and engraved images used to illustrate European accounts of discovery and exploration, which were one of the earliest recorded outlets for the production and reproduction of ethnographic fantasies.

## Travel Literature and the Diffusion of Culture

> There is but one merit I insist upon, that of a steady
> adherence to veracity. . . . I may be detected in many
> mistakes; because a foreigner must often be exposed
> to receive partial accounts of things from natives
> who have an interest in hiding the nakedness of
> their country and in exaggerating its advantages; but
> I shall never be detected in a wilful perversion of the
> truth.
> — Henry Swinburne (1779)

As a narrative genre, travel literature can be traced back at least to the writings of Herodotus in the fifth century B.C.E. His *Histories* represents one of the first serious attempts at ethnological writing. Accompanying trading expeditions as far east as Persia and as far west as Italy, Herodotus recorded his observations carefully, duly noting local variations in taste, social custom, climate, and diet.[6] As the genre continued into the Middle Ages, travel accounts began to draw more on fantastic legends than on actual observations. Rather than survey nearby European "barbarians" or "savages" (as Herodotus had done in ancient Greece), medieval copyists and epitomizers dwelt on the savagery of antiquity, focusing on occasional remarks in the classics concerning distant lands said to be inhabited by dragons, giants, and various sorts of anthropomorphic monsters. Because these writers did not travel, they were forced to describe places they knew virtually nothing about, and the result was that they populated the world with dark creatures of their own imaginations.[7]

With the discovery of the New World in the fifteenth century and the many subsequent voyages of exploration across the globe, Europeans began to expand their cultural and geographic horizons. Descriptions of distant lands and peoples were increasingly based on firsthand observation rather than on flights of fancy or the distortion of classic sources. It is in this context that the illustrated travel account came into being.

Although the fifteenth century heralded a new era in Europe's empirical knowledge about the rest of the world, fictions of the primitive nevertheless persisted in illustrated accounts of voyages and exploration. A pair of examples illustrates just how "fictional" representations of the primitive could be. In 1634, Fortunio Liceti published an illustrated edition of *De Monstris*,

FIGS. 1 & 2. *Left*: "The Elephant-Headed Man," from *De Monstris*, by Fortunio Liceti (Padua, 1668 ed.). Reproduced by permission of the Houghton Library, Harvard University. *Right*: "The Hirsute Aborigine," from *Anthropometamorphosis*, by John Bulwer (London, 1653). Reproduced by permission of the Houghton Library, Harvard University.

a "scientific" study of the monstrous races of mankind. Intrigued by cases of deformed or so-called monstrous births in Europe, Liceti put together an encyclopaedic reference work on human abnormality.[8] This fantastic collection of grotesque body imagery contained an illustration by Ambroise Paré of a figure described in the text as an "elephant-headed man" (Fig. 1). Although based on a single case of human deformity (and, I would suggest, perhaps also on the image of the Hindu god Ganesh), Liceti extrapolated this medical conundrum into a visual trope that stood for the condition of savagery in general. Another image that illustrates how the dark side of the visual imagination could block out the enlightenment of discovery may be found in John Bulwer's *Anthropometamorphosis*, in which, nearly two centuries after the European encounter with the New World, the author presents a serious depiction of the so-called hirsute aborigine (Fig. 2), a native of the "Hairy Nation" described by Pliny the Elder in the *Historia naturalis*.

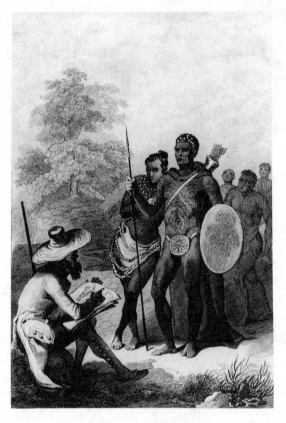

FIG. 3. "Levaillant dessine une Kobobiquois et sa femme," from *Nouvelle Bibliothèque des voyages anciens et modernes* (Paris, 1842), vol. 8, plate 7, facing p. 361. Reproduced by permission of the Harvard College Library.

Illustrations were important to travel accounts in part because they added a very powerful element of realism to the narrative description of distant peoples and foreign lands. Particularly after the introduction of a sophisticated form of copperplate intaglio engraving in the late sixteenth century—which permitted far more detail and verisimilitude than had been possible earlier—the illustrations in accounts of voyages and travels made images of non-Western peoples more tangible and lifelike. As art historian Barbara Maria Stafford has noted, "The writer alone, no matter how indefatigable his powers of perception, could not hope to give a complete representation of all the facets of a scene."[9] Hence, like the authority inherent in the field photograph of the ethnographic text, the engraving (in an earlier era) was intended to signal to the reader that the account was authentic and that the observer had indeed once been among those observed.[10]

Though some expeditions included an artist who was brought along to record, in visual form, the customs, costumes, and other colorful aspects of "native" life (Fig. 3), more often than not travel accounts were illustrated by European artists who had never set foot among the people they were commissioned to portray. Put at an obvious disadvantage by not seeing their subjects, they were forced to create an impression of realism with only scant knowledge of the reality they were charged to depict. These artists tried to overcome their ignorance by resorting to a combination of two techniques: borrowing and conventionalizing.[11] In the first instance, illustrators simply "borrowed" or copied images directly from earlier sources. Sometimes minor and seemingly insignificant details were altered. Witness, for example, the two renditions of the punishment of one of the King of Whydah's wives and her gallant, in which the French version of the image (Fig. 4) is a faithful

FIG. 4. "Punition d'une des femmes du roi de Juida, et de son amant," from *Abrégé de l'histoire générale des voyages,* by Jean François de La Harpe (Paris, 1780), vol. 3, plate 3, facing p. 261. Private collection.

FIG. 5. "Punishment of one of yᵉ King of Whidahs Wives, & her Gallant," from *A General History of Voyages* (London, ca. 1760), vol. 3, plate 2, facing p. 38. Private collection.

reproduction of the earlier English version (Fig. 5), except that the spit (driven, perhaps, by a penchant for culinary detail) has been rotated in the French edition so that the victim's body roasts evenly on a different side.

Artists also borrowed specific elements from earlier visual representations, inserting them, sometimes quite haphazardly, into their own images. This kind of ethnological *bricolage* often produced some rather unexpected combinations. Thus, for example, an African "fetish temple" at Porto Novo, Benin, was depicted in 1885 (Fig. 6) with supporting houseposts that appear to be lifted directly from a Sepik River hook figure from New Guinea (Fig. 7). At the expense of ethnographic accuracy, the illustrator created a pastiche of primitive symbols — a mixed metaphor, as it were, alluding to the universality of idolatry and paganism in the non-European world.[12]

Illustrators of travel accounts also resorted to conventional canons of composition to represent the non-European subjects they had never seen. Although not pirated *directly* from one another, these archetypes became visual signals to readers that the illustration was about something or someone exotic. The increasing popularity of the illustrated travel account engendered

FIGS. 6 & 7. *Above:* "The Goddess Odudua, and Fetish Temple at Porto Novo," from *Fetishism and Fetish Wor-
shippers*, by Noel Baudin (London, 1885). Reproduced by
permission of the Harvard College Library.

*Right:* Hook Figure, Sepik River, New Guinea. Reproduced by permission of the Natural History Museum of
Los Angeles County. Photograph by Donald Meyer.

a whole body of conventional criteria that effectively created the very standards by which the subject of a picture could be identified (and verified) as primitive.

Illustrators were able to use conventionalized images without sacrificing a sense of realism because few of their readers had ever seen the peoples and places described in the text. Since neither artist nor reader had much knowledge of what the subject ought to look like, it is easy to understand how a system of imaginary signs could come into being to represent any culture deemed primitive. All that was necessary was that the image producer and image consumer agree on the meaning of these newly constructed signs.

Given the ignorance of its reader, the caption that accompanied a picture assumed a powerful function. As art historian E. H. Gombrich has argued, the caption effectively determines the truth of an image. The reader compares the caption to the picture and either agrees or disagrees with the veracity of the label. In the Age of Discovery, the public had few opportunities to check the truthfulness of captions. "How many people," Gombrich asks rhetorically, "ever saw their ruler in the flesh at sufficiently close quarters to recognize his likeness? How many traveled widely enough to tell one city from another?" Captions and pictures were matched and rematched with sovereign disregard for truth. The print sold on the market as a portrait of a king would only need to be altered slightly (if at all) to represent his successor — or enemy.[13]

In the illustrated travel account, such indifference to truthful captions was wedded to the use of conventional images. Gombrich locates an excellent example of this phenomenon in Hartmann Schedel's 1493 publication, the *Nuremberg Chronicle*, one of the first illustrated accounts of the manners and customs of foreign peoples. Gombrich writes:

What an opportunity such a volume should give the historian to see what the world was like at the time of Columbus! But as we turn the pages of this big folio we find the same woodcut of a medieval city recurring with different captions as Damascus, Ferrara, Milan, and Mantua. Unless we are prepared to believe these cities were as indistinguishable from one another as their suburbs may be today, we must conclude that neither the publisher nor the public minded whether the captions told the truth. All they were expected to do was to bring home to the reader that these names stood for cities.[14]

The analogy between the cities of the *Nuremberg Chronicle* and the scenes representing primitives in the illustrated travel account is compelling. The stereotyped and conventionalized illustrations from the *Nuremberg Chronicle* signal to the reader that places like Damascus and Milan are "cities," while at the same time granting the reader the illusion of seeing *each* city in its uniqueness. Similarly, the standardized pattern evident in the representation of primitives conveys a general message of Otherness, while at the same time letting the reader believe that each locale has genuinely been captured. The price illustrators must pay to create such standardized conventions is indifference to local detail. But the authority inherent in the very conventions so established yields, by a somewhat curious and ironic twist, a substantial return: tipped off by a caption, the reader is more likely to believe that the unique, local identity of the scene has been portrayed with fidelity not to convention but to reality itself.

Although the conventional themes of travel-account illustrations are many, in my research eight stand out as particularly prominent within the overall iconographic repertoire. The first two concern the relationship between Europeans and non-Europeans: (1) "the inhospitable reception" usually shows a scene of debarkation in which seafaring Europeans are pelted with stones and other projectiles by "hostile natives" on the land, and (2) "the conquest" (a logical sequel, given the history of Western expansionism) shows the European dominating the foreigner—as the now "subjugated natives" welcome the Europeans and accept with open arms the brave new riches of the Western commodity world. The remaining themes relate to perceived aspects of non-Western cultures themselves: (3) scenes of torture and unnatural mutilation; (4) scenes of execution, cannibalism, or human sacrifice; (5) scenes of exaggerated piety, either in the face of indigenous royalty or in the face of idolatry; (6) scenes of serpentine, seemingly mindless processions; (7) strange acts of courtship or evidence of unbridled sexual appetite and dishonest behavior; and (8) scenes of savage merriment focused principally on drumming and dancing.

## The Beat in the Heart of Darkness

The art of dance is bad everywhere because one
does not suspect that she is the art of imitation.
— Diderot (1757)

Of all the motifs in the illustrated travel account that were stamped by the European observer as key symbols of the exotic Other, one of the most arresting and pervasive is the iconography of music and dance. Dating as far back as ancient Rome, and in particular the writings of Cicero, percussion and dancing were associated with the cultures of foreign and allegedly inferior peoples. Writing in the late sixteenth century, a Christian observer con-

FIG. 8. "The Adoration of the Golden Calf," from *Figure de la Biblia*, by Gabriello Simeoni (Lyons, 1565). Reproduced by permission of the Bibliothèque Nationale, Paris.

demned dancing as the "vilest vice of all," associating it with pagan rituals performed by the ancient peoples of Israel, who, before the descent of Moses, danced in a circle around the Golden Calf (cf. Fig. 8). "They dance," he wrote in 1577,

> with disordinate gestures, and with monstrous thumping of the feet, to unpleasant sounds, to wanton songs, to dishonest verses: maidens and matrons are groped and handled with unchaste hands, and kissed, and dishonestly embraced; and the things which nature hath hidden, modesty covered, are then oftentimes, by means of lasciviousness, made naked, and ribaldry, under the color of pastime, dissembled.[15]

Writing nearly two centuries later, in 1788, another observer noted in his article for the third edition of *The Encyclopaedia Britannica*: "As barbarous people are observed to have the strongest passions, so they are also observed to be the most easily affected by sounds, and the most addicted to dancing."[16] Another century later, in 1876, the illustrator of Reverend W. W. Gill's *Life in the Southern Isles* captured in visual form the negative Victorian attitude toward music and dance. Divided into two panels, the image depicts a "before scene" (Fig. 9) that shows the village under heathenism, and an "after scene" (Fig. 10) that shows the same village under Christianity.

By this time, dancing had indeed become a leitmotif in the Western image of non-Christian or primitive behavior. Combing through accounts of

FIG. 9. "A Village in Pukapuka, Under Heathenism," from *Life in the Southern Isles*, by W. W. Gill (London, 1876), plate on p. 18. Reproduced by permission of the Harvard College Library.

FIG. 10. "The Same Village, Under Christianity," from *Life in the Southern Isles*, by W. W. Gill (London, 1876), plate on p. 19. Reproduced by permission of the Harvard College Library.

travel and exploration, which date from the early sixteenth to late nineteenth century, it is possible to identify and isolate a single, recurring scene of one or more musicians (often drummers) and a circle or procession of dancers. Some new elements are occasionally added, and older ones sometimes dropped, but the basic iconographic motif of the primitive dance can be traced through strata of visual archaeology along an unbroken continuum for nearly four hundred years of art history. Although its earliest roots are linked ultimately to a classical Greek genre represented in particular by the ancient Bacchic dancers,[17] beginning in the early sixteenth century a very specific image — a circle or line of dancers accompanied by one or more musicians — is associated uniformly with the visual anthropology of non-Western peoples in nearly every corner of the so-called primitive world.

The series of visual representations that I explore here begins sometime in the mid-sixteenth century with the production of two very specific iconographic genres: (1) the heathenism and spirit of temptation associated with the adoration of the Golden Calf, and (2) the lasciviousness identified with the feasting and ribaldry of European peasantry. One of the earliest depictions of the followers of Aaron dancing around the Golden Calf at the foot of Mount Sinai is Lucas van Leyden's *The Dance Around the Golden Calf* (1529–30). Painted in the form of a small triptych, the center panel shows a circle of dancers moving in a wild gesticulant manner around an elevated sculpture of the dreaded graven image. The subject of the painting is the ultimate form of idolatry. "A false image," as David Freedberg describes it, "made in the teeth of the prohibition against graven images, is surrounded by visible evidence of the debauched sensuality into which men and women fell as a result of their adoration of the artistic, manmade, golden substitute for the God they could never see. . . . Debauchery and unbridled sensuality is chiefly represented by dancing."[18] Commenting on the same triptych, Carel van Mander noted in 1604 that "Amidst the festivities and banqueting one sees the dissolute nature of the people depicted very realistically, and the unchaste lust shining forth from their eyes."[19] Although van Leyden's painting is not, strictly speaking, a representation of primitive society, it eventually served as a major iconographic template for the visual representation of "true" primitive cultures.[20]

A second source for the visual representation of carnal music and orgiastic dance emerged at about the same time. Beginning in the early sixteenth century, a number of European engravers turned their artistic gaze toward the rural peasantry. For the most part, the peasants were depicted wildly dancing or drunkenly carousing. Some of the most noteworthy representations in this genre include Sebald Beham's woodcuts *The Nose Dance at Fools' Town* (1534) and *Large Peasant Holiday* (1535), Pieter van der Borcht's engraving *Peasant Holiday* (1559), Pieter Bruegel the Elder's engraving *The Wedding Dance* (1570), and Theodor de Bry's engraving *Peasant Holiday* (1590).[21] Like the heathen idol worshipers of the Old Testament, the peasants were portrayed as a "godless" people who heeded neither spiritual nor temporal authority as they feasted in a savage and untamed manner.

The first use of the music-making and dancing motif in the portrayal of a "real" primitive society is found in an engraving entitled "The Manner of Serving Food and Drink, and the Dance of Savages Before Their King" (Fig. 11), which was made about 1600 in the studio of the Flemish engraver Theodor de Bry. Set on Hoorn Island in the South Pacific, the image was first published in *Grands Voyages*, a series published in Germany between

FIG. 11. "The Manner of Serving Food and Drink, and the Dance of Savages Before Their King," from *Grands Voyages*, vol. 4, by Theodor de Bry (Frankfurt, 1619), part 11, plate 8. Reproduced by permission of the Bibliothèque Nationale, Paris.

1590 and 1634 by de Bry and later his sons Johan Israel and Johan Theodor. The *Grands Voyages* was the first comprehensive, printed and engraved, factual travel account. It was, as such, the earliest serious attempt to provide the European public with a pictorial image of newly discovered and newly conquered lands.[22] The content and layout of "The Manner of Serving Food"—in particular, the central circle of dancers and the little crouched drummer in the corner of the scene—are clearly related to both the Golden Calf and the "carousing peasantry" prototypes, and appear over and over again in subsequent iconographic representations of non-Europeans.

In analyzing de Bry's interpretation of what I argue are his alleged visual models, it is interesting to note that he replaced the dancing men and women of both the Old Testament and the peasant feast with small, putti-like figures who are set in sharp contrast to the full-stature figures congregated in the background and on the perimeter. Drawn from themes in antiquity, the putto figure was a childlike creature whose strong little limbs could drive it into artless mischief and gleeful antics.[23] Although the *dancing* putto is by no means uncommon in Renaissance painting and sculpture (and is typically depicted as dancing around the Christ child), what is novel here is its association with a remote, non-European culture. The intent of the artist, I would submit, was to portray the inhabitants of Hoorn Island as belonging to the so-called childhood of mankind—not in the Victorian sense of a retarded civilization low on the evolutionary ladder, but in the classical sense of an otherworldly epoch characterized by wonder and magic. Thus the association of non-Europeans with drumming and dancing is not intended here as a strictly pejorative judgment, but rather as the result of a complex reformulation of geography and chronology. That is to say, distance through uncharted space is signaled to the viewer through a familiar (art) historical reference to distance through time.[24]

The fact that de Bry turned to the representation of peasants (and its associated portrayal of collective worship and dance around the Golden Calf) for an appropriate way to depict a distant and unfamiliar non-Western culture can be explained, I believe, by the attitude of Europeans at that time toward the peasantry. Just as the European peasantry would later come to serve Victorian anthropologists as a critical link between modern (civilized) and primitive (savage) man, so in the late sixteenth century the putatively boorish behavior of the peasantry, with its own brand of vulgar and provincial customs, seemed to provide a logical source from which to envision the hedonistic practices of non-Europeans described by traveling adventurers and missionaries.[25]

FIG. 12. "Danse et musique des Hottentots," from *Histoire générale des voyages*, by Antoine François Prévost (Paris, 1748), vol. 5, plate 27, facing p. 155. Reproduced by permission of the Harvard College Library.

A compelling model for the visual representation of non-Western societies, de Bry's image was borrowed again and again by illustrators of factual travel accounts. A century after publication of the *Grands Voyages*, we find an engraving entitled "Hottentot Dancing and Music" (Fig. 12), originally issued in 1731 in Peter Kolben's account of *The Present State of the Cape of Good Hope*. Though limited to two dancers in the foreground, the scene shares many of de Bry's compositional standards: the crouched drummer in the corner of the image, the contrapposto structure of the dancing body, and the palm-leaf canopy that frames the picture. In this rendering of the scene, the drummer has been moved from the lower right to the lower left, but in later editions he is moved back to the right.

Ten years later, in 1741, we find yet another scene of drummers and dancers, this one engraved by Bernard Picart and published in Jean-François Bernard's encyclopedia of world religions. Entitled "Réjouissances des mexicains, au commencement du siècle" (Fig. 13), the image is supposed to depict a celebratory ceremony among the ancient Aztecs. The drummer and other musicians have been placed at the bottom right corner of the scene, and the dancers, most of whom are portrayed with bent legs and upraised arms, fill the central portion of the image. The dancing putti from de Bry's model are hinted at by two small figures in the lower left corner.

In 1754, we find Bernard Direxit's engraving, also set in Mexico, of the

FIG. 13. "Réjouissances des mexicains, au commencement du siècle," from *Cérémonies et coûtumes religieuses de tous les peuples du monde*, by J.-F. Bernard (Paris, 1741), vol. 7. Reproduced by permission of the Harvard College Library.

FIG. 14. "Amusemens de l'empereur après son diner," from *Histoire générale des voyages*, by Antoine François Prévost (Paris, 1754), vol. 12, plate 14, facing p. 532. Reproduced by permission of the Harvard College Library.

"Amusemens de l'empereur après son diner" (Fig. 14). The affinities to de Bry's original image are again striking: the drummer is crouched in the lower right corner of the scene; a royal host sits under cover, wearing a feather bonnet; and the dancers, with bent legs and upraised arms, occupy a central place in the composition.

Several decades later, in 1793, we return to the west coast of Africa in a scene commissioned to illustrate Archibald Dalzel's narrative *The History of Dahomey* (Fig. 15). Again we find a central composition of drummers and dancers and a monarch seated under cover (in this case a parasol to shade him from the sun). Although the image is clearly part of the visual legacy of primitive musicians and dancers, Dalzel's oeuvre is the first in our series in which dance is used to convey a transparently racist image. As it turns out, Dalzel had invested heavily in the Atlantic slave trade. Following the British anti-slave-trade movement in Parliament in 1789, he set out to "prove" that Africans were naturally inclined toward war, human sacrifice, and cannibalism. A careful reading of Dalzel's narrative reveals a subtext arguing that the

FIG. 15. "Victims for Sacrifice," from *The History of Dahomey*, by Archibald Dalzel (London, 1793), plate facing p. 130. Reproduced by permission of the Houghton Library, Harvard University.

slave trade was in fact a form of divine intervention through which individuals were saved from a potentially worse fate at the hands of their own people.[26] The text accompanying the engraving tells us that this fanfare and merriment are not being conducted in a "Christian spirit": indeed, the dancers are all lining up for their own sacrifice. The cruel contradiction of men dancing on the way to their deaths was meant to underscore the putative barbarism of these African people.

Following in Dalzel's footsteps, we move in 1806 to the exploration of Sierra Leone, where an unnamed artist "discovered" yet another circle of dancers and group of drummers (Fig. 16). Although the musicians in this composition have been moved to the upper corner of the scene, the basic elements from de Bry's model are repeated clearly once again. The image also reflects the racism inherent in Dalzel's representation: the dancers' blackened faces, with exaggerated large white eyes and gaping mouths, anticipates the racist representation of African Americans in the blackface routines of the minstrel shows that began in the mid-nineteenth century in the United States.

In 1884, James Buel included an image of "Music-Charmed Savages" (Fig. 17) in his book *The World's Wonders as Seen by the Great Tropical and Polar Explorers*. The drummers are tucked away in the back left corner and the thatched roof from de Bry's original composition has been replaced by some sort of circus tent, but the dancers are still in a circle, their gestures and positions basically unchanged. In the text, the author stresses the women's ridiculous behavior, suggesting that even the primitive men present at the dance recognized the wantonness of their mothers, sisters, and mates:

Women were observed racing down from their villages. . . . In a short time the buglers could hardly blow their instruments for laughing at the extraordinary effect of their performance. A fantastic crowd surrounded them, and every minute added to their number. The women were entirely naked; thus the effect of a female crowd, bound-

FIG. 16. "The Cullemgee of the Negroes," from *A Collection of Modern and Contemporary Voyages and Travels*, by Richard Phillip (London, 1806). Reproduced by permission of the Harvard College Library.

ing madly about as musical enthusiasts, was very extraordinary. Even the babies were brought out to dance; and these infants . . . were jolted about without the slightest consideration for the weakness of their necks by their infatuated mothers. As usual, among all tribes in Central Africa, the old women were even more determined dancers than the young girls. Several old Venuses were making themselves extremely ridiculous, as they sometimes do in civilized countries when attempting the allurements of younger days. The men did not share in the dance.[27]

The author uses his description of the primitive women's dance to explore his own gender prejudice, inviting the (Victorian male) reader to share his momentary delight in discovering that women throughout the world are incapable of controlling their passions. European women are thus reduced to primitives and their unchecked emotions understood as a kind of survival from an earlier stage of cultural evolution.

FIG. 17. "Music-Charmed Savages," from *The World's Wonders as Seen by the Great Tropical and Polar Explorers*, by J. W. Buel (St. Louis, 1884), plate on p. 248. Reproduced by permission of the Harvard College Library.

FIG. 18. "Danse des Ba-Ngala," from *Sur le Haut-Congo*, by Camille Coquilhat (Paris, 1888), plate facing p. 297. Reproduced by permission of the Harvard College Library.

Finally, in 1888, shortly before photographs completely replaced engraved prints in illustrated travel accounts, an image of a drummer and group of dancers appeared in Camille Coquilhat's book *Sur le Haut-Congo* (Fig. 18). Although the vegetation has grown considerably more dense — dimming, in its shadow, the clarity of de Bry's original scene — the picture of the Ngala dance from Coquilhat's book has changed very little in either form or content during the course of nearly three hundred years of European discovery and exploration. What were presented to readers as "discoveries" in the factual travel account did not consist of previously unreported truths about other cultures. Rather, in each account the artist simply discovered the work of an earlier period — a prior formula or trope used by the image-maker to signal, through a kind of iconographic shorthand, the Otherness and "primitivism" of the people being represented.

## Conclusion

To appreciate the pervasiveness of drumming and dancing in the Western image of primitive society, one need only look as far as Emile Durkheim's classic treatise on the origin of religion. In 1912, Durkheim wrote, in *The Elementary Forms of the Religious Life,*

> Commencing at nightfall, all sorts of processions, dances and songs had taken place by torchlight; the general effervescence was constantly increasing. . . . The men leaped and pranced about, uttering savage yells all the time; the burning torches continually came crashing down on the heads and bodies of the men, scattering lighted sparks in every direction. . . . It is in the midst of these effervescent social environments and out of this effervescence itself that the religious idea seems to be born.[28]

Throughout the book, Durkheim notes that his vision of the primitive dance was informed largely by the Australian ethnographies of Baldwin Spencer and F. J. Gillen. Besides containing a richly detailed textual narrative of Australian customs and beliefs, Spencer and Gillen's principal works, *The Native Tribes of Central Australia* (1899) and *Wanderings in Wild Australia* (1928), are heavily illustrated with visual images — not, however, with woodcuts or engravings but with black-and-white field photographs.

Spencer and Gillen comment in their work on the limitations of both writing and photography as modes of ethnographic representation. In one place they note that "the smoke, the blazing torches, the showers of sparks falling in all directions and the masses of dancing, yelling men formed altogether a genuinely wild and savage scene of which it is *impossible to convey any adequate idea in words.*"[29] Elsewhere, Spencer remarks that "the scene at night, in front of the camp fires when also the performers were encouraged by the presence of a large and excited audience of women, was *much more picturesque than the photographs give any idea of.*"[30]

Thus, in their own estimation, Spencer and Gillen concede that neither words nor photographic images are capable of capturing the passion and intensity of the primitive ritual dance. Yet, ironically, for several centuries prior to this, a far more "artificial" mode of representation — woodcuts and engravings made by European artists who had never seen the people they were attempting to portray — somehow communicated with great immediacy the apparent "savagery" and "primitivism" of those inhabiting the remote shores that were being newly charted by European explorers. What the engraving lacked in absolute realism (in contrast to the verisimilitude of its modern cousin, the field photograph) it made up for by recourse to conventions of composition and visual redundancy. Through constant repetition of vaguely familiar scenes, the engraving engendered its own canons of authenticity and its own lexicon of visual emotion.

Because engravings were drawn from the mind, they were not judged by the same standards as photographs. They were genuine not because they captured an immediate truth but because they drew on deep-seated sentiments and expectations shared by both their producers and their consumers. Whether or not Durkheim knew it, his vision of primitive religion emerging from the bliss of the savage, dancing crowd was one handed down to him not simply from the ethnographies of Spencer and Gillen but from the cumulative sediment deposited in the collective unconscious by centuries of iconographic representation — visual metaphors born in the intellectual effervescence of the European imagination.

NANCY PERLOFF

# Gauguin's French Baggage
## *Decadence and Colonialism in Tahiti*

Before sailing for Tahiti in 1891, Paul Gauguin informed his friend Odilon Redon, "The European Gauguin has ceased to exist and nobody will ever see any more of his works here again."[1] Four years later, in a letter to August Strindberg that Gauguin included as the preface to an exhibition catalogue of his Tahitian works, he spoke of the "clash between your civilisation and my barbarism. . . . A civilisation from which you are suffering; a barbarism which spells rejuvenation for me." In the same letter, Gauguin eulogized the Tahitian "Paradise" that he was discovering and sketching out, and contrasted his "naturally naked Eve" with Strindberg's ashamed one. The language spoken by Strindberg's Eve is a "language with inflections, European language," Gauguin observed, whereas "everything is bare and primordial in the languages of Oceania."[2] Beginning in about 1887, with his travels to Panama and to Martinique, and continuing through his Tahitian sojourn, Gauguin's letters repeatedly invoke this opposition between the civilized and the barbaric, the European and the savage, the sensitive and the Indian. Art historians take the civilized/primitive dichotomy at face value, making it the mainstay of their argument that Gauguin struggled to leave the corrupt European world behind and find a new identity among the natives.[3] They read Gauguin's later Breton and his Tahitian works as attempts to understand primitive symbolism and superstition, to explore the kinship between the unsophisticated mind and the creativity of the modern artist, and to recapture an ancient and simple worldview.

Yet how do we reconcile such claims of Gauguin's self-discovery far from Europe with the enigmatic, fantastic imagery that haunts his paintings, wood reliefs, and ceramics from about 1889 on? Serpents, apples, foxes, cocks and hens, and exotic or shamefaced Eves of the later Brittany period (1889 to early 1891) are joined, in the Tahitian scenes, by images that advance the themes of guilt and corruption, but with greater subtlety and mystery: tall plants with flower-eyes resembling peacock tail feathers; spirits with death masks; disembodied eyes among plants and floral sprays. Art historians from Kirk Varnedoe and Jehanne Teilhet-Fisk to Wayne Andersen and Henri Dorra interpret this dreamlike, often ghoulish imagery as part of a complex web of symbols that Gauguin used to convey fertility, carnality, sin, and superstition, all within the context of a "primitive" Eden.[4] According to this general interpretation, Gauguin's sexual encounter with "savage" woman becomes naturalized and even virtuous, because it is instinctive.

Recently, Abigail Solomon-Godeau has stepped out to question assumptions about Gauguin's "organic, natural imagery" and to challenge the art-historical myth of his primitivism. She identifies this myth as a "patriarchal" view that disturbingly echoes Gauguin's written accounts of his experiences with desirable, healthy, "naturally naked" Eves.[5] She traces the "primitive" myth to Gauguin's self-portrait as a "savage" artist. And she rightly questions art historians' uncritical acceptance and adoption of what Gauguin *said*. By focusing exclusively on the gendered discourse of primitivism, however, Solomon-Godeau ignores sources other than patriarchal attitudes for the imagery in Gauguin's later Brittany and Tahitian works. She does not consider that Gauguin might have chosen any number of images to express his patriarchal views, and thus it is important to ask why he seized upon foxes, serpents, peacock tail feathers, death masks, and naked Eves, and what source or setting inspired this particular imagery.

I propose that Gauguin culled his imagery from his own Parisian literary milieu. Like the French decadent artists and writers who were his contemporaries, he invented dreamlike, artificial landscapes with fantastic vegetation and unearthly creatures in order to escape the modern world. He shared the decadents' urge to find erotic stimulation in visions of tainted flesh and corruption; the fallen woman, once pure but now sullied, had a perverse and tantalizing charm. And he joined his fellow decadents in exploring the myths of ancient civilizations, which lured him with their exoticism and their death spirits. In steeping himself in scenes of corruption, Gauguin became especially fascinated by the impact of colonial corruption on pure Tahitian natives. Moreover, by imposing decadent European themes and imagery on dark-skinned natives, Gauguin exerted his control over the Tahitian and expressed a paternalistic attitude typical of late nineteenth-century French colonialism. Decadence and colonialism thus worked in tandem as cultural determinants for the modes of representation that he introduced into his art around 1889 and after.

Two examples will begin to illustrate my point. The canvas entitled *The*

FIG. 1. Paul Gauguin, *The Loss of Virginity*, 1890–91, oil on canvas, 35 1/2 × 55 1/2 inches. The Chrysler Museum, Norfolk, Virginia, Gift of Walter P. Chrysler, Jr.

*Loss of Virginity* (Fig. 1), which Gauguin completed in late 1890–91, while still in Brittany, presents a naked girl with black hair and full, sensual lips lying rigidly on her back in an exotic, fantastic landscape, the dark ocean in the distance. One hand holds a plucked flower while the other embraces a fox with devilish eyes who plants his paw firmly on her breast. The contrast between the healthy brown hue of the girl's face and neck and the pallor of the rest of her body suggests that her flesh is in the process of decaying or rotting. An artificial light on her body intensifies the taut whiteness of her skin. What is the meaning of this enigmatic scene? For Gauguin, the fox had explicit connotations of lewdness and the loss of female purity. In a letter to Emile Bernard, he called it the "Indian symbol of perversity" (*Letters*, no. 87). The girl, with her dark-skinned face, which Gauguin may have based on the Tahitian or Javanese women he met during the Paris Exposition of 1889, is an exotic Eve who has plucked the flower of evil and succumbed to the devil's sexual temptation. Gauguin contrasts her motionless white body with the lush, vibrant greens and blues of the dreamlike landscape behind her. The fox gazes ambiguously both at the girl and out at the viewer. The painting's images of corruption, evil, sickly flesh, voyeurism, and fantasy move it far away from the simple, "primitive" virtues and the instinctive, "primitive" carnality celebrated in Gauguin's writings.

The canvas *Tahitian Women* (Fig. 2), which Gauguin painted in 1891 in Tahiti, is also mysterious. Two women, both drawn from the same model, are seated on the sand in a constricted space. Their overlapping positions intensify the sense of crowding. Gauguin gives no clues as to the kind of painting he is making. Is *Tahitian Women* a portrait, an ethnographic document of Tahitian life, a genre or domestic scene, a scene about the working class or the aristocracy? None of the categories applies. Despite Gauguin's isolation and monumentalization of the two women, he has not created a portrait. Rather, the women emerge as types, as young Tahitian beauties. The painting's close-up view encourages a physical examination of the women's dark skin tone, the gleaming light on their black hair, their full torsos and bosoms; facial expressions, quite sketchy in the case of the woman on the left, reveal little about individual character. Nor does the context offer any clue about the women's identity or the nature of their activity. The two are clothed but idle; one muses while the other languidly braids strips of

FIG. 2. Paul Gauguin, *Tahitian Women*, 1891, oil on fine-weave canvas, 26 7/8 × 35 1/2 inches. Musée d'Orsay, Paris.

palm leaf. By compressing the space, moreover, Gauguin avoids even a suggestion of the possible proximity of huts, spouses, and children, and of work from which the women may be enjoying a momentary respite. Instead he plucks them out of their context, confines them to a claustrophobic setting, and displays them as exotic curios.

Kirk Varnedoe and Jehanne Teilhet-Fisk would have it that, in seeking to understand the myths, beliefs, and customs of native peoples of Brittany and Tahiti, Gauguin shunned the theories of progress and evolution that prevailed in late nineteenth-century France. He fought against the tide, they argue, challenging contemporary French views of the debased "savage" who must be colonized by a higher, civilized culture. Varnedoe and Teilhet-Fisk assume a dichotomy between European and Polynesian cultures, and claim that Gauguin tried to replace his European identity with some definable Tahitian essence. Such interpretations ignore the twentieth-century predicament in which cultures no longer exist as separate essences with fixed boundaries; rather, they intersect and fuse, precluding the notion of an isolated position from which one culture views another.[6]

Moreover, Gauguin's visual art suggests that a European's cultural rebirth as a Tahitian "savage" is not possible. It tells a different story, a story of visionary landscapes, despoiled Eves, and nightmarish images. It also choreographs its native subjects and places them on show as a spectacle for the viewer's consumption. Has Gauguin really embraced the "savage" life and left his European side behind? Is his attitude toward the primitive Bretons and Tahitians one of pure empathy? Or are Gauguin's visual images expressions of a fin-de-siècle European idiom superimposed on an Oceanic people? In 1889 Gauguin paid many visits to the Paris Universal Exposition, where the colonial exhibit with its staged display of imported natives had a startling impact on his depiction of anonymous Tahitians as appropriated objects for our viewing. The fair served as a crucial catalyst for Gauguin's attitudes toward corruption and his view of France's colonized peoples. I will examine the French decadence and colonialism that Gauguin encountered and explore their convergence in his visual art, in order to present a reconfiguration of Gauguin's work.

I

Until his late thirties, Paul Gauguin lived the life of a prosperous member of the French bourgeoisie. After serving in the French Navy, he settled in Paris in 1872 and took a position as an *agent de change* for a stockbroker. The following year he married a Danish woman, Mette Gad, and assumed the full trappings of a bourgeois existence in Paris. He painted on Sundays and on vacations, and otherwise worked full time as a broker, succeeding so well during the boom years of the 1870's that he sometimes cleared several thousand francs a day.[7] In late 1876 or early 1877, Gauguin took up work first in banking and then in the sale and purchase of insurance company stocks, until the bankruptcy of the Union Générale and the collapse of the Stock Market in 1882 put an abrupt end to his thriving financial career. At this point, having lost much of his earnings, which he had kept in stocks, Gauguin vacillated between financial and artistic paths. He worked in sales and at other odd jobs through 1885, but increasingly tried to earn his living through his art, and by 1886 he had abandoned his business career for life as an artist. The shift to full-time painting did not bring a newfound disdain for monetary gain, however. On the contrary, Gauguin's obsession with money and his expectation that he would sell enough art to be able to live well remained stubborn concerns throughout his life. Camille Pissarro describes Gauguin's mercantile attitude, with specific reference to his wish to paint in Rouen, in the following terms:

He is naive enough to think that since the people in Rouen are very wealthy, they can easily be induced to buy some paintings. . . . Gauguin disturbs me very much, at least he gives that impression. I haven't the heart to point out to him how false and unpromising is his attitude; true, his needs are great, his family being used to luxury, just the same his attitude can only hurt him. Not that I think we ought not try to sell, but I regard it a waste of time to think *only* of selling.[8]

Gauguin was away at sea during the Prussian victory over France and the Paris Commune of 1870–71. In the ensuing volatile years, French monarchists tried to overturn the Third Republic and restore the king. By 1879 they succumbed to a group of republicans then called Opportunists, who believed firmly in national consolidation.[9] One of these Opportunists, Jules Ferry, became Prime Minister in 1880. It was Ferry who laid the foundations for a new colonial empire. Since the early seventeenth century, France had held colonial possessions in Senegal, part of Haiti, part of Canada, and Martinique. Tahiti became a protectorate in 1842. During his two terms as Prime Minister (1880–85), Ferry made large expansions in this colonial territory. France acquired Tunisia and most of Indochina, began to penetrate Madagascar, and moved out into the Sahara from bases along the African coast. The imperial drive rallied public attention around Ferry's principal theme during his ministerial terms: France's great progress and advancement as a cultural, military, and industrial power since the Franco-Prussian War and the Commune. He channeled this theme into plans for a grand Universal Exhibition, in the tradition of Britain's Crystal Palace Exhibition of 1851, the Philadelphia Centennial of 1876, and later world's fairs in the United States designed to celebrate new technology, give impetus to manufactures and industry, and promote foreign trade. Ferry scheduled the Universal Exhibition to open in Paris in 1889, in commemoration of the hundredth anniversary of the French Revolution.[10]

His cabinet fell, however, in 1885, and responsibility for constructing the exhibition was placed in the hands of four successive governments between 1886 and 1889. Beleaguered by political divisions and economic decline at home, and disturbed by an international situation which by 1889 took the form of an "armed peace" between France, Germany, England, and their European neighbors, the Third Republic hoped to use the exhibition to restore its prestige and to demonstrate the strength of imperial France to European rivals.[11]

Gauguin had several reasons for joining the twenty-eight million visitors who flocked to the Paris Exhibition between its May 1889 opening and its November close.[12] On the Champ-de-Mars, next to the fair's official art section and facing the press pavilion, he obtained use of a café owned by the Italian Volpini for an exhibition of seventeen of his own paintings, drawings, and watercolors, as well as works by Emile Schuffenecker, Emile Bernard, and other fellow "Impressionists and Synthetists" who had not been invited to show at the official art section.[13] The exhibition at the Café Volpini opened sometime in late May or early June. Gauguin naturally wandered from there to other parts of the fairground. He had a remarkable choice of pavilions to visit, for the 1889 Exposition continued the encyclopedic tradition of previous nineteenth-century world's fairs in its display of the latest achievements in French trade, industry, agriculture, science, education, the arts—indeed, every aspect of society and culture.[14] The visitor entered the fair through the colossal arches of the Eiffel Tower, commissioned and built specifically for the 1889 Exposition as a symbol of liberalism's successes under the Third Republic. Strolling along the Champ-de-Mars, one witnessed exhibits of the fine arts, the liberal arts, and manufacturing processes. Directly in front of the Eiffel Tower and facing the Seine stood the vast History of Human Habitations Exhibit, comprising a chronological re-creation of human dwellings according to evolutionary stages (stone, bronze, iron) and ages of civilization.

Northeast of the Champ-de-Mars, on the Esplanade des Invalides, the fair's sponsors grouped three major exhibits that drew big crowds: the Ministry of War, held in a pavilion designed as a medieval castle and displaying examples of the latest weapons, introduced since the Franco-Prussian War; the Exhibit of Social Economy, featuring housing, hygienic, and recreational structures for French industrial workers; and the Exhibit of the French Colonies, a collection of reconstituted exotic villages with typical human dwellings and architectural forms, and with native peoples from four ethnic groups — Asian, African, Oceanic, and Arabic.[15]

Of all these displays, Gauguin found the Colonial Exhibit most intriguing and visited it many times. Years spent in the middle-class business world predisposed him to favor the fair's message of French imperialism. And the exhibit hit a raw nerve, for he had spent the past two years longing to escape Paris for remote haunts. No longer financially prosperous, Gauguin became increasingly obsessed with finding a place where he could do without money while still enjoying some of the comforts to which he had grown accustomed during his days as a successful stock agent. His goal, moreover, was always to return to Paris and sell his art. In a letter written to Mette before he left for Panama in the spring of 1887, he described how he would live there like a native, take his paints and his brushes to an almost uninhabited islet, and "rejuvenate myself far from the haunts of men." Plans for founding a studio in the tropics began to surface in letters of 1888 (*Letters*, no. 48, to Mette Gauguin, and no. 68, to Emile Bernard). Gauguin thus arrived at the Paris Expostion with a great urge to learn more about exotic cultures, their visual art, and their peoples, and to choose a country where he could seek a post sponsored by the French government. At the Colonial Exhibit he encountered Java, India, and Tonkin for the first time — in microcosm of course. In letters to Bernard, he expressed delight in the "Hindu" dances at the Javanese "village" and in the "Indian" sculpture shown both in original examples and in replica (ibid., no. 81). According to Charles Chassé, Gauguin picked up a fragment of a frieze that had fallen from a building of the Javanese Village and took it back with him to Le Pouldu in Brittany.[16] He was also captivated by the huts he saw in the colonial "villages"; in a letter discussing his studio in the tropics, he explained, "With the money I shall have I can buy a hut of the kind you saw at the Universal Exhibition. An affair of wood and clay, thatched, near the town but in the country. This would cost almost nothing." And he took full advantage of the presence of native women imported from the colonies, reporting to Bernard about his appointment with a mulatto girl (ibid., nos. 105 and 81).

At the time of his visits to the Universal Exposition, Gauguin had not yet developed a particular interest in Tahiti. He was fascinated by all the colonial lands and quite unfamiliar with them. The Commissioner of the Colonial Exhibit had designed his spectacle for precisely such a captive, uncritical audience; the villages erected on the Esplanade des Invalides represented countries most Europeans had never seen and — in the cases of Madagascar, Tonkin, and Annam — countries and states that France had acquired as recently as 1884 and 1885. Everything about the exhibit was designed to boost French pride in the exotic lands that formed the nation's growing overseas empire and to convert the French to the cause of national imperialism. At the African "villages" and pavilions, for example, one could walk through simulated African streets with thatched huts; natives transported to Paris for the duration of the Universal Exposition lived and worked in the market, the restaurants, and throughout the "village."[17]

The Colonial Exhibit also demonstrated the state's use of paternalism in treating members of the empire.[18] Far from being a collaborative venture or even a project directed by France in consultation with the colonies, the exhibit was run entirely by official commissioners of the French government. The fair's commissioners summoned native peoples to France, chose and designed the architectural forms and streets they deemed representative of the different countries, and confined the people to a special exhibit on the fairgrounds. This paternalism found subtler expression, moreover, in the idyll of social and racial harmony that emerged from the planners' arrangement of the various pavilions and "villages." Pavilions of Algeria, Tunisia, and Annam-Tonkin stood across from the "village" of Senegal, the factory of Gabon, Tahitian huts, and the pavilion of Guadalupe.[19] Pavilions of Indochina were located close by. French visitors strolled through these displays. Thus the French empire appeared as one glorious and peaceful family, with France at the helm. The fair's planners intended this image of an imperial community to impress the African, Arabic, Asian, and Oceanic natives in the Colonial Exhibit just as strongly as the French public. In his report on the Universal Exposition, E. Monod declared: "[The colonial peoples] will carry back a deep impression of the greatness of our country. . . . With the exposure of their minds to new ideas, the edifying role of France for the peoples has been defined."[20]

The message of white superiority over the colonized and the "primitive," so central to the Colonial Exhibit, reverberated throughout the Universal Exposition and influenced such impressionable visitors as Paul Gauguin. By devoting so many of the exhibits to France's latest achievements, the fair's sponsors encouraged visitors to celebrate the contrast between the curios, artifacts, and primitive arts of the Asians, Africans, and Native Americans and the technological advances of the whites. The History of Human Habitations Exhibit and a display at the Palace of the Liberal Arts on the evolution of man from primitive toolmaker to civilized technological expert took as their theme the progress of man the thinker.[21] In this way the Paris fair carried the assumption that the "high" civilizations, deemed so because of their industrial production, had a right to oversee colonialism and the expansion of world trade. In the eyes of the fair's commissioners, the advanced development of imperialist nations in every aspect of society and culture wholly justified their administration of colonized peoples, indeed, normalized it as part of the course of civilized life.

## II

Before the fair, Gauguin's dreams of founding a studio in the tropics had focused on Martinique (*Letters*, no. 68, to Emile Bernard). His visits to the Colonial Exhibit, however, introduced a host of new countries where he might reside under the auspices of an official post from the French colonial administration. The prospect of settling in one of the new French colonies must have seemed particularly exotic; after the fair, Gauguin's letters make no further mention of Martinique, and by early November 1889—the last month of the exhibition—he had already obtained a recommendation for a position in Tonkin, a protectorate in Indochina that France had acquired in 1883. Around this time, Gauguin's letters express increasing hostility toward Europe. He contrasts the East, where he "shall be rejuvenated," with the "corrupt" West. He presents himself as an outsider, uncomfortable with the aged, corrupt, Western civilization that spawned him and eager to "gain new strength in touching the soil of the East" (ibid., no. 106, to Bernard). Yet the paradox—as Gauguin would quickly learn—was that unmediated contact with the East was a mirage. As a Frenchman, he could not simply sail for the East. He could only reside in countries that were French colonies, and even then, the choice of country was entirely the decision of the colonial administration. Moreover, without France's vast colonial empire, Gauguin could never have considered taking up residence in an exotic Eastern land. Certainly, he had no qualms about benefiting from the colonial system directed by the country he found so corrupt. Indeed, the prospect of free or reduced rate of passage and part-time work was quite appealing.

The French government did not respond favorably to Gauguin's application to go to Tonkin, and when he went directly to the Colonial Department in Paris in February 1890, they turned him down. Encouraged by Odilon Redon, and especially by Redon's wife Ari, who came from the island of Réunion in the Indian Ocean and who had visited Madagascar several times from France, Gauguin now set his sights on Madagascar as the tropical island for his artists' studio.[22] He hoped to sell 38 paintings to the inventor Dr. Charlopin and to use the money from the sale to found his colony. He tried to persuade Emile Bernard to join him:

I have made up my mind to go to Madagascar. I intend to buy a little place in the country which I can enlarge myself, to plant and live simply. . . . It costs nothing to live for those prepared to live like the natives. One can easily obtain all one's food from hunting alone. So, if things can be arranged, I will go there and do what I say — live in freedom and practise art. . . . [All] my heart goes out to the man who is suffering, to the artist who cannot work at his art here in Europe. . . . [Come] and seek me out." (ibid., no. 102)

Gauguin assured his friend that women were, "so to speak, obligatory" in Madagascar; hence the artist would have both a native woman and a daily model at his disposal. He wrote of his plans to buy a hut in Madagascar just like the Malagasy thatched dwellings he had seen in the colonial "village" at the Paris fair. And he reported to Bernard quite authoritatively that, once they had set up their hut, with cows, poultry, and fruit, they would be able to live for nothing. "Where life is primitive," he wrote, "you can subsist upon the fruits of the earth gathered without toil" (ibid., no. 105).

What gave Gauguin the impression that natives of the French colonies lived without money and without toil? To some extent, he gleaned this view from the fair, which, if it showed natives carrying baskets, chiseling wood, making curios and artifacts, or quaintly tending their huts, did not display signs of hardship, poverty, or dwellings in disrepair. The image was deliberately utopian, since the fair's sponsors wished to attract potential traders and colonists. The fair's official handbooks strongly reinforced this idyllic image, painting scenes of a colonial paradise where life was simple and struggle unknown. Gauguin had access to these handbooks when Bernard, after showing no interest in Madagascar, suddenly proposed sailing to Tahiti instead.

To entice Gauguin, Bernard sent him the best-selling travel romance of a naval officer's love affair in Tahiti, Le Mariage de Loti, written by Pierre Loti and published in 1881. When Gauguin requested more objective information, Bernard forwarded an official handbook on the Society Islands published in 1889 by the Colonial Department for the exhibition. According to Bengt Danielsson, Bernard must also have sent his friend Les Colonies fran-

*çaises* by Louis Henrique et al. (1889), because this handbook contains descriptions that recur almost verbatim in Gauguin's letters of the time. Only one of the handbook's authors had actually traveled to Tahiti; the others wrote from their imagination. They described Tahitian life in the following terms: "The Tahitians have only to lift their hands in order to harvest the bread-fruits and wild bananas which form their staple food. Consequently, they have no need to work." And "while men and women on the opposite side of the globe toil to earn their living, . . . the lucky inhabitants of the remote South Sea paradise of Tahiti know life only at its brightest. For them, to live is to sing and love." The handbook also praised the "rather high level of culture" of the Tahitian race, "remarkable above all for its affability, gentleness, and hospitality. Theft and murder are in Tahiti almost unknown." [23]

Whether through these descriptions, the prose of Loti, or the recommendations of Ari Redon, Gauguin shifted his preference from Madagascar to Tahiti. His letters to his wife and to the artist J. F. Willumsen are steeped in language nearly identical to the official handbook's reports on the Society Islands. He dreams of the day when he "shall go fleeing to the woods of an island of Oceania, live there off ecstasy, quiet and art, surrounded by a new family, far from this European struggle for money." He yearns to be "free at last, with no money troubles, and able to love, to sing and to die." And he eulogizes the Tahitians who "sing; they never steal . . . they do not kill." [24] The official handbook's descriptions of Tahitian natives, and especially of the Tahitian woman — a "perfect model for a sculptor," with "open and composed" features that show "never a hint of worry or concern" — expressed a paternalism that was rampant at the exhibition. Gauguin felt the impact of such views and adopted them himself; he lavished praise on the women of Madagascar, for instance, for lacking the "calculation" of French women. [25]

Emile Bernard ultimately chose to stay in Paris rather than join Gauguin in founding his tropical studio. Not dissuaded from his plan, Gauguin wrote to the Minister of Public Education and Fine Arts on March 15, 1891 to request a government-sponsored artistic mission to Tahiti. On March 18 his request was endorsed by Georges Clemenceau, and by March 26 the Ministry notified him that it would grant funding for his mission to "study and ultimately paint the customs and landscapes of [Tahiti]". Two days later, the Director of Fine Arts requested that the Compagnie des Messageries Maritimes issue Gauguin a second-class ticket at a 30 percent discount from Marseilles to Noumea. Armed with a recommendation from the Director of Fine Arts to the Under-Secretary of State for the Colonies, Gauguin left Marseilles on April 1. [26] His colonial mission had begun.

## III

When Gauguin arrived in Tahiti, his head was full of the colonial sites he had visited at the Paris Exposition, the exotic accounts of the island in Louis Henrique's official handbook, and the Tahitian romance conjured by Pierre Loti. He may have dismissed Loti's prose as superficial and the novel as an unreliable source, but he read the book all the same, and it clearly had an influence on the particular Tahiti he began to sketch.[27] Loti's Tahiti, like the Tahiti of Henrique and his coauthors, was an island where one could wander without weapons, provisions, or money; where hospitality and cordiality greeted one everywhere. Loti's *vahine*, Rarahu, enjoyed an utterly idle existence, free of responsibilities and concerns save to dream, bathe, sing, and wander through the woods.[28]

Yet the Tahiti of Loti's novel also had sensual, ghostly, and corruptive elements that made it both more alluring and more ambiguous than Henrique's South Sea paradise. Polynesian mythology, for example, contained words signifying "spirits, bewitchment, malignancy, evil eye, secret foe, the smell of the dead." These fantastic beliefs were exotic in their mysteriousness and enticed Loti because they took him back to a dim Tahitian past. He came to see Tahiti as a paradise embedded in ancient mythology, where "primitive peoples" sat and dreamed like "tattooed ancients with the look of sphinxes." The spectacle of young Tahitian girls shouting "Toupapahou," the "uncanny name, terrifying and untranslatable," for one of the Tahitian spirits, titillated Loti with its mystery and its nightmarish edge.[29]

Much of Tahiti's charm for Loti lay in its tension between tropical beauty, calm, and languor and the decay caused by the intrusion of European civilization. As a typical late nineteenth-century paternalist, he wished to preserve Rarahu's "mysterious savagery," her difference, while at the same time encouraging a European demeanor. His remarks after glimpsing her a final time before departing for England reveal how provocative he found the effect of colonialism on the once-pure Tahitian native: "There was really exquisite and perfect distinction in her little savage physiognomy. Her face seemed to have gained the ultra-terrestrial charm of those doomed to die."[30]

*Le Mariage de Loti* weaves a romantic, colonialist tale of a naval officer's sojourn in Tahiti and his obsession with a "wild," "primitive" girl. It is also a fantasy of escape to an exotic land. In its fascination with myth and fantasy, with night spirits, with erotic and sensory stimulation, and with the unnatural taint of corruption, the novel shows a mind immersed in the sensibility of late nineteenth-century Parisian decadence. Decadence, the literary movement that reached its peak in 1884, with the publication of Joris-Karl Huysmans's novel *A rebours*, subverted Romantic associations of nature, virtue, and the primitive by cultivating their opposite: artificiality, vice, and human superiority over nature. The movement played a central role in late nineteenth-century French literary and artistic thought. Just as Gauguin read Loti's novel, so he perused Huysmans's book of art criticism, *Certains* (1889), and wrote articles assessing Gustave Moreau and Odilon Redon, both of whom Huysmans praised for fleeing to an imaginary past full of the "tumultuous spaces of nightmares and dreams."[31] The affinity between the enigmatic, disquieting imagery of Gauguin's later Brittany and Tahitian works and the visions of corruption, artifice, and the fallen woman that haunted Parisian decadents places Gauguin firmly within the fin-de-siècle climate of his time. Despite his claims to the contrary, Gauguin never left this European perspective behind.

One of the first statements on the decadent aesthetic in France appeared in the preface written by the French poet and critic Théophile Gautier for the 1868 edition of Baudelaire's *Les Fleurs du mal*. Gautier opened his preface by defining the "decadent style" embraced by Baudelaire as the "necessary and fatal idiom of peoples and civilizations where artificial life has replaced natural life." Decadent artists reveled in excess, in pushing every sensation to its extreme. They craved artifice and escape. Thus they discarded the light of the classical style for a world of shadows inhabited by superstitions, weary and insomniac phantoms, nocturnal terrors, monstrous dreams, fantasies, and "everything that the mind, at the bottom of its deepest and last cavern, contains of the gloomy, the deformed, and the vaguely horrible."[32]

Gautier described how, in addition to nightmarish visions, the taste for the artificial prompted Baudelaire's creation of wholly fabricated, man-made landscapes comprised of metal, marble, and water and shorn of vegetal and organic elements. Such eerie vistas, although invented by humans, bore no trace of nature or of men and women. Rather, Gautier observed, Baudelaire envisioned "a virgin and pure air, immaculate whiteness, snow on the Himalayas," a scene in which "everything is rigid, polished, glistening under a sky without sun, without moon and without stars."[33] Even more than Baudelaire, Gautier wished to escape modern civilization for the past. His nostalgia typified the sentiments of his fin-de-siècle generation, which imagined and savored the ancient as a storehouse for extreme sensory experiences, fantastic opulence, and primitive myth and ritual. The poet Jean Lorrain invoked this vision of ancient civilizations in a commentary on Gustave Moreau and his contemporaries: [34]

He infected a whole generation, sick today with a mystical nostalgia for the Beyond, with a dangerous passion for dead beauties, beauties of bygone ages which he resuscitated. . . . And that painful obsession with the symbols and perversions of the old theogonies, that curiosity about the divine debaucheries worshipped in the dead religions, has become the exquisite sickness of the refined souls of this *fin-de-siècle*.

Joris-Karl Huysmans shared the ambivalent attitude of Baudelaire and Gautier toward contemporary urban living. Count Des Esseintes, the jaded hero of Huysmans's *A Rebours*, is the only surviving member of an interbred, aristocratic family. As a young man, he mingled among the different strata of society, seeking compatriots in temperament and intellect. One by one, he dismisses the various groups. Disgusted by the banal, hypocritical, and materialistic values he encounters in each instance, and full of disdain for all humanity, he resolves to escape. He finds a retreat far enough from Paris that no one can reach him, but close enough to confirm his solitude by way of contrast. [35]

Once settled in his hermitage, Des Esseintes experiments with exotic and artificial methods to stimulate his senses and imagination and wrench himself from the boredom of modern existence. In the chapter on Gustave Moreau's 1876 *Salome Dancing Before Herod* (Fig. 3), for example, Huysmans describes how his hero selected paintings for his retreat:

Once he had cut himself off from contemporary life, he had resolved to allow nothing to enter his hermitage which might breed repugnance or regret, and so he had set his heart on finding a few pictures of subtle, exquisite refinement, steeped in an atmosphere of ancient fantasy, wrapped in an aura of antique corruption, divorced from modern times and modern society.

Seeking to pique his mind as well as his senses, Des Esseintes looks for evocative paintings that will "point the way to new possibilities, and shake up his nervous system by means of erudite fancies, complicated nightmares, suave and sinister visions." Moreau delights him more than any other painter and, after selecting two of the artist's works, Des Esseintes becomes riveted to the painting of Salome and stands dreaming before it night after night. Huysmans's poetic description creates a story around every detail of the painting, gleaning visions of tactile flesh, "heady odours," "overheated" temperatures, and gleaming, phosphorescent altars — each of which arouses a different sensation in the viewer. [36]

FIG. 3. Gustave Moreau, *Salome Dancing Before Herod*, oil on canvas, 56 1/2 × 41 1/16 inches. The Armand Hammer Collection, The Armand Hammer Museum of Art and Cultural Center, Los Angeles, California.

Huysmans's comments on Salome echo the decadent aesthetic of Baudelaire and Gautier. He describes Moreau's portrayal of phantoms and images from the world of nightmare: the sleepwalker, Salome; her mother, the "ferocious Herodias"; the "hermaphrodite or eunuch who stands sabre in hand at the foot of the throne, a terrifying creature . . . with its sexless dugs hanging like gourds under its orange-striped tunic." He attributes to Moreau an obsessive fascination with the ancient. Moreau goes back to the "beginnings of racial tradition, to the sources of mythologies," Huysmans argues, selecting legends from the Middle East and fusing them into one, as well as blending them with the beliefs of other peoples — Christians, Indians, Byzantines. All of Moreau's ingredients, moreover, are artificial. He intoxicates the senses by painting Romanesque columns "set with lapis lazuli and sardonyx," by giving Salome a "triumphal robe, sewn with pearls, patterned with silver, spangled with gold" and a "jewelled cuirass . . . ablaze with little snakes of fire." Moreau paints clouds of incense vapor and perfume. Gold beams of sunlight are the only natural light source that enters Herod's palace.[37]

Huysmans's decadent vision also enlarges slightly on Baudelaire's and Gautier's. He observes that the escapist aura of the Salome painting stems not only from Moreau's use of dark fantasy, ancient mythology, and artifice but from his intention to remain "outside the bounds of time." Moreau gives "no precise indication of race or country or period," Huysmans observes, "setting as he did his Salome inside this extraordinary palace with its grandiose, heterogeneous architecture, clothing her in sumptuous, fanciful robes." According to Huysmans's interpretation, then, Moreau's use of legend, nightmare, lust, timelessness, and artificial sources of light and smell elevates the mind and the senses to a heightened state of receptivity and excitement.

Along with Moreau's *Salome*, Des Esseintes loves the prints of Odilon Redon, which hang in a separate room of his hermitage amidst engravings by Dutch and Italian artists. Des Esseintes is both impressed and appalled by the frightening, often grotesque creatures in Redon's drawings. He describes a "horrible spider, with a human face lodged in the middle of its body," that seems to belong to the "horrors of a nightmare dream." He places Redon's "ape-like" human beings and faces with wild, insane eyes "outside of any known category; most of them leap beyond the boundaries of painting, innovating a very special fantasy, a fantasy of sickness and delirium." He argues that Redon's choice of imagery reflects a wish to escape to prehistoric times and places populated by ancestral figures; he has already noted Moreau's similar concern with the ancient. Redon's "mirages of hallucination and effects of terror" remind Des Esseintes of the stories of Edgar Allan Poe.[38]

The images of fantasy, nightmare, and artificiality articulated so brilliantly by Huysmans in his interpretations of Moreau and Redon came to define French decadence at its peak in the 1880's. Moreover, contemporaries of Huysmans, such as Octave Mirbeau and Camille Pissarro, analyzed Gauguin's paintings in terms astonishingly similar to those that Huysmans had applied to Moreau and Redon. In February 1891, urged by the critic Charles Morice, Mirbeau wrote an article as a kind of promotional piece to help with the auction of Gauguin's paintings from Martinique, Arles, and Brittany before his first trip to Tahiti. Speaking of Gauguin's recent work, Mirbeau evoked its mystery:

Sometimes it rises to the height of a mystical act of faith; sometimes it shrinks and grimaces in the frightening gloom of doubt. And always it emits the bitter and violent aroma of the poisons of the flesh. There is in his work a disquieting and savory mixture of barbaric splendor, of Catholic liturgy, of Hindu reverie, of Gothic imagery, of obscure and subtle symbolism.[39]

Pissarro's critique of Gauguin's Brittany painting, *The Vision after the Sermon* (1888), did not invoke the same values of carnality and excess but decried the "mystical," "authoritarian," "anti-social" philosophy of Gauguin's painting and called it a "step backward" rather than a modernist statement.[40]

The commentary of Mirbeau and Pissarro indicates that some of Gauguin's contemporaries viewed him within the context of French decadence. The coincidence between Mirbeau's references to disquieting mixtures of barbaric splendor and poisons of the flesh in Gauguin's paintings and the decadent sensibility articulated by Baudelaire, Gautier, Huysmans, and Loti affirms the presence in Gauguin's art of visual allusions to depravity and nightmare — not merely as elements naturalized in a "primitive" setting but as values of decadence. Five points of intersection are telling. First, both Gauguin and the decadents sought to escape and to isolate themselves from modern civilization, from the "prisons," as Gauguin termed European houses. Second, both explored the realm of fantasy and, specifically, the dark world of nightly terrors, phantoms, and superstitions. This absorption with spirits brought with it a yearning to make contact with the myths and legends of ancient civilizations, appealing for their exoticism, their origin in a distant past, and their mystery. Third, both defied the natural in favor of artifice, fabricating dreamlike landscapes with mysterious vegetation, fantastic, unearthly creatures, and ambiguous lighting. Fourth, both were simultaneously intrigued and repelled by the effects of modern European corruption. Loti and Gauguin deplored the evil effects of civilization but were also titillated by the image of a healthy native woman succumbing to the taint of colonial corruption; they and their decadent compatriots sought erotic stimulation from sullied flesh and from heightened sensory experiences. Finally, Gauguin shared some of Moreau's fascination with a host of references to different cultures and religions, and with scenes existing outside the bounds of time. No doubt, Gauguin located his "primitive" landscapes unambiguously in Martinique, Brittany, and Tahiti. Yet their timeless quality, and their allusion to Christian, Buddhist, and Maori images, may have served to promote the same escapism that characterized Moreau's *Salome*.

## IV

Decadent imagery began to emerge in Gauguin's visual art in 1889. The coincidence between these allusions to paradise, sin, and depravity and Gauguin's exposure to the Colonial Exhibit at the Paris fair suggests that the exhibition may have been a catalyst for his new interest in decadence. Certainly the displays from the French colonies were a staged artifice that put forth messages about the appeal of exotic peoples and their lands, about the possibility of escape to one of these lands, and about the curiosity of witnessing civilizations at a "primitive" or ancient stage of development. Gauguin's rendezvous with native women at the time of the fair, in addition to the obvious sensual pleasures they offered, introduced the provocative theme of the healthy primitive sullied by white European corruption.

In his first experiments with decadent imagery in 1889, Gauguin explored themes of paradise and paradise lost. The oil painting on wood, *Self-Portrait with Halo* (Fig. 4), for example, shows the artist in the dual role of Satan and fallen angel. The mane of black hair, the slanted eyebrows, and the exaggeratedly crooked nose all convey Gauguin's demonic powers, while the yellow halo represents his angelic persona. The painting is divided, moreover, between the fiery red of hell and the mass of yellow, with its stylized suggestion of angel's wings.[41] Gauguin toys somewhat humorously with his predicament as both tempter and tempted. The delicate serpent held between his mannequin-like fingers may be his deadly weapon or the evil to which he has succumbed. The fantastic, papyrus-shaped flowers and the green, red, and purple apples — representing various stages of ripeness for plucking — may be his satanic attributes or fruits of temptation looming and beckoning on either side of him.

*Self-Portrait with Halo* employs an abstract, highly symbolic visual language to introduce the decadent themes of corruption and evil. Gauguin implies sexual temptation through his juxtaposition of the serpent, the flowers, and the fruit nearly ready for plucking, but he shows us neither sullied flesh, nor evil spirits, nor feelings of shame and guilt. The painting is equivo-

FIG. 4. Paul Gauguin, *Self-Portrait with Halo*, 1889, oil on wood, 31 1/4 × 20 1/4 inches. Chester Dale Collection, National Gallery of Art, Washington, D.C.

cal, dreamlike, and possibly self-mocking. A wood panel that Gauguin created in the fall of 1889 and entitled *Soyez amoureuses vous serez heureuses* (Be in Love and You Will Be Happy; Fig. 5) continues to explore the artist's relationship to corruption but makes more direct reference to disquieting sexual images by including a host of different female figures, all of them "exotic." The head of Gauguin appears in the upper right, sucking his thumb and reaching with his other hand to take the hand of a fleshy, naked woman with African or Polynesian features, who pulls back in fear.[42] A fox, Gauguin's symbol of lewdness and male sexual power, gazes boldly out at the viewer as if guarding the scene of seduction. Gauguin places the fox on the panel's lower right, hence aligning and linking the creature with the artist's head above. Between the fox and Gauguin's large head appears another "ex-

FIG. 5. Paul Gauguin, *Soyez amoureuses vous serez heureuses* (Be in Love and You Will Be Happy), 1889, painted linden-wood, 37 1/2 × 28 1/2 inches. Courtesy, Museum of Fine Arts, Boston, Arthur Tracy Cabot Fund.

otic" woman who crouches and holds her face in despair. Branches of a tree with large full flowers sway around her, suggesting an atmosphere of heady perfume and sensuality. The suffering woman in this particular pose recurred many times in Gauguin's work as a symbol of female misery, desolation, and sin, and as a representation of Eve. Her sources are "exotic"; Gauguin based her fetal pose on the customary burial position of a Peruvian mummy, which he saw at the Musée d'Ethnologie de Trocadero in Paris and which appeared prominently in displays at the 1889 fair.[43] Surrounded here by the fox, the blossoms, and the huge head of Gauguin, the woman tries to protect herself from the lure and the taint of male sexuality.

The crouching woman's anguish, the fearful expression of the "savage" on her right, and the general mood of mystery and eeriness are compounded by the presence of six other women, all with African or Oceanic features and shown either as staring, disembodied heads in contorted positions, or with faces partially hidden.[44] As voyeurs of a brutal seduction scene, they intensify its illicit, evil aura. A phallic shape, which projects below the railing where Gauguin's hand and the large woman's elbow converge, continues the panel's imagery of dismembered body parts. It also poises the scene at the moment of sexual anticipation.

In *Soyez amoureuses vous serez heureuses* decadence and colonialism begin to converge where Gauguin imposes European feelings of guilt and temptation on dark-skinned women from Africa and Oceania, and where he inserts a component of evil voyeurism into the native's world. Gauguin's depiction, in a panel predating his Tahitian journey, of the female's fear of sin and her pliancy in the face of male sensuality and seduction indicates that he did not find these themes in African or Pacific lore. Rather, he took them from the Judaic and Christian writings of the Old Testament, specifically the Genesis story of the Fall of Adam and Eve and their Expulsion from the Garden of Eden, and ascribed them to a nonwhite culture. Gauguin's panel thus shows native women from a European vantage — namely, the perspective of original sin. Moreover, in order to accentuate Eve's guilt, as well as her ambivalent feelings of attraction to and fear of evil, Gauguin alters the Genesis story. Whereas in Genesis Eve is innocent until she submits to the serpent and tastes the apple, in Gauguin's panel Eve's state of anguish precedes and anticipates the Fall.[45] In this way, Gauguin turns the story of Eve into a decadent tale of temptation and corruption.

Three works that Gauguin produced in 1889, a few months before the Paris fair, indicate that he emphasized themes of guilt and moral ambivalence in the Eve story before he gave his crouching Eve the dark skin and exotic physical features that she displays in *Soyez amoureuses*. In April 1889, a month before the opening of the Paris Exposition, Gauguin painted two canvases of identical dimensions, which he may have conceived of as pendants. One was exhibited at the Café Volpini under the title *In the Waves*; the other Gauguin entitled *Life and Death*. In *Life and Death*, a white Eve in the Peruvian mummy pose sits against an ominous expanse of black that may be a tree trunk or the shadow of a tree. The serpent is gone. His evil influence is implied, however, in the bluish-grey quality of Eve's skin, which looks sickly and deathly, especially in contrast with the healthy pink tones of her female companion. In *In the Waves*, this female personification of life abandons herself to the green waves.

At the Café Volpini, Gauguin exhibited a pastel that bore the caption *Pas écouter li . . . li . . . menteur* (Don't Listen to the Liar; Fig. 6). In it he conflated white and nonwhite worlds. Eve is a white woman leaning against a tree from which the serpent emerges. She sits in the pose of the Peruvian

FIG. 6. Paul Gauguin, *Pas écouter li . . . li . . . menteur* (Don't Listen to the Liar), 1889, pastel and watercolor on paper. McNay Art Museum, San Antonio, Texas, bequest of Marion Koogler McNay.

mummy, a non-Western imposition and a possible intimation of her impending sin, expulsion, and symbolic death as a virgin. She is white, but the caption suggests that she speaks to herself in a fanciful French that Gauguin intended to evoke the speech of nonwhite cultures. In his review of the Café Volpini exhibition, the critic Jules Antoine asked of this pastel, "On what evidence does Gauguin base his assumption that Eve spoke negro?" — thus calling into question the inconsistency and, indeed, the utter fantasy of transforming the Old Testament Eve into an exotic "primitive." A letter from Gauguin to Emile Bernard contained his scornful retort: "What a silly article! . . . So Eve did not speak negro; but for heaven's sake what language did she speak with the serpent?"[46]

After the Paris fair, Gauguin introduced dark-skinned Eves, often with negroid features, into his work, and cast them in poses borrowed from Southeast Asia. The world he created looks more exotic, even though his use of the Eve story continued the colonial imposition of European themes and hence the colonial representation of nonwhite peoples from a Western perspective. Gauguin had seen photographs of the carved figures at the Javanese temple of Borobudur — probably in 1889, some time before the exhibition opened — and he studied the plaster casts from the Borobudur reliefs exhibited at the fair.[47] In addition, the "Hindu" dancers performing at the Javanese "village" intrigued him. In his glazed stoneware statuette representing an Eve figure (Fig. 7), his gouache entitled *Eve Exotique*, and his stoneware pot decorated with a bathing woman and trees (Fig. 8), Gauguin introduced gestures and standing poses clearly influenced by the Borobudur relief figures. Eve appears as an exotic Easterner. Moreover, the attention in each work to a beautiful, seductive Eve draped in black tresses and surrounded by images of fertility and sexuality — on the stoneware pot, for example, the tree sprouts a phallus — creates a duality that would increasingly characterize Gauguin's Tahitian Eves. She is the tempted woman who succumbs to corruption, but she also incarnates the femme fatale, the evil temptress.

In one of his early canvases of a Tahitian Eve, *Te nave nave fenua* (The Delightful Land; Fig. 9), Gauguin painted a lizard hovering threateningly next to Eve's ear. She is dark-skinned and stands in the pose of a Borobudur statue. According to the heroine in *Le Mariage de Loti*, missionaries in Tahiti described the serpent who tempted Eve as a "long lizard without feet," because serpents were unknown in Polynesia.[48] Gauguin's lizard may have been inspired by Loti's novel, but its scarlet red wings make it an utterly fantastic invention. The tall flowers that resemble peacock tail feathers are

FIG. 7. Paul Gauguin, *Eve*, 1890, ceramic, painted, 23 5/8 × 11 × 10 5/8 inches. National Gallery of Art, Washington, D.C., Ailsa Mellon Bruce Fund.

equally fantastic. A year after Gauguin completed this painting, two critics in Paris remarked on its visionary qualities. Achille Delaroche wrote: "a fictive orchard offers its insidious flora to the desire of an Eve from Eden whose arm extends timorously to pluck a flower of evil, while the beating red wings of the chimera whisper at her temples." Charles Morice, who probably conferred with Gauguin before writing his commentary, compared the flowers to "the dazzling eyes of peacock feathers, flowers of pride."[49]

Certainly, the flower bears a striking resemblance to the fantastic plant — part eyeball, part peacock feather — in Odilon Redon's lithograph from *Les Origines* (1883), subtitled *Il y eut peut-être une vision première es-*

FIG. 8. Paul Gauguin, *Pot Decorated with a Bathing Woman and Trees*, 1889–90, stoneware, 5 1/4 inches high. Musée d'Orsay, Paris.

*sayée dans la fleur* (Fig. 10).[50] The flower also resembles the peacock feather appearing as the final plate in Redon's lithograph album *Les Fleurs du mal* (1890; Fig. 11). At the turn of the century, the peacock was an important symbol of artificial beauty, indolent luxury, and eroticism. In Oscar Wilde's *Salome* (1891–92), for example, Herod offers Salome fifty white peacocks in the hope of quenching the lust that has goaded her to demand the head of John the Baptist.

The affinity between Gauguin's flowers and peacock feathers thus casts a perverse, erotic aura over *Te nave nave fenua*. Gauguin reinforces this mood by juxtaposing the flowers with the mysterious red-winged lizard above. Both are sources of temptation and corruption for Eve. Both make contact with her flesh. Redon may again have influenced Gauguin, this time in the choice and placement of the winged creature: in a lithograph from Redon's album *Tentation de Saint-Antoine* (1888), a large, dark, menacing bird hovers directly above a woman's head, poised to land (Fig. 12). The lithograph's title describes the bird "hurling itself" onto the woman's hair. Gauguin substitutes a flying lizard and uses a very similar compositional format, placing the lizard to one side of Eve's head.[51]

F I G . 9 . Paul Gauguin, *Te nave nave fenua* (The Delightful Land), 1892, oil on coarse canvas, 35 1/2 × 28 inches. Ohara Museum of Art, Kurashiki, Japan.

The flower-eyes and the winged creatures of Redon and Gauguin are symbols of doom and fatality. Yet Redon leaves the identity of the bird and the cause of doom mysterious, whereas the implications of corruption in Gauguin's scene are unmistakable. His huge fleshy Eve, her breasts and pubic hair boldly confronting the viewer, finds the lizard's words enticing even as she averts her eyes and backs away. She reaches to pluck the flower. The tinge of red in her black hair and the reddish flower behind her left ear suggest that the winged monster's scarlet color has already tainted her. She has absorbed his black and red colors, just as black and red have infiltrated the bark of the tree on her right, the mound she stands on, and the ground beneath her. Her heavy nudity, her sensuality, and her indolence accentuate the impression that she has yielded to temptation and sin. Gauguin does not saturate his painting with images of corruption; his use of blacks and reds — rather than sickly flesh — to express defilement is abstracted. The

FIG. 10. Odilon Redon, *Il y eut peut-être une vision première essayée dans la fleur*, from his album *Les Origines* (1883), lithograph.

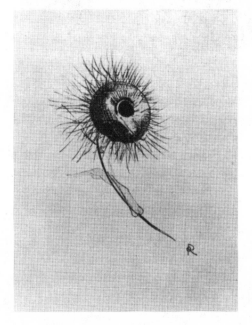

FIG. 11. Odilon Redon, *Cul-de-lampe*, from his album *Les Fleurs du mal* (Paris, 1890), lithograph.

FIG. 12. Odilon Redon, *Et un grand oiseau qui descend du ciel vient s'abattre sur le sommet de sa chevelure . . .* , from his album *Tentation de Saint-Antoine* (première série, 1888), lithograph, 1888. Reprinted courtesy of the Stickney Collection, 1920, no. 1635. Photograph © 1993, the Art Institute of Chicago. All rights reserved.

painting's decadent, erotic edge emerges in the provocative tension between Eve's hesitation and her attraction to evil, between pure, naked flesh and defilement, and in the contrast and even contradiction between the lush, vibrantly colored, tropical vegetation and the onset of depravity.

In *Te nave nave fenua*, the ghoulish lizard, with its disproportionately huge wings and tiny body, and the inflections of red in Eve's hair add to the scene's frightening quality. By painting such a huge Eve, Gauguin effects a strange contrast between her very real presence and the miniaturized, dreamlike quality of the surrounding vegetation. Eve is a victim of the lizard's corruption, but she also dwarfs her tempter as a sensual and potent temptress in her own right.

In the 1892 canvas *Parau na te varua ino* (Words of the Devil), eyes and the act of watching become a central theme (Fig. 13). Here eyes acquire their special power not in the context of the Redonian flower or peacock feather, but in the face of an evil spirit and in a death mask. The painting depicts a self-conscious Eve haunted from behind by the fixed stares of a kneeling evil spirit and a mysterious, red-and-green death mask suspended above a tree branch. Richard Field and Jehanne Teilhet-Fisk have interpreted this painting as Gauguin's representation of the intrusion of "civilized" Western concepts on "natural Tahitians." Both scholars imply that Gauguin adopted a strong moral position, condemning the evil West in favor of virtuous Polynesia. Yet in positing this neat opposition between West and East, such arguments overlook the nature of modern cultural identities, which are relational rather than authentic. They assume that Gauguin was able to step outside the West and attack it from an essential Tahitian perspective. In fact, the colonial enterprise made it increasingly difficult to maintain such an outside position. Gauguin could not become a Tahitian, any more than Tahitians could discard the Christian beliefs and the missionary dress that had entered their culture. Many elements of *Parau na te varua ino* — the smile flickering on Eve's face, the enigmatic death mask, the utterly dreamlike and artificial landscape — express this cultural intersection, suggesting that the painting documents not only Tahitian fears and superstitions but Western views as well.

For example, in his treatment of the Tahitian Eve, Gauguin expresses a typically decadent interest in the world of depravity. The moment he shows us is the sequel to *Te nave nave fenua*. It is the awakening of shame after plucking the flower, when the no longer innocent Eve covers herself for the first time. Yet in contrast to Eve's separation and mark of the sinner in traditional Western depictions, Gauguin's painting integrates Eve into the setting with the spirits, positioning her head on a diagonal between the red-and-green death mask on the upper right and the evil spirit seated below. Her black hair also merges with the greens and blacks of the background vegetation. Moreover, Gauguin's Eve does not bawl or hide her face in shame. She modestly covers her sexual parts but allows a hint of a smile to play on her lips and in her eyes. Although she has been seduced, she bears the alluring gaze of the temptress rather than the ashamed expression of the sinner. The phallic tree trunk behind her enhances the mood of sexual desire, as do the

FIG. 13. Paul Gauguin, *Parau na te varua ino* (Words of the Devil), 1892, oil on coarse canvas, 36 1/8 × 27 inches. © 1993, National Gallery of Art, Washington, D.C., gift of the W. Averell Harriman Foundation in memory of Marie N. Harriman.

activities of watching and voyeurism in the painting: Eve's eyes strain to look behind her, while the death mask and evil spirit straddle her with their all-seeing eyes. Eyes in *Parau na te varua ino* serve in part to express themes of lust, sexual fantasy, and titillation.

They also contribute to the painting's darker and equally decadent expression of nightmare. Here Gauguin's treatment recalls a similar kind of eye imagery in the works of Redon. In the charcoal drawing *Eyes in the Forest* (1885), for example, Redon displays large, disembodied eyes gazing out from an aura of white light amidst the dark sky and tree trunks of the forest (Fig. 14). The same device of open, disembodied eyes staring out beyond the scene of the painting operates in Gauguin's death mask. Like Redon, moreover, Gauguin strengthens the nightmarish and fantastic element by juxta-

FIG. 14. Odilon Redon, *Eyes in the Forest*, 1885, charcoal drawing on pale brown paper, 13 1/4 × 10 3/4 inches. The Saint Louis Art Museum, gift of Mr. and Mrs. Morton D. May.

posing the death mask, bearing animate, humanlike eyes, with the inanimate curve of a tree branch. In a charcoal entitled *Marsh Flower* (ca. 1885), Redon drew a pale angular face with eyes closed, growing like a flower from the branch of a tree. Gauguin may have absorbed this strange contrast between animate and inanimate, human and vegetable, in *Parau na te varua ino*. He may also have been intrigued by another aspect of eye symbolism that applies to Redon's drawings. According to Philippe Jullian, Redon's eyes were a means of entering into a different world.[52]

Two elements link *Parau na te varua ino* with Gauguin's earlier wood panel, *Soyez amoureuses vous serez heureuses* (see Fig. 4). First, the hand and thumb barely visible beneath the red-and-green death mask recall Gauguin's self-portrait sucking his thumb, which appears in the upper right portion of the wood panel. Gauguin even frames both with a compositional division: the diagonal branch in the panel and the tree branch in the painting. The similarity between the images suggests some new meanings for the death mask in *Parau na te varua ino*: Gauguin as voyeur, as seducer of Eve, and as Western colonizer and seducer of Tahitian natives. His dramatic and some-what comical choice of the death mask to disguise these roles conveys his fascination — neither approving nor condemning — with the impact of Western values on Oceania. From the wood panel he also brings back his staring fox, the Indian symbol of perversity, which appears in the form of the evil spirit sitting in a similar frontal position.[53]

Gauguin's preoccupation in *Parau na te varua ino* with evil spirits and with his own evil suggests that a fear of his decadent, European side may have impelled him to "Edenic" climes, only to find that he couldn't escape his identity. The Tahitian paintings show this confrontation between a decadent European and a tropical island by contrasting images of death, perversity, and corruption with the lush Tahitian vegetation.

Moreover, the landscape in *Parau na te varua ino* looks vibrant but also forbidding. Its artificiality recalls Gautier's description of the ideal scenery painted in Baudelaire's *Rêve parisien*, in which everything is rigid, polished, and glistening under a sky without sun, moon, or stars. The source of light in the painting is uncertain. It could be the moon, or the dreamlike white floral sprays and the purplish sand. Is this a nighttime scene, or has Gauguin merely plunged his Eve and spirits into a dark portion of the forest? What is the relationship between the forest vegetation and the purplish foreground, which some critics have identified as sand?[54] The ambiguity and unreality of the setting enhance the painting's expression of fantasy, superstition, and escape.

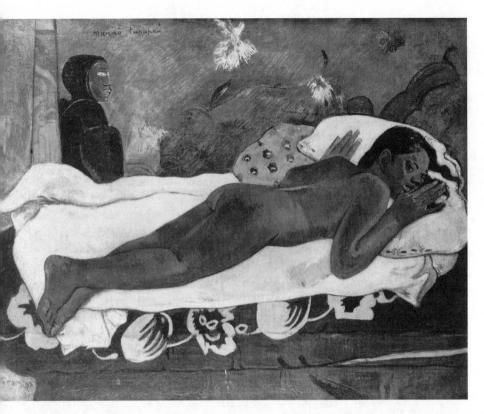

FIG. 15. Paul Gauguin, *Manao tupapau* (Spirit of the Dead Watching), 1892, oil on burlap mounted on canvas, 28 1/2 × 36 3/8 inches. Albright-Knox Art Gallery, Buffalo, New York, A. Conger Goodyear Collection, 1965.

*Manao tupapau* (Spirit of the Dead Watching), painted in 1892, is equally enigmatic and suggestive (Fig. 15). An anecdote in his Tahitian journal *Noa Noa* (1893) describes the incident that inspired it. Gauguin writes that he returned late one night to his hut in Papeete to discover his Tahitian mistress Tehura lying terrified on the bed, possibly mistaking Gauguin for "one of those legendary demons or specters, the *tupapaus*."[55] In *Manao tupapau*, Gauguin contrasts this sinister world of phantoms and apparitions that bring corruption with native nudity, purity, and health. He uses eye imagery and themes of watching, expressed in the painting's title, to elicit a sensation of terror and infuse it with a sexual, voyeuristic component. The tupapau, dark-skinned and cloaked in black, leans against a bedpost which is decorated as a totem with large, blue, staring eyes. Gauguin opposes the frontal eye of the *tupapau*'s profile head with another frontal eye seen in a faintly outlined

259

head to the right. The eye of this mysterious head aligns itself with the spirit's hand. Is the *tupapau* about to pluck this eye, just as the lizard beckons Eve to pluck the peacock-tail flower-eye in *Te nave nave fenua*? Gauguin may be linking the act of plucking eyes and flowers with the spirit's act of watching Tehura, and hence with the end of purity and virginity.[56] The unearthly purple, blue, and black hues of the backdrop, the inflection of these hues in the white bedsheets, and the evil *tupapau's* mysterious role express, metaphorically, the native girl's encounter with corruption. The eye of the *tupapau* and those of the enigmatic head, set amidst floral sprays and an oval leaf resembling an eye, may also be metaphorical eyes of escape that will abduct Tehura to another world. Gauguin's association of eyes with flowers recalls Redon.

In *Manao tupapau*, Gauguin's interest in the terror of his young Tahitian mistress when she beholds the *tupapau* recalls Pierre Loti's ecstatic descriptions in *Le Mariage de Loti* of Tahitian superstition and of the "uncanny" name of *tupapau*, which young Tahitian girls shout when they glimpse the spirit during their night-bathing. The emphasis in Gauguin's painting on the frightening implications of the *tupapau's* presence — the spirit's evil powers, its voyeurism, and its defilement of "primitive" girls — suggests that, like Loti, Gauguin found the bewitchment and the death apparitions in Polynesian mythology mysterious and sexually stimulating. They introduced a realm of nightmare that aroused the imagination and the senses by celebrating vice and perversity. Gauguin's interest in the *tupapau* also resonates with Moreau's interest, according to Huysmans, in returning to the sources of mythologies. Ancient myth, with its mysteries and its "primitive" rituals, offered a marvelous escape from the torpid and numbing predicament of modern living.

*Tahitian Pastorals* (1892) likewise invokes the religious rituals and beliefs of ancient cultures (Fig. 16). The painting is one in a series of three containing figures in white in a visionary, tropical setting. The other two paintings show a statue to the Tahitian moon-goddess Hina in the background. Charles Stucky surmises that Gauguin conceived of the series as an imaginary representation of the pre-European civilization in the South Seas, with islanders worshiping the moon and playing musical instruments. Although the statue of Hina does not appear in *Tahitian Pastorals*, this painting is possibly also a nocturnal scene illuminated by a full moon.[57] The title *Once Upon a Time*, which Gauguin inscribed on one of the other paintings in the series, underscores that absorption with fantasy, legend, and the origins of civilizations that aligns Gauguin with his decadent contemporaries.

F I G . 1 6. Paul Gauguin, *Tahitian Pastorals*, 1892, oil on canvas, 34 1/8 × 44 1/2 inches. State Hermitage Museum, St. Petersburg.

When the three paintings were first shown at the Paris Exhibition in 1893, the critic Achille Delaroche wrote a review that Gauguin apparently liked. Here Delaroche referred to the mysterious orange-red dog in each painting as a heraldic genie of evil. Certainly the dog recalls the fox in such earlier works as the 1889 woodcut *Soyez amoureuses vous serez heureuses* (Fig. 5) and the 1890 painting *The Loss of Virginity* (Fig. 1). For Gauguin, the fox had explicit connotations of lewdness. Yet even without associations of sexual depravity, the dog in *Tahitian Pastorals* imparts a disturbing mood. The standing girl looks toward the dog, who sniffs and looks away. Both appear to respond to something happening outside of the painting. Their responses create an impression of evil portents, all the more uneasy because Gauguin leaves so few clues. In choosing to represent an ancient, pastoral scene of moon worship, he is less interested in portraying bucolic paradise than in the juxtapositions of innocence and imminent evil, of the vibrant display of tropical colors, white dresses, and pink blossoms versus the darkness of corruption.

*Ta matete* (Market Day; Fig. 17), also created in 1892, looks utterly differ-

FIG. 17. Paul Gauguin, *Ta matete* (Market Day), 1892, oil on canvas, 28 3/4 ×
36 1/8 inches. Oeffentliche Kunstsammlung Basel, Kunstmuseum, gift of Dr. h. c.
Robert von Hirsch, 1941.

ent from a decadent painting such as Moreau's *Salome Dancing Before
Herod* (Fig. 3). Gauguin chooses an outdoor tropical setting, broad areas of
bright color, and wide sweeps of colored forms rather than Moreau's tiny,
glittering details and two-dimensional space. Yet *Ta matete* contains a syncre-
tism similar to the mixture of different cultures that so impressed Huysmans
in Moreau's *Salome*: the palace resembling a "basilica built in both the Mos-
lem and the Byzantine styles"; the countless arches of the ceiling "springing
from thick-set, almost Romanesque columns"; the Tetrarch Herod "frozen
like some Hindu god." Similarly, in *Ta matete* Gauguin models his figures
on an Eighteenth Dynasty Egyptian tomb painting reproduced in one of
the photos he owned in Tahiti. Tahitian natives in the painting thus assume the stylized, profile position of figures in an Egyptian frieze. Gauguin
clothes his Tahitians not in Egyptian dress but in decorative Christian-
missionary garb, and introduces a Tahitian woman on the far right wearing
a native floral dress (*pareu*). This free mixture of allusions to Tahitian, Egyp-

tian, and Christian cultures produces an effect of fantasy and temporal displacement similar to Moreau's in *Salome*.

## V

The fantasy pervading *Ta matete* and, indeed, all of Gauguin's decadent scenes also plays an important role in his views of Tahiti, which show natives, usually female, lounging, holding fruit, or musing. In their careful rendering of skin tone, body type, facial features, hair, and native dress, these paintings seem to give the Tahitians a tactile, physically palpable presence. Yet the context in which we find the women and the motivation for their activity or inactivity are not explained. Titles such as *Vahine no te miti* (Woman at the Sea; Fig. 18) or *Aha oe feii?* (What! Are You Jealous?; Fig. 19) reveal nothing

FIG. 18. Paul Gauguin, *Vahine no te miti* (Woman at the Sea), 1892, oil on coarse canvas, 36 1/4 × 29 inches. Museo Nacional de Bellas Artes, Buenos Aires.

FIG. 19. Paul Gauguin, *Aha oe feii?* (What! Are You Jealous?), 1892, oil on coarse canvas, 26 1/2 × 35 7/8 inches. Pushkin State Museum of Fine Arts, Moscow.

about their subjects' identity, nor does Gauguin introduce facial expressions, postures, or styles of clothing that would individualize the Tahitian and make the painting a character study or portrait of a particular social class. Rather, he stages the women in poses of his choice, isolates them, and exposes them for our scrutiny. The mystery surrounding their identities, their relationships to one another, and their activities adds to the dreamlike, decadent quality of the scene.

Critics take their interpretive lead from references to marriage and jealousy in the paintings' titles and speak of many of these works as genre scenes.[58] I would argue, on the contrary, that Gauguin has devised a mode of representation that eludes the conventional categories of portrait, narrative, or genre painting. The impetus may well have come from his experience at the Paris Exhibition, with its staged spectacle of imported natives in re-created Arabic, Javanese, or African "villages."

Gauguin's visual art continues the fair's colonial perspective by imposing postures familiar from nineteenth-century European painting on dark-skinned Tahitian women for whom such poses are quite alien. In *Vahine no te miti*, for example, his rendering of a Tahitian nude from the back imitates

Degas's representations of nudes turned away from the spectator, with faces hidden from view. For Degas, such a mode of representation has a clear purpose. He shows women in the attitudes they typically adopt when absorbed in bathing, washing, drying, combing their hair. Wash basins, water pitchers, and drying cloths function as tools in these activities. In *Vahine no te miti*, however, the woman's position prevents the viewer from seeing why she raises her arms or what she might be doing. Her stance does not indicate absorption in a particular bathing activity, and the flowers on her left serve not as props but as decorative forms. Moreover, Gauguin's isolation and compression of his monumental nude within a constricted space deprive the figure of the context that Degas offers, recalling instead the confined stage on which natives were paraded at the fair's Colonial Exhibit. His is not a genre scene, but what kind of painting is it? In its close study of the female torso and its choice of a pose in which the nude sits with her back to the viewer, head turned slightly and curve of the buttocks barely visible, the painting draws on Ingres's famous oil, *The Bather of Valpinçon* (1808). Thus Gauguin chooses a pose that clearly originates in nineteenth-century French painting, and in so doing he translates Tahitian beauty into European terms. Only the dark hair, dark skin, and floral *pareu* draped on the woman's knee identify her as a Tahitian.

Charles Stucky is the only critic who has remarked on the unusual composition of this and many of Gauguin's Tahitian paintings. The bather dwarfs her spatial setting, which Gauguin treats almost as an afterthought. Such a figure might have appeared as a detail in a more populated nineteenth-century painting, but Gauguin's isolation and monumentalization of her arbitrary activity has no precedent.[59] Although Stucky does not speculate about the reasons for this unusual compositional treatment, it seems quite likely that Gauguin's cropping of the Tahitian bather in a close-up view reinforces his intention to create, in lieu of a portrait or genre scene, a dreamy colonial spectacle, an exposition of Tahitian nudity to be examined and admired by Europeans.

The painting *Aha oe feii?* shows two women who may be bathers reclining on pink sand next to the water (see Fig. 19). The strip of sand and the flat, decorative patterns of water and leaves contrast with the heavy, palpable presence of the nudes, who thrust outward like sculptures or figures in a relief. Gauguin based the pose of the seated figure on a photograph that he owned of the frieze from the Theater of Dionysus in Athens; European prototypes again become the filter through which he views Tahitians.[60] Although the nudes may be bathers, the painting's principal focus is not the acts of washing and drying but a timeless scene of indolence and repose. Imbued with the descriptions of Tahitian life that he had read in 1889 colonial handbooks, Gauguin painted a dreamlike scene of natives freed from the responsibility of work. Yet the utter stillness of the figures and their lack of interaction inflects the painting with a drugged stupor that is eerie rather than tranquil. Moreover, the claustrophobic space confines the figures like caged creatures on view. Is Gauguin condoning the paternalistic, colonial treatment of these women as appropriated objects, or is he critical of this view? Certainly, the smooth, highly tactile flesh of each nude figure encourages the kind of physical scrutiny prompted by *Vahine no te miti* (Fig. 18), *Tahitian Women* (Fig. 2), and a host of Gauguin's other colonial Tahitian scenes.

This physical appeal is offset, however, by the seated figure's dark, melancholy expression and by the passive, heavy languor and listless inactivity of both nudes. A people living in their sensuous and savage past have run up against the intrusion of European civilization. They find themselves trapped in this space. Without taking a stand, Gauguin explores the titillating, decadent image of a "primitive" race on the brink of decay. The natives look fleshy and robust, but they have already been corrupted. The words of Pierre Loti come to mind: "Strange is the fate of these Polynesian races, the forgotten leavings of a primitive people; there they remain, living in immobility and contemplation, gently dying out under the touch of civilized nations."[61] Indeed, *Aha oe feii?* expresses an ambivalence toward the effects of European corruption — both a fascination and a distaste — that resonates with the sensibility of Loti and Gauguin's other decadent contemporaries. The painting also becomes an enigmatic commentary — neither approving nor condemning — on the nature of colonial spectacle at the Paris fair.

*Aha oe feii?* bypasses the nineteenth-century categories of portrait and genre. Gauguin introduces no idiosyncratic facial expressions, postures, or props to reveal the character or identity of the individual Tahitian and hence produce a portrait. Rather, the women are conceived of as types, as composites of the young Tahitian beauty with physical traits meticulously rendered. The anonymity of this painting — and of *Tahitian Women, Nafea faaipoipo* (When Will You Marry?, 1892), and Gauguin's other Tahitian scenes — extends to social class. Unlike such works of Jean-François Millet as *Man with a Hoe* (1860–62; Fig. 20) and *The Sower* (ca. 1849–50), which portray the quintessential French peasant at work in his or her barren landscape, Gauguin shows no interest in variations of clothing, distinctions in age, or special qualities of the landscape that tell the viewer something of the sub-

FIG. 20. Jean-François Millet, *Man with a Hoe*, 1860–62, oil on canvas, 31 1/2 × 39 inches. Collection of the J. Paul Getty Museum, Malibu, California.

ject's social class and circumstances. Nor does he present his figures engaged in activity—whether domestic work, childcare, physical labor, or socializing—in the manner of a genre painting. Instead, he conflates European poses with dark-skinned natives whose age, physical features, and passivity remain constant from painting to painting.

*Te faaturuma* (The Brooding Woman; Fig. 21), painted in 1891, brings the melancholy bather indoors, where she sits musing in a colonial-style hut. Gauguin clothes her, scatters a few objects on the floor, and places her in a more expansive space than that occupied by the figures in *Aho oe feii?* In this way, he shifts attention from a close physical scrutiny, recalling the paternalistic examination of natives at the fair, to a consideration of why she sits there and what the various props, the dog or fox on the verandah, and the man outside on horseback might mean. Yet nothing in the painting provides any clue about the woman's identity or the motivation for her weary, brooding

FIG. 21. Paul Gauguin, *Te faaturuma* (The Brooding Woman), 1891, oil on fine-weave canvas, 35 1/2 × 26 1/2 inches. Worcester Art Museum, Worcester, Massachusetts.

stance. Gauguin's clear disregard for conventional portraiture is apparent from his sketchy treatment of facial features; the woman's eyes and eyebrows are merely undulating lines. How, then, do we interpret *Te faaturuma*? Like *Aha oe feii?*, it is a painting in which decadence and colonialism converge. Gauguin combines the colonial perspective of the anonymous portrait with a decadent's interest in images of temptation and sullied purity. The woman gazes in the direction of two pieces of fruit, possibly apples, and a bowl holding a burning cigar. The phallic cigar lies on a diagonal with the woman's head and the mysterious black fox on the verandah. By juxtaposing the cigar with the ripening fruit and by linking both with the woman and the fox, Gauguin suggests the lurking presence of corruption. The heavy-bodied Tahitian woman dressed in white has yielded to the fruit's temptation. The cigar, a symbol of the French presence in Tahiti, evokes lewdness and male sexuality; colonial corruption has invaded the Tahitian woman's world.

## VI

Gauguin saw and painted the South Sea island of Tahiti through the filters of French decadence and colonialism. His position between cultures typifies the twentieth-century cultural predicament, analyzed by James Clifford, of "offcenteredness in a world of distinct meaning systems, a state of being in culture while looking at culture."[62]

Gauguin's artistic persona defines itself neither in his rejection of the West and immersion in Tahitian superstition, nor in his European perspective. It exists, rather, in the intersection between the two, in the distinctive overlay of European themes and values on a distant culture increasingly entangled in the colonialist enterprise. Moreover, his complex fusion of decadence and colonialism with the tropical Tahitian setting is symptomatic of our twentieth-century condition, in which there are no lost authenticities, no essences to redeem. "Identity, considered ethnographically, must always be mixed, relational, and inventive," writes Clifford.[63] Gauguin could not abandon an essential European culture, any more than he could embrace an authentic Tahitian one. Claims that he did so overlook the startling cultural tensions and differences expressed in his visual art. Such differences are critical not only to Gauguin's "primitivism" but to the modernist "primitivism" of the Fauves, Expressionists, and Cubists that followed.

# Modernism's African Mask
## *The Stein-Picasso Collaboration*

### I

"The modern movement in art gets its inspiration undoubtedly from African art, and it could not be otherwise." Such, at any rate, was the opinion of Paul Guillaume, who may not have been entirely disinterested, since it was his business to sell African art to European collectors. According to Guillaume, the effect of African art on European modernism was no less than that of classical art on the Renaissance.[1] Though current scholarly opinion is a good deal cooler on the subject, it still acknowledges the force of European fascination with African masks and statues.[2] Even so, there is significant disagreement about the nature and effect of that fascination. Was it primarily ethnographic, fixated on the culture that could be rather luridly imagined behind a single African artifact, or was it aesthetic, with the artifact seen as a new arrangement of shapes in space? Was it part of an escapist daydream or a radical disruption of European representational conventions?

One way of beginning to answer these questions is to examine the role of Africa in one of the most celebrated relationships in European modernism: Pablo Picasso and Gertrude Stein. Their meeting took place at a crucial moment both for them and for the arts they practiced, Stein just beginning to write under the influence of post-Impressionism, Picasso on the verge of disrupting his canvases with actual words. This crossing of old boundaries had a lot to do with the beginnings of modernism, but it was accompanied by another, rather different crossing as Stein and Picasso simultaneously discovered African art. Though the first of these "transgressions" seems aesthetic and the second ethnographic, it may be that their relationship is more than coincidental.

Both Stein and Picasso came to resent the myth that modernism began on the day Matisse showed them an African figurine he had found in a second-hand shop.[3] Late in life, Picasso strenuously denied that he had been crucially influenced by African art, and Stein said of herself in *The Autobi-ography of Alice B. Toklas*: "She was not at any time interested in African sculpture."[4] And yet the original frontispiece of this very work shows Stein ensconced behind her writing desk, awaiting Alice, with a piece of African sculpture prominently displayed before her (Fig. 1). This is perhaps one of a group of objects Stein purchased for Picasso at Nîmes in 1918,[5] an act that is emblematic, despite the disclaimers, of their collaborative use of African models in inventing modernism.

One of the most important episodes in the birth of that movement oc-curred shortly before Matisse brought his find to Stein's studio. In the winter of 1906, Picasso ended a long struggle with his portrait of Stein by painting out a likeness he had labored over for as many as 92 sittings. Over this gen-erally realistic portrait, he imposed a flat, expressionless mask with two eye slits cut against the angle of the rest of the face and body, a mask derived from ancient Iberian reliefs he had seen at the Louvre. This portrait (Fig. 2) was the first in a series of paintings, all featuring rock-solid figures with im-passive faces, that culminated in the masked women of *Les Demoiselles d'Avignon* (1907), some of whom have faces much like the mask Picasso fash-ioned for Stein, and others of whom wear masks inspired by his visit to the Musée d'Ethnographie at the Palais du Trocadéro. In its finished state, there-fore, *Les Demoiselles* is a virtual map of Picasso's progress from 1905 to 1907, from the Stein portrait, through Africa, to the first intimations of "what two years later would become Cubism."[6]

Even while sitting for Picasso, Stein was composing the work she would herself call, with a disarming lack of modesty, "the first definite step away from the nineteenth century and into the twentieth century in literature."[7] Stein took this step in a way remarkably like that of Picasso, for she composed this crucial work by covering a failed self-portrait with an ethnic mask. Having struggled unsuccessfully to account for an unhappy love affair in *Q.E.D.*, a book that remained unpublished until after her death, Stein re-wrote the work, sometimes leaving whole lines of dialogue nearly intact, as "Melanctha," the story of a young black woman's emotional trials.[8]

Thus, Stein and Picasso take the first steps into Cubism and literary mod-ernism by performing uncannily similar transformations on the figure of Gertrude Stein herself. Placing a painted mask over his naturalistic portrait, Picasso duplicates the linguistic mask Stein was simultaneously devising for herself. By rewriting her own story for black characters, Stein anticipates, and perhaps even motivates, Picasso's use of African masks in *Les Demoiselles d'Avignon*. In each case, in painting and in literature, the step away from conventional verisimilitude into abstraction is accomplished by a figurative change of race.

Of course, Picasso's immediate models are not the same as Stein's, but the fact that Stein drew her inspiration not from Africa but from black Baltimoreans she encountered as a medical student would not have mattered

FIG. 1. Man Ray, "Gertrude Stein and Alice B. Toklas" (ca. 1922). Frontispiece, *The Autobiography of Alice B. Toklas* (1933). © 1993 ARS, New York / ADAGP / Man Ray Trust, Paris.

FIG. 2. Pablo Picasso, *Portrait of Gertrude Stein* (1906). The Metropolitan Museum of Art, Bequest of Gertrude Stein, 1946. © ARS, New York / SPADEM, Paris.

much at the time.[9] "Melanctha" was composed in a time of growing pan-Africanism, from the international pan-African conference in London in 1900, which W. E. B. Du Bois attended as American representative, to the collapse of Marcus Garvey's movement in the early 1920's.[10] Stylized African masks drawn by the American Aaron Douglas figure prominently in the decorative artwork of *The New Negro* (1925), the inaugural anthology of the Harlem Renaissance, and similar masks were at one time commissioned for Carl Van Vechten's controversial success, *Nigger Heaven* (1926).[11] In that work itself, the main character, who fitted Van Vechten's image of an up-to-date young black woman, collects African sculpture and quotes a long stretch of "Melanctha" from memory.[12]

For Van Vechten, apparently, the difference between sculpture and literature was no more important than that between Africa and America. In fact, it was common in the early years of the century for critics as different as I. A.

Richards and Zora Neale Hurston to draw a line of comparison from African art to African-American language and literature without bothering over-much about differences between the arts.[13] Thus the other difference be-tween Picasso and Stein, that his masks were visual while hers were verbal, might not have mattered much either. But, in fact, it is just this crossing of ordinary aesthetic boundaries, this jump from the visual to the verbal and back again, that the African mask makes possible — not, of course, by eliding the actual processes of representation, but by highlighting them. This is one reason why the African mask can stand as a sign of the aesthetic collaboration of Picasso and Stein.

From the very beginning, however, this mask has inspired quite different, even contradictory, reactions among Europeans and Euro-Americans. One sort of response to Picasso's version of Africa is felt by William Rubin, who finds in Les Demoiselles d'Avignon "something ominous and monstrous such as Conrad's Kurtz discovered in the heart of darkness."[14] To sum up his own very similar reaction, Leo Steinberg applies to the painting a phrase bor-rowed from Nietzsche: "wild naked nature with the bold face of truth."[15] So insistent are these metaphors of exposure and discovery, nakedness and wild-ness, that it is almost impossible to recall that the figures so described are wearing masks. What Steinberg calls "the bold face of truth" is in fact an African mask, clapped violently over the face of Picasso's prostitute. Yet there is no real contradiction here because in Steinberg's account the mask is the bold face of truth, revealing inner depths that flesh ordinarily conceals. The mask is not really a cultural artifact, worn for purposes of concealment or adornment, but a psychological revelation exposing what usually lies behind the face.

On the other hand, André Salmon saw Les Demoiselles as "almost entirely freed from humanity . . . white signs on a blackboard."[16] The same metaphor is used by D. H. Kahnweiler, Picasso's early dealer, who insisted that African art had revealed the true nature of all art, "which is that of handwriting."[17] Quite independently, it seems, Stein decided that African art had made Pi-casso's painting "calligraphic."[18] In this interpretation, the African mask is convention embodied, the sign of signs. As such, it inaugurates Western ab-straction by exposing the conventional nature of all art. Yet it is at least strange that a continent widely perceived in Europe as analphabetic and illiterate should have helped transform European art into calligraphy. At a time when colonized Africans were systematically denied instruction in the European languages, how could African art teach European art how to write?[19]

These are just a few of the contradictions in the feelings of Europeans about the African art they began to incorporate into their own in 1907. African art is portrayed as both abstract and naturalistic, highly conventional and thrillingly crude, opaque and yet more naked than any merely unadorned face. Such contradictions have survived even the most recent developments in cultural criticism. After placing Picasso's primitivism in the context of colonialist controversies of 1905–6, Patricia Leighten concludes that Picasso was a kind of "shaman" whose painting expressed the "anxiety that civilization had done its work too well, made us too tame, and thus cut us off from sources of magic, fear, and dread."[20] In Leighten's account, Picasso's paintings seem to have no formal properties at all, just resonance within a context, but for Yve-Alain Bois, the same paintings are formalist exercises par excellence, made so by their exposure to an African art that is morphologically provocative because it is so arbitrary.[21] It is no accident that Bois's article is entitled "Kahnweiler's Lesson," because it repeats the analysis in which the African mask is a collection of arbitrary signs, a semiotic exercise curiously unconnected to the people who must have made it, just as Leighten repeats that part of Steinberg and Rubin's work that breathes heavily over revelations of "the heart of darkness."

Similar inconsistencies occur in interpretations of Stein's story of African-American life in a fictionalized Baltimore. Stein herself said, in a 1909 notebook, "I believe in reality as Cezanne or Caliban believe in it."[22] Is she claiming that Cézanne introduces us to a reality as basic as that lived by Caliban, or that Caliban has as unsettling an effect on our notions of reality as Cézanne? "Melanctha" seems to be the first representation of this paradoxical reality, presided over as it was by Cézanne, Stein's first aesthetic model, and by Caliban, the freakishly distorted stereotype who mixes "strong black curses" with "the wide abandoned laughter that gives the broad glow to negro sunshine."[23] But how are critics to understand this mixture of aesthetic experimentation and racist crudity? Very rarely have they been up to the implications of Stein's statement that Cézanne and Caliban see the same reality. It is far easier to concentrate on aesthetics, as critics of *Three Lives* have for so long, or to demolish the racism of "Melanctha," as is now becoming more common.[24]

These are the difficulties critics face when they attempt to understand the role of Caliban in the art that follows Cézanne. On the one hand, how could the works of a people supposedly so close to primal realities, so "authentic," in a word, awaken a jaded European intelligentsia to the arbitrariness of its own semiotic system? On the other hand, how could an art so morphologically arbitrary, so semiotically vertiginous, beat jungle drums in the hearts of European art critics? And what sort of movement was it that, if the critics are to be believed, appropriated African models to make its own art both more immediate and more consciously artificial? Like many masks, the African mask that Stein and Picasso drew across the face of European art reveals a good deal about what it is supposed to conceal. It reveals, of course, the deeply contradictory response of Europe to the cultures it was colonizing as the first modernists were born. It also reveals the mixed motives behind the rebellion of early modernism against that dominating European culture. Like the culture they challenged, Stein and Picasso found African art to be both elemental and intriguingly artificial: modernism is, at least in part, what they made of this contradiction.

## II

From the very first, contradictions existed in the reactions of Europeans to the cultures they discovered in Africa and America. Columbus first found the people he called Indians to be remarkably generous and peaceable, "the best people in the world"; only later did he decide that these same people were wicked and deceitful.[25] Three hundred years later, European invaders of the deepest Amazon remarked that the people they found there were "unreliable, betraying under different circumstances, and often apparently under the same, . . . all the opposite traits of character."[26] What these explorers discovered in the Amazon was, of course, their own preconceptions oscillating mysteriously before their very eyes. Europeans like Columbus were charmed at first by how easy it was to fit the aboriginal inhabitants of the strange continent into European molds; as this fit became less and less satisfactory, charm gave way to disquiet and unease, the people who had seemed comfortingly familiar becoming odd and unaccountable. Hundreds of years later, European notions of the other continents still waver between these linked opposites of identity and difference, since the first impulse of assimilation seems to have no more moderate an alternative than utter, blank incomprehension.

For Sara Suleri, one important version of this dichotomy is "the great contradiction of the excessive literalism or the excessive metaphoricity of the racial body." The colonial subject is either a part of nature, utterly literal and therefore soothingly simple, or menacingly unreadable, mysterious, and suggestive of some vast unknown. In the latter case, the signs of the colonized culture appear for the moment *as* signs — hieroglyphs, handwriting, calligraphy, whatever — because they can't be read except as signifying the European's own fascination with the unreadable.[27] European reactions to other cultures tend to oscillate between these two poles, and thus the same culture can seem simple, authentic, concrete, or, in contrast, odd, uncanny, and arbitrary.[28]

These incompatible but strongly linked alternatives persist even in the reaction of the avant-garde against Eurocentrism. The avant-garde certainly used Africa to make its rebellion seem a return to nature. Sometimes this involved pretending to *be* African. After his interest in African art became well known, Picasso enjoyed spreading the rumor that he was himself of African descent.[29] Stein had toyed with such notions from the time of her undergraduate days at Radcliffe. The "dark-skinned" alter ego named Hortense Sänger who appears in one of the themes she wrote there lives a life that is strangely mirrored in the racial genre pieces Stein wrote just before and just after: on the one hand, Hortense's frustrated sensuality is echoed in the "sensuous sunshine" filled with "the voices of negroes singing"; on the other hand, her melancholy is shared by a "melancholy looking porter" who is abused because he is black.[30] Stein retained this superficial sense of identification later in life, when she was wont to sprinkle her letters with Joel Chandler Harris–style dialect: "The cakes did arrive and dey was damn good, so says us and the Matthewses and little Roger who got a piece."[31] Though there is very little of this sort of dialect in "Melanctha," its publisher did boast that "the reader himself, for the time, is a coloured person too."[32] Apparently, racial role-playing appealed as much to the common reader, who is assumed to be white and male, as it did to Stein and Picasso.

Nonetheless, this kind of racial mask functioned for Stein and Picasso as a sign of expatriation. Rubin speculates that Picasso's adoption of African motifs completed a necessary estrangement from Barcelona. Though "Picasso's father was not around to be shocked when the young painter's primitivism culminated in *Les Demoiselles d'Avignon*," the painting violated all the bourgeois artistic conventions inherited from the father, a professor at the Fine Arts Academy, breaking a hold that was for Picasso both aesthetic and familial.[33] Stein's father was also safely dead by the time *Les Demoiselles* was painted, but the picture freed her from a far more thorough domination by disgusting her brother Leo. The "Negroid things" were a dead end, he felt, and thus began the split that would leave his sister with all the Picassos they had jointly collected.[34] Thus *Les Demoiselles* became the occasion for a break that had to come sooner or later were Stein to continue with the avant-garde writing that exasperated her brother as much as Picasso's painting did.

For Stein and Picasso, identification with Africa replaced identification with countries and families whose traditions seemed stifling. The affectation of racial difference represents the radical difference Stein and Picasso felt between themselves and those to whom they had been born. Thus Picasso told Malraux that the African sculptures he saw at the Trocadéro were "against everything" and that they supported him in his feeling that "I too am against everything. . . . Everything is an enemy! Everything!" Yet these fearsome and violent figures also became protective, totemic, for those bound together by their opposition to everyone else. Just because they stood with him against a hostile world, the African pieces were "*intercesseurs*, mediators" for Picasso.[35] Thus they also protected those whom they isolated. In this way, African figures became the totem of the European avant-garde, that tiny tribe unified by its shared opposition to the rest of European society. It is no accident, then, that the earliest propaganda for aesthetic modernism often represented its practitioners as racially alien to Europe, as "The Wild Men of Paris" or "the heirs of the witch doctor and the voodoo."[36]

The role of racial alien was a very flexible one for this branch of the European expatriate avant-garde. Insofar as its expatriation was willed, in revolt against the social constraints and falsehoods of Europe and America, this role completed the process of exile. As Nathan Huggins says of certain white devotees of the Harlem Renaissance: "They defected, became apostates; they became Negroes."[37] Insofar as exile is simply an extreme version of the "transcendental homelessness" of all modern citizens, an unwelcome and even tragic condition, the black role promises another home, very much like the one intellectuals have searched for ever since the German Romantics.[38] The avant-garde rejects European society and thus enjoys the freedom of living outside the law, while simultaneously savoring a connection to something more authentic found in Africa.

## III

And yet, a mask of authenticity seems a contradiction in terms. The very transformation by which a deracinated European bourgeois becomes a vital African tribalist must appear in its own right as a duality, a tension between what is and what might be. Modernism sometimes seemed to base itself on such tensions. In 1907, the year of *Les Demoiselles*, Ezra Pound wrote a poem called "Masks," as W. B. Yeats did a year or two later.[39] These poems are versions of what would become one of the recurrent motifs of modernism, a movement obsessed with personae, metamorphoses, doubles, mythic parallels. This obsession with what Robert Langbaum once called the "mysteries of identity" was especially strong, for obvious reasons, among the expatriates who formed such a large proportion of the early generation of modernists. To feel oneself in two places at once, at home and abroad, is almost to feel as two persons and thus to acquire a skepticism about the possibility of ever having an identity, if that means being just one thing. Seen in this light, a mask is the embodiment of the variability and indeterminacy of human identity.[40]

This might be considered a quality of all masks, which are, as A. David Napier maintains, "devices for analyzing the relationship between illusion on one hand and the recognition and integrity of a human face on the other."[41] But the African mask is a particular case of rare power for Europeans, because it is for them only partly distinguishable from the African face. The hero of Conrad's *The Nigger of the "Narcissus"* is described as having "a head powerful and misshapen, with a tormented and flattened face — a face pathetic and brutal; the tragic, the mysterious, the repulsive mask of a nigger's soul."[42] For a writer like Conrad, an African face *is* a mask because there is something essentially mysterious about it, something paradoxical and ambiguous. It is at once brutally repulsive, far too real, and mysteriously elusive, abstract and distant. It is no accident that the name of this character appears in the ship's log and thus in the novel as an indecipherable blot, an unreadable sign, because the character himself is an unreadable sign.

The African mask that appears in Picasso's works is, like this one, much more than a metaphor for some primitive authenticity. The figure at the far left of *Les Demoiselles*, for example, wears a mask that has been variously identified as Iberian, African, and Oceanic (Fig. 3). If, however, one were to lift this mask, an act made possible by the survival of Picasso's studies for the painting, one would see under it another mask much like the one Picasso used to finish the Stein portrait. The evidence suggests that Picasso painted over this first mask at about the same time he repainted the two figures on the far right, sometime after his famous trip to the ethnographic collections at the Trocadéro.[43] Even beneath this layer, however, there is yet another, this time male, for the figure began its life in Picasso's studies for the painting as a male medical student who was apparently hesitating on the edge of dissipation. In fact, the figure apparently represented Picasso himself until he

FIG. 3. Pablo Picasso, *Les Demoiselles d'Avignon* (1907). Oil on canvas, 8' × 7'8". The Museum of Modern Art, New York, acquired through the Lillie P. Bliss Bequest. © ARS New York / SPADEM, Paris.

changed its sex and gave it a mask (Fig. 4).[44] Steinberg says of this mask that it "protects a secret history," by which he means that the "sex change" the figure undergoes is obscured. And yet it may be that the mask expresses Picasso's secret as succinctly as possible, that a mask is in itself expressive of the way that "conventional sexual character traits seem reversed."[45]

The mask worn by Stein in her portrait apparently expressed certain complex feelings raised in Picasso by her unconventional sexuality. As John Richardson puts it, Stein appeared to Picasso as an "hommesse," at once "more feminine and more masculine than the adolescent waifs of 1905."[46] The mask she wears is a sign of this sexual ambiguity, the impersonal immobility of it associated in Picasso's work of the time with a physical bulk and power not at all conventionally feminine. Between the Stein portrait and *Les Demoiselles*, there stands a whole line of solid, sometimes openly phallic, women, often in intimate pairs, their masklike faces expressive only of this sexual indeterminacy. Picasso shares in this indeterminacy himself by using the same mask to change the sex of his alter ego, creating an ambiguity that remains visible in *Les Demoiselles* in the hesitation of the masked figure on the threshold of the brothel. This figure, raising a curtain on the edge of the painting, is both inside and outside the brothel, both male and female, customer and commodity.

Though the "secret history" behind the mask is no longer fully apparent to the audience, a good deal of the power of *Les Demoiselles* resides in the way it challenges, both physically and figuratively, conventional notions of female passivity. Much of this challenge comes from the primal savagery of the masks, which seem weirdly alive, contorted as if in the act of moving. Something even more radical happens as the masks communicate their ge-

FIG. 4. Pablo Picasso, study for *Les Demoiselles d'Avignon* (1907). © ARS, New York / SPADEM, Paris.

ometry to the unclothed bodies of the prostitutes, which can seem no less composed, no less artificial, than the masks themselves. The difference between mask and nakedness is removed by the geometric angularity of the composition, so the body comes to seem as arbitrary, as constructed, as the painted mask. And once the bodies become twisted geometric forms, even their nakedness is not enough to reveal their gender. As Brigitte Leal says in her edition of Picasso's sketchbook for *Les Demoiselles*, once the figures "undergo this primitive stylization," there is nothing but hairstyle to distinguish the women from their male customers: "Like them, they have that aura of sorrowful dignity — with their impassive faces and absent gaze — which Gertrude Stein so admired."[47] Perhaps Stein admired this masklike stillness precisely because of the sexual ambiguity it brought to the painting, making gender a matter of convention, of art, rather than a biological necessity. The tension in the painting between mask and nakedness seems to break down the difference between surface and depth and to make gender a matter of role-playing rather than of essence. Thus the body is no longer a natural and inescapable datum, and gender is no longer a given, but rather something much more like clothes — or a mask.

Stein created a version of this mask for herself in "Melanctha." Just as Picasso had performed a sex change on one of his own alter egos to produce *Les Demoiselles*, so Stein, in rewriting *Q.E.D.*, transformed Adele, her mouthpiece, into Dr. Jeff Campbell. On the one hand, this change provides a convenient mask for the sexual feelings that disorder *Q.E.D.*, since it changes the lesbian relationships of that book into heterosexual ones. On the other hand, the revisionary masquerade sets up an uncanny oscillation, especially in that all of Adele's most conventional fears and prejudices have been transferred to Dr. Jeff, as if Stein chose to represent the more retrograde parts of her own psyche as male. Certainly, much of the shock value of "Melanctha" comes from the blithe reversal by which the woman "wanders" while the man fidgets at home.

One of the most objectionable aspects of "Melanctha" is certainly its fixation on the sexual lives of its subjects, as if African-American characters are to be understood primarily in sensual terms. Yet the shift of race seemed to make it easier for Stein to see the senses, even the body itself, as ruled by convention. Perhaps Stein, like her publishers, invites her predominantly white readership to identify with the characters and thus play a black role, and yet presenting race *as* a role seems an open invitation to consider it as culturally constituted — and perhaps to consider gender as a role as well. The residual ambiguity created by the racial masquerade makes gender and, finally, the body itself seem a mask. Once again, then, the mask is not a cover for an unconventional sexuality but a revelation of it, even a means of achieving it. Like other forms of masquerade, particularly cross-dressing, the racial mask highlights what Kaja Silverman calls "the dislocation between subjectivity and the role."[48] The ambiguous relationship between mask and face, costume and body, makes it impossible to see biology as destiny.

Like the Arab robes of T. E. Lawrence or the Indian regalia of E. M. Forster, the racial masks that Stein and Picasso give to their own sexual ambiguity have a complex motivation and effect. On the one hand, there is, no doubt in each case, a longing for a certain kind of sensual freedom, found in Africa or Arabia or India because such freedom is always found "elsewhere," just as the natural is always found "elsewhere."[49] On the other hand, the mask maintains a tension between nature and convention, essence and accident, that expresses, even if it does not explain, the very process of displacement that simultaneously links and separates the two halves of each pair. The virtue of works like *Les Demoiselles* and "Melanctha" is that they bring out into the open the dialectical relationship between the mask as raw nature and the mask as cultural convention, and thus approximate the power of the African mask in its own context.

According to Henry Louis Gates, Jr., the African mask is a dialectical synthesis of all sorts of discordant qualities: "Mask is the essence of immobility fused with the essence of mobility, fixity with transience, order with chaos, permanence with the transitory, the substantial with the evanescent."[50] Picasso seems to have sensed similar possibilities in the African art he found in Paris, since he spoke of that art as both *raisonnable* (that is to say, formally ordered) and *magicaux* (uncanny, mysterious, occult).[51] Stein also spoke of African art as "natural, direct and civilised," as if to defy the usual contrast between the natural and the civilized.[52] These modernists were attracted to African art because it seemed to promise direct access to nature, but also because it broke down the whole dichotomy between nature and culture.

Thus the mask that Picasso gives first to Stein is both ancient and impersonal, while also somehow being a perfectly individual likeness, "the only reproduction of me which is always I, for me," as Stein put it.[53] A representation that is so obviously a "reproduction" can hardly be a perfect likeness as well, but Stein's insistence that the portrait *is* her is more than merely playful. What the portrait most faithfully represents is the tension, the slippage, between mask and face, between impersonality and individuality, between conventional representation and likeness that it was Stein's program in life and art to explore. Picasso's mask presents this program by only indirectly representing Stein's face.

In other words, the duality of the mask forces a confrontation between representation by likeness and representation by convention or habit. Kahnweiler once said that "in certain Ivory Coast masks, the Cubist painters discovered marks which, without recourse to imitation, compelled the spectator to imagine the face whose 'real' shape these masks did not imitate."[54] This is how the mask erases the distinction between writing and painting so as to make the latter "calligraphic," by confronting the viewer both with marks that imitate because they seem real and with marks that imitate because they allow us to imagine the real. By questioning the presumed difference between these two kinds of marks, which is the difference between conventional and natural signification, the mask becomes what Walter Benjamin called a "dialectical image."[55] It is in this sense that the mask is the most characteristic sign of the collaboration of Stein and Picasso, because it was the means by which their different arts could unsettle each other and, by eliding their own differences, make a modernism that would transform both.

## IV

According to Adam Gopnick, the mask that Picasso painted over the Stein portrait became, in its mixture of styles and forms, "a kind of creole." The beginnings of modernism are thus compared to what happens when two different dialect groups exchange vocabularies.[56] The same comparison between mask and dialect is frequently made from the other direction. For example, Gates has used the African mask as a metaphor for certain American linguistic and literary tactics. According to Gates, the literary version of the mask is dialect, which he calls "a verbal mask."

Yet the "self-conscious switch of linguistic codes" that Gates identifies as one of the primary strategies of dialect-speakers is a mask that does more than just cover or obscure.[57] Under this definition, dialect is not a particular kind of language, not a mere deviation or deformation, but a particular use of language. It puts the standard language in conflict with itself, "constructing a continuum of variation," to quote Gilles Deleuze and Félix Guattari, "negotiating all of the variables both to constrict the constants and to expand the variables."[58] Social linguists such as Shirley Brice Heath have discovered the same thing in the course of empirical studies: different social and ethnic groups use language for different purposes, call on it for different reasons, and only a very few of these have to do with correctness of expression.[59] Dialect is most like "a verbal mask" when it plays against such correctness, because then it approximates the mask's uncanny power to focus the natural and the arbitrary in a single spot. Instead of merely setting up a screen behind which nonstandard speakers might plot or smirk, dialect actively contrasts what poses as natural to its own conventions. It is this play between dialect and the standard language that resembles the tension the mask creates between the face and its facsimile.

It is in this sense that Stein creates a mask of dialect in "Melanctha." The language in this work has been called "photographically exact."[60] Though this may seem a bit extreme, the first publishers of the story did send a representative to Stein's studio to determine whether she was in fact an educated native speaker, the language apparently coming a bit too close to crude reality for perfect comfort.[61] But when Stein wanted to write in dialect, as she did rather frequently in her letters, she used the same phonological and syntactical conventions that white American writers had been using for decades: "We is doin business too."[62] There is very little of this sort of dialect in "Melanctha" itself.[63] What Stein does instead is to create a dialect in which conventions of verbal verisimilitude are played against themselves so that the speech seems simultaneously concrete and highly artificial.

The first readers of "Melanctha" were promised photographic realism because it was inconceivable at the time that writing about black people could have any other purpose than ethnographic representation. Stein seems to feed this appetite for the real and the concrete by trapping her characters within a round of numbing repetition. Repetition itself signifies the exigency of the real. In his study of colloquial language in American literature, Richard Bridgman observes that "In the dialogue of uninstructed characters, iteration is understood to result from their inability or superstitious unwillingness to substitute synonyms, pronouns or verbal auxiliaries for the concrete terms of their discussion. This steady, relentless hewing to a line of particulars suggests then that material reality is all that is trusted, all that can be depended upon to convey meaning."[64] Stein seems to make the same point by choosing a particular class of words for repeated repetition, words like "real," "regular," and "certainly." Particularly in the speech of Jeff Campbell, reliance on these words suggests a desire to stabilize reality by fastening language to it ineluctably.

Yet, as Kenneth Burke observes, "The most clear-sounding of words can be used for the vaguest of reference, quite as we speak of 'a certain thing' when we have no particular thing in mind." Burke points out that when we say that something is "essentially" true we often mean that it isn't true at all.[65] In the same way, when we protest that something is "really" true, our emphasis suggests that there is some reason for doubt. Stein wedges an entire argument into the minute space between the adjective and its adverbial qualification. What does it mean, for example, that Rose Johnson is "married really" to her husband (*Three Lives*, p. 88)? Why is it necessary for her to assure her friends that she is not married "falsely"? There are even more possibilities in the negative case, as, for example, when the narrator assures us that, for all her wandering, Melanctha never did anything "really wrong" (ibid., p. 96).

In such cases, it seems that the very effort to nail language to a single, unequivocal reality defeats itself, as if the very act of invoking the real over and over again actually multiplies it. "It was all so nearly alike it must be different and it is different," as Stein says elsewhere.[66] Repetition of simple, basic words often has this effect in Stein, as, for example, when Melanctha accuses Jeff Campbell: "You want to have a good time just like all us others, and then you just keep on saying that it's right to be good" (p. 118). To have "a good time" is obviously the very opposite of being "good," as becomes clear at the end of the story, when Rose Johnson observes that Melanctha "never come to no good" because she insisted on her right "to have a good time" (p. 235). If "good" can mean both bad and good, then it seems that very little is stable in the system of language or in the morality it supports.

By taking the real and the good and transforming them into terms of qualification, Stein raises a general suspicion about the way language attaches attributes to things. Several times in the course of this story, Stein calls Jane Harden "a roughened woman" (pp. 104, 107). Thus it would seem that her name is an appropriate one, designating some essential hardness in her nature. Yet she is called "roughened," not "rough," and if what Stein says elsewhere is true and "people can be made by their names,"[67] then perhaps Jane was roughed up by her own name. Perhaps her "roughness" is merely an impression that others have about her. Or perhaps it designates her ability to "harden" others. But when Jeff Campbell accuses Melanctha of having "hard" ways like Jane, he exclaims, "I can't believe you mean them hardly" (p. 138), so that "hardly" means both hardly and hardly at all.

Thus the paradox on which Stein constructs the peculiar dialect of "Melanctha." A patois with a very restricted vocabulary and a repetitious, looping sentence structure, it seems on the surface to correspond to Bridgman's description of a kind of speech that sticks almost superstitiously to the known and familiar. And yet, the more Stein's speakers reiterate the few simple words allotted to them, the more unstable those words become. Even in the act of assuring their hearers that they can speak the truth, speakers like Jeff Campbell convict themselves of lying: "It's easy enough for me always to be honest, Miss Melanctha. All I got to do is always just to say right out what I am thinking. I certainly never have got any real reason for not saying it right out like that to anybody" (p. 128).[68] The more he uses "certainly," "real," and "right" as magical intensifiers, the more one begins to doubt what he is saying. In fact Jeff has just admitted, in the same paragraph, "I just can't say that right out that way to you."

So much of the drama of "Melanctha" is about what characters say, instead of what they do, that this conflict between the sayable and the unsayable comes to dominate the story. It is Jeff's destructive habit of using words to pull intimate emotions to the surface that threatens and finally destroys his relationship with Melanctha. "You always wanting to have it all clear out in words always, what everybody is always feeling," Melanctha complains. "I certainly don't see a reason, why I should always be explaining to you what I mean by what I am just saying" (p. 171). The phraseology here clarifies the conflict between the characters. Jeff demands words that justly represent habitual feelings, words that commit the speaker. For Melanctha, however, words are something that she is "just saying." If Jeff maintains that it is easy "just to say" what he is thinking, Melanctha counters that whatever she is "just saying" need not represent her innermost thoughts.

This sexual conflict might also be seen as an interracial difference of the kind Heath documents in her study of language acquisition. The white families Heath describes emphasize saying "the right thing." One way that parents school their children in this discipline is by rejecting "children's descriptions of things by their attributes before they have learned to respond with the *name* of the item."[69] This clears away the inessential (the attribute) and emphasizes the single essential designation (the name). But, as Stein says, "the reason that slang exists is to change the nouns which have been names for so long."[70] The dialect Stein puts in the mouths of her black speakers does correspond to the black speech Heath describes in her study, in that it multiplies attributes and uses them, moreover, to undermine the solidity of the name.

Long before Stein came to it, the conflict between dialect and the rigidity of the standard language was fought across lines of race and gender. Dialect that could trace itself back to Anglo-Saxon was always referred to as "manly."[71] Its concrete reliability corresponded to a sacred myth of sturdy yeomanry. In contrast, the languages of foreigners and the dialects spoken by blacks were seen as effeminate. The Italian language itself, according to G. P. Marsh, was "inconsistent with being bold and manly and generous and truthful."[72] And it was no accident that the influence of slave speech was so often perceived as coming through the domestic household, through the idle women who prattled thoughtlessly with their servants.[73]

In "Melanctha," however, the male and female use the same words: only tiny differences of arrangement separate what Jeff wants so badly "just to say" from what Melanctha is "just saying." How can the difference between truth and falsehood, concrete reality and fantasy, male and female hinge on such minute differences? By making her dialect both direct and indirect, distinct and very slippery, Stein also undermines the associated differences of race and gender. The masks worn by her characters, which transform Stein herself into Dr. Jeff, correspond to these verbal masks. Like the dislocations of Picasso's finished canvas, which preserve in altered form the secret history of race and sex change, Stein's verbal dislocations represent, in the final text, the indeterminacy that made her hover between male and female, white and black.

## V

Zora Neale Hurston, among many others, lists, as one of the "characteristics of negro expression," a "will to adorn," to embellish, to bring an angularity and asymmetry to language that she traces to African sculpture. But Hurston also tells her readers that the terms of "negro expression" are all "close fitting."[74] How can there be a close fit between word and thing and, at the same time, room for angularity and asymmetry? Gates says more explicitly what Hurston seems to be suggesting, that what truly distinguishes "negro expression" is the ability to play back and forth between the close-fitting and the loosely approximate. According to Gates, the "masking function of dialect" is its "self-conscious switch of linguistic codes from white to black or, more properly, from standard English to the black vernacular."[75] At the most general level, such switching moves back and forth between signs that seem to be motivated and signs that advertize and even revel in their conventional nature. Though Stein includes in "Melanctha" very little that could be recognized as actual black dialect, her whole linguistic strategy is to produce this tension between two quite different kinds of language.[76]

Perhaps it was something like this that Richard Wright meant when he said of "Melanctha" that "Miss Stein's struggling words made the speech of the people around me vivid."[77] Critics have always had a hard time accepting this testimony because the speech in "Melanctha" is so clearly inauthentic and because Wright's work seems so little like Stein's, despite the extravagance of his praise for her. But perhaps Wright valued the way Stein's "struggling words" struggled against one another, producing the tension that Gates identifies as the "masking function of dialect." If so, then the step that Stein had taken in 1905 by assuming an African mask had opened the way to a far more radical twentieth century than even she had imagined.

In Picasso's case, it becomes clear that the African mask is an aesthetic element, like the stenciled numerals or the squares of real newsprint that Rosalind Krauss credits with bringing into modern art its most fundamental representational tension.[78] But this is not because of the purely formal properties of the mask, and surely not because the arrangements of African masks are, as Bois suggests, somehow more "arbitrary" than European forms. The mask can become a radically disturbing image because of the ethnographic generalizations attached to it, because these contain contradictions so acute and because these contradictions match so closely other contradictions of gender, nationality, and genre that modernism made it its business to explore. Modernism could not escape the contradictions of European colonialism; indeed, it was only because it pushed these to extremes that it could exist as a movement at all.

# PART V

# Culture and Displacements

ROBERT DAWIDOFF

# The Kind of Person You Have to Sound Like to Sing "Alexander's Ragtime Band"

In 1910, Irving Berlin wrote a song that would sweep the Western world. "Alexander's Ragtime Band" remains the archetype of the American popular song, an appropriative, Creole genre in which the conflicting claims of European and African traditions are settled in songs and unsettled in interpretations. The songs reflect the status of the blending. The combination of African and Western is an unstable union, reflecting the riddled, horrific history of the formation of American racial culture.

The role of the artist in this appropriation, however, needs attention. The generic and creative artist chooses among available cultural traditions — in the American instance, largely among diasporas. The modern popular artist, as a broker in cultural transaction, a half breed, a "white" black or "black" white, and the signifier of sophisticated cosmopolitanism, is the subject of American popular songs. Their singer (whatever the immediate concern stated in the song — usually love) becomes a certain kind of person in the singing, much as the lieder singer must be a certain kind of singer as a way of "becoming" what the song describes. That kind of person, the modern kind of person, a creation of American cultural brokerage, is the kind of person you have to be to sing the song.

To some extent, being the kind of person who can sing the modern song is the ingredient that modernism sought in its primitivism. While modernism was doing its appropriative thing, it was already beguiled by the musical appropriations of the likes of Irving Berlin. They are the very essence of the modern, not least because they substitute cosmopolitan for provincial traditions. This story of Irving Berlin and "Alexander's Ragtime Band" concentrates much that was widespread in early twentieth-century taste and culture; it is also an instance of how deliberate the connections between cultural traditions were and how conscious the modern choice among them.

The key challenge for the modern American songwriter was to make a song that white folks could sing, not in blackface but in whiteface. The African-American tradition was sophisticated and various. The cultural production typified by "Alexander's Ragtime Band" recognized the value of that tradition and a need to simplify and stereotype it. The American song in its golden age is the textual equivalent of a somewhat liberated place. The particular black people in the songs are given greater scope and a more humane role than in Jim Crow society. But these are still givens, not rights, let alone equality. The white performer remains the vehicle of this tradition, inspired by and surrounded by blacks. Some African-American performers, like Bert Williams, Ethel Waters, and Paul Robeson, were given a restricted place in this scheme of things. Individual African Americans or stylized groups appear in the tableaux of America presented by popular entertainments, toting barges or standing respectfully before the statue of Father Abraham in the Lincoln Memorial. (See Frank Capra and Robert Riskin's *Mr. Smith Goes to Washington* for the latter image.) Lena Horne's appearances in MGM musicals were fashioned so they could be cut from prints that were to be shown in the South. But, in general, the music was still about the omnipresence of the largely invisible and always subordinate black persona.

This musical appropriation was an appropriation of the "primitive" because of its sophistication, because the African diaspora had the ingredients to shake up the American, white, European normal. The autonomy of the black was subverted by the songwriter, who was usually an outsider and frequently second-generation American Jewish (Berlin was a first-generation exception to this). Such appropriation formed part of the Jewish project of making America more sophisticated, more hospitable, and more tolerant.

North American elegance and sophistication — and, it turns out, the musical element that moved the whole modernist, Africanist safari — were undertaken in code: the supposedly primitive was taken on in order to increase sophistication. The actual moment of canonic discovery involved a substitution of African-American cultural complexity for something less complicated, producing an appropriative blend. The sophistication of this blend, verbal and intellectual as well as musical, was remarkable vis-à-vis the United States, and was often the work of songwriters working in the borrowed African-American mode. Elegance and sophistication were the very elements that African-American musicians could reactivate, by taking them back to the musical impulses that had inspired them. Thus songwriters imitated a black presence in the music and language of the songs in order to take ironic, sophisticated, earthy, comic views of American life, simplifying and commodifying what was specially available to the African American.

The invisibility, controlled rendition, or faked presence of the African and African American in American music was exactly what jazz came up against and what bebop challenged. The history of American music lies in the shifting blend and unequal exchange of such appropriations and repossessions.[1] The key modernist moment was an appropriation of the African to make a sophisticated popular music. The sophistication resided not in a taste for the "primitive" but in the traditions being appropriated. The plundering of the African-American tradition for its hard-won sophistication, which expressed in matchless fashion the ironic mix of participation in and distance from American convention, gave the crucial ingredient to the American song — its breeziness, its cool, and its room for improvisational freedom. The modern American moment, however, still preferred to assign that song to a white singer in blackface or, in time, to singers like Fred Astaire, whose incorporation of the African American was subtler and less advertised.

The African American in the appropriative mix retains artistic advantage and ultimately drives the creative game. The canonic American choice was between an Old World and a New. In fact, the American choice was between several Old Worlds. The elimination of the Native American distinguished America's first few centuries. In place of the flourishing North American civilizations, the European colonial and successor states introduced waves and classes of immigration. In place of native hierarchies, European Americans instituted distinctions based on race, religion, date of arrival, economic success, and so on. The cultural history of this New World constituted itself as a series of choices between available cultural traditions and among prototypical agents of culture.

Here are the words to "Alexander's Ragtime Band":

> Oh my honey, Oh my honey
> You better hurry and let's meander
> Ain't you going, ain't you going
> Up to the leader man, the ragged meter man,
> Oh my honey, let me take you to Alexander's grand slam,
>     brass band, ain't you coming along
> Come on and hear, Come on and hear
> Alexander's Ragtime Band
> Come on and hear, come on and hear
> It's the best band in the land
> They can play a bugle call, like you never heard before
> So natural that you want to go to war
> That's just the bestest band what am

> Oh my honey lamb
> Come on and hear, Come on and hear
> Let me take you by the hand
> Up to the man, up to the man
> Who is the leader of the band
> And if you care to hear *The Swanee River* played in Ragtime
> Come on and hear, come on and hear
> Alexander's Ragtime Band.

Irving Berlin had been fooling around with the melody that became "Alexander's Ragtime Band" for some years.[2] Russian-born Israel Baline had begun his career as a singing waiter and song plugger but realized that songwriting was the way for him to make his mark and that Irving Berlin was the name under which to do it. (It is worth recalling here that the names Irving, Howard, Milton, Morris, Seymour, and Sidney became common names given to American Jewish males from immigrant families.) Berlin had inspired facility and a good ear but no musical training. He was as dependent on transcribers in his early work, as many of his compatriots were on scribes to write their letters: "There is the fellow who creates the song and there is the fellow who is a technical man, just the same as there is someone who's skilled at typing your letter. Now you may not be able to type your own letter, but somebody else can do it for you. But they can't make it up for you."[3] Berlin, of course, took dictation from the culture with his inner ear, but that is what expressive cultural agency is — knowing how to take dictation from a culture in musical and lyrical shorthand.

Berlin had experienced frustration in his early career. He was a successful vaudeville songwriter who wrote with other people, putting words to their tunes, but, as he himself said, his hits were just passing things. He compared his work to Stephen Foster's: "Folks are still singing 'Swanee River' and 'My Old Kentucky Home.' It's something to be known like Stephen C. Foster." The key to Foster's great appeal lay in his effective combination of the sentiments and melodies of American Creole culture: his pastoral songs combine touches of African-American minstrelsy with doses of Euro-American sentiment; you can't have Foster without racial diversity, and you can't have Foster without racial hierarchy; "darkies" add color to the music and the lyrics, setting off the sentiments about home and family that this gay composer understood as only outsiders can understand the sentimental needs of cultures in formation.[4]

Berlin shared Foster's ambition of creating, from the outside, a music that would make room for him and appeal to the country's essence. The driven immigrant was certainly an outsider, and however much he was beguiled by its European characteristics, Berlin knew that what made American music go was the African element. He wanted to harness that element in his music. He also knew that novelty was part of the formula: popular culture had to be new and traditional at the same time; like Social Darwinism in America, it had to offer new ways of saying things people believed.

Berlin fooled around with several formulas for a hit. He tried to liberate himself from cowriters and composers by writing words for a melody in the public domain. Hence Mendelssohn's "Spring Song" emerged as "That Mesmerizing Mendelssohn Tune" (or "Rag"). In 1909, Berlin adapted the 1890's updating of this classic and added his own words: an invitation to hear that lovely Mendelssohn tune. It was a hit, but nothing remarkable.[5] Berlin was more than a *macher*, moved by more than his ambition; he really wanted what he perceived as Foster's permanence, the security of a popular master, the safety of an American creative endeavor, and he was a phenomenally gifted songwriter who pursued his craft with the singlemindedness of a genius.

Berlin liked what he knew of black music. Although the ragtime craze had passed, he knew that "ragtime" as whites understood it was far from exhausted. Ragtime as Scott Joplin, James Scott, Artie Mathews, and others had developed it was a complicated, written-down music, arguably the most sophisticated blend of African and European-American music ever achieved — the stuff, its composers believed, of opera and concert halls.[6] Berlin, like many white listeners, heard the lilt of ragtime and yearned for its syncopations in popular music, not just in that old concert-hall stuff. Berlin did not have the musical training to grasp the complexities of ragtime. He couldn't write it; he couldn't even read it. What he called ragtime was its syncopation and some of its chords, not the composed music or its elements.

Depending on composer Ted Snyder for the melodies, he tried several ways of using ragtime to Americanize (i.e., to enliven) ethnic ditties: "The Opera Rag," "Sweet Marie, Make a Rag-a-time Dance with me," "Yiddle on Your Fiddle, Play Some Ragtime." The songs were not hits, but his method is significant. Berlin tried to mate ethnicities, to broker the exchange through juxtaposition; to take one group's beat and another's stereotypically ethnic behavior. This, in essence, tries to liberate black music from the black person's image, like Sophie Tucker's saga of trying to sing hot music in white-face, not blackface. But it didn't work, probably in part because Berlin could not make something real out of two artificial elements — a black music he could not master and a series of ethnic stereotypes he was equally ill-placed to manipulate — not to mention attempting to do so in a culture that re-mained devoted to restricting African Americans to demeaning roles.[7]

The first thing Berlin solved was the music writing. He was a roughhouse pianist — Jimmy Durante was the classic of the breed — playing the black keys, which were easier to control ("the nigger keys," as they were called). This apparently restricted him to the key of F-sharp major: "The black keys are there under your fingers. The key of C is for people who study music," said Berlin. His biographer Lawrence Bergreen says "playing only the black keys deprived him of the ability to explore a wide range of musical subtleties. Nor could he embellish his tunes without harmonies. Without some way of manipulating his melodies, he would never be able to call himself a song-writer, and he would never be able to match the standard set by Stephen Foster" (As Thousands Cheer, p. 57).

Luckily for Berlin, there was the transposing piano, the cotton gin of American music, which could change keys when the player moved a con-cealed lever. George M. Cohan had three. It solved Berlin's musical prob-lem, although he still depended on transcribers to write the music down. The music, he said, was in him: "I know rhythm" (ibid., pp. 57–58). What Berlin did, of course, was to take the rhythm and the harmonies of black music — music that Joplin, Scott, Mathews, and James Reese Europe, to mention only a few, had elaborated with great sophistication into a written, classical African-American music — and plunder it for its beat and for its cul-tural meaning.

"Plunder" is what composers and writers do, of course, and Berlin's bor-rowings across American culture were standard operating procedure. But part of that cultural-production-as-usual must be understood as doing with African-American music things that (1) African Americans were not free to do; (2) reinforced restricted and demeaning stereotypes about black Ameri-cans for purposes of popularity; (3) simplified to the point of crudity a flourishing African-American musical tradition and culture; and (4) claimed sole credit for something borrowed, not invented. By the twentieth century, it must be recalled, there was already an elaborated and developed, compos-ing and performing black American tradition that included popular and for-mal music, church music, street music, work music, and so forth. Its masters were African American, but their mastery did not coincide with the patron-age that really counted, either institutional or popular. Therefore, although the music was there, the culture within which it might happen was not. White American culture was not prepared to accept black musicians except in musical equivalents of their racist images — even, alas, when those images were benign; indeed, it was still the case that America preferred its "black" musicians to be whites in blackface masquerade.[8]

Irving Berlin took his own creative advantage of a situation for which he was not responsible. He was not motivated by racism, but he did have a quality other than his genius that suited him to be the agent of this most influential of appropriations of African-American music, namely, its transformation into the rhythms and harmonic capital on which the golden age of American songwriting and musical theater could confidently draw. Berlin was the key musical figure of the American musical theater and popular song tradition. Asked to define Berlin's place in American music, Jerome Kern said he "was American music." The Savannah-born Southern gentleman Johnny Mercer remembered as a child asking his older brother Walter who the greatest composer alive was and being told it was Irving Berlin.[9] Berlin was that good. But he could stand for American music precisely because his black contemporaries could not, since white American culture was in no way prepared to grant agency or cultural identity to African Americans.

The music that resulted from this mating is terrific. But what Berlin created — and Jerome Kern, Cole Porter, George and Ira Gershwin, Richard Rodgers, Lorenz Hart and Oscar Hammerstein II, Harold Arlen and Johnny Mercer distinguished — was mastered by Thomas "Fats" Waller and Andy Razaf and Duke Ellington and Noble Sissle and Eubie Blake. Their mastery was acknowledged, but their work and autonomous creativity were discouraged, if not prohibited, because of their color. Berlin, Kern, and the Gershwins did not intend racism, as they understood it. A genuine part of their project was to eliminate what they felt was American race prejudice, to respect what they recognized as African-American racial genius, to express a fellow feeling as victims of oppression. Of the songs that resulted, Berlin's extraordinary "Suppertime," his musical monologue of a woman giving her children supper while trying to figure out how to tell them that their father had been lynched, which he wrote for Ethel Waters, is the most politically direct. Yet the fact remains that even the best-intentioned songwriters had to write music for negro characters like Porgy in *Porgy and Bess* or Joe in *Show Boat* (Universal Studios 1936). No matter how good these songs were, they remained specific set pieces that assigned a particular, restricted place to black people. Moreover, adapting black music for white audiences at that time generally meant that it was also performed by whites. The original *Show Boat* had blackface performers; American popular music still had no room for black artists.[10]

The seriousness of the ethnic project of Americanizing the European does not deserve to be understated. The Jews, for instance, who leapfrogged over native blacks into acculturation and assimilation, knew that their road to Americanization was an obstacle course that had a finish line, yet for Native Americans and African Americans this was not the case. In fact, the Jewish immigrants took over from the African Americans as acceptable blacks. One might even speculate that, contrary to too much received opinion, the obstacle to black progress was black progress, the success American blacks had achieved in elaborating cultural and educational institutions; Howard University preceded not only Brandeis University but the removal of anti-Jewish religious quotas from the Ivy League as well.

One reason European immigrants could do so well is that they were willing to be white blacks: Bert Williams was never as acceptable as Al Jolson as a coon-shouting performer for many reasons, predominantly the absence in Jolson of the inescapable racial inventiveness and irony that distinguished African-American playing of the American racial game. When Jolson, Sophie Tucker, Tess Gardella, Jimmy Durante, Eddie Cantor, and Bing Crosby took on a black persona, it did not include the sophisticated irony that always accompanied African-American culture, and that lurked in the rags of Joplin as well. Berlin's assimilation of the black keys coincided with a shifting of the culturally visible African-American musical project decisively away from the institutions and purposes of African-American culture itself.

What distinguished this assimilation was its adopting the black musical impetus into a narrative song tradition that emphasized common Americanization values like Christmas, love, and Mother. This adoption process had two distinct phases. The first phase, Irving Berlin's (and Tucker and Jolson's moment) was dominated by second-class white people, Jewish immigrants who were more acceptable aliens than were blacks, whose parroting of American ideals was more successful / less threatening, and whose barriers to Americanization were less sturdy. Jews played the "coon," a role beneath most sophisticated black performers that also replaced them on the stages of a mainstream culture that preferred them static if visible and invisible if there was a substitute. Anti-Jewish, anti-Irish, anti-Italian, and anti-Catholic prejudice persisted. But the cosmopolitan values immigrants represented managed to take hold, and the creative fact of the matter is that the immigrant playing the black came to represent cosmopolitan America because the European diaspora was acceptable in a way that the African diaspora was not.[11]

The second phase in the adoption of black music occurred when two kinds of simplification took place: the music was simplified, and the implications of a black artistic agency were simplified. Berlin's motto for songwriting was easy to sing, easy to say, easy to remember, and applicable to the everyday. "Alexander's Ragtime Band" was all those things. According to Bergreen, Berlin thought he could have better luck with the tune "if he included words that could help sell the idea of ragtime to audiences." The song took some time but, reversing the common pattern, caught on throughout the country: coon-shouters and minstrels, Emma Carus, Lew Dockstader, and Al Jolson took to it; it then spread to England and Europe and became the best-selling song of its day, the song that established Irving Berlin. It was the quintessential song about the phenomenon it represented, namely, white people's interest in black music (ibid., pp. 65–70).

The song, a catchy, raggy march, doesn't tell a story like "Some of These Days"; rather, it simply takes place: "Let's go hear some hot sounds, I'll take you to hear this great new group, Alexander's Ragtime Band." Right away, we know a few things: ragged meter, ragtime, and the diction of the opening "Ain't you going" tell us this is about black musicians. The lyrics are meant to be "coon-shouted," and they are clearly about how anyone can Africanize him- or herself. The singer talks that talk not as evidence of his own blackness (that much we don't know) but because he is familiar with the black side of town. The singer is an agent of cultural appropriation, as we say, or hip and cool — a tour guide to the wrong side of town. He pioneers Norman Mailer's "white negro" and much of the modern American youth culture which follows, which happens in relation to black style, and which is the explicit narrative of jazz history.

Critic Gilbert Seldes judged Berlin's accomplishment acutely:

How much ragtime had been sung and played before, no man may calculate; it had been heard in every minstrel show, and its musical elements were thoroughly familiar. What was needed was a crystallization, was one song which should take the whole dash and energy of ragtime and carry it to its apotheosis; with a characteristic turn of mind Berlin accomplished this in a song which had no other topic than ragtime itself. *Alexander's Ragtime Band* appeared with its bow to negro music and its introduction of *Swanee River*; it was simple and passionate and utterly unsentimental and the whole country responded to its masterful cry, *Come on and hear!*[12]

And our guide knows Alexander, a personal friend of his, although we have no reason to think they are actual compadres. He is, like Berlin, enthusiastic about the sound of ragtime and eager for us to get into the swing of it, but he is not himself of it. The visit is mediated, the tour guide is hipper than we — cosmopolitan, in the know — but not part of the culture being visited. The distinction is a subtle one, but even "the bestest band what am, oh my

honey lamb" is not to be taken as Alexander's own talk but as the appropriated slang of the cool visitor. It sounds odd to us now, but contemporary
sources, such as Carl Van Vechten and Blair Niles, suggest how the archaic
blackspeak that we associate with blackface performers had some of the aura
of the later white appropriations of black speech.[13]

What Berlin had done was to present the story of the song as a way and a
persona via which whites could listen to black speech. "Alexander's Ragtime
Band" eliminates the voice of the black person whose music, recognition,
even friendship it appropriates — with whatever demeaning restraints and
whatever redeeming, transforming ironies — and substitutes a presence that
acts out a black person that whites can be. Both coon-shouting and minstrelsy allow the black person to be eliminated so that the white person can
assume the part of one he wishes to be. The African American is occasional
and peripheral to the appropriated African-American persona. The black
performer has the choice of tacit assent to a rigid, restricted racial stereotype
or ghettoization, that ghetto being a kind of permanent minor league where
white people go to hear Alexander's band so they can copy it. The fact that
the ghetto became a shrine for well-meaning whites, even talented and
black-acknowledging whites, carries little weight when both the society and
the culture are structured racially. In "Alexander's Ragtime Band," the black
performer becomes the touchstone for the white appropriation of the song.
From now on, the game will be who gets to sing the song: how black a white
person need be and, in a subsidiary way, how white a black person must be
to sing it. The manners for listening to African-American music are as clear
as in opera or chamber music — there are body moves and snaps and shakes
that distinguish the hearer. The African-American source of these manners
has also been appropriated as learned behavior by American whites.

Calling the bandleader "Alexander" was one of Irving Berlin's master
strokes. The name sounds right in the song and has the "darky" ring to it,
but think of what else it does. Who was Berlin's Alexander? He probably
didn't know of Alexander the Great but of Alexander, the Czar of Russia.
Like the slaveholders who degraded both their slaves and the political aspects
of their own cultural baggage by naming their chattel Caesar or Pompey,
Berlin calls his "darky" Alexander, making the terrifying ridiculous, as he
was later to do when he had the *goyim* march down Fifth Avenue showing
off their fashion finery in *The Easter Parade* (MGM 1948) instead of rampag-
ing on a pogrom in the Lower East Side. It is interesting to compare this to
Shelton Brooks's "Darktown Strutters Ball," a wonderful case of a black song-

writer writing a coon song for white performers, and a good song at that. Alexander's Ragtime Band may well be playing at the Darktown Strutters Ball, but the latter's lyrics do not catch, as the former's do, the distancing of that trip to the ball. "Darktown" is after the event.

The success of "Alexander's Ragtime Band" was phenomenal and lasting. It preserves in lively lyric and tune a perennial moment in American life, when white America has to find the best band in the land and all that "signifies," as Professor Henry Louis Gates has shown us. The terms on which that visit takes place have changed; indeed, the history of American music lines the history of that moment. The terms of the appropriative exchange have improved from the African-American point of view. The broker's role has changed, it is a target of opportunity position in a cultural sense, although commercially it is for the most part still restricted. Berlin's success with it was, ironically, sealed by a persistent rumor that he had not written the song himself but employed a "little colored boy" who wrote the melodies for him. Berlin's response was furious and curious:

Songwriters don't steal, at least those of reputation don't. Why should they? But the public, by some freak of mind, would rather believe that the fellow who is getting the credit isn't the one who is doing the work. . . . Someone started the report that I had paid a negro ten dollars for it and then published it under my own name. I asked them to tell me from whom I bought successes, twenty-five or thirty of them. And I wanted to know, if a negro could write "Alexander," why couldn't I? Then I told them if they could produce the negro and he had another hit like "Alexander" in his system, I would choke it out of him and give him twenty thousand dollars in the bargain. If the other fellow deserves the credit, why doesn't he go get it? (ibid., p. 69)

Yet the rumor didn't die; even Berlin's publisher believed it (ibid.).

The rumor but specified, in unproved allegation, the cultural truth that Berlin had taken negro music and put it to his own use. That use transformed the music into what would be the standard text for the next generation. Berlin became "The Ragtime King" but remained baffled by the complexities of ragtime. He gave the name of a sophisticated music to some of its ruder gears. "I never did find out what ragtime was," he said. Berlin was offended by the notion that he needed a black person to write his music — hey, anyone could. "The reason our American composers have done nothing highly significant is because they won't write American music. They're as ashamed of it as if it were a country relative. So they write imitation European music which doesn't mean anything. Ignorant as I am, from their standpoints, I'm doing something they all refuse to do: I'm writing American music!" (ibid.,

p. 68). And so he was. But he took the name for the serious American music that African-American writers were writing and gave it to the more accessible, appropriated, and shared music he was writing.

Berlin acknowledged the widespread rumor that an African American wrote his songs at the fortieth anniversary celebration of the founding of the American Society of Composers, Authors, and Publishers (ASCAP). Berlin offered his remarks as a parodic medley of his own hit songs and included the lines "I'd like to express my gratitude / To a man in my employ, / I'm speaking of THE LITTLE COLORED BOY!" Berlin continued "Sweetest Little Fella" / And can he compose! / No one's ever seen him / But He's Mighty "Lak" a Rose! / He wrote "Come On and Hear, Come On and Hear" and a / Hundred other hits!" In the audience that night was Andy Razaf, the songwriter who many on Tin Pan Alley had credited with being Berlin's "little colored boy." Andrea Razafkeriefo was most famous for his collaborations with Fats Waller on such songs as "Black and Blue," "Ain't Misbehavin'," and "Honeysuckle Rose," and with Eubie Blake on "Memories of You." He was one of the best songwriters of the classic age — and a classic illustration of the neglect, discrimination, and frustration that African-American songwriters endured during the heyday of a music that was, in fact if not in deed, specially their own to write. The subject of an excellent new biography by Barry Singer, Razaf's experiences and creative output are indispensable to understanding the history of the American song and its cultural context. He replied to Berlin in the *Amsterdam News* on May 8, 1954:

Please permit me to comment on the legend of the "colored boy" who was supposed to write Irving Berlin's songs.

As a writer who virtually lived in Tin Pan Alley from 1913 until 1948, and who owed much of his inspiration to Irving Berlin, I, for one, would like to see this ridiculous legend placed in a coffin and given a permanent burial.

Berlin, as a writer, is to Tin Pan Alley what Louis is to boxing, Edison to inventions and Einstein to science. Their kind of genius comes along once in a lifetime. Few writers can write a great tune and a great lyric. This guy does both — and how! Of all his breathtaking list of socko hits, I'd be happy to settle for just two of them — "God Bless America" and "White Christmas."

Yes, if such a "colored boy" existed, many would-be writers today could really use him. To think of it, I could give him some part-time work, myself.

In closing, I would like to say to anyone who still insists this legend is true, that if a "colored boy" wrote Irving Berlin's songs, then a "white boy" wrote mine![14]

There is no evidence that Berlin didn't do his own writing. He did the culture's work, brokered the exchange, denying autonomy to the very part of the music that entranced the world, trying to limit the quality that made it music, to patent it, name it, own it, control it, apply it, use it. Like Sophie Tucker, who made it a point to take off her glove so people would know this "colored gal" was white, Berlin resented being considered negro, although the music he wrote invited the thought and its most interesting composers and performers also had to cope with it. The white black person succeeded the blackface performer. What that person learned from the music was not the syncopation fix Berlin imagined but a taste, the most sophisticated taste Americans could have, one that competed with and replaced the European sophistication that had been the hallmark of American cosmopolitanism since Jefferson and Franklin. The Old World, like the New, was finding out about Africa.

The African-American path not taken by American popular and formal culture remained thwarted but by no means deadened. What Berlin and his fellows, black and white, did was to establish the canonic text or blend or standard for American popular song. It was characterized by an American foreground—the plantation South, the country, the city—by European, Asian, and African locales, and by a European/African-American background. The American musical, like the generic song, was always balancing operetta and jazz with contemporary American lingo and up-to-date references, which were in turn competing with the traditional lyric beauties of English and the subtle, ironic, democratic, streetwise African-American language.

Different mixes were achieved. Jerome Kern was the most European, Harold Arlen the most Afrocentric among white songwriters; among black songwriters, it is harder to say. Duke Ellington let whites write the words as often as not; the result is a body of song about which the standard thing to say is how little the words measure up to the music; one might also say that Ellington wrote music that preempted lyrics. Fats Waller and Andy Razaf, like the Johnson brothers, Shelton Brooks, and Noble Sissle and Eubie Blake, wrote terrific songs but were prevented by Broadway Jim Crow from gaining anything like equal access to the kinds of job opportunities that made songwriting a possible career for white men with talent.

Two rough paths emerge: white writers keep going back to hear Alexander's band and get that inspiration; black writers develop something different, the application to the standard, accepted, appropriated text of the very energies—ironic, rococo, racial, coded, artistic—that escaped Berlin. Until the atom bomb and the emergence of bebop and the Civil Rights movement, American popular music established itself within the song's circumference, the song as Berlin set it, seeking rhythmic and setting updates from blacks. The number of whites who are black "wannabes" in this culture is extraordinary. "Alexander's Ragtime Band" is interesting because it signifies the fixing of the "classic" American song, the text that would stabilize racial harmonies for a generation.

What ensued, of course, was a history of exchange. White artists and black artists had something in common, something shared, a place — unlike in the movies, let alone literature and life — where America developed cultural exchange. It was Louis Armstrong, of course, singing his monumentally deconstructed and rhythmically restored version of "I Can't Give You Anything But Love, Baby," who captured the moment of exchange with an irony that subverted the blackface purpose and launched jazz's reappropriation of African-American music. Improvisation, not imitation, is freedom. And freedom is what even the best song of that era must deny the African American. The freedom to improvise, to change the melody, to reinvent the words, to alter the nature of drama and self-presentation, to play a new game on the given ground — this freedom is what African Americans before the Second World War were still denied.

Look for black people in American culture in that era and you'll find them in music, especially on instruments and surrounding certain white stars — but not, incidentally, musical stars. Mae West sounded like she learned it from Sophie Tucker (or whoever taught Sophie), but she knew enough to hire Duke Ellington to accompany her in a movie and to keep black women around her to allay suspicion and get her into the mood. The American blonde had more African American in her composition than meets the eye. Peggy Lee, Marilyn Monroe, and even Doris Day borrowed from their black sisters; Peggy Lee sued Walt Disney for stealing her song stylings when she herself had taken them from Billie Holiday and Lil Green. The greatest white black man of them all (until Elvis) was Fred Astaire, who remains the classic singer of the Berlin, Kern, Gershwin, Porter, Arlen song. He presented black-inspired rhythm in singing and dancing at its most complete and evolved. His vaunted style shares African- and Anglo-American roots. In white tie and tails, Fred is somewhere between master and servant, always at ease but never quite at home. His memorable and embarrassing blackface homage to Bill "Bojangles" Robinson in *Swingtime* ("Bojangles of Harlem" by Dorothy Fields and Jerome Kern) is alarming because the good song and the terrific dancing are mired in weird, degrading settings and associations that set off the artistic connection between these two giants and express Astaire's own (and through him the dominant culture's) debt to Robinson and to the African-American traditions he represented. Astaire became what Robinson couldn't, except in the movie *Stormy Weather,* which is a fictionalized biography of a black entertainer like Bill Robinson. The reason Astaire succeeded where Robinson did not is simply that Robinson was black in a racist society. Bojangles could dance with Shirley Temple because, although society did not trust the adult black men from whom it kept its women (and its citizenship) with its girls and boys, young black boys and old black men were welcome (the African-American man in his prime was simply not seen on screen except in chains or some other form of slave drag). To dance with Shirley Temple was, of course, pace Graham Greene, to dance at a distance from acknowledged sex. Fred Astaire touched the women he didn't kiss more than Errol Flynn touched the women he did. Moreover, Astaire's romantic, sexy moves were borrowed — yet forbidden to those from whom they were appropriated.

Lincoln Kirstein identified African America as the source of American elegance in remarks that follow the journey in "Alexander's Ragtime Band": "[Carl] Van Vechten helped me explore the marvellous dark continent where shone those magnificent palaces, the Savoy Dance Hall and the Apollo Theater. It was a Harlem then oddly unresentful, open and welcoming to the Prince of Wales, to Miguel Covarrubias, to Muriel Draper, and to all writers and artists who recognized in its shadows the only authentic elegance in America." [15] The African American had access to elegance, to that irony which keeps one aware of the double standard behind the stated connection between having class and being good. The black knew, as a condition of life (not just a canon of taste), that you could be as good as could be, have style, and yet remain an outsider, unranked; the lie of taste in a racist society is first and foremost the connection between individual merit and accomplishment. The black irony that gives subtlety almost automatically to the most ordinary exchange, movement to the most static of postures, danger to the safe — that very irony is the hallmark of American sophistication, which sees the real truth behind the lie of the things of the world and, it must be said, does not seek recourse in revolution. The elegance involved is one that is circumscribed by the appropriative setting. One is an agent of a cultural element rather than a free agent of self. Elegance is always distinguished by formal limits and style. American elegance plays the details of such style, ruling against the free and open, democratic range of feeling, against the democratic human type. American sophistication piques rather than lays down a rule, but it is a piquing that is deeply formed by and knowledgeable about the rule — and committed, somehow, to something other than a simple personification of it.

The black American knows the rules, had better know the rules better than anybody else — just ask Mammy. But the black American is not able to be what she or he knows so completely. Even a black servant has to watch it, has to caper in between the formal ministrations. Thus the immigrant playing black is a more sentimental creation than the black playing black. African-American elegance derives from a situational irony that makes any African-American utterance at once supportive of and ironic about the rules. Compare, for instance, what Kern and the Gershwins did for Fred Astaire with what they wanted to do but couldn't do for black performers. Paul Robeson struggled with the limitations of his generic role in *Show Boat.* "Old Man River" is a memorable aria, right up there with "Summertime." But it is an aria in an allegorical setting, imposed rather than free. Astaire had the freedom that the African American created in music and in tone, plus the text served him well. But Astaire, like Mae West, had to keep black people around. Singing and dancing "Shine on Your Shoes" in *The Band Wagon* (MGM 1953), Astaire is paired with a black shoe-shine man who has that rhythm and is cool, and who lends these qualities to Astaire's lively, rhythmic, but somewhat archaic tap. It is a great scene that dramatizes what "Alexander's Ragtime Band" canonized: the source of the hip white in actual contact with the black. Given the insistent racial hierarchy of American society, such totemic contact was a kind of renewal, and its best art — the songs of Berlin, Gershwin, and so on — keeps coming back to it.

Attempts to stage the authentic scene itself, for all their interest, suffer from the inevitable, deadening weight of the nature of the black status quo in white America; this is as true of Gertrude Stein's *Four Saints in Three Acts* as it is of Virgil Thomson's *Porgy and Bess* and Joplin's *Treemonisha.* These are cultural productions that do not allow for freedom. The black white, like Astaire or Mae West or earlier versions of them, borrows from the black in order to be more sexually and physically and rhythmically free, more playful, more all sorts of things. In doing so, he or she opts for a kind of freedom, an expansion of what the society already grants its racially privileged members.

The black choice was widened as well. The text of the American song, with its appropriative blend, created places for African-American artists to improvise, thus reasserting their agency and the independent interest of the African diaspora's commentary on these cultural goings-on. The way to hear it is to listen to Louis Armstrong, Sidney Bechet, Coleman Hawkins, Art

Tatum, Lester Young, Billie Holiday, and how they play and sing the songs that emerged from the great "Alexander's Ragtime Band" moment. They loved those songs and played them. The quality of improvisation that is brought to the proceedings is an assertion of the true nature of African-American sophistication, which unsettles the song with the surprising appearance of its destined singer.

The key to jazz, as it evolved within the larger American cultural marketplace, is that its story, at least until bebop, was the liberation of African-American creative energies within the set form of the American popular song. Its genius was in part original, and lay also in its imposed, ironic, improvisatory commentary. Jazz narrated an American setting that would not yet acknowledge it. Bessie Smith's 1928 version of "Alexander's Ragtime Band" takes this hybrid original song back to its truest sources and expresses the musical impulses that Berlin borrowed. Hers was a relatively straightforward blues reclamation, a magnificent pledge of things to come.

# "Remembering the Jungle"
## Josephine Baker and
## Modernist Parody

Josephine Baker is one of the very few black women to have lived a favorite American myth, the rags to riches story — in her case, rags to riches, back to rags, and then riches again. Instead of replicating the masculine model of hard work and virtue exemplified by Benjamin Franklin and Andrew Carnegie, Baker's narrative depends on the conventions that underlie the construction of traditional feminine sexuality; that is, on the cultural equation in which women use sexuality in order to obtain the protection — often defined as wealth — of men. Successful femininity in this paradigm is demonstrated by the exchange of attractiveness and sexual accessibility for wealth and social status. As Thorsten Veblen has observed in *Theory of The Leisure Class* (1899), the function of women in this context is to display the wealth of men. This conspicuous consumption of masculine wealth is explored in such nineteenth-century novels as Edith Wharton's *The House of Mirth* and Kate Chopin's *The Awakening*, and was spoofed by Marilyn Monroe in the 1953 film *Gentlemen Prefer Blondes*. Three decades before Monroe's comic portrait of the decorative woman, Josephine Baker effectively deployed feminine artifice to create a stage persona that parodied yet depended on the display of masculine wealth. Indeed, as a young Afro-American woman in the 1920's, a period of intense racism in the United States, her strategy was necessarily more complex than Monroe's.

A recent biography of Josephine Baker, *Jazz Cleopatra*, by Phyllis Rose, and a PBS documentary, *Chasing a Rainbow*, tell the story of a poor black girl born in the slums of St. Louis in 1906 to parents Carrie McDonald and Eddie Carson, who had been part of the migration from the rural South to the industrial North at the turn of the century.[1] While still a teenager, she ran away with Eddie Baker, a railroad conductor, and joined a touring vaudeville troupe that ended up in New York City, where, from 1922 to 1924, she gained notoriety for her antics at the end of the chorus line in Noble Sissle and Eubie Blake's *Shuffle Along*. Half urchin, half hobo, wearing ragged stockings and abbreviated overalls, she rolled her eyes, contorted her face, and swiveled her body in a deliberate parody of the blackface vaudeville routines and the conventions of the Negro minstrel show. In the touring company and on the New York stage, she hammed it up — pigeon-toed, knock-kneed, rump out, she wiggled, shimmied, slithered, and bumped her way to fame (Fig. 1).

When the *Revue Nègre* went on tour to Paris in 1925 (Fig. 2), Josephine Baker experienced, for the first time in her life, freedom from overt racial hostility. Instead of reviling her, Parisians celebrated her blackness. Of course, the French fascination with Baker was also based on a conviction of racial superiority — the superiority of the colonizer toward the colonized — but it was played out in terms of the fascinated, often admiring gaze of the white audience on the primitive Other, who represents erotic energy repressed by European civilization.[2]

In many respects, Josephine Baker's experience of racial hostility in the United States and her special status as patronized exotic in Europe parallel those of Helga Crane, the protagonist in Nella Larsen's novel *Quicksand*, published by Alfred A. Knopf in 1929. Indeed, it is possible that Larsen used Baker's life as a model for her character. Like Josephine Baker, Helga Crane desires to be "in different strange places, among approving and admiring people, where she would be appreciated, and understood."[3] In Larsen's novel, Helga Crane is viewed as a "strange species" to be "proudly exhibited. . . . Here she was a curiosity, a stunt, at which people came and gazed" (*Quicksand*, pp. 70–71). Encouraged to wear bright colors, dangling earrings, and thick enameled bracelets, Helga Crane becomes a curiosity. But whereas Crane is dismayed by her objectification, Baker exploited her status as libidinous primitive to create a career that reenacted the commodification of Africa by Europe.

Once in Paris, Josephine Baker secured her special status by deploying conventions of the burlesque to create a *danse sauvage* that played with the paradigm of the black exotic in the context of white colonialism. Deliberately constructing her stage persona, incorporating colonial (and racist) definitions of the primitive in her theatrical repertoire, she created the legend of her exotic sexuality. French audiences were riveted by her "lithe" body and her vitality (Fig. 3). As one French journalist observed, "She was so natural — she moved like an animal."[4] In an essay about her in the September 1926 *Vanity Fair*, the poet e. e. cummings said that, looking at Baker's performance, "we find ourselves remembering the jungle."[5] Baker was widely

FIGS. 1 & 2. *Left:* Josephine Baker, ca. 1925. Courtesy of Roger-Viollet, Paris. *Right:* Poster for *La Revue Nègre*, 1925. Courtesy of the Bibliothèque Nationale, Paris.

FIG. 3. Josephine Baker and Joe Alex in the *danse sauvage* of *La Revue Nègre*, 1926. Joe Alex was a member of the dance troupe. Courtesy of the Bibliothèque Nationale, Paris.

perceived by Parisians as a vibrant creature of natural instincts, in contrast to what was seen as the pallid, fatigued gentility of overbred Europe. At the same time, the audience assured itself of its civilized status as it vicariously experienced the savage through Baker's performance. In a distorted version of Social Darwinism, race and gender became markers for the bifurcation of the human psyche and soma; in this scheme, the person of color, especially a woman of color, was less evolved, and therefore less civilized. Baker's display of natural vitality and lack of inhibition made the audience feel in control and superior, while at the same time her performance provided vicarious release for "culturally unacceptable behavior." Yet the "natural creature" proved to be a complex construction indeed, and, as already suggested, Josephine Baker worked hard to create her image. One humorous and perhaps offensive example of her deliberate manipulation of the trope of the black exotic is the publicity release by her press agent which states that Baker's "favorite dishes are plover eggs and a cannibal sandwich (raw chopped meat and onions)."[6]

While Josephine Baker was empowered by the French fascination with her coffee-colored skin and performance as uninhibited savage, there was also a dimension of exploitation in her reification as exotic object. Nevertheless, despite becoming part of the process of commodification, Baker also took advantage of the situation by deliberately manipulating the conventions of primitivism to gain a considerable measure of control over her audience. In this exchange, it is not altogether clear who was the exploiter and who the exploited. Certainly, Baker's performances brought financial rewards — by 1929, she was a millionairess. What needs to be emphasized here is that Josephine Baker used the conventions of gender as well as those of race to achieve success; that is, in addition to playing with the trope of the black savage, she used feminine artifice to successfully arouse the sexual appetites of the white male audience. Through the dramatic persona of the black female primitive who held the promise of endless libidinousness, Josephine Baker achieved the American Dream — paradoxically, in Paris.

In her decades in Paris, Baker reconstructed her image from that of a jungle creature to queen of the Folies-Bergère (Fig. 4). As she herself put it, "The *danse sauvage* is over." Befitting a queen, she wore tiaras and regal trains and bought a chateau in the Dordogne reputed to contain a bed that had belonged to Marie Antoinette. Now it was reported that she dined on "fish heads and rooster's combs served with special sauces."[7] And legend has it that she drank only champagne. This transformation from primitive Other to regal presence recapitulates the theories of cultural evolution popular at

F I G . 4. Queenlike Josephine Baker entrances her suitors. Courtesy of Roger-Viollet, Paris.

the time. It was generally felt that it was necessary to bring products of the European marketplace to backward tribes in an effort to civilize the natives — that is, to enable them to realize the capitalist / modernist promise. By conspicuously displaying artifacts associated with royalty, Josephine Baker exemplified the civilizing power of European culture; by wearing the diadem and scepter, she demonstrated that even the most unrepressed savage could be tamed. It is noteworthy that this trajectory from parodic savagery to parodic royalty has characterized the lives of other Afro-American performers, notably Louis "Rex" Armstrong, Billie Holiday (Lady Day), Count Basie, and Duke Ellington. The tradition persists today in the personae and performances of the funk-rock singer Prince and Rap artist Queen Latifah.[8]

Once in her chateau, Les Milandes, Baker created a utopian family by adopting her "rainbow tribe" of children from many races and nationalities.

It was her hope that the international community she created could transcend antagonism and polarization based on racial and ethnic difference.
When asked in 1973 by Henry Louis Gates, Jr., whether she regretted leaving
the United States and missing the Civil Rights era there, she responded: "I've
thought often about your question, about running away from the problem.
At first, I wondered if it was cowardice, wondered whether I should have
stayed to fight. But I couldn't have done anything. I would have been
thwarted in ways in which I was free in France. I probably would have been
killed. But really I belong to the world now."[9] In the novel *Quicksand*, Helga
Crane makes similar observations:

Go back to America, where they hated Negroes! To America, where Negroes were
not people. To America, where Negroes were allowed to be beggars only, of life, of
happiness, of security. To America, where everything had been taken from those
dark ones, liberty, respect, even the labor of their hands. To America, where if one
had Negro blood, one mustn't expect money, education, or sometimes even work
whereby one might earn bread. Perhaps she was wrong to bother about it now that
she was so far away. Helga couldn't, however, help it. Never could she recall the
shames and often the absolute horrors of the black man's existence in America without the quickening of her heart's beating and a sensation of a disturbing nausea. It
was too awful. The sense of dread of it was almost a tangible thing in her throat."
(ibid., p. 83)

As already noted, France was not free of racism, but public displays of violence against blacks — beatings and lynchings — and the abject poverty of
ghetto life did not characterize black/white relations when Josephine Baker
lived there.

At Les Milandes and in the theatrical performances of her later years,
Baker brought her belief in racial equality and a nurturing ethos to an international arena. During World War II, she was very active in the Resistance
movement, and the French government awarded her a medal of honor in
recognition of her humanitarianism and heroism. Unfortunately, her in-
come did not meet her extraordinary expenses, and eventually her creditors
foreclosed on her castle, literally putting her out on the street. There is a
poignant photograph of Josephine Baker sitting outside her kitchen door
wearing a shabby skirt, sweater, and slippers. Her hair in curlers, she is surrounded by bags filled with miscellaneous belongings: she could be a domestic servant sitting on the stoop of a Harlem brownstone. Her life seems
to have come full circle.

But the story does not end there. Josephine Baker returned to the Paris
stage, where once again she was celebrated. One evening, after a festive party

in honor of the fiftieth anniversary of her debut, she died in her sleep as a result of heart failure. Her funeral in Paris was worthy of a head of state: there was a procession of flower-shrouded limousines down the Champs Elysées, with thousands of her admirers lining the street to bid her a final farewell. Baker had become a national symbol of the civilizing mission of France. Significantly, tributes to Baker emphasized her unusual humanitarianism and dignity. Referring to her origins as "a plain ghetto girl," Ishmael Reed observed in his eulogy that "She never forgot who she was, though, and held her head high and if she wasn't a goddess she was certainly a Queen, which is almost like being a goddess." [10]

Although this dramatic story is fascinating in itself, Josephine Baker used the modernist concept of self-construction as well as the modernist interest in primitivism to create a series of dramatic personae that both parodied and challenged notions of essentialism in the arenas of race, class, and gender. In particular, it is instructive to consider the construction of Baker's personae by analyzing the semiotics of her costumes, makeup, and stage settings, beginning with her role as clown at the end of the chorus line, through the wild gyrations of the *danse sauvage*, to the elegant poses of her regal years at the *Folies*.

To understand Baker's challenge to essentialist thinking, it is necessary to examine the assumptions underlying racist beliefs in the 1920's. Apocalyptic studies of the demise of civilization were published in the United States and Europe in the wake of the rapid social change following World War I. Madison Grant's *The Passing of the Great Race, or the Racial Bias of European History* (1918) is the prototypical racist study, in which a hierarchy based on race and nationality divides Europeans into three categories — the best being Nordic, followed by the Alpines, then the Mediterraneans. Grant argues that civilization will come to an end unless the Nordic people assert "the pride of race and the right of merit to rule." F. Scott Fitzgerald used such studies as Grant's in a scene in *The Great Gatsby*, in which Tom Buchanan summarizes the book he is reading:

"Civilization's going to pieces," broke out Tom violently. "I've gotten to be a terrible pessimist about things. Have you read *The Rise of the Colored Empires* by this man Goddard?"

"Why, no," I answered, rather surprised by his tone.

"Well, it's a fine book, and everybody ought to read it. The idea is if we don't look out the white race will be — will be utterly submerged. It's all scientific stuff; it's been proved. This idea is that we're Nordics. I am, and you are, and — " After an infinitesimal hesitation he included Daisy with a slight nod, and she winked at me again.

"— And we've produced all the things that go to make civilization — oh, science and art, and all that. Do you see?"[11]

Daisy Buchanan's wink constitutes an effort to resist Tom's monomaniacal vision and, as such, is similar to Baker's parody of the colonized and colonizing.

In the 1920's, many books similar to Grant's study were published. Lothrop Stoddard's *The Rising Tide of Color: Against White-World Supremacy* (1920), Emile Fournier-Fabre's *The Greatest Shock, or The Mixing of the Races* (1921), and Maurice Muret's *The Twilight of the White Races* (1926) reveal the extraordinary degree of anxiety and hostility about race and ethnicity on both sides of the Atlantic.[12] As has been observed, France was not necessarily less racist than the United States, but there certainly was less racial violence there in the 1920's, at least. In France, there was a different paradigm for black/white relationships because the French were responding not in the context of a history of slavery but in terms of their colonial empire. For the most part, colonized populations did not inhabit Paris or France but resided, in the European view, on distant, dark continents.

In spite of the fact that slavery was no longer legal in the United States, subordination of blacks remained intact. There was a widespread perception that Afro-Americans were beasts of burden, inferior forms of life, creatures who inhabited a lower position on the phylogenetic scale. American newspapers and periodicals from the turn of the century through the 1920's are filled with disturbing expressions of the belief in the inferiority of non-Caucasians in general and Afro-Americans in particular. For example, in 1936, *Life* magazine ran a cartoon showing a corpulent, balding man in a swivel chair in his office, which has in its window the sign "colored man wanted." Before him stands a pigtailed Chinese coolie. The caption reads: "Boss: Mercy me! What we need is a Colored Boy. Applicant: Ain't I Yellow Enough?"[13]

After World War I, lynchings were commonplace in the South, and race riots were increasingly frequent in the industrial cities of the North. In 1917, when Josephine Baker was 11, she witnessed race riots in East St. Louis that were among the worst during this era. In addition to widespread burning of homes, 39 people died. "One of the first things I remember," Baker told Henry Louis Gates, Jr., "was the East St. Louis Race Riots. I was hanging on to my mother's skirts, I was so little. All the sky was red with people's houses burning. On the bridge, there were running people with their tongues cut out. There was a woman who'd been pregnant with her insides cut out."[14]

Although, as we have seen, anxiety about social change was expressed through the paradigm of race relations in Europe as in the United States, the model was different. Colonialism and the sentimentalized belief in the primitive as exotic, as well as belief in the civilizing mission of the nation, actually gave Baker more latitude in shaping her dramatic personae, whereas in the United States she was limited to variations on the theme of master/slave relations. As an Afro-American, she was able to engage Parisian fascination with jungle themes, which of course included tropes of Anglo-European men in white suits and pith helmets whose mission it was to plunder the riches of their colonies as well as to ravish the untamed, libidinous women of the subcontinent. This European conviction of cultural superiority created yet another dramatic arena for Baker — that of the savage tamed and molded by a superior civilization. At the same time that Baker enacted this range of roles, she also effectively engaged French fascination with American modes of improvisation and flexibility — the emblems of freedom — as represented by jazz culture.

In the post–World War I United States, Afro-American culture became inscribed with complex and charged meanings. As middle-class American culture became increasingly aligned with technology, immigrant — and especially black — culture was increasingly associated with noncerebral, nonrational values. The black body represented unrestrained, illicit desire, and black sexuality was associated with satanic chaos and bestiality. At the same time, black culture represented freedom from routine, predictability, rigidity. Jazz culture and Harlem in the 1920's represented liminal space — a continual carnival where whites could go slumming to "let off steam." That is, black jazz culture and Harlem became the cultural equivalent of the American libido. What Josephine Baker did at the end of the chorus line, through her comic rendering of irrepressible and uncontainable energy, was to manipulate expectations of black sexuality. Afro-American culture signified liberation from restraint.

To align Anglo-European and American society with the superior realm of reason and control, the nonrational components of the psyche were split off and projected onto women, immigrants, and people of non-European origins, particularly blacks. In its crudest form, this cultural equation assigns the following characteristics, defined as superior, to Caucasians: reason, logic, mastery, control, and law. Those defined as inferior are associated with non-Caucasians: disorder, spontaneity, and abandon. As I have noted, non-Caucasian women represent an intensified form of these culturally inferior values.[15] In Nella Larsen's *Passing*, Helga Crane succinctly describes the bifurcation when she observes that she moves between the "prejudiced restrictions of the New World to the easy formality of the Old, from the pale calm of Copenhagen to the colorful lure of Harlem."[16] Although Larsen spatializes this cultural divide by contrasting Copenhagen with Harlem, the novel makes it clear that the schism transcends national and geographical boundaries. Meditating further on arbitrary definitions of racial difference, Helga Crane probes the construction of racial and cultural superiority and inferiority:

But later, when she was alone, it became quite clear to her that all along they had divined its presence, had known that in her was something, some characteristic, different from any that they themselves possessed. Else why had they decked her out as they had? Why subtly indicated that she was different? And they hadn't despised it. No, they had admired it, rated it as a precious thing, a thing to be enhanced, preserved. Why? She, Helga Crane, didn't admire it. She suspected that no Negroes, no Americans, did. Else why their constant slavish imitation of traits not their own? Why their constant begging to be considered as exact copies of other people? Even the enlightened, the intelligent ones demanded nothing more. (*Passing*, p. 83)

In Copenhagen, Helga Crane attends a Negro vaudeville act in a traveling circus: "And how the singers danced, pounding their hands together, twisting their legs, waving their abnormally long arms, throwing their bodies about with loose ease! And how the enchanted spectators clapped and howled and shouted for more!" (ibid., pp. 82–83). While Helga feels ashamed and exposed "as if these pale pink and white people among whom she lived had suddenly been invited to look upon something in her which she had hidden away and wanted to forget" (ibid., p. 83), she also knows that the energy and physical joy of the dancers is part of her and part of the white audience as well. The fascination of the members of the audience lies in the fact that they see before them the display of their own hidden, buried energies. Although initially repelled and driven to deny the full range of her humanity, Helga Crane is repeatedly drawn back to the spectacle of these dancers whose performance embodies the self-denied: "But she returned again and again to the Circus, always alone, gazing intently and solemnly at the gesticulating black figures, an ironical and silently speculative spectator. For she knew that into her plan for her life had thrust itself a suspensive conflict in which were fused doubts, rebellion, expediency, and urgent longings" (ibid).

The way audiences responded to Josephine Baker certainly has parallels with Larsen's description of the reception of the vaudeville act in Copenhagen. As mentioned, the French repeatedly used the adjective "lithe" to describe Josephine Baker. Partly, they were responding to a trope of wildness and erotic abandon that confirmed their definitions of the primitive, as we have seen. And partly they were responding to the casual fluidity of American manners and the informality of American physical expression — in the minds of many, another form of primitivism. In contrast to the extraordinary stylization of body movements in Anglo-European culture, Afro-American dance seemed to epitomize abandon or, at the very least, freedom from restraint. If Americans were casual, then Afro-Americans were spontaneity itself. The popularity of the dances of the 1920's that black culture created — the mooch, the black bottom, the shake, the shimmy, the mess-around — also demonstrated Anglo-Europeans' general fascination with pushing the limits of the ritualized range of physical movement. During World War II, to be an admirer of Josephine Baker was a code for the Resistance. Because her choreography disrupted the static poses prescribed by European tradition, supporters of the Resistance saw her as a symbol of freedom in opposition to the forces of Nazism.[17]

Perhaps the paradigmatic moment of Josephine Baker's repertoire for the Folies-Bergère in Paris was the first time she appeared on stage bare-breasted, wearing a G-string made of satin bananas (Fig. 5). In this sequence, Baker

FIG. 5. Josephine Baker in 1927. Here Baker is shown in the banana skirt, first worn in the Folies-Bergère in 1926–27. Courtesy of the Bibliothèque Nationale, Paris.

brilliantly combines tropes of civilization and savagery. The scene is set in the jungle, thick with foliage and vines and a fringe of beach. Two exceptionally fit black men wearing loincloths beat tom-toms under a palm tree that leans toward the sand. As they play, there is a rustle in the upper corner of the frame; the spectator glimpses a bare foot, then an ankle, leg; finally, torso, arms, and head appear. As this jungle creature descends the tree, one is aware that she is not wearing clothes to speak of, but it is not until she begins a series of undulating motions on the sand that it is obvious that she is bare-breasted. (This fact made international headlines; the American film clip of this dance was touched up in order to meet the censors' requirement that Baker wear a brassiere.) As the savage woman gyrates toward the tent where the pith-helmeted colonialist sleeps, she is the incarnation of unfettered physicality, uninhibited sexuality; a promise of gratification of primal needs, of a return to prelapsarian days of unself-conscious sexuality, before the repression exacted by civilization robbed life of its joy and vitality.

The idea of the primitive has a lengthy tradition in Western civilization, predating the description of the acorn-eating primeval man in Boethius's *Consolation of Philosophy* (535 A.C.E.). In medieval and Renaissance times, the wild man was imaged as a precursor of the noble savage: in the medieval period, he inhabited the borderlands between civilization and nature; in the Renaissance, he represented the prelinguistic human being whose mode of communication is gestural and whose instincts are benign. In Spenser's *Faerie Queene* (Book VI), for example, the wild man is benign, optimistic, with an intuitive sense of good and evil; he is a fundamentally constructive being and represents a positive force. In his *Essay on Cannibals*, written in the late 1580's, Montaigne was among the first to relativize the concept of the barbarian by insisting that the context be taken into account. Arguing that "barbaric" simply means different, Montaigne pointed out that, for example, even though Brazilians eat human flesh, they eat it only after death; on the other hand, Europeans torture living human beings. "Which is more civilized?" he asked.

Increasingly, Baker played with these relative concepts of civilization and barbarism in an effort to gain more and more control over her reification as primitive. By juxtaposing images of the jungle and the royal court, the carnal and the cerebral, she subverted the trope of cultural evolution and progress. Instead of costumes of animal skins, which blur the distinction between the tribal and the bestial, she consciously separated herself from association with the bestial and displayed her control over the animal realm by walking leopards (and sometimes swans) on leashes in the streets of Paris and Berlin

FIGS. 6 & 7. *Left:* Josephine Baker with Mildred, her pet leopard. Baker also kept a pet panther named Sheik. Courtesy of Roger-Viollet, Paris. *Right:* Josephine Baker. Courtesy of Roger-Viollet, Paris.

(Fig. 6). Here she signaled that, in her own process of becoming tamed and civilized, she had gained the authority to tame the panther. Teasing out the ambiguities involved in the attempt to distinguish the physical from the bestial, Baker playfully asserted the distinction by simply draping her bejeweled and partially nude body on a tiger skin (Fig. 7). On the one hand, this image suggests the repressed beast within the civilized person — or, as Freud would put it, the id controlled by the ego, if not the superego — by creating a visual hierarchy in which the human being dominates the animal world; on the other hand, the connection between the two worlds is all too apparent.

Establishing herself as the reigning presence of the Folies-Bergère, Baker enjoyed the oxymoronic status of queen of the burlesque and manipulated tropes of royalty to create a legend in which she was the living embodiment of the civilizing process. Wearing a jeweled tiara, she descended an illuminated staircase with a twelve-foot egret feather train trailing behind her, becoming a living tribute to France and the entire colonial enterprise (Fig. 8).

This conspicuous display of costly feathers represents the commodification of nature as well as of the female body. The iconography of the egret train is especially significant: the feathers used for capes and hats are grown by the egret only during mating season. In 1905, a suitcase of this rare mating plumage cost $5,000. The fact that Baker became known for this kind of display of rare and costly bird feathers and animal skins signals her triumph over the natural world; that is, as a black she has transcended the bestial. But not as a female. Having attained the status of decorative woman of the highest order, she wore extravagantly expensive clothes and ornaments — gowns by Poiret, Dior, and Chanel, and jewelry by Tiffany and Cartier (Fig. 9). Of course, the irony was that, while she achieved considerable mastery in the realm of race, and even class to some extent, she remained mastered by the traditional gender system. Although she achieved the highest levels of ornamental femininity, she was a woman dependent on men for her status.

Again, especially in the case of the feathered woman who is black, the

FIGS. 8 & 9. *Left*: Josephine Baker, be-plumed and bejeweled at the Folies-Bergère. The egret-feather train became her signature. Courtesy of Roger-Viollet, Paris. *Right*: Josephine Baker, ca. 1932, in a Dior gown. Courtesy of Roger-Viollet, Paris.

FIGS. 10 & 11. *Above:* Josephine Baker performing. Courtesy of Beinecke Rare Book and Manuscript Library, Yale University, James Weldon Johnson Collection, and of Keystone, Paris.

FIG. 12. *Left:* Josephine Baker in her dressing room. Courtesy of Keystone, Paris.

subtext of colonization remains, and with it the added twist of exotic sexuality tamed. Baker transcended the sphere in which, as primitive, she was conflated with the animal world (the nonrational, the carnal); she no longer represented herself as the lithe, sinuous, unrepressed animal. Yet even though she displayed plumage as an emblem of potential status and privilege, she was still associated with the theatrical tradition in which feathered women are equated with barnyard fowl — hens, chicks, ducks, and so forth. Jewelry, too, conveys an ambiguous message — think of the diamond necklace that is commonly referred to as a choker. Thus, as a beplumed, bejeweled, ornamental woman (Fig. 10), Baker was still mastered by the male gaze. While the *danse sauvage* suggests a wild abandon that lacks self-consciousness, and that therefore embodies potential freedom, the ornamental feathered woman suggests self-restraint and, if not control, at least choice — she is a prize to be won. The illusion here is that she gives herself to the highest bidder. On the one hand, this conflation of female sexuality with feathered creatures creates an illusion of tamed eroticism; on the other, the female display of costly feathers confers status on the man who possesses her.

In her later and even more commanding years, Josephine Baker wore jewel-encrusted dresses and less plumage (Fig. 11). The care of her multiracial family took up more of her attention, and instead of her theme song, *I Have Two Loves, My Country and Paris*, she sang about the utopia she had hoped to create at Les Milandes. She spurned racism and ridiculed the taboo of miscegenation. In an ironic and powerful reversal of convention, she stated: "I think they must mix blood, otherwise the human race is bound to degenerate. Mixing blood is marvelous. It makes strong intelligent men and takes away tired spirits."[18]

Josephine Baker's career is a compelling study in modernist self-construction and the conscious manipulation of cultural tropes. Finally, her life and her art celebrate the triumph of the comic spirit as well as her extraordinary achievements in the art of play, whether on or off the stage (Fig. 12).

# Primitive Self

## Colonial Impulses in Michel Leiris's
## "L'Afrique fantôme"

The concept of the primitive or savage constitutes one of the most identifiable threads that runs through French intellectual thought. From Montaigne
to Deleuze, Rousseau to Breton, the philosophers of the Enlightenment to
Lévy-Bruhl and Lévi-Strauss, this notion has occupied a central place in
French discourse on nature, culture, and the identity of (Western) man. The
primitive — for which the African has become, in the European imagination,
the ultimate incarnation — can be said to have played for the French or the
European the role of a looking glass in which his own image is refracted as
civilized. To play this role, the primitive so imagined must remain the silent
and radically different Other, whether viewed negatively or positively. As
V. Y. Mudimbe observed, in the primitivist conception, "the figure of the
African was taken both as an empirical fact and as the sign of absolute
otherness."[1]

The period of the 1920's and 1930's in France was marked by an intense
activity around the notion of primitivity. Poets and artists in the throes of a
spiritual crisis scrambled over the globe in search of different models of humanity. Convinced of the existence of a primitive world that was the ante-
type of Europe, they went to find it in Africa, Oceania, the Americas —
wherever there were non-whites subjugated to European colonial rule. Paul
Morand, Blaise Cendrars, Jean Paulhan, and Georges Bataille, to cite only a
few, succumbed to the appeal of the so-called primitive world. The particular revolt of the Dadaists and surrealists was postulated on the same synthetic
experience. Confronted with the savagery of World War I, these poets, singing the *de profundis* of Western civilization, declared themselves savages,
cannibals. "*Monde occidental, tu es condamné à mort,*"[2] Louis Aragon
exclaimed.

However, this period was also the triumphant era of European colonialism. In 1931, the French Government inaugurated the Exposition Coloniale,

bringing to Paris replicas of African cities, mosques, pagodas, Buddhist temples, and "natives" of all sorts in their "natural" habitats. A mesmerized public came to observe, learn, and be informed about the munificence of the colonial enterprise. Even the U.S. took part in this grandiose colonial circus, displaying in the Washington pavilion its civilizing influence over Puerto Rico, Hawaii, Samoa, and Guam. A monument to imperialist public relations, the Exposition Coloniale was also the apotheosis of the primitivist idea. Spectators were invited to experience in one day the thrill and excitement of the "jungle." African and New Caledonian schoolteachers and civil servants were enrolled to pose as "authentic" savages.[3] Euphoric artists and intellectuals, eager to renew their inspiration, came to admire these "false" savages. This masquerade, officially organized by the Ministry of the Colonies, summarizes in a lapidary fashion the primitivist program. The internal principle of primitivism is based on this game of mirrors, illusion, and inversion, at the end of which appears the Other. In this confusion, modern primitivism emerged out of two contradictory propositions: the poetic, which claims that Western culture is deficient and moribund, and the official, which affirms it as the perfect and ultimate state of humanity.

L'Afrique fantôme (1934) by Michel Leiris offers a particularly instructive example of the use of the primitivist concept in modern literature. This book is the account of the famous 1931–33 Dakar-Djibouti ethnographic mission led by Marcel Griaule, for which Leiris served as secretary-archivist. Thirty years old and unemployed, Leiris went to Africa because there was nothing for him to do in Europe. His formal connection with surrealism had come to an end. His literary career at the time amounted to relatively little: some playful poetic exercises, the transcriptions of his dreams in "Le Pays de mes rêves" (1925),[4] and a novel, Aurora, "at the bottom of his drawer." His life had reached an impasse; ethnology held great hope for career and glory.

L'Afrique fantôme enjoyed subsequent editions in 1950 and 1981; the latter contains, along with the fieldnotes per se, a preamble, a preface, and endnotes added in 1950. The preamble and preface purport to place the text in perspective for the present-day reader. In them a seemingly wiser, much older Leiris acts as censor and critic of the younger Leiris who authored the book we are about to examine. He insists on the dramatic differences between the man he has become and the man he was when he undertook the journey to Africa in 1931, whom he describes as a disillusioned young European who "foolishly" sought an antidote to the poisons of Western civilization in Africa. In the 1981 edition, Leiris claims to be a transformed person with a broader humanitarian perspective and deeper understanding of the "legitimate aspirations" of colonized people: "This perspective is far removed from what I sought when I understood this journey out of which came 'L'Afrique Fantôme'. The primary motivation is no longer the fallacious attempt to be different by plunging — even though symbolically — into a "primitive mentality."[5]

The preface, written in 1950, also offers explanations and caveats to prevent a misunderstanding of the text. Acknowledging his own insensitivity, blindness, and prejudice, a contrite Leiris places himself beyond the pale of reprobation and critical judgment. In so doing, the "ghost" of the past is exorcised, and the poet — redeemed, as it were — starts with a clean slate:

> One will find that in several instances . . . I appear morose, difficult, prejudiced — even unjust — inhuman (or "human, too human"), ungrateful, a traitor, and much more. . . . I will add today that in several instances also I let transpire the arrogance of the Westerner, no matter what disdain he pretends to have for his own civilization; here and there . . . I acted as a spoiled brat or with effeminate nervousness, which at times translated into impatient gestures which could, for a brief moment, confuse me with the brutal colonizer that I never was. (*L'Afrique fantôme*, p. 9)

In view of such a confession, one could argue that Leiris, anticipating absolution, is asking the reader to look elsewhere for the meaning of the text. No longer is it necessary to uncover what he himself has already admitted. His racist and colonialist viewpoint, once established, should be considered the residue of a distant past that must be kept at a distance. Placed in this light, *L'Afrique fantôme* becomes a sort of *confession d'un enfant du siècle*, which, as such, has intrinsic epistemological value. Leiris remains convinced of its documentary and poetic value for today's reader. He argues, however, that his oeuvre is not meant for the run-of-the-mill reader, who would content herself with a literal interpretation of the written word. Toward this vulgar reader, Leiris exhibits scorn and impatience. His book, he declares, is not for everyone; it is "presented to the appreciation obviously not of the entire human species, but at least those of its members who speak French and are not illiterate" (ibid., p. 5).

Confronted with a text so armored with a barrage of explanations, caveats, acts of contrition, and retractions, the reader "who reads French and is not illiterate" is naturally intrigued — all the more so by Leiris's comment that his journey, and therefore the writing of his book, would have been inconceivable in an Africa not yet "tamed" (ibid., p. 8). Moreover, it is not superfluous to note that the Dakar-Djibouti team was preparing for departure just as the "enormous panoply of exotic worlds [was] being laid out in the Bois de Vincennes."[6] These two events are interrelated and emerged from the same historical and political conditions created by colonialism.

With *L'Afrique fantôme*, we are in the presence of a hybrid document that combines self-representation with ethnological analysis. In it, the author exhibits the tragi-romantic sense of alienation of the modernist poet while retaining the detached, often cynical stance of the "scientific" observer. Poetry, dreams, and stream of consciousness alternate with matter-of-fact notations on the activities of the mission and life occurrences in colonial Africa, from the most banal to the most unusual. The internal logic of *L'Afrique fantôme* is based on a principle of indecision and indeterminacy. It is fairly obvious that throughout his fieldnotes, Leiris attempted to establish a climate of dualism, uncertainty, and subjectivity. Primary value is ascribed to moods, sensations, and feelings rather than actions and ideas. The "scientific" project is not forgotten, however, since it provides the ultimate justification for the narrative. Multiplying the angles of vision, Leiris operates on seemingly contradictory registers: confessional and ethnographic, poetic and utilitarian, one blurring the contours of the other, one engulfing the other. Few have focused on Leiris's ethnological practices and his discourse on the "Dark Continent."[7] Most commonly, critics have recast the elements of *L'Afrique fantôme* in a modernist project of self-construction. Philippe Lejeune, for instance, views it merely as an exercise in "auto-ethnography," an attempt by Leiris to explore the dark continent of the self:

Obsessed with his personal problems, Leiris saw the journey as a way of breaking the constraints imposed by his European personality in order to find a primitive mentality, for which he had a nostalgia. His attitude, especially at the end of the journey, was to search for contact with the authentic sacred. This was an attitude of identification, a lyrical desire to be initiated, as if African civilization reflected the deeply buried self he was attempting to recover.[8]

James Clifford, though setting Leiris's account in the historical context of colonialism, leaves implicit the actual acts by which Leiris and his fellow travelers produced knowledge about Africa. In fact, Clifford somewhat cursorily sets aside Leiris's "colonial standpoint," preferring to see *L'Afrique fantôme* as a mise-en-scène — albeit an inconclusive one — by means of which Leiris attempted to narrativize an existential experience. Leiris, he concludes, searched "for a satisfactory way of telling — of collecting and displaying — an existence" (*Predicament of Culture*, p. 170). A similar idea is conveyed by George Marcus, who finds the meaning of Leiris's text in a surrealist attempt to shape modern consciousness through personal experience.[9] For the Martinican poet Edouard Glissant, Leiris's journey to Africa was first and foremost motivated by the poet's "desire to find himself." While he acknowledges Leiris's problematic representation of Africa, Glissant nonetheless salutes him as "an essential figure of modern humanism."[10] A similar conclusion is reached by Jacques Darras, who, comparing Leiris to Conrad and Gide, also favors the idea of "self-search."[11]

One can understand why *L'Afrique fantôme* has often been considered an exercise in self-investigation. Leiris himself insists that his fieldnotes represent nothing but "a personal chronicle, an intimate journal which could as well have been written in Paris but happened to have been kept during a stroll through Africa" (*L'Afrique fantôme*, p. 213). Indeed, when leafing through the book, one is struck at times by the intimate nature of the narrative. Dreams are recorded here and there, according to the surrealist belief in the power of the primitive unconscious. The subject's fear of coitus and his erotic obsessions are displayed in spurts of uncontradicted shamelessness. The image projected is that of a poet, a dreamer who exhibits himself in absolute innocence. We are confronted with the image of the European who, in contact with Africa, slowly peels away the layers of civilization that separate him from natural and unobstructed life. The undressing of the self is both metaphorical and literal. Leiris wants to be naked and savage. He rejoices at the idea of sleeping naked, "in a savage state" (ibid., p. 194). The Africa he yearns for is "the land of 115 degrees in the shade, of slave convoys, cannibalistic feasts, empty skulls, of all things that are eaten, corroded, lost" (ibid., p. 225). The narrative is sprinkled with evocations of Conrad's *Heart of Darkness*, Kipling, and the Rimbaud of Abyssinia, which by inference should naturalize Leiris into the family of notable vagabonds of European literature. The journey is depicted as a descent to the end of the world, a farewell to civilization, as Leiris pursues the primitive Other near him, inside of him, and yet so far from him in time and space. This is what Alain-Michel Boyer believes when he says that, for Leiris, "L'homme des lointains est une introduction aux lointains intérieurs de l'homme. L'enquête est aussi une quête; bien plus une conquête." ("The man from distant places is an introduction to distant places within man. The exploration is also a quest, or more properly a conquest.")[12] Everything occurs as if the expedition through Africa was first and foremost an exploration in the jungle of the inner self, rather than a well-planned, well-protected mission organized by the Institute of Ethnology of the University of Paris and the National Museum of Natural History.

Once a climate of subjectivity has been established, the lines of the narrative become blurred. However, no intricate decoding strategy is needed to discover what we are not supposed to acknowledge. The solitary voyager in revolt against the values of Western civilization that Leiris claims to be is, all things considered, a constructed persona that does not hold up under scrutiny. Something rings false about his exhibitionism when it is placed in the objective context of the ethnographic mission. Indeed, the Dakar-Djibouti mission was not "a solitary promenade" but a quasi-militaristic expedition financed and approved by the French Senate and heavily subsidized by private organizations, notably the Rockefeller Foundation.[13] In this context the dreams, poems, streams of consciousness, and erotic obsessions interspersed in the fieldnotes appear at best as aesthetic games, at worst as exasperating tics.

Though one can say that Leiris's book covers a great variety of subjects and can mean a great variety of things, one must not display unnecessary skepticism about what the text says and how it says it. Rather than indulging in a doubtful deciphering of Leiris's inner self, it might be useful to examine what he says about what he saw and did during the 21 months he spent in Africa. An account of his full participation in the activities of the mission is not absent despite the subjective mode of the narrative, although it is rendered somewhat less discernible by the constant oscillation of the text between the inside and outside world, nonproductive reverie and systematic notations. The reader can be confounded and wonder which of the two Michel Leirises presented in the book is the real one? Is he the poet whose mode of thinking is "nondirected" in the fashion of the primitives imagined by Lévy-Bruhl? Or is he the methodical archivist and aggressive collector of artifacts whose thoughts are focused on the specific project of the mission? They are, of course, one and the same person; one picks up, in a real sense, where the other leaves off. Yet Leiris demands that we not be misled by this apparent dualism. He argues that his colonial accoutrements and behavior should not destroy his true essence, which is that of a dilettante and an artist: "With my colonial hat, my khaki shirt, my hunting pants, I remain the same man, riddled with anxiety, whom some consider a nice chap, quiet and colorful, a kind of 'bourgeois' artist" (ibid., p. 130).

While Leiris insists on a reading that would give primary importance to the self faced with the absurdity of life, L'Afrique fantôme remains a precious document on the articulation of ethnographic discourse within the colonized space. Indeed, the significance of L'Afrique fantôme resides in its blunt, naked exposition of the practice of field research during the first third of the twentieth century. Through Leiris's account, the reader accedes to the very unsavory nature of the "scientific" project undertaken on the Dakar-Djibouti mission. Leiris in fact identifies it in unambiguous terms with robbery and profanation, which are shown to be the normal modus operandi of the expedition. As Leiris notes tongue in cheek, the mere sight of the ethnographers created in the villages they crossed a turmoil comparable only to the disorganization caused in a conquered land by enemy troops bent on destruction: "During our visit in Koura (a village where we spent the night), all the villagers were terrified. For quite some time now, in many of the villages we have crossed, we have witnessed the same type of panic" (ibid., p. 94).

The reaction is understandable. On their path, Leiris and his fellow travelers sowed terror and desolation. Houses, altars, and churches were looted with determination and lawlessness. Utensils, costumes, toys, headdresses were spirited away or brutally snatched from their owners. Sanctuaries were violated. Masks, fetishes, and other sacred objects were stolen as the ethnographers brazenly operated under the horrified gaze of powerless villagers. "The fumes of sacrilege go to our head" (ibid., p. 87), exclaimed a delirious Leiris after a particularly terroristic raid. The vocabulary throughout his fieldnotes is telling: "looting," kidnapping," "raid," "robbery," and "bootlegging" are often used to describe the "scientific" operations of the mission. A journal entry of September 7, 1931, among many others, reveals quite forthrightly the system of gathering and data collection used by the Mission.

Before leaving Dyabougou, visit to the village and kidnapping of a second Kono, which Griaule had discovered by surreptitiously entering the sacred hut. This time, Lutten and I are in charge of the operation. . . . In the next village, I discover a Kono hut with a broken door. I show it to Griaule and the deed is done. . . . Shortly after the raid, we arrive at San. We eat lunch, then make contact in a neighboring village with the Bobo Oules, who are charming people. Idyllic nudity and jewelry made of straw or shells, young men with hair very nicely woven and women with their heads often shaven (mainly the older ones); all that is more than enough to seduce me, and make me indulge in all acts of piracy while thinking only of Robinson Crusoe and Paul and Virginie. (ibid., p. 83)

*L'Afrique fantôme* is replete with incidents of the brutal assertion of power. When any resistance was met from the Africans, the response of the "missionaries" was swift, surgical. The size of the object to be "removed" from its legitimate owners in the name of scientific knowledge did not seem to act as a deterrent. Hence, in the name of art preservation, Griaule and his companions stole entire mural walls decorating an Abyssinian church in Gondar. Whereas Leiris represents Griaule and his fellow travelers as motivated primarily by greed and the desire for lucre, he says that for him the compelling force remained "the idea of profanation."[14] After stealing a statue from a sanctuary, Leiris experiences a sort of orgasmic jouissance: "Nouvelle pollution nocturne. Rêvé par ailleurs que je me reconciliais avec André Breton" ("Another wet dream. Dreamed also that I made up with André Breton.") (ibid., p. 126), he notes in his journal on that day. This reference to Breton is no doubt meant to remind us of the days when surrealism used blasphemy and scandal as its mode of expression. It displaces attention from the brutality and atrocity of the ethnographers' practices to the poetic mischief of the past. Figures of European Romanticism — Robinson Crusoe, Paul and Virginie — are invoked in the same manner to readjust the focus. They appear providentially to rescue the ethnologist from the moral wreckage of his enterprise.

For the sake of historical accuracy, it is fair to note that the data-collection techniques used by the Dakar-Djibouti mission were not unusual schemes promoted by a derelict bunch. Quite to the contrary. Leiris and his friends were not renegades rejecting the conventional laws of a profession. They acted in conformity with the "scientific" norms of the time, which celebrated the image of the ethnologist as militant rogue:

Such abductions were also going on in other sites of Western exploration. Contemporaneous with the Dakar-Djibouti expedition, for example, André Malraux was engaging in activities of a similar nature in Cambodia, for which he served a brief term in jail; . . . the Imperial National History Museum in Vienna was installing a New Zealand collection that included mummies stolen by Maoris recruited for the job; . . . and Melville and Frances Herskovits were wheedling carvings from distraught Maroon women in the interior of Suriname. These are the encounters that have supplied our museums, from the Musée de l'Homme to the Metropolitan Museum of Art, with the great bulk of their non-Western artistic treasures.[15]

Yet Leiris did find himself at odds with his newly adopted profession. "Why is the ethnographic investigation so often connected in my mind to a police inquiry?" he asks (ibid., p. 210). He is frustrated by the distance between the subject/ethnographer and its object, the African, who remains "stubbornly opaque." He deplores the spiritual and temporal distancing of the ethnologist from the "primitive" Other. The research on *zâr* rituals in Ethiopia is often viewed as the culminating point of *L'Afrique fantôme* and as a significant moment in the history of French ethnography. There Leiris asserts the value of the ethnographer identifying with the culture he studies: the idea is to encounter the "primitive" Other on his own, predefined territory and to put oneself in his skin. Hence Leiris participated in the zâr ceremony—which he also financed and arranged—seeking the experience of religious trances and possession. Exotic, strange, and magical, this was the Africa he had hoped to encounter from the outset, the Africa that generations of European travelers, adventurers, and missionaries of all stripes had accredited. Animals are sacrificed. Leiris submits obediently to the rituals. He has the priestess place the bloody entrails on his head. He tastes animal blood in communion, eats chicken livers, all the while taking notes, all the while adding up the cost to him of the ceremonial arrangement.

For Leiris the poet, this is, presumably, *l'expérience des limites* so dear to Bataille. For Leiris the ethnographer, it is an application of the avant-garde doxology that substitutes transcultural identification for scientific objectivity in the name of truth and authenticity. As Trinh T. Minh-Ha points out, however, the (neo)colonial power relation which obtains between subject and object in such anthropological encounters invalidates the claim to authenticity: "The move from obnoxious exteriority to obtrusive interiority, the race for the so-called hidden values of a person or a culture, has given rise to a form of legitimized (but unacknowledged as such) voyeurism and subtle arrogance—namely, the pretense to see into or own the others' minds."[16] The feelings that prevailed at the end of this *corps à corps* with the primitive sacred were ennui and resentment: "The study was beginning to bore me. I was increasingly unable to see magi and Atrides in these peasants, who were simply sordidly avaricious" (ibid., p. 446). Much of Leiris's discontent after the zâr episode was linked to the question of money, to the legitimate insistence of his African informants or actors to be remunerated for their services.

Of course, Leiris's attitude toward the Africans is itself the most eloquent refutation of the myth of communion with the Other. According to his detailed account, the theory and practices of the Dakar-Djibouti expedition systematically violated and brutalized the very object of its study. It is therefore surprising to read James Clifford's dithyrambic statement that "the work of Griaule and his followers is one of the classic achievements of twentieth-century ethnography" (*Predicament of Culture*, p. 58). Such a claim forces us to meditate somberly on the theories and ethos that govern the discipline of ethnology. In any case, during their journey through Africa, Griaule and his companions, if not outwardly violent, displayed generally unsympathetic or frankly racist feelings toward Africans. Leiris's journal is sprinkled with predictable images of Africans and with indicting moral judgments of them as persons. He repeatedly expresses his anger at their "shiftiness," "unreliability," and "laziness." Measuring the extent of his irritation, Leiris questions his own capacity for restraint: "Will I end up saying also that 'these

Negroes are all the same' and that the only way to make them behave is the whip?" (*L'Afrique fantôme*, p. 172).

The African woman finds little redemption in the bestiary where Leiris imprisons her. Sometimes she is described as being as "pretty as a monkey" or as "beautiful as a beautiful cow"; at other times "she is not, properly speaking, a woman" (ibid., pp. 74, 119).

In front of the Africans, Leiris wants to remain the European, feared and obeyed. As he conducts his interviews, bribing and coercing informants, he poses dramatically as the superior Other, at times reproducing quite literally the language of colonialism, which demands the recognition of clear, unequivocal distinctions between Europeans and Africans, white and black, in the colonized space. "I realize full well how much they would despise me if I placed myself at their level, if I let myself go" (ibid., p. 349), he reasons. When unable to assert his authority and superiority, the poet/ethnographer feels like an unarmed target. The idea communicated, explicitly or implicitly, throughout his journal is that the line which separates him (the white European) from "them" (the black Africans) must never be crossed if the authority of the ethnographer is to remain unchallenged. As Leiris amply demonstrates, this fundamental precept of the colonial order governed the activities of the mission as a whole.

At other times, Leiris's verdict against the Africans is irremediable because of the ordinariness of their lives and the environment in which they live. Instead of the marvelous and the magical he had anticipated, Leiris for the most part encountered dispossessed farmers subjugated to colonial rule. Reality thus came into violent collision with the ethnological project, vitiating it, as it were. The Africa pursued by ethnology, at each moment, threatens to dissolve into nothingness. By an artificial process, this elusive object was captured, however. Through the lens of his camera, Leiris discovered the permanent, invariable Africa of the primitivists. "I must look at the pictures that have just been developed to realize that I am somewhere which resembles Africa" (ibid., p. 171), he notes with feigned ingenuousness.

The brigandage perpetrated by the Griaule mission throughout its journey is most often presented by Leiris as childish pranks or as the fulfillment of some obscure erotic desire. Leiris does express discomfort at the scandalous practices of the ethnographic team. Yet he claims innocence when measuring the mission's methods of exploration against the colonial authorities' methods of subjugation: "To the officials, however, who would take us to task because of our dealings with the Negroes, it would be easy to answer that as long as Africa is subjected to a system as repugnant as the one of levies and military service, without anything in return, they can not be disturbed with regards to a few objects, stolen or bought at a bargain price" (ibid., pp. 89–90). Here we see the complicity of ethnography with the colonial enterprise. On the one hand, the colonial structure ensures the safety and success of the fieldwork by providing the Griaule team with the administrative and military protection necessary to keep the "native" in his place. On the other hand, colonialism, thanks to its oppressive apparatus, absolves Leiris of all blame.

One does find entries in *L'Afrique fantôme* where Leiris decries the brutal nature of colonization and appears to refute the myth of France's *mission civilisatrice*. However, Leiris's anti-colonialism often takes an ambiguous form. Observing the colonial fauna encountered during his peregrinations, he proclaims an affinity for its most aggressive members, the military police. Their close contact with the Africans, albeit brutal, places them in a special category: "In the colonies, I prefer the military to the civilians. They are closer to the natives and more like them, by the very fact that their profession consists in fighting with them" (ibid., p. 154). Leiris's indictment of colonialism is thus transformed into a form of defense, and the focus displaced from the reality of oppression and exploitation to a question of existential authenticity. According to this logic, colonized and colonizers, living in fraternal hatred, become united in a common project. Such logic, of course, normalizes the very system that Leiris purports to denounce.

Leiris could not encounter the African even at the philosophical level because he was imbued with the ideology of Otherness, which asserts as evident the radical opposition of civilized and primitive, reason and instinct, European and African. His representation of Africa and Africans in *L'Afrique fantôme* is based on the belief in the timeless truth of these terms as antinomies inscribed in Nature. Like other European primitivists who thrived on ambiguity, Leiris saw in the contemporary African "at once a 'brother' and an 'other.'"[17] This "brother," of course, had only one raison d'être — to reconnect Western man with his mythical, prehistorical past. The *"je est un autre"* of Rimbaud is one of the earliest examples of modernism's celebration of the "primitive" alter ego that lies both inside and outside of Western man. It must be emphasized, however, that the operative language of primitivism rests on this very contradiction, which can never be eliminated. In the final analysis, primitivism recognizes only one axiomatic proposition: whatever is black all over cannot be white, and therefore equal. It is on this simple principle that colonialist Europe structured its basic argument for domination and power. The idea of European superiority and African inferiority found its justification in this simple proposition. A similar logic governed the eth-nographic assumptions of Leiris and his friends, who affirmed by their deeds that the "I" of the European is the absolute subject and the African the ob-ject, deprived of self-consciousness. In this scheme, the culture of Europe is posited as everything, and that of Africa, as a vague, irrational chaos.

L'Afrique fantôme records the stages of a journey that took Leiris, Griaule, and their companions to French Equatorial Africa, Nigeria, the Cameroons, the Belgian Congo, the Sudan, Abyssinia, and the Somalian Coast. The ex-pedition was proclaimed a success. In the second issue of Le Minotaure, which is devoted entirely to the Dakar-Djibouti mission, there is an over-whelming inventory of the "loot" brought back to Paris. Among other things, there were thirty-five hundred "ethnographic objects"; an important collec-tion of Abyssinian paintings, including the murals from the church in Gon-dar; three hundred Ethiopian manuscripts and amulets, which went to the Bibliothèque Nationale; a zoological and botanical collection comprising several live animals, trees, and plants; and six thousand photographs. "Such is the booty brought back by this expedition, which accomplished in spite of numerous difficulties its assigned mission," wrote Paul Rivet and George-Henri Rivière, Director and Assistant Director of the Museum of Ethnogra-phy.[18] The sheer volume of these acquisitions should put to rest the notion that Leiris came back from Africa empty-handed and confused, having found only the phantom of himself and Africa. At the end of the journey, no an-guish or feeling of alienation eclipses his sense of accomplishment. As he prepares to return to his bourgeois world, whose trappings, he says, seduce him as much as the glare of "tin mesmerizes the Negro," Leiris appears con-tent, serene: "I filed away my paper in the box-desk, closed my luggage, pre-pared my clothes for tomorrow morning. I write these lines on my couchette. The boat sways slightly. I have a clear mind, a tranquil heart. All I have left to do is to close this notebook, turn off the light, lie down, sleep and dream" (ibid., p. 525).

L'Afrique fantôme is an ambivalent text that has been subjected to differ-ent readings and interpretations. For some, its value resides in the author's self-representation. Others say that it is a valuable contribution to modern ethnology and must be appreciated as such. There are also those who suggest that it illustrates the subversive spirit of surrealism and the modernist concep-tion of freedom. They argue that Leiris, like a number of avant-garde poets preoccupied with Eros, magic, and the primitive, found gratification in sym-bols and the practice of aggression. The analysis proposed here does not necessarily contradict these interpretations, nor does it preclude the possibility of other encounters with Leiris, the man and the poet. In considering *L'Afrique fantôme*, my intention has been to make explicit the conditions of emergence of the primitivist discourse. This discourse, as I have attempted to show, tends to silence its own truth. Yet some critics have been reluctant to acknowledge the obvious content of Leiris's text, as though an implicit censoring rule had been promulgated by members of the same tribe. As Johannes Fabian observes, "the silence and secrecy surrounding the ethnographic act are comparable to the removal of fundamental religious acts from the everyday sphere."[19] In the 1950 preamble and preface of *L'Afrique fantôme*, Leiris also tried to "white-out" from his 1934 text the historical and the political, and to valorize the personal and existential. Throughout his account, he minimizes his own responsibility in the mission's activities. Playful or disarmingly frank, he vaunts the uniqueness of his position not as agent but as spectator.

To read *l'Afrique fantôme* only in terms of an individualized quest, as some have done, is to distort its meaning and erase its syntax, which is at once mystifying and revealing. The indirection and indefiniteness of the text, which oscillates between the self and the world, lucidity and duplicity, define its character. The excess of truth about the self often blurs the reality of the world, the colonial space and the ethnographic practice. Leiris, as we have seen, was not a mere voyeur or somnambulist crossing a phantasmatic Africa. On the contrary, if we are to believe his own account, he was one of the mission's most intrepid agents. *L'Afrique fantôme* records much more than the angst of a morose man engulfed by his obsessions. It can be read both as an extended and exuberant celebration of European colonial power and as a testimony to that authorized mayhem in colonized Africa which for a long time passed for scientific investigation. A composite account of ethnological notations, dastardly deeds, poetic reflections, and erotic broodings, *L'Afrique fantôme* provides insight into the primitivist mentality. It poses in a troubling manner the question of the writer's involvement in promoting the colonialist worldview in the politics of meaning and knowledge.

MARJORIE PERLOFF

# Tolerance and Taboo
## Modernist Primitivisms
## and Postmodernist Pieties

Combien de kilomètres a-t-il fallu que nous fas-
sions pour nous sentir enfin au seuil de l'exotisme!
— Michel Leiris, *L'Afrique fantôme*

Exoticism, as Leiris knew, can take many forms, not the least of which is the
contemporary urge to eliminate it once and for all, to demonstrate that we
are all equal and that, so far as history goes, an enlightened "we" who live at
the end of the twentieth century can see the hidden and not-so-hidden colonialism, racism, and sexism of the early twentieth century as in themselves
they really were. In her highly praised study, *Gone Primitive: Savage Intellects, Modern Lives* (1990), for example, Marianna Torgovnick is scornful of
modernist definitions and ideas about the primitive, which "all take the West
as norm and define the rest as inferior, different, deviant, subordinate, and
subordinatable."[1] "We simply do not have," she mourns, "a neutral, politically acceptable vocabulary," the "best we can do" thus being "to uncover,
from a political and cultural perspective, the kinds of work key terms like
*primitive* have performed within modern and postmodern culture and the
kinds of work they have evaded and short-changed" (*Gone Primitive*, p. 21).

But of course words like "evaded" and "short-changed" are themselves
loaded, suggesting that there is a correct (as in politically correct) way to
regard "the primitive" and the "work" it *should* perform in our culture.
Oddly — and I shall come back to this issue — *Gone Primitive* seems to have
learned little from a book that appeared just two years earlier and on which
it is heavily dependent for its information, subject matter, and even its specific examples, namely, James Clifford's *The Predicament of Culture* (1988),
which argued eloquently that "the words of ethnographic writing . . . cannot

be construed as monological, as the authoritative statement about, or interpretation of, an abstracted, textualized reality."[2] When Torgovnick does cite
Clifford, it is to remark (accurately enough) about his omission of the role
gender plays in the construction of "the primitive," an omission that places
Clifford in the long line of those First World male (and sometimes, like Margaret Mead, even female) ethnographers who have victimized the Other.[3]
Thus, in an ironic reversal, the ethnographer takes the place of the "primitive" in the "them" versus "us" game.

Fieldwork, in this scheme of things, is devalued as old-fashionedly em-
piricist, as is any sort of firsthand experience of ethnographic acts and their
objects of investigation, the knowledge, for starters, of the languages of both
the investigators and the investigated. The preferred method is to know what
one wants to prove — in this case, that modernism was riddled with racism,
sexism, and colonialism — and then to collect one's supporting exempla, the
game being to ignore all "evidence" that might point in a contrary direction.
Ironically, then, we are now witnessing an increasing body of scholarship on
oppressed groups that, in its zeal to track down the oppressors, reinscribes
the very oppression and subordination it seeks to descry. Furthermore, such
would-be oppositional discourse curiously reverts to the very binary model
that poststructuralist critics have assiduously claimed to be undermining. In
what follows, I take Torgovnick's interrogation of modernist primitivism as
my example.

Chapter 5 of *Gone Primitive*, "The Many Obsessions of Michel Leiris,"
begins with the following thumbnail sketch:

Michel Leiris is a French novelist, poet, and man of letters, but also and by profession, an ethnographer who has written a massive and important book on African art.
Intellectually, he has traveled with his culture, moving from Surrealism in the twenties and thirties, to Existentialism after World War II, to, more recently, a poststructuralist concern with language. He has been the intellectual bridesmaid of figures
better known in this country, like Georges Bataille and Jean-Paul Sartre. (p. 105)

Whatever audience Torgovnick is writing for here, surely it cannot be an
audience in any way familiar with French literature or culture, much less
with Michel Leiris or problems of African ethnography. "A graduate seminar
at Duke in Spring 1988," explains this professor of English in her preface,
"was indefatigable in providing me with information and with evidence that
primitivism was everywhere present in contemporary culture" (p. x). Hers,
one surmises, is a projected readership not likely to be offended by such
inaccuracies as that Leiris was a "bridesmaid" (an odd vulgarism) of Sartre,

or that Leiris's interest in language *followed* his surrealist phase (which was, incidentally, never fully surrealist), when in fact it coincided with it. And further: only a fairly narrowly drawn American audience would not question Torgovnick's assertion that the "best-known work in English on Leiris," a special issue of *SubStance* edited by Jean-Jacques Thomas, conceives of the writer as "ethnographic hero" and ignores (in the case of Mary Ann Caws's essay) his terrible misogyny. What Torgovnick doesn't say is that this issue appeared as long ago as 1975, when gender theory was in its infancy, and that, from the 1960's to the present, a rich secondary literature on Leiris has come into being, critics from Maurice Blanchot, Philip Lejeune, and Susan Sontag to Rosalind Krauss, James Clifford, and Dennis Hollier writing major commentary on this complex and brilliant writer.[4]

Then, too, the cultural production Torgovnick investigates seems oddly unrelated to questions of the actual production and reception of Leiris's autobiography. The critic bases her entire reading of Leiris's *Manhood* (*L'Age d'homme*, 1939) on its "inspiring icon" in the form of Lucas Cranach's diptych *Lucrece and Judith* (1536), reproduced on the book's cover (see *Gone Primitive*, p. 109). But although Cranach's diptych is indeed central to Leiris's autobiography, the original 1939 edition published in Paris by Gallimard does not reproduce the painting at all (it first appeared in the 1946 edition, where *L'Age d'homme* is preceded by the introductory essay, "De la littérature considérée comme une tauromachie"), whereas the 1966 Livre de Poche edition has on its cover a blown-up detail of Judith's torso, the gender of the headless figure, holding what seems to be its own head in its left hand, being ambiguous; and the 1973 Folio paperback edition depicts Judith as a semi-abstract playing-card figure, a kind of Queen of Hearts.[5] Indeed, the first time Cranach's Lucrece and Judith become, so to speak, Leiris cover girls is in the 1984 North Point Press translation by Richard Howard (a translation originally published by Grossman in 1968). And when the University of Chicago Press recently reissued this edition, North Point having gone out of business, the cover design and format were retained.

Leiris's "misogynist" cover (which was not in fact his cover at all) thus finds itself juxtaposed to Torgovnick's own Chicago cover, in her case of Man Ray's 1926 photograph *Kiki* (also called *Noire et blanche*), an egregious example, no doubt, of modernist "primitivism" in its juxtaposition of the oval head of Man Ray's sleeping mistress (Kiki) and the oval African mask with its sightless eyes—both the "white" face, underneath jet-black hair, and the black mask, silhouetted against Kiki's naked white arm and shoulder, being rendered as fetishized objects controlled by the male artist-photographer

Man Ray. What the Leiris–Man Ray juxtaposition masks, however, is that, unlike Man Ray, whose passionate love life was legendary, Michel Leiris had, by his own account, enormous sexual difficulties; his erotic fantasies of dismemberment, far from being directed outward — say, toward African women who would have to submit to his will — were primarily directed at his own person.

The aim of Torgovnick's chapter, in any case, is to debunk the myth of Leiris as "intellectual hero," a term that I have never seen applied to Leiris but that Torgovnick uses a number of times, interchangeably with "postmodern ethnographic hero." In his famous essay of 1950, "L'ethnographe devant le colonialisme," Leiris "correctly" (the word is Torgovnick's) "notes the colonized would begin to 'speak back' to the once monologic West," and "admirably" (again her word) "maintains that the ethnographer's role should be that of facilitating the future that the formerly colonized imagine for themselves" (*Gone Primitive*, p. 106). But such "admirable" and "correct" ideas are evidently not enough to redeem a writer whose early autobiographical work, *Manhood*, when read in conjunction with his ostensibly anti-colonialist *African Art* (1967), reveals "a spillage between sexuality and Western interest in African art — a spillage we too often take for granted, and take for granted to our shame" (ibid., p. 107).

Let us see what we should be ashamed about. *Manhood*, Torgovnick claims, cannot just be read as an arresting, fictionalized autobiography; on the contrary, "the terms Leiris chooses for his exposure of self should be taken seriously and count as facts about his brand of primitivism, even if they are 'invented' or 'constructed' facts" (ibid., p. 108). The word *facts* is interesting in this context. One such "fact," evidently, is Leiris's reading of Cranach's *Lucrece and Judith*, a double painting that, so the author tells us, represents the two erotic poles that haunted his adolescence and young manhood. Here, taken out of its context, which I shall discuss in a moment, is Leiris's description:

the first, Lucrece, pressing to the center of her white chest, between two marvelously hard round breasts (whose nipples seem as rigid as the stones decorating a gorget or cuirass at the same place), the narrow blade of a dagger whose tip is already beaded, like the most intimate gift appearing at the end of the male member, with a few drops of blood, and about to annihilate the effect of the rape she has suffered by a similar gesture: one that will thrust into a warm sheath of flesh, and for a bloody death, the weapon at its maximum degree of stiffness, like the rapist's inexorable virility when it enters by force the orifice already gaping between her thighs, the gentle pink wound that soon after returned the libation in full measure, just as the wound — deeper, wickeder too, but perhaps even more intoxicating — made by the dagger will release, from Lucrece's very heart as she faints or fails, a torrent of blood; the second, Judith, in her right hand a sword naked as herself, its point piercing the ground close to her slender toes and its firm broad blade having just severed Holofernes' head, which hangs, sinister trophy, from the heroine's left hand, fingers and hair mingled in hideous union — Judith, wearing a necklace as heavy as a convict's chain, whose coldness around her voluptuous neck recalls that of the sword close to her feet — Judith, placid and already seeming to ignore the bearded ball she holds like a phallic glans she could have sundered merely by pressing her legs together with Holofernes' floodgates opened; or which, an ogress at the height of her madness, she might have cut from the powerful member of the drunken (and perhaps vomiting) man with a sudden snap of her teeth.[6]

Interestingly, Cranach's paintings have little of the violence and horror that Leiris ascribes to them; his astonishing ekphrasis teases out meanings largely submerged, if not absent, in the diptych, where the myths are primarily vehicles for the painter's exhibition of the female body in all its sensuous nudity. The reference to Judith's "fingers and [Holofernes's] hair mingled in hideous union," for instance, is a pure invention on Leiris's part, the calm expression on Judith's lovely face all but belying what has just taken place. But Torgovnick pays no attention to these anomalies, concerned as she is with what she takes to be the "repellent" "pornographic violence" of Leiris's description, and concluding that he must have come to ethnography "via sensual associations very much like those which attract him to Cranach's Lucrece and Judith."[7]

Accordingly, when she reads the later, seemingly objective account in *African Art* of the tribal signification of scarification and tattooing, as well as circumcision and, in the case of young women, excision of the clitoris and the labia majora, Torgovnick detects an ulterior motive. Leiris is not, she argues, writing a disinterested account of African tribal customs; he is enjoying what she calls the "prophylactic effect" inherent in his "ethnographic approach to the primitive" (*Gone Primitive*, p. 114). Like Judith and Lucrece, the native women who are described with seeming scientific detachment cannot "talk back," the male viewer thus being able to gaze at them voyeuristically. "They are object; he is subject. He is in control, empowered, unthreatened" (ibid.). The attraction of Africa for Leiris turns out to be pornographic, a vehicle for his diseased sexual fantasies about women. Such ethnographic work, Torgovnick concludes, is finally "perverse," a model we who are enlightened must abjure. Its "structures of mastery" must give way to those of "mutuality; a reaching out to the natural world as our home and mother, not the exploitation of that world for profit." "Primitive societies," after all, should be "allowed to exist in their own times and spaces, within their own *conceptions of* time and space, not transposed and filtered into Western terms." Indeed, a correct history of primitive societies would acknowledge these societies "as full and valid alternatives to Western cultures" (ibid., p. 247).

On what planet, one wonders, do these utopian conditions obtain? Where are the "structures of mutuality," where the "natural world" that is "our home and mother," where each society exists "in [its] own time and space"? Not, assuredly, in Leiris's France, a France that was engaged during his high-school years in the horrific trench warfare of World War I, a France that, by the time he published *Manhood*, was months away from the Nazi occupation of World War II. Under these circumstances, "structures of mutuality" and "full and valid alternatives" (themselves, incidentally, nothing if not Western, post-Enlightenment norms) may have seemed just slightly out of reach.

Here is where history comes in, history which is the great absence in the branch of cultural studies practiced by Torgovnick.[8] Her reasoning goes something like this: (1) enlightened narrative about so-called primitive societies is directly related to "enlightened" personal morality; (2) Leiris had curious sexual obsessions, judging from the revelations in his autobiography, which must count as relevant "facts" in any assessment of his "character"; and therefore, (3) even though Leiris later writes explicitly and eloquently against colonialism, his accounts of such matters as African tattoo and scarification rituals are not to be trusted. To put it crudely, anyone so preoccupied with what may well be kinky sex, and who persists in seeing sex in its relationship to death, cannot be the kind of "ethnographic hero" "we" want.

I wish I could say my summary of Torgovnick's argument was simplified. But the fact is that the colonialist Joseph Conrad, the racist D. H. Lawrence, the voyeuristic Bronislaw Malinowski, and even the cowardly Margaret Mead, who, despite her own lesbian leanings, "stop[ped] short of explicitly writing against homophobia" (ibid., p. 238) — all these are found wanting according to the severe, puritanic yardstick applied to them in *Gone Primitive*. How Conrad's representations of the European experience of the Congo in the early twentieth century relate to other accounts of the period is considered beside the point, the point being, it seems, that Conrad refused to spell out what lay behind Kurtz's famous phrase, "the horror, the horror," that he ignored "ugly facts, facts like how those heads [of the natives] got on the palisade, facts like the African woman's relation to Kurtz" (ibid., p. 152).

"Conrad's version of the primitive," declares Torgovnick with great moral authority, "is a cheat" (ibid., p. 153).

So, it seems, was the "phantom Africa" of Michel Leiris. Born in 1901, Leiris grew up in bourgeois comfort in Paris, where his father was a banker. The young Leiris was seemingly insulated from the Great War, which broke out, let us remember, when he was at the impressionable age of thirteen. Not that *Manhood* is overtly a war book. Indeed, its foreword, "De la littérature considérée comme une tauromachie" (in the English translation, "The Autobiographer as *Torero*" becomes the afterword), begins with a nonchalant reference to Leiris's coming to legal maturity "four years after the war which like so many other boys of his generation, he had experienced as scarcely more than a long vacation" (*Manhood*, p. 154; *L'Age d'homme*, p. 9). But in the very next paragraph, we read, "Now in 1939, when the young men of the post-war period see the utter collapse of that structure of facility which they despaired of trying to invest with not only an authentic fervor but a terrible distinction as well, the author freely acknowledges that his true 'manhood' still remains to be written, when he will have suffered, in one form or another the same bitter ordeal his elders faced." And on the following page, the narrative breaks off abruptly with the following remarks:

> This was the preface I was writing for *Manhood* on the eve of the "phony war." I am rereading it today [evidently 1945] in Le Havre, a city I have often visited for a few days' vacation and to which I am bound by many old ties (my friends Limbour, Queneau, and Salacrou, who were born here; Sartre, who taught here and with whom I became associated in 1941 when most of the writers remaining in occupied France united against the Nazi oppression). Le Havre is now largely destroyed, as I can see from my balcony, which overlooks the harbor from a sufficient height and distance to give a true picture of the terrible *tabula rasa* the bombs made in the center of the city, as if there has been an attempt to repeat in the real world, on a terrain populated by living beings, the famous Cartesian operation. On this scale, the personal problems with which *Manhood* is concerned are obviously insignificant: whatever might have been, in the best cases, its strength and its sincerity, the poet's inner agony, weighed against the horrors of war, count for no more than a toothache over which it would be graceless to groan. (*Manhood*, pp. 154–55; cf. *L'Age d'homme*, p. 11)

Such speculations might have led to silence — the "no poetry after Auschwitz" stance. Or they might have led, as indeed they did, to the use of "the toothache over which it would be graceless to groan," and related aches and wounds, as synecdoches and analogues for those "horrors of war" and, in a larger sense, horrors of being human which are, in any case, always seen as paradoxical. "Even in Le Havre," Leiris remarks in the foreword, "things continue, urban life persists. Above the still intact houses as above the site of the ruins there shines intermittently, despite the rainy weather, a bright, beautiful sun" (*Manhood*, p. 155). Just so, the imagery of death, of shame and horror, of the abject, which is so prominent in *Manhood*, is made poignant by its association with desire and pleasure, with the longing for voluptuous gratification. And to complicate matters further, what makes modern, "civilized" urban life so terrifying is that the orderly and familiar rituals of bourgeois family life to which the child is exposed, the boredoms of normal everyday existence, provide only the flimsiest screen for the violence beneath the surface.[9]

In assessing Leiris's authorial position in *African Art*, read retrospectively, in the light of his autobiography, Torgovnick writes "They [the African women] are object; he is subject. He is in control, empowered, unthreatened" (*Gone Primitive*, p. 114). Presumably Leiris has this position because he is a white man, describing the tribal mutilation practices of black women.[10] But surely no one is less "in control" and "unthreatened" than the hero of *Manhood*, who, from the opening page of the book, presents himself as having a "head . . . rather large for my body," legs "a little short for the length of my torso," and thin, hairy hands, "the veins distinct; my two middle fingers, curving inward toward the tips, [which] must denote something rather weak and evasive in my character." And further: "Sexually, I am not, I believe, abnormal — simply a man of rather cold temperament — but I have long tended to regard myself as virtually impotent. It has been some time, in any case, since I have ceased to consider the sexual act as a simple matter, but rather as a relatively exceptional event" (*Manhood*, p. 5). Here is the personal predisposition that colors so many of the book's subsequent events and memories.

Take the memory of the boy's first erection, when he was six or seven, on a family picnic in the woods near Paris. "The event which caused my excitement was the sight of a group of children . . . climbing trees barefoot. . . . Much later, it seemed to me that the strange sensation I experienced then came from imagining what must have been both a pleasant and painful feeling for the children in question, the feeling caused by the contact of the soles of their feet and their bare toes with the rough bark" (ibid., pp. 13–14). We may consider such confessions as, in Torgovnick's words, "a disturbing reminder of how this linking of sex and violence . . . pervades Western culture and provides a psyche like Leiris's with ready simulacra" (*Gone Primitive*, p. 110). Or we may try to understand Leiris's collage of "disturbing" images as by no means "simulacra" but, on the contrary, images with specific reference to a time and place when pretensions of a protected childhood and "civilized" behavior, of paternal and church authority and training, of fixed class divisions and the seemingly incontrovertible gap between masters and servants were all playing themselves out against the backdrop of a world war that was a persistent but barely alluded to subtext.

We can see this anomaly most clearly in the short sequence called "Throat Cut," in the chapter "The Head of Holofernes." The incident in question could hardly be more ordinary. Yet the autobiographer, who has presented his childhood self as acquiring knowledge of violence and tragedy largely from spectatorship, whether at the opera, the theater, or the museum, recalls it as "the most painful of all my childhood memories":

At the age of five or six, I was the victim of an assault. I mean that I endured an operation on my throat to remove certain growths; the operation took place in a very brutal manner, without my being anesthetized. My parents had first made the mistake of taking me to the surgeon without telling me where we were going. If my recollections are correct, I believed we were on the way to the circus; I was therefore far from anticipating the nasty trick about to be played on me by our family doctor, who assisted the surgeon, as well as by the latter himself. The occasion went off, point by point, like a play that had been rehearsed, and I had the feeling that I had been lured into a hideous ambush. Matters proceeded as follows: leaving my parents in the waiting room, the old doctor led me into another room where the surgeon was waiting for me, wearing a huge black beard and a white gown. . . . I saw various sharp instruments and must have looked frightened, for the old doctor took me on his lap and said to reassure me: "Come here, *mon petit coco*! Now we're going to play kitchen." From this moment on I can remember nothing except the sudden assault of the surgeon, who plunged some kind of sharp instrument into my throat, the pain that I felt, and the scream — like that of a slaughtered animal — that I uttered. My mother, who heard me from the next room, was terrified.

On the way home in the carriage, I did not speak a word; the shock had been so violent that for twenty-four hours it was impossible to get a word out of me; my mother, completely disoriented, wondered if I had become mute. All I can remember about the period immediately following the operation is the carriage ride, my parents' vain attempts to make me speak, and then, back at the house, my mother holding me in her arms in front of the living-room fireplace, the sherbets she had me swallow, the blood I spat up at each mouthful and which mingled with the raspberry color of the sherbets. (*Manhood*, pp. 64–65)

"My whole image of life," remarks Leiris, "has been scarred by the incident: the world, full of traps, is nothing but a huge prison or an operating theater; I am on earth only to become a specimen for doctors, cannon fodder, food for worms" (ibid., p. 65). What justifies this seemingly excessive response is that the incident in question depended on a terrible deception, on the collusion of his parents with the doctor's "enlightened" view that children are to be manipulated and coerced into acquiescence. But the curious phrase in the above sentence is "cannon fodder" (*chair à canons*; *L'Age d'homme*, p. 112). The world as prison, as operating theater — these classic metaphors emerge naturally from the tonsillectomy, but the image of cannon fodder relates the ordinary childhood incident to the extraordinary circumstance of the war outside the nursery. The child is lured by the promise of a circus, just as the young medical student in Celine's *Voyage au bout de la nuit* is promised adventure and a beautiful uniform only to end up, like little Leiris, in the place of dismemberment, where the red of raspberry sorbets is mixed with blood.

The memory of the throat operation foreshadows another seemingly trivial, "suburban" incident:

One day a cousin whose parents lived in the villa next door to ours was bitten by a dog. One detail made me shudder: I was told that the bite had been so deep "a piece of buttock had remained in the child's underwear." I cannot think of this cousin — who was subsequently killed in the war — without remembering what he was like when the incident occurred: a big, well-built, heavy-set boy whose parents adored him because he represented, from a certain point of view, the ideal of beauty and health, and whose chubby calves were the admiration of almost everyone in the family, except for my mother, who said he was a "big softy" and thought her sons "more delicate." (*Manhood*, p. 67)

It is against the backdrop of such incidents that we must understand the attraction-repulsion associated for Leiris with "Lucrece the chaste and Judith the patriot prostitute," as depicted in Cranach's diptych:

One might . . . suspect that their two apparently distinct gestures were at bottom identical, and that both were supremely concerned to cleanse in blood the taint of an erotic act, the one expiating by her suicide the shame of having been violated (and perhaps of having enjoyed that violation), the other expiating by murder the shame of having prostituted herself to her victim. So that it would not be out of mere caprice, but by virtue of profound analogies, that Cranach painted the two as pendants, both similarly naked and desirable, at one in that complete absence of moral hierarchy which is the necessary concomitant of nakedness, and shown on the verge of committing particularly arousing actions. (ibid., pp. 93–94)

"The passage repels most," writes Torgovnick, "by its suggestion that Lucrece enjoyed (must have enjoyed) her rape . . . and its parallel suggestion that Judith castrates Holofernes to punish him for his sexuality, rather than kills him as a political act" (*Gone Primitive*, p. 110). The either/or of the latter statement (i.e., it's either politics *or* sex) would be quite alien to Leiris's radius of discourse, but the former statement, with its very contemporary (and justified) complaint about the still-prevalent male assumption that women who are raped somehow "want" it, is also misconceived. The death of Cleopatra, who represents for Leiris a kind of symbolic union of the Lucrece and Judith prototypes, is apposite here:

On the one hand the murderous serpent, the male symbol par excellence — on the other the figs beneath which [the asp] was concealed, the common image of the female organ. . . . I cannot help noting with what exactitude this meeting of symbols corresponds to what for me is the profound meaning of suicide: to become at the same time *oneself and the other*, male and female, subject and object, killed and killer — the only possibility of communion with oneself. (*Manhood*, p. 93)

Leiris relates this image of "the right to love oneself to excess" to "that of Prometheus punished for having stolen fire" (ibid.).

Leiris is not, then, subscribing to anything so vulgar as the patriarchal belief that woman is the subject who "enjoys" rape. He identifies, after all, not with Lucrece's rapist but with Lucrece; not with Holofernes but with Judith, his case being for the dissolution of gender boundaries in the love act and for the inseparability of Eros and Thanatos. The issue is not whether or not this particular vision of human sexuality is "true" but whether Leiris's powerful self-examination and pitiless self-critique carry conviction. The aim of *Manhood*, after all, is not to provide moral uplift or to present the reader with "full and valid alternatives," but to depict an especially demonic (because so seemingly placid and bourgeois) world, the world *entre deux guerres*, in all its excesses and contradictions.

Can a writer like Leiris be a "good" ethnographer and an important source for our understanding of the "primitive"? In the final chapter of *Manhood*, Leiris tells us that, in response to a crisis period in his twenties, he decided to engage in "a more strenuous life for a while," and "went to Africa for almost two years, as a member of an ethnographical expedition. After months of chastity and emotional weaning, I fell in love while in Gondar with an Ethiopian woman who corresponded physically and morally to my double image of Lucrece and Judith" (ibid., p. 40). This woman's face, Leiris recalls, was "beautiful but her breasts ravaged"; she was "wrapped in a filthy gray toga, smelled of sour milk, and owned a young Negro slave girl"; he dwells further on the "bluish" tattoos around the neck of this "syphilitic" witch, and notes that, "her clitoris extirpated, like all the women of her race, she must have been frigid, at least from a European point of view." "I never," he concludes, "made love to her, but when the sacrifice took place it seemed to me that a relation more intimate than any carnal link was established between her and myself" (ibid., p. 140).

It is interesting to compare this retrospective description of the Gondar woman to the diary version recorded just a few years earlier and published in *L'Afrique fantôme* (1934). Emawayish, as the woman in question was called, was the daughter of Malkam Ayyahou, the charismatic leader of a group of initiates possessed by *zâr* genies. Leiris's entry for August 25, 1932 records a dark mood: "Bitterness. Resentment against ethnography, which makes you take so inhuman a position, that of an observer, in situations where it would be best to let go."[11] As James Clifford recounts in his notes to the translation, "Three days later, during an intense possession seance, Emawayish contrives to leave her mother, comes over to the bed on which Leiris is sitting and, in a gesture of apparent intimacy, places his hand under her armpit. The ethnographer is entranced by the songs she sings while possessed and wants her to write them down so that he and his Ethiopian co-worker Abba Jérome can make translations" (headnote to "Phantom Africa," p. 42). Here is the beginning of Leiris's entry for August 31:

During the morning, letter from Emawayish. She would be pleased if I made her a gift of a blanket. Quite a natural wish, following my courtly declarations of devotion. . . . I'll never accuse a native of venality. Just imagine how insanely wealthy a European must seem to such poor people and how they must look obsessively on his smallest objects of comfort, as if they were treasures! (Leiris, "Phantom Africa," pp. 42–43)

Leiris now brings Emawayish pens, ink, and a notebook "so she can record for herself—or dictate to her son—the manuscript [of her songs]"; he is upset that another member of the expedition, Lutten (for whom "making love is only a matter of pleasure or hygiene!") wants to sleep with her, whereas he himself finds it "impossible . . . to treat love with nonchalance." Isolated, lonely, unable to find anyone to whom he "can speak from the bottom of [his] heart," he is all but suicidal. When he urges her to record her love songs, Emawayish asks pointedly: "Does poetry exist in France?" And then, as if challenging Leiris's manhood: "Does love exist in France?" (ibid., p. 43; *L'Afrique fantôme*, p. 359).

The very next entry (September 1) begins: "Very bad night. First insomnia, then, very late, a little sleep," which is haunted by guilty dreams. "During the day," Leiris notes, "though tired and enervated, I feel better. I realize

I've been overworked, that I've been too caught up with research in a dangerous area." And he admits his doubts as to the methods of gathering material, the poetry collected "probably not as beautiful as I had thought, the possession states not as intense . . . and also covering up quite a bit of merchandizing. . . . But above all, and in contradiction to all this, an ardent sensation of being at the edge of something whose depths I will never touch." Then, after describing Emawayish's belief that "one of the spirits inhabiting the head of her mother is capable of killing her son," he remarks sadly that he cannot really enter her spirit world, "imbued whatever I do with a civilization that leads one to give everything a moral rather than a magical tint. And this is the great boundary I will never cross" ("Phantom Africa," p. 44; *L'Afrique fantôme*, p. 360).

Is this the white man who Torgovnick takes to be wholly "in control, empowered, unthreatened" in his relation to African women? Who voyeuristically revels in the sight of their naked breasts and colorful tattoos? One wonders what sort of relationship between the Leiris of 1932 and this particular Ethiopian woman critics like Torgovnick would consider acceptable. The West, she asserts, might have developed a "history in which primitive societies were allowed to exist in all their multiplicity, not reduced to a seamless Western fantasy, . . . [a history in which] the majority of Euro-Americans can accept that our nations — for all their present comforts and power — exist on the same plane with other social and political entities" (*Gone Primitive*, p. 147). But perhaps this optimistic trust in an "openness," so to speak by fiat, "to alternative conceptions of knowledge and social reality" is itself the ultimate "seamless Western fantasy."

How, asks James Clifford in a critique of Edward Said's 1978 *Orientalism*, "can one ultimately escape procedures of dichotomizing, restructuring, and textualizing in the making of interpretive statements about foreign cultures and traditions?" (*Predicament of Culture*, p. 261). If, that is to say, Said presents Orientalism as "a corporate institution for dealing with the Orient" — an institution that has wielded the power of "dominating, restructuring, and having authority over the Orient" (ibid., p. 259) from the late eighteenth century to the present — how can his own account avoid the essentialism inherent in the unstated assumption that the "oppressed" Orient is in fact *not* like the one produced by the Orientalist myth? The critique of Orientalism presupposes, in other words, an Orient with such and such specific characteristics, characteristics that have been *misrepresented* by the West. And further: "The Western culture of which Orientalism is an exemplar [is viewed] as a discrete entity capable of generating knowledge and institutional power *over* the rest of the planet. Western order, seen this way, is imperial, unreciprocal, aggressive, and potentially hegemonic" (ibid., p. 272). Against this binary opposition, an opposition Said himself begins to doubt as his argument proceeds, Clifford makes the case for a "West" that is itself "a play of projections, doublings, idealizings, and rejections of a complex, shifting otherness." "Europe," in this case, may be seen as a false stereotype of the Orient, the question being, in Clifford's words, "How . . . is an oppositional critique of Orientalism to avoid falling into 'Occidentalism'"? (ibid., p. 259).

There are no easy answers to such questions. That colonialist "fictions of the primitive" have been used for at least a century to bolster the West's own self-image is incontrovertible. But that we can now enter a utopia where we approach "primitive" cultures as "full and valid alternatives" to our own is perhaps an even more dangerous myth. If I have dwelt at such length on the argument of *Gone Primitive*, it is because this well-meaning study epitomizes the wrong turn the new "cultural studies" take when they ignore both history and common sense. In her attack on Leiris, as on the "primitivism" of Conrad and Lawrence, Freud and Roger Fry, Malinowski and Mead, Torgovnick's root assumption is that a good writer (or ethnographer) is equivalent to a good person, and, concomitantly, that a "good" book is one that is a repository of the "right" cultural values. But, as John Guillory has recently argued, we must beware of equating "the values expressed in a work with the value *of* the work," of assuming that a given work is simply the "container of such and such values": "The reversion to moralism is determined by the equation of text-selection with value-selection. For this reason much of what passes for political analysis of historically canonical works is nothing more than the passing of moral judgment on them. The critique of the canon moves quickly to reassert absolutist notions of good and evil." [12]

One thinks, here, not only of a study of primitivism like Torgovnick's but of such recent studies of minority writing as Cary Nelson's 1989 *Repression and Recovery*,[13] with its eloquent but ultimately absolutist replacement therapy, the canonical "greats" (Eliot, Pound, Frost, Stevens, Williams, etc.) being swept under the rug to make room for a large body of "neglected" and hence, ipso facto, "deserving" poets of the period: women, African Americans, Communist activists.

Perhaps a more satisfactory critique of primitivism and its analogues would begin with the recognition that primitivisms, like the modernisms to which they are related, can only be plural. How, to take just one example, does the Russian "neo-primitivism" of the artists Goncharova and Larionov,

Tatlin and Malevich, or the poets Khlebnikov and Kruchenykh, square with the "primitivism" of Leiris and his colleagues at the Paris Collège de Sociologie? Why does the Russian avant-garde's "primitivist" concern for peasant and folk art, the *lubok* (woodblock) and the icon, and the "primitivist" quest of Khlebnikov "to find the magic stone for transforming all Slavic words, the magic that transforms one into another without breaking the circle of verbal roots,"[14] take a spiritualist turn so unlike the erotic "primitivism" of a Picasso, who gives two of his androgynous "demoiselles d'Avignon" African masks for faces?

We cannot hope to address such questions without a consideration of history as well as geography. Khlebnikov, descended from Mongolian Buddhists who inhabited the grassy steppes on the west bank of the Caspian Sea; Khlebnikov, the son of a prominent naturalist and ornithologist who studied the biological sciences and mathematics before he ever came to poetry in St. Petersburg; Khlebnikov, whose first publication in St. Petersburg (1908) was an anonymous manifesto posted in a university corridor, a call to defend the Slavic countries of Bosnia and Herzegovina against annexation by Austria, declaring "Holy War! Unavoidable, approaching, immediate — war for the trampled rights of the Slavs, I salute you! Down with the Hapsburgs! Hold back the Hohenzollerns!"[15] — Khlebnikov was inevitably attracted to a homegrown "primitivism" quite alien to the disillusioned postwar musings of the author of *L'Afrique fantôme*. Yet — and this is the irony — Leiris's surrealist compilation of language games and concrete poems, called *Glossaire*, is nothing if not Khlebnikovian. Here is one such passage, published in *La Révolution surréaliste* in 1925:

By dissecting the words we like, without bothering about conforming either to their etymologies or to their accepted significations, we discover their most hidden qualities and the secret ramifications that are propagated through the whole language, channeled by associations of sounds, forms, and ideas. Then language changes into an oracle and there we have a thread (however slender it may be) to guide us through the Babel of our minds.[16]

This might be one of Khlebnikov's descriptions of *Zaum* (trans-rational) language, were it not that Khlebnikov takes etymology to be the key to *Zaum* language formation, a view that perhaps classifies the Russian poet as more of a "primitivist" than the primitivist Leiris. At the same time, Khlebnikov's primitivism has none of the eroticism central to Leiris's, and it is hard to call it "racist" because the primitive race invoked and "exoticized" is Khlebnikov's own.

But the exotic is, of course, always a contested site. I recall meeting Margaret Mead once, at a Washington dinner party in the 1960's. She was wearing a long, colorful cotton dress and lots of wooden jewelry and supported herself on a large shepherd's crook, which she tapped emphatically on the floor when she wanted to make a particular point. I found her extremely exotic — a powerful, individual presence. Marianna Torgovnick, however, scolds her for such things as "never fully mingl[ing] with the Samoans" or for "referring routinely to male graduate students as 'men' and females at the same stage of professional life as 'girls.'" It seems that the poor Margaret of memoir and historical record is not allowed to dwell, as are the "primitives" toward whom Torgovnick expresses such tolerance, in her "own *conception of* time and space"; nor is hers judged to be one of those "full and valid alternatives" the author wants us to respect. The "full range of human sexual possibilities and variations in belief" (*Gone Primitive*, p. 246) — these are evidently available only to the still exotic Others.

Surely there are more satisfying ways of approaching the Other. I conclude with some lines from "Chapter 217" of Lyn Hejinian's long poem *Oxota: A Short Russian Novel*,[17] which tells the story of the American poet's gradual initiation into the otherness of the then Soviet Union:

Recognition in itself is a source of great excitement
I discovered I knew *Tekhnologicheskii Institut* as well as *Ploshad Lenina*
Deductions are directions
Truths change, things develop
I felt a thrill of gratitude — to whom or what it may refer
Lurking with competence, I was familiar with the future.

# PART VI

# Modernism Reconsidered

FRANK KERMODE

# Modernism, Postmodernism, and Explanation

> The reason that there is so much satisfaction in explanation [is that] consciousness being there, if we may use such an expression, in direct communion with itself, enjoys itself only. No doubt it there seemed to be occupied with something else, but in point of fact it is busied all the while merely with itself.
>
> — Hegel, *The Phenomenology of Mind*

Postmodernism, an idea whose time is widely thought to have come, is a bundle of concepts of style or period that seems to be credited with all the more explanatory power because it refers to so many disparate phenomena. Some exponents have sought to reduce it to a few principles, but for most it is a loose association of scattered ideas. However, it is said to represent a pretty clean break from the phase of cultural history that preceded it, which they identify with modernism. Unlike modernism — elitist, restrictive, and unhealthily obsessed with the past — postmodernism is conscientiously opposed to hierarchies and careless of the past, or at any rate takes a very different and less monolithic view of it than modernism. My floruit fell in what they call the modernist period — it may astonish you to learn that I was born before the publication of *Ulysses* and *The Waste Land* — and although I don't much care what they say about it, I have a feeling that the straw-period they have set up isn't altogether what modernism was (or is) like. Indeed, I suspect that we may think differently about postmodernism if we improve our notion of what its predecessor was really like, not least in respect to its dealing with the past.

Of course we don't expect period descriptions to be watertight; there are too many examples to the contrary. "Baroque" is a familiar instance of a

357

stylistic and period category extensible almost to the point of uselessness. And although it constitutes an important difference that people do call themselves postmodernists and didn't call themselves Baroquists — this is the difference, as E. H. Gombrich remarked, between a period and a movement — there is still an inevitable spread of sense. What began as a simple way of describing architecture in revolt against the architecture of the soidisant Modern Movement now has implications involving the whole of culture and politics. The term *postmodernism* can be applied opportunistically to almost anything. It can be said to have brought philosophy to an end, leveled the arts, and deliberately trivialized the past, though it does occasionally show some concern for its own historical antecedents — its origins being, as usual, sought in favored works of modernism.

Nevertheless, it would be foolish to imagine that one could be rid of a self-proclaimed paradigm change merely by claiming that it isn't as novel as it pretends to be. As all literary historians know, the same can be said of the Renaissance and Romanticism, and to say it is not exactly tantamount to saying there were no such things. To believe that one is a part of some such revolutionary change necessarily affects the thinking not only of its missionaries but of all who attend to the historical movement of thought but who cannot so easily accept an alteration in the whole body of our culture and our relation to the past — especially the old habit of devoting special attention to some parts of the past as they have been preserved, changed, and enriched for us by what we call tradition. So we have to consider these claims seriously. Those of us who deplore what may seem an insult to our interests, an attempted falsification of our least questioned assumptions, must remember that we have allowed ourselves to become vulnerable precisely by insufficiently questioning those assumptions — for example, by not thinking strongly enough about such issues as the relation of our own historical situation to past historical situations, and the source of authority within our institutions; and by attending too little to those popular forms of culture now said to have the same right to attention as our "high" variety. We also need to consider whether or not the modernism of which we are described as the very conservative defenders was indeed tainted by the faults of which it is now accused. In particular, was its view of the past as it is now described, or did it in fact (as I believe) effect the large shift in our attitudes for which postmodernism now claims the credit? Is postmodernism dining on the crumbs from the table of modernism?

Let me offer a suitably trivial preliminary illustration. Some of you have seen the film *Dead Poets' Society* and may remember the scene in which the teacher jumps up onto his desk and makes the boys do likewise because he wants them to understand, in this immediate way, just what it is to see a familiar scene under a changed aspect. At the end of the movie the teacher has been fired. When he returns to the classroom to collect his things, he finds his unbending, old-fashioned boss taking the class. The older man has reverted to teaching methods the hero had urged the boys to despise, and to textbooks he encouraged them to tear up. As the young teacher leaves with his bag, the boys, one after another, stand on their desks in tribute. The older man cannot make them get down. Simply by seeing for themselves how different the room looks from up there, they have learned a lesson about change of aspect, and the lesson has stuck. Watching this final scene I wondered a moment whether the author of the story could have had in mind the example of some passionate advocate of changed aspects — perhaps William James, for the film was American, or even Ludwig Wittgenstein, whom I happened to be reading at the time, along with Ray Monk's superb biography.[1] I shall wind myself into the subject of change of aspect by talking a bit about Wittgenstein as an exemplar of the change of aspect we associate with modernism.

Behind all of Wittgenstein's agonized attempts to think matters through to their limits, there was a conviction he doubted other philosophers could share, namely, that the attempt to utter the unutterable was futile. This by no means meant that the unutterable didn't exist. The final words of his first book, the *Tractatus Logico-Philosophicus*, are famous: "Whereof we cannot speak thereof we must be silent."[2] This doesn't mean that that of which we cannot speak is unworthy of our attention; it is, on the contrary, the most important consideration of all. One thing modernism taught us was just this: that writing can be taught to take account of what it cannot explicitly express.

Wittgenstein once explained to a prospective publisher that the manuscript he had submitted was only half the book; the other, the much more important half, was of necessity unwritten. One cannot say what can only be shown. To recognize that fact implies an understanding that there is something vital that is not said, and ought not to be said: "The nonsense that results from trying to say what can only be shown is not only logically untenable but ethically undesirable" (Monk, *Wittgenstein*, p. xx).

These rules applied very generally. For instance, though Wittgenstein was an exceptionally religious man, he held the view that religious experience simply could not be usefully talked about. All theology was entirely beside the point; so too with poetry. He liked poetry that was inexplicit, poetry that did not try to say everything. "If only you do not try to utter the unutterable then nothing gets lost. But the unutterable will be — unutterably — contained in what has been uttered." It followed, he thought, that philosophy should ideally be written as poetry, similarly inexplicit even when offering propositions.

The feeling conveyed by the *Philosophical Investigations*, at any rate to a non-philosopher, is often the feeling of reading a strange poem, a poem in which one detects at one moment a suspicious simplicity — why is he bothering to say that? — and at another (possibly in the same passage) a difficult insight that is protected by that apparent simplicity. Hence Wittgenstein's gloomy conviction, even during his admittedly overage undergraduate education at Cambridge, that nobody, or hardly anybody, would understand him, even world-class philosophers such as Bertrand Russell and Gottlob Frege; they could not accept the change of aspect, even though they surely had the intellectual equipment to do so, for both men, in his view, were stuck with an unreconstructed, wrongly aspected idea of mathematical logic, just as others were unable to free themselves from the urge to produce causal explanations.

The *Philosophical Investigations* travel, as Wittgenstein says, "over a wide field of thought criss-cross in every direction." Their emotional background is what he calls in the preface "the darkness of this time," but it remains background; he does not comment again, or try to explain, that general darkness.[3] The darkness the book considers is the darkness of philosophic thought; and this, he argued, could only be dispelled by eliminating the characteristic errors of philosophical thinking. These are many-headed, which is why the book has such a restless quality, sometimes issuing a string of disconnected aphorisms, questions, and comments, occasionally sticking to one theme for several entries.

One such sequence is the celebrated discussion of games (sections 65 ff.). Here he argues that the general form of propositions is like that of games. What is common to everything we give that name to (board games, football, card games, chess, ring-around-the-rosy)? If we look we find no common feature — balls, cards, boards, and so on — but rather a series of relationships, a "family resemblance" (section 67). And we perceive this precisely by looking, not by thinking, as a philosopher might. If we object that this is avoiding the job of saying what a game is, or what a proposition is, or complain that the concept is "uncircumscribed," Wittgenstein replies that this introduces a false notion of exactness. If we call it a "blurred concept," he answers that an indistinct photograph of a person is still a photograph of that person: "Is it even always an advantage to replace an indistinct picture by a sharp one? Isn't the indistinct one often exactly what we need?" (section 71).

To this defense of the indistinct we may add the famous recommendation of roughness: "We need friction. Back to the rough ground!" (section 107). If what is necessary to us is indistinct, approximate, rough, and if explanatory clarity is somehow false, we need not be surprised to be told in another passage that we must "do without all *explanation* [*Erklärung*], and description alone must take its place" (section 109). This leads directly to another celebrated saying, that "philosophy is a battle against the bewitchment of our intelligence by means of language" (section 109), because language prevents silence and offers explanations.

I am dwelling on Wittgenstein here precisely because he thought so insistently about the concepts of aspect, relationship, and explanation. He is as difficult as poetry, especially modernist poetry, can be. His simplicities are obscure; his method involves omission — not uttering — and the withholding of explanations of the omissions.

How can we relate these characteristics to the art of modernism (in which, incidentally, Wittgenstein showed very little interest)? Perhaps we can do it by turning to his native Vienna and consulting his elder contemporary, Freud.

Wittgenstein admired Freud, but with reservations that warn us of a gulf, a paradigmatic disparity, between them. What he admired was precisely the originality and force with which Freud compelled us to undertake a change of aspect. He made us look, which is what Wittgenstein also hoped to do. What he criticized was Freud's wrongly aspected ambition to provide a *general theory* of dreams. Such a theory would necessarily be false, a surrender to what Wittgenstein called a craving for generality. He deplores the reductionism of Freud's sexual reading of dreams in *The Interpretation of Dreams* but commends the work on jokes, because there the comments rely not on causal explanations but on juxtapositions of word or sense, the perception of these relations, as it were, *synoptically*; he even says that this kind of perception should be a model for aesthetic appreciation. But it is quite inconsistent with a "craving for generality," and Freud was caught between the two. That craving, which entails a quest for total explanations of a causal kind, was, in Wittgenstein's view, fatal to the truth. Of all the arts the most important for him, as might be expected, was music, which does not try to say, for it can only contain, the unutterable. If he were to be asked what is valuable in a Beethoven sonata — the sequence of notes, the feelings Beethoven had

when he was composing it, the state of mind produced by listening to it —
Wittgenstein would reply that "whatever I was told I would reject, and that
not because the explanation was false, but because it was an explanation. If I
were told anything that was a theory, I would say, No, no! That does not
interest me."

In this sense he is, of course, the opposite of Freud with his "craving for
generality," for explanatory theory. What interested Wittgenstein was the relations of things viewed synoptically, not in causal depth. He rejected explanation in favor of looking.

Goethe had entertained the notion that his *Urpflanze* should be thought
of as having real existence, so that he might even find it in Italy. That is, he
imagined there was an actual plant from which all other plants had evolved
over time. But then he accepted a change of aspect: instead of seeking mor-
phological causality, Goethe thinks of his ur-plant as a model: "with this
model it will be possible to go on forever inventing plants and know that
their existence is logical; that is to say, if they do not actually exist, they
could" (Monk, *Wittgenstein*, p. 510). Thus instead of seeking empirically
verifiable laws of evolution, Goethe offers a synoptic view of plant life.
"Goethe's morphology provided Wittgenstein with an example of a study that
seeks to *clarify without explaining* the phenomena with which it deals"
(ibid., p. 511, my emphasis).

Goethe at first sought the kind of explanation that requires long historical
views: how did things get to be this way? It is an understandable response. To
suppress what, given the cultural presuppositions, seems a natural desire for
causal explanations, and ask rather how things are, what connections can be
perceived between them, constitutes a change of aspect so great, in the case
of Wittgenstein, that highly intelligent and expert philosophers, though
quick to recognize his superior genius, could not be sure that he wasn't talking nonsense, wantonly throwing away, or dismissing as pseudo-problems,
the intellectual labors of his predecessors.

Let me dwell for a moment on the kind of inheritance Wittgenstein
seemed to be squandering by referring again to the situation in which Freud
found himself. Freud clung obstinately to the idea that psychoanalysis was a
science, a natural science. From the eighteenth century on, science had
learned to take a long view of the past. When the history of the earth was no
longer the six thousand years worked out by the biblical chronologists, long
stretches of time became available in which great changes, previously un-
thinkable, could occur; Darwin's explanation of evolution would of course
be inconceivable without that geological donnée. The scientific habit, the

new way of using time, was adopted also by the humanities. Linguistics became a science, with etymology doing the work of geology. Biblical criticism could speculate on the changes overtaking biblical documents at the hands of revisers, so that the biblical canon, long conceived as in some sense one global work, was fragmented; it lost that quality of inspired connectedness and interrelation; it dissolved into separate documents behind each of which there lay a historical origin long obscured by the action of time, but now to be revealed by explanatory detective work. And Freud, as nineteenth-century biologist and physician, drew on this long past when he set out to satisfy that "craving for generality" of which Wittgenstein was to complain. He accepted Ernst Heinrich Haeckel's principle that ontogeny repeats phylogeny, that the development of the individual organism recapitulates that of the species. This enabled him to extend the history of neurosis beyond an individual life and to confer on fantasy "a phylogenetic heritage," giving his interpretation of it the status of historical truth: according to these lights, incredibly long historical processes are recapitulated in the psychic history of the individual. Thus Freud could hope, as he put it, to "fill a gap in individual truth with prehistoric truth."

Freud — like Frazer and Einstein in their different enterprises — was, as it were, caught between aspects. His thought was extraordinarily novel, yet it grew from nineteenth-century presuppositions he could not abandon; hence he made many compromises, always maintaining his scientific claims while moving progressively toward a position which more or less tacitly allowed that the long past was not really where the psychoanalytic action was. It was in the present, in the transference.

In 1915 a book was published whose true importance took a long time to emerge. Ferdinand de Saussure's *Course in General Linguistics* represents a major change of aspect, a renunciation of explanation in the sense of conjectures of historical causation, for Saussure saw that the speaker of a language, when he looks at that language, is confronted not with a history but with a state. And "the linguist who wishes to understand a state must discard all knowledge of everything that produced it," since what produced it is not a part of the state.[4] He must instead examine, synchronically, the interconnectedness of that state.

I cite Saussure not only because of his importance to later semiotics, his central place in structuralist and poststructuralist thought, but because he instituted the change of aspect that made them possible, giving up the old diachronic linguistics for synchrony. Later psychoanalysis was to stress the configurations, the copresences, of the transference, here and now, and to ignore the Freudian calling up of prehistory to fill gaps in the explanation of the analysand's narrative. The past, in analysis, is something that is constructed here and now. The dialogue of transference and countertransference is all there is, and its relation to the historical or prehistorical is essentially no different from that of a fiction, a poem or a novel.

The shift of aspect that Saussure's book so dramatically illustrates took longer to happen in psychoanalysis. Freud could very well have read Saussure, but he didn't—in fact never mentions him; having invested quite heavily in the old diachronic linguistics, Freud would probably have resisted the synchronic method, though he might have enjoyed Saussure's later work on paragrams (hidden names buried in texts). As it was, Saussure did not enter the psychoanalytic field until he was rather spectacularly introduced into it by Jacques Lacan. Although a shadow of the old diachronic view persists, the Saussurian "turn," or change of aspect, has in time prevailed. It asks us to *look* at rather than to conjecture historical causes.

I am giving a few instances of major aspect-changes in the modernist past, and I think their long-term effects include postmodernism. I will stay a moment longer with the modernist aspect-changes, the downgrading of explanation in the old sense of historical causality, as exemplified by Wittgenstein. He was a loner, though not, in this matter, quite alone, save in the bewildering simplicity of his formulations.

Reading Sanford Schwartz's *The Matrix of Modernism*,[5] one cannot avoid noting changes of aspect not altogether dissimilar from those for which Wittgenstein was striving, though they are usually expressed rather differently. Schwartz's concern is primarily to show that they provide a general philosophical basis for much literary modernism. But in the course of doing so, he repeatedly shows how such philosophers as Dilthey and Bergson and F. H. Bradley—the subject of T. S. Eliot's thesis—felt the need to replace explanatory with descriptive psychology, on the assumption that explanation distorts. All these people, and William James also, felt that theory, being isolated from "lived experience," could not but introduce falsity. Like Wittgenstein, though each in his own way, they distrusted explanations and valued indistinctness.

It is important to such discussions that causal explanations are in one sense necessarily invalidated by a failure to account for much that does not present itself for empirical examination. And it is obvious that this fact has a bearing on the modernist preoccupation with the primitive. The rejection of causal explanation was in part an attack on the inheritance of science—and of all the forces of technology and the market that combined to give an impression of mechanization (culture reduced to civilization, etc.), and decadence. Wittgenstein, born in fin-de-siècle Vienna, assumed the fact of decadence, read Spengler with approval, and lamented the threatened disappearance, in this dark time, of a world or "form of life" in which his kind of art and thought were possible; the world was now such that genius, which sees things as they are, had no company, could choose only solitude. Perhaps the importance of the kind of thinking he wanted to pursue was no longer very obvious; perhaps it drew whatever importance it had from a system of values inseparable from a culture that was disappearing. Yet that culture — the culture of Kakania, as Malcolm Bowie calls it, borrowing the name given by the novelist Musil to the Austro-Hungarian Empire in its dying phase — was the very culture in which psychoanalysis (called by the satirical Karl Kraus the disease of which it professed to be the cure) could develop. It cultivated neurosis in a culture of neurosis, and it offered, by the investigation of individual miseries, to discover the power of the unperceived primitive. And soon there would be an immense revaluation of primitive images from the real past of the world, or from parts of it that did not much resemble Vienna — images, African sculpture and the rest, themselves perceptible as alien, as related to primordial life and culture, and yet, in the hands of modern men, suggesting not only nostalgic primitivism but also an awareness of decadence, as a remarkable scene in *Women in Love* suggests. They were the primitive, *external* foreign objects that corresponded to what Freud called the "internal foreign territory."

The primitive has several uses. On the one hand, it can be a mode of explanation, as it was for Freud — a "construction" claiming to be historical. On the other hand, it can be a model of that which is not discursive, not explanatory, that which baffles us by its isolation, its manifest inexplicitness, its apparent indifference to our concerns, its masks — in short, by its possession of an indistinct power that seems alien but that calls on us — with an urgency that we only now, under a changed aspect, apprehend — to interpret it in such a way that we may discover the significance for us that we sense it must have, namely, the unutterable contained in it, which it does not attempt to utter. It is thus sharply contrasted with inherited ("Victorian") forms of art. There are related contrasts: Romans utter the unutterable, Etruscan primitives do not. Or, in Wilhelm Worringer's once-famous formula, there are societies (stable) of abstraction, and there are (post-Renaissance) societies of expression (indeed, one side effect of the modernist change of aspect was that it became fashionable to deplore the Renaissance). The former do not explain, they repeat: archaic sculpture; inexpressive, hieratic Byzantine art.

The latter are contaminated by human, nonhieratic mess — T. E. Hulme famously called Romanticism, as a descendant of the art of the Renaissance and after, "split religion" — and by sentimental explanations that disperse hieratic presence. Bad art is dependent on external explanation, external reference, on trying to utter what is unutterable. But the primitive feels no need to explain itself; it is not required to give us a sense that it is thinking about what it is doing or feeling. It does not need to change, to evolve.

We are now on the familiar ground that saw the invention of the dissociation of sensibility — the invention of a past time when thinking and feeling went on simultaneously and it wasn't necessary to use one to support or make available the other. A Frazer could work the primitive into a quasi-evolutionary scheme, although I think it was not his quasi-scientific explanations that won him so much fame but the materials he collected, materials from all over the place, synoptically available, that could be used by those who wanted to bypass the decadence of explanation, skip over the Renaissance to the mysteriousness of what was to be supplanted by self-regarding, humanistic explanation. Thus there grew up a new veneration for art that leaves out, and so has a chance of containing, the unutterable — art under a new aspect, indistinct, calling one back to rough ground, demanding that one look, and see what is not palpably there: connections, interrelations, gaps signifying the unuttered. Hence there is a sense that to represent the truth, to be in the truth, is to write what must be looked at, rather than explained; the ground must be rough to give the reader friction; there must be interrelations the purpose of which the viewer or the reader must discern.

Consider a very simple and, in a way, too familiar contrast: the dramatic monologue as practiced by Robert Browning and by T. S. Eliot. Browning can be difficult, but he delivers strong hints as to the character of what he doesn't utter. Eliot is difficult in another way. What is left out of "My Last Duchess" is fairly easy to infer from what is left in. The commentators can tell us who the duke was, and who the last duchess, and who the duke wanted to marry next. But the poem makes all this redundant. It makes the flush of the dead woman at once beautiful in art and unforgivable in life, an offense to the speaker's rank, something that he feels no need to define or excuse. His last duchess died because he could not screen her beauty and grace from others as he can now screen the portrait in which, he is pleased to remark, she stands "as if alive." Having made himself clear on the point — his attitude to such possessions as wife and picture, the fineness of a taste that cannot be separated from personal vanity and possessiveness — he assumes that the messenger has gotten the message and proceeds to negotiating the next dowry. Claus of Innsbruck's representation of Neptune among seahorses ("thought a rarity") ends the poem, apparently, but only apparently, an irrelevance, for it invites us to regard the portrait of the dead woman as an equal rarity (and now a rarity of the only kind the duke can tolerate: to be seen only with his express permission, something commissioned and owned by him, like the seahorses). The duke is as candid as he needs to be, has been as cruel as he needs to be, is formidable in his dedication to selfish interest — and yet, we may reflect, perhaps no more so than the other party to the next proposed dynastic marriage, who must be willing to give another woman into the duke's deadly possession. Subtle and suggestive as it is, the poem leaves us in no doubt as to our bearings; it invites, but it also circumscribes, our interpretations.

"The Love Song of J. Alfred Prufrock" is recognizably in the tradition of such dramatic monologues, but it introduces a deliberate dispersity, reflected in its oblique epigraph, in its renunciation of the unobtrusive couplets of Browning. The rhymes are now intermittent, yet emphatic or banal ("come and go . . . Michelangelo"), the metaphors bizarre (the evening as "a patient etherised upon a table," the fog as an animal, its behavior elaborately described), the transitions unmotivated:

There will be time, there will be time
To prepare a face to meet the faces that you meet;
There will be time to murder and create,
And time for all the works and days of hands
That lift and drop a question on your plate;
Time for you and time for me,

And so on; the familiarity of the lines can disguise their random motions, their apparently irrelevant allusions, their deviations from sense and their slips into bathos. Where are "we"? What is this dim, unexplained, visit? How does disturbing the universe get into the plot? We feel entitled to explain Browning's poem by dwelling on the position, the ruthlessness, the collector's taste, the psychology of the speaker, the Renaissance blend of art and acquisitiveness. Here we can do nothing strictly comparable: we cannot accommodate by explanation the pin on which the speaker wriggles (is "formulated") and the arms seen by lamplight and the lonely men in shirtsleeves and the ragged claws, the cakes and ices (rhyming bathetically with "crisis," so that the tone is deliberately hard to identify), the marmalade and the rolling up of the universe, the attendant lords and the mermaids singing. Explanations are regularly offered, out of habit, and all fail. Here we have crisscrossing, sudden ironies, unstated associations, all to be synoptically viewed. We have rough ground, friction; we are invited to look. We remember that secrets are to be sought in the condensations and displacements of certain distorted discourses, and not on their surface, although they can be intuited by steady concentration on that surface — or perhaps by what Freud called "evenly-hovering attention." And we remember, too, that a moment of lived experience can, as Eliot notoriously remarked, contain a reading of Spinoza, the noise of a typewriter, and the smell of cooking, and that to apprehend them together — but not, of course, to "explain" their collocation — is somehow a victory over the world of "disparate particulars" and "disconnected impulses." The poem is less a record or a narrative or a representation than an invitation to a kind of victory, that kind of victory.

When we move on to Eliot's "Gerontion" we find an even deeper obscurity: a bleaker denial of facilitating transitions, a denial of the significance of all signs, a set of unacknowledged quotations, unmotivated ellipses. No identifiable subject speaks these words; it will not help to know who Madame de Tornquist was; if we track down the source of the old man waiting for rain, or explain the origin of the hot gates, we are no wiser. This is a poetry not to be read like that. And not the least interesting aspect of its history was its immediate reception — at any rate by Ezra Pound — as truly a new thing, the wanted thing, the realization of what had been, until it appeared, an unformulated aspiration, a form of the modern that properly defied explanation. Pound was himself to produce a summa that likewise challenged the reader, canto by canto, to take a synoptic view, to provide a kind of reading that did not depend on the old explanation by origin. He was Nietzschean in his mistrust of history as a ground for explaining the modern. He was a lover of the luminous detail — the enigmatic ideogram, as Ernest F. Fenollosa explained it — and of the research methods of Louis Agassiz. I have sometimes wondered whether Pound's admiration for Agassiz was not enhanced by the knowledge that Agassiz was a great biologist who resisted Darwin and clung to the notion of simultaneous creation, as if the world could be explained as Georges Cuvier wished to explain it, by intense contemplation of successive synchronic systems of fossils commemorating each successive creation, systems discontinuous and unrelated to one another, like Michel Foucault's epochs. Pound had ideas but also a prejudice against ideas, with their trails of probably false or prejudiced history, and so had Eliot, who commended Henry James's intelligence by pronouncing him divinely void of ideas.

Thus far I have left out an important part of this sketch of the modern as defiant of explanation; but I obviously must at least mention it. Insofar as art was taken to be involved with great ideas, subservient to what are now called the *grands récits*, or discredited metanarratives, it was violently attacked, not from Vienna or London but from Zürich, and later from Paris and New York. Futurism had embraced the modern, condemned the book and the past. Apollinaire and his friends rejoiced to be anti-passéiste. In Wyndham Lewis's BLAST there were lists of what must be blasted or blessed, and the blasted included much that was venerated, canonical. But these movements were tentative compared with Dada, which had a program not for art but for anti-art; it broke more decisively with the art of the past, or tried to, than had anything before it.

Dada was certainly thought to be a change of aspect that reflected a more general change. It was avowedly a reaction to the Great War, which itself seemed to insist on the senselessness of, even as it destroyed the monuments to, history as it had been understood. Yet Dada had a kind of irresponsible or carnival gaiety, and one aspect of its new aspect was that it eroded the old, obvious divisions between art and jokes about art. Whereas the history of Picasso's *Les Demoiselles d'Avignon* (1907) can be told as an evolution from one stage of painting to another—a tale of developing new attitudes to illusion, to explicitness, to distinctness, of a new understanding of the picture plane and conventional ways of treating it—and even Schönberg's twelve-tone music can be understood as a historical consequence of the gradual erosion, after Wagner, of older ideas of tonality, Dada really was revolutionary. It could not, in the end, escape being itself drawn back into the history of art, but the wild permissiveness of its practitioners invented virtually every possible variety of protest against history and convention, as we observe from the fact that later movements with similar ambitions call themselves Neo-Dada or recreate Dadaist "forms," as did the Happenings of the 1960's. The sort of aesthetic problem posed by Marcel Duchamp is still with us; as I write, an article in *The New York Times* discusses in quite the old way a three-seater toilet decorated by William De Kooning, with help from Jackson Pollock, maybe: is it art or a joke? If the former, how much is it worth? The price could be the $50 the present owner paid for it; or it might be $3,000,000. Of course this shows that Dada, whatever it was meant to be, is now Art.

Dada was, it said, "Art without sense." It had no program except to abolish the past, was devoid of ideas except the idea that old ideas associated with art were wrong. It cultivated the operations of chance with an assiduity that caused Hans Richter to say that this above anything else marked Dada off "from all preceding artistic movements"[6]—another change of aspect. Dada cultivated the ready-made and the collage and the photomontage, which destroyed point of view, mixed flat surface with perspective; it introduced the abstract or phonetic poem — pure jargon. It turned into Surrealism, thus incorporating part of the Freudian past, and it is claimed that these two movements together brought about "a change in our field of vision that corresponds to a revolutionary change in the nature of our civilisation" (Richter, *Dada*, p. 195). What both movements, or both phases of the same movement, had — and it is the basis for the claim that they produced a valid "change of aspect" — was just that abrogation of the past, of inherited ideas of order that, roughly at the same time, though in such different ways, interested Dilthey and Bergson and James, and Wittgenstein.

It is surely in this sense — the revaluation of the inexplicit, the rejection, by one means or another, of the cause-haunted past — that we understand the foundation of the modern, though we have to add that here, as elsewhere, programs to abolish the past are usually accompanied by newly created views of it — less continuous ones perhaps, more scattered, more open to synoptic viewing, yet offered as valid pasts all the same. Probably this is unavoidable. Dada did not succeed in abolishing the past; for us it has become part of it.

Exponents and explainers of postmodernism also claim to have effected, or recorded, a change of aspect. Postmodernism is anti-foundationalist, it mistrusts diachronic explanations and those metanarratives it regards as the enslavers of modernism. It is suspicious of theory, though dedicated to the idea of interweaving discursive practices in the here and now, a time notable for what Fredric Jameson calls "the waning of affect," Wittgenstein's time of darkness. It is interested in fragments and discontinuities, as against totalities and continuities; it asserts the impossibility of diachronic explanations. It denies traditional hierarchies, political or cultural. And it holds that the aspect it is changing, superannuating, is in fact the aspect of modernism, now described as the faith of the official culture, against which postmodernists see themselves as in revolt.

Obviously I am here conferring a single identity on a movement that has many different interests, not all compatible. But there is enough truth in the formula to suggest that the anti-modernist stance is very unstable. Much postmodernist thinking seems continuous with varieties of modernist thought, and this is acknowledged by some theorists of the postmodern. The cult of discontinuity, rupture, limit, for which Foucault has been the postmodern source, is perceptible, in less schematic forms, in Dada, as indeed it is, in an admittedly different mode, in Wittgenstein. It is true that, in modernism, certain of the texts and objects traditionally venerated continued to be valued; they were joined by others, newly revalued, to replace some that were expelled from the canon. But that remains the case, however surreptitiously, as we see from the choice of philosophical or anti-philosophical guides, and from the persistent search for earlier and earlier instances of the postmodern. It may well be that postmodernism is modernism described in a new dialect, that the great drive toward changed aspects happened in the past, and that postmodernists have only found new ways of talking about the same thing; if so, it is of course admitted that, in the process of redescription, that thing is somewhat altered.

Jürgen Habermas, who voices opposition to some postmodernist ideas, argues that "modernity" can be seen as a continuation of the Enlightenment. It began, he says, with Baudelaire, and reached its climax with Dada and the "new value placed on the transitory, the elusive and the ephemeral."[7] Habermas asks whether the end of the old avant-garde, as described by Peter Bürger, is indeed the end of modernity. The continuation of the Enlightenment project meant the splitting off of experts from the rest, so that arts and aesthetics became the privilege of a few. Surrealism (and Dada) disputed this, and consequently there have been attempts to democratize art. But these, he believes, have only emphasized "the structures of art they were meant to dissolve." And Habermas believes that such attempts prove the unwisdom of abandoning the "project of modernity." Although he wants the discourse of modern art to blend with those of current political and social practice, he sees in his idea of modernity a rival to that of the postmodernists. For him the great change of aspect was a slow one, not a violent rupture; and he pushes it back to Walter Benjamin and beyond.

We have grown accustomed to news of frequent paradigm-shifts, of irreversible and discontinuous epochal mutations, deconstructive aspect-changes in law, politics, and religion as well as in literature. Such claims and announcements are not difficult to make, and most of them involve the destruction of a past. Some, as it happens, do not, asking only for a new hermeneutic relation with that past, or new ways of reading it in the light of negotiations between what are called discursive practices, in the light of what we take to be our newly acquired and superior knowledge of the ways in which power operates. These often have the merit of being unsensational and decently argued. Not all the claims and announcements deserve the same commendation. But it is easier to talk about changes of aspect than to effect them.

I began by talking about Wittgenstein because he struggled to change an aspect and to make us see just how difficult it is both to do it and to talk coherently about it. He was my way into the problem, not — expressly not — because he explained it, but because he tried to show how such changes should properly be apprehended: frictionally, synoptically, synchronically, obscurely but without alienating jargon, without the presupposition that the past is what must be dismissed (he insisted on the need, if such work as his was to be done at all, for a historically formed community of understanding). We recognize in the *Philosophical Investigations* an essential obscurity that arises because different language-games, despite family resemblances, have different rules. Yet in all I have been considering there is a rule concerning the use of the past. It may be a command to abolish it, or a command to retain it and view it under a newly aspected light, as in Picasso. Modernism of different sorts used both these rules — and so, with the proviso that it also rule against past modernism, does postmodernism. Yet a great change is announced. And it may be that our desire to live at the moment of universal, epochal change can only be understood by the consideration that people have been claiming to do that, off and on, for a very long time. It gives some point to their lives, and would not do so if that point were the same one that gave point to the lives of their predecessors. And yet, if there can genuinely be such a point, it may well have occurred at the time of modernism.

# Reference Matter

# Notes

BARKAN AND BUSH: Introduction

1. Elazar Barkan, "Benin Art, Imperialism, and the Birth of Modernism," unpublished manuscript.

2. In this essay, as ought to be self-evident, the terms *primitive, savage* and *civilized* are always to be understood as constructions, never as "reality."

3. See, for example, Adam Kuper, *The Invention of Primitive Society: Transformations of an Illusion* (New York: Routledge, 1988), and Robert Young, *White Mythologies: Writing History in the West* (New York: Routledge, 1990).

4. Christopher Herbert, *Culture and Anomie: Ethnographic Imagination in the Nineteenth Century* (Chicago: University of Chicago Press, 1991), chap. 4.

5. Edward Said, "Representing the Colonized: Anthropology's Interlocutors," *Critical Inquiry* 15 (Winter 1989): 222–23.

BUSH: The Presence of the Past

1. T. S. Eliot, *The Sacred Wood: Essays on Poetry and Criticism* (1920; rpt., New York: Barnes and Noble, 1966), pp. 49, 51.

2. T. S. Eliot, "Ulysses, Order and Myth," *The Dial* 75 (1923), 483.

3. For a more elaborate statement of this argument, see Ronald Bush, "T. S. Eliot and Modernism at the Present Time: A Provocation," in Ronald Bush, ed., *T. S. Eliot: The Modernist in History* (Cambridge: Cambridge University Press, 1991), pp. 191–204. Subsequent references are indicated parenthetically in the text.

4. My citations are taken from the classic New Critical reading of *The Waste Land*, Cleanth Brooks's essay, "*The Waste Land*: Critique of the Myth," originally published in *The Southern Review* 3 (Summer 1937): 106–36 and reprinted as chap. 7 of Brooks's *Modern Poetry and the Tradition* (1939; rpt. New York: Oxford University Press, 1965), pp. 136–72, esp. pp. 171–2.

5. See Terry Eagleton, *Criticism and Ideology* (1976; rpt., London: Verso, 1985), pp. 145–51.

6. Eliot's anthropological interests are evident from his collected and uncollected prose. However, ever since Grover Smith edited and annotated *Josiah Royce's Seminar, 1913–1914: As Recorded in the Notebooks of Harry T. Costello* (New Brunswick: Rutgers University Press, 1963), it has been clear just how serious they were. The

notebooks in Smith's volume refer most strikingly to a graduate seminar paper Eliot wrote for Royce's class, "The Interpretation of Primitive Ritual," which was excavated and treated as a turning point of Eliot's early writing by Piers Gray in *T. S. Eliot's Intellectual and Poetic Development, 1909–1922* (Atlantic Highlands, N.J.: Humanities Press, 1982). Concurrently, William Skaff addressed the connections between Eliot's anthropological and philosophical writings in *The Philosophy of T. S. Eliot: From Skepticism to a Surrealist Poetic, 1909–1927* (Philadelphia: University of Pennsylvania Press, 1986), esp. chaps. 5, 6, and 7. Then Robert Crawford's *The Savage and the City in the Work of T. S. Eliot* (Oxford: Oxford University Press, 1987) attempted to integrate the subject with Eliot's adolescent reading and added considerably to the evidence of his anthropological reading and its significance. Most recently, Marc Manganaro has conveniently condensed much of this material in "'Beating a Drum in a Jungle': T. S. Eliot on the Artist as Primitive," *Modern Language Quarterly* 47 (1986): 293–421.

7. For the details of Eliot's visit and response to the St. Louis World's Fair, see Tatsushi Narita, "Eliot and the World's Fair of St. Louis — His 'Stockholder's Coupon Ticket,'" *Studies in Social Sciences and Humanities*, Nagoya City University, Nagoya, Japan, 26 (March 1982): 1–24; and idem, in later volumes of the same journal, "Eliot and the World's Fair of St. Louis — Collateral Evidence of his Fair Outings," 28 (March 1984): 1–23; "Eliot and the St. Louis Fair's Philippine Exposition — Another New Piece of Fact," 29 (March 1985): 33–46; "Eliot's Imagined World of Matahiva: A Hidden Aspect — On His 'The Man Who Was King,'" 30 (March 1986): 59–82; "Eliot and His First Beating of the 'Bhghong,'" 32 (March 1988): 39–47; and "T. S. Eliot's 'The Man Who Was King' and Some Cross-Cultural Documentary Evidence," 34 (March 1990): 71–87. Subsequent references *by year* are indicated parenthetically in the text.

8. On the introduction of "native villages" and their relation to the growth of the academic discipline of anthropology, see Paul Greenhalgh, *Ephemeral Vistas: The Expositions Universelles, Great Exhibitions and World's Fairs, 1851–1939* (Manchester: Manchester University Press, 1988), chap. 4 ("Human Showcases"), pp. 82–111; citation from p. 102.

9. See Robert W. Rydell, *All the World's a Fair: Visions of Empire at American International Expositions, 1876–1916* (Chicago: University of Chicago Press, 1984), p. 160. Subsequent references are indicated parenthetically in the text.

10. *History of the Louisiana Purchase Exposition*, Compiled From Official Sources By Mark Bennitt and Frank Parker Stockbridge and Illustrated With More Than Four Thousand Engravings (St. Louis: Universal Exposition Publishing Company, 1905), pp. 463–65.

11. The seventeen-year-old Eliot published "The Man Who Was King" in his high-school literary magazine, *The Smith Academy Record* (June 1905): 1–3. A large portion of the story is quoted in Narita 1990, pp. 76–78 (see also Narita 1986, 1988). Eliot's story had been previously discussed in Neville Braybrook, "T. S. Eliot in the

South Seas," in Allen Tate, ed., *T. S. Eliot: The Man and His Work* (New York: Dell, 1966), pp. 386–87 and in Crawford, *The Savage and the City*, pp. 18–19. Crawford locates its literary provenance in the tales of Mayne Reed.

12. On the turn-of-the-century evolutionist consensus among anthropologists, see Adam Kuper, *The Invention of Primitive Society: Transformations of an Illusion* (New York: Routledge, 1988), pp. 6–7, 64–65; the citation from Lewis Henry Morgan's *Ancient Society* can be found on p. 65. For Boas's impending critique, see Kuper's chap. 7, "The Boasians and the Critique of Evolutionism," pp. 125–51.

13. From Eliot's "Commentary" in *The Criterion*, April 1934, as quoted in Herbert Howarth, *Notes on Some Figures Behind T. S. Eliot* (Boston: Houghton Mifflin, 1964), pp. 151–52. Howarth's chapter, "Some Gifts of France," provides an excellent introduction to the intellectual ambiance of Eliot's French year.

14. The citation is from Eliot's manuscript "The Interpretation of Primitive Ritual," p. 3 (see note 6), as given in Piers Gray, *T. S. Eliot's Development*, p. 115.

15. From Eliot's review of Clement C. J. Webb's *Group Theories of Religion and the Individual*, *International Journal of Ethics* 27 (1916): 116, as cited by Manganaro, "'Beating a Drum,'" p. 396.

16. The Eliot citations in this paragraph are drawn from Manganaro, "Beating a Drum": for the first, from Eliot's *The Use of Poetry and the Use of Criticism*, see p. 396; for the second (from Eliot's review of Wyndham Lewis's novel *Tarr* in the September 1918 *Egoist*), p. 395. Eliot's phrase, "the beating of a drum," is quoted by Manganaro (p. 403) from an essay of that title Eliot published in the October 6, 1923 *Nation and Athenaeum*.

17. T. S. Eliot, "Warpaint and Feathers," *The Athenaeum*, October 17, 1919, p. 1036. Subsequent references are indicated parenthetically in the text.

18. The manuscript can be found in the John Hayward Bequest of T. S. Eliot papers in King's College Library, Cambridge, and is cited at length in Piers Gray, *T. S. Eliot's Development*. An incomplete transcription of the paper is also available, along with a transcription of the seminar discussion it provoked, in the notebooks of Eliot's fellow student at Harvard, Harry T. Costello, as edited by Grover Smith under the title *Josiah Royce's Seminar* (see note 6).

19. From a lengthy reference Eliot made to "The Interpretation of Primitive Ritual" in his 1923 "Introduction" to his mother's poem "Savonarola." Cited in Smith's edition of the Costello notebook, *Josiah Royce's Seminar*, p. 73

20. "The Interpretation of Primitive Ritual," ms. p. 5, as cited in Gray, *T. S. Eliot's Development*, p. 122. Costello's transcription and comment appears in Smith, *Josiah Royce's Seminar*, p. 74.

21. From "The Interpretation of Primitive Ritual," ms. p. 12, quoted in Gray, *T. S. Eliot's Development*, p. 130. Eliot's words translate Durkheim's 1895 *Les Règles de la méthode sociologique*, p. 117.

22. From Eliot's "Introduction" to "Savonarola," p. viii, as quoted in Smith, *Josiah Royce's Seminar*, pp. 74–75.

23. Emile Durkheim, *The Elementary Forms of the Religious Life*, trans. Joseph Ward Swain (1915; rpt., New York: The Free Press, 1965). Subsequent references are to page numbers from this edition, cited parenthetically in the text.

24. T. S. Eliot, "Durkheim: A Review of *The Elementary Forms of the Religious Life. A Study in Religious Society*. By Emile Durkheim, Professor of the Faculty of Letters at the University of Paris," *Saturday Westminster Gazette*, August 19, 1916, p. 14; idem, review of the same, *Monist* 28 (Jan. 1918): 158–59. The *Westminster Gazette* review was identified by Louis Menand and Sanford Schwartz and reprinted with a substantial introduction in *Modern Philology* 79.3 (February 1982): 309–15. (All references here, however, are to the original.) The *Monist* review was one of a series Eliot published between July 1917 and October 1918, signed only with the Greek letter η. Other books he reviewed include, interestingly, Georges Sorel's *Reflections on Violence* (July 1917), Stanley A. Cook's *The Study of Religions* (July 1917), and J. T. Merz's *Religion and Science* (April 1918). A more complete list of the anthropological studies Eliot reviewed or referred to between 1913 and 1918 can be found in Crawford, *The Savage and the City*, pp. 88–89.

25. See Steven Lukes, *Emile Durkheim: His Life and Work* (New York: Harper and Row, 1972), pp. 450–84.

26. It is worth noting that Eliot cites this phrase in his *Monist* review, p. 159 (see note 24).

27. Eliot made this infamous remark during the 1933 Page-Barbour Lectures at the University of Virginia, which were published as *After Strange Gods: A Primer of Modern Heresy* (New York: Harcourt Brace and Company, 1934); see p. 20. It is to Eliot's credit that he sensed the offensiveness of his discussion and prevented the book from being reprinted. For a recent discussion of the passage, see Christopher Ricks, *T. S. Eliot and Prejudice* (London: Faber and Faber, 1988), pp. 40 ff.

28. Quoted in Skaff, *Philosophy of T. S. Eliot*, p. 71, from Eliot's 1924 "A Prediction in Regard to Three English Authors, Writers Who, though Masters of Thought, are likewise Masters of Art," *Vanity Fair* 21.6 (February 1924): 29. The three authors Eliot referred to were Henry James, James Frazer, and F. H. Bradley.

## NYE: Savage Crowds

1. Elias Canetti, *The Torch in My Ear*, trans. Herman Neugroschel (New York: Farrar, Straus, Giroux, 1982), p. 246. Subsequent references are indicated parenthetically in the text.

2. For references to the imitative and hallucinatory qualities of some crowds, see Elias Canetti, *Crowds and Power*, trans. Carol Stewart (New York: Viking, 1963), pp. 358–65, 369, 373.

3. See George Rudé, *The Crowd in History: A Study of Popular Disturbances in France and England* (New York: Wiley, 1964).

4. Colin Lucas, "The Crowd and Politics Between *Ancien Régime* and Revolu-

tion in France," *Journal of Modern History* 60, 3 (Sept. 1988): 421–57. See also George Rudé, *The Crowd in the French Revolution* (New York: Oxford, 1959).

5. Alessandro Manzoni, *The Betrothed*, trans. Archibald Colquhoun (New York: Dutton, 1961), pp. 181, 188–89, 195, 202–3.

6. Gustave Flaubert, *The Sentimental Education*, trans. Perdita Burlingame (New York: Signet, 1972), pp. 285–87. Subsequent references are indicated parenthetically in the text. On Flaubert's knowledge and use of the language of the clinic, see Roger L. Williams, *The Horror of Life* (Chicago: University of Chicago Press, 1980), pp. 111–216.

7. François Guizot, *De La Démocratie* (Paris: Masson, 1849), pp. 90–91.

8. Edmond de Goncourt, *Paris Under Siege, 1870–71: From the Goncourt Journal*, ed. and trans. George J. Becker (Ithaca, N.Y.: Cornell University Press, 1969), pp. 54, 75.

9. Hippolyte Taine, *The Ancient Regime*, vol. I, trans. John Durand, rev. ed. (New York: Henry Holt, 1891), p. 251. On Taine and crowds, see Jaap van Ginneken, *Crowds, Psychology and Politics 1871–1899* (Cambridge: Cambridge University Press, 1992), pp. 20–51.

10. Henrik Ibsen, *Ibsen: Plays*, vol. 2, trans. Michael Meyer (London: Methuen, 1974), pp. 195–99. Even so, Stockmann concedes that "individuals" are shaped "out of the raw material of the masses" (ibid., p. 195), and in the last act he declares he will educate a band of street urchins to be the "free men and aristocrats" of the future (pp. 221–22).

11. Ibsen, *Plays*, pp. 193–94. For this aspect of the beliefs and behavior of modern avant-gardes, see Renato Poggioli, *The Theory of the Avant-Garde*, trans. Gerald Fitzgerald (Cambridge: Harvard University Press, 1968), pp. 79–84. Subsequent references are indicated parenthetically in the text.

12. On Zola's crowds, see Susanna Barrows, *Distorting Mirrors: Visions of the Crowd in Late Nineteenth-Century France* (New Haven, Conn.: Yale University Press, 1981), pp. 93–113; and Naomi Schor, *Zola's Crowds* (Baltimore, Md.: Johns Hopkins University Press, 1978). Subsequent references are indicated parenthetically in the text.

13. See George L. Mosse, *The Nationalization of the Masses: Political Symbolism and Mass Movements in Germany from the Napoleonic Wars Through the Third Reich* (New York: New American Library, 1975), pp. 75–126; Eric Hobsbawm and Terence Ranger, *The Invention of Tradition* (Cambridge: Cambridge University Press, 1984); and Michael Biddiss, *The Age of the Masses: Ideas and Society in Europe Since 1870* (New York: Harper, 1977), pp. 29–182.

14. On French strikes and their political implications in the 1890's, see Michelle Perrot, *Les Ouvriers en grève*, 2 vols. (Paris: Mouton, 1974).

15. Enzo Collotti, "Nationalism, Anti-Semitism, Socialism and Political Catholicism as Expressions of Mass Politics in the Twentieth Century," in Mikulas Teich

and Roy Porter, eds., *Fin-de-Siècle and Its Legacy* (Cambridge: Cambridge University Press, 1990), pp. 90–91.

16. For England, see Reba Soffer's discussion of Martin Conway, Wilfred Trotter, Graham Wallas, and William McDougall in her *Ethics and Society in England: The Revolution in the Social Sciences* (Berkeley: University of California Press, 1978), pp. 217–52. For Italy and France, see especially the discussion of Scipio Sighele and Alfred Fournial in van Ginneken, *Crowds and Politics*, pp. 52–129.

17. On the influence of hypnosis, see Serge Moscovici, "The Discovery of the Masses," pp. 13–15, and Erika Apfelbaum and Gregory R. McGuire, "Suggestive Influence and the Disqualification of the Crowd," pp. 44–47, both in Carl F. Graumann and Serge Moscovici, eds., *Changing Conceptions of Crowd Mind and Behavior* (New York: Springer Verlag, 1986).

18. Patrick Brantlinger quotes the British socialist Graham Wallas, writing in 1914, that crowd psychology "now enjoys in the social philosophy of the newspapers some of the old authority of the Laws of Political Economy." See Brantlinger, "Mass Media and Culture in *Fin-de-siècle* Europe," in Teich and Porter, eds., *Fin-de-Siècle and Its Legacy*, p. 109.

19. On LeBon, see Robert A. Nye, *The Origins of Crowd Psychology: Gustave LeBon and the Crisis of Mass Democracy in the Third Republic* (London: Sage, 1975); also, Barrows, *Distorting Mirrors*, pp. 162–88; and van Ginneken, *Crowds and Politics*, pp. 130–87. On crowd psychology in general, see Nye, *Origins of Crowd Psychology*, pp. 59–81; Roger L. Geiger, "Democracy and the Crowd: The Social History of an Idea in France and Italy," *Societas* 7, 1 (Winter 1977): 47–71; and Serge Moscovici, *L'Age des foules* (Paris: Fayard, 1981).

20. Gustave LeBon, *The Crowd* (New York: Viking, 1960), pp. 14–16, 151–53. Subsequent references are indicated parenthetically in the text. See also his *La Psychologie du socialisme* (Paris: Alcan, 1898).

21. On this point, see Gabriel Tarde, *L'Opinion et la foule* (Paris: Alcan, 1901); Terry N. Clark, ed., *On Communication and Social Influence* (Chicago: University of Chicago Press, 1969); and Serge Moscovici, "The Discovery of the Masses," in Graumann and Moscovici, *Conceptions of Crowd Mind*, pp. 19–23.

22. See also LeBon, *The Crowd*, pp. 65, 71, 106, 110, 113.

23. Cesare Lombroso, "Introduction," in Gina Lombroso Ferrero, *Criminal Man According to the Classification of Cesare Lombroso* (New York: Putnam's, 1911), pp. xiv–xv. On atavism, see Steven Jay Gould, *The Mismeasure of Man* (New York: Norton, 1981), pp. 122–27. On Lombrosan criminology, see Robert A. Nye, *Crime, Madness, and Politics in Modern France: The Medical Concept of National Decline* (Princeton, N.J.: Princeton University Press, 1984), pp. 97–116.

24. Sigmund Freud, *Group Psychology and the Analysis of the Ego* (New York: Norton, 1959), p. 49; on LeBon, see pp. 4–15. LeBon himself uses a similar metaphor in *The Crowd*, pp. 46–50, equating the crowd mind to that of "primitives," "women," and "children."

25. Anson Rabinbach, *The Human Motor: Energy, Fatigue, and the Origins of Modernity* (New York: Basic Books, 1990), pp. 19–45, 146–78.

26. Jennifer Birkett, "*Fin-de-Siècle* Painting," in Teich and Porter, *Fin-de-Siècle*, p. 148. Subsequent references are indicated parenthetically in the text.

27. Richard Drake, *Byzantium for Rome: The Politics of Nostalgia in Umbertian Italy, 1878–1900* (Chapel Hill: University of North Carolina Press, 1980), p. 221.

28. Poggioli, *Theory of the Avant-Garde*, pp. 75–76. See also Patrick Brantlinger, *Bread and Circuses: Theories of Mass Culture as Social Decay* (Ithaca: Cornell University Press, 1983), pp. 113–53, and Frederick R. Karl, *Modern and Modernism: The Sovereignty of the Artist, 1885–1925* (New York: Atheneum, 1985), pp. 82–85.

29. Matei Calinescu, "Modernism and Ideology," in Monique Chefdor, Ricardo Quinones, and Albert Wachtel, eds., *Modernism: Challenges and Perspectives* (Urbana: University of Illinois Press, 1986), p. 79. For related arguments, see in the same volume Russell Berman, "Modernism, Fascism, and the Institution of Literature," pp. 95–96, and Robert Wohl, "The Generation of 1914 and Modernism," p. 74.

30. See, in particular, the sections on attention and fixations in Max Nordau, *Degeneration*, 2nd ed. (London: Heinemann, 1913), pp. 52–66. Subsequent references are indicated parenthetically in the text. On the predominance of hysteria and the hysteria diagnosis in this era, see Ruth Harris's "Introduction" to Jean-Marie Charcot, *Clinical Lectures on Diseases of the Nervous System* (London: Tavistock, 1991), pp. ix–lxviii, and Jan Goldstein, "The Hysteria Diagnosis and the Politics of Anti-Clericalism in Late Nineteenth-Century France," *Journal of Modern History* 54 (1982): 209–39. On degeneration, see Robert A. Nye, *Crime, Madness, and Politics*, and, in general, Ian Dowbiggin, *Inheriting Madness: Professionalization and Psychiatric Knowledge in Nineteenth-Century France* (Berkeley: University of California Press, 1991), pp. 118–71.

31. As Nordau said of the so-called higher degenerate, he resembles "intellectually the type of the primitive man of the most remote stone age; or in the worst case, as an idiot, that of an animal far anterior to man" (*Degeneration*, p. 556).

32. LeBon was precise in the practical guidance he offered leaders: "To bring home conviction to crowds it is necessary first of all to comprehend thoroughly the sentiments by which they are animated, to pretend to share these sentiments, then to endeavor to modify them by calling up, by means of rudimentary associations, certain eminently suggestive notions, to be capable, if need be, of going back to the point of view from which a start was made, and above all, to divine from instant to instant the sentiments to which one's discourse is giving birth. This necessity of ceaselessly varying one's language in accordance with the effect produced at the moment of speaking deprives from the outset a prepared and studied harangue of all efficaciousness" (*The Crowd*, p. 113).

33. On the relationship of Sorel and LeBon, see Nye, *Origins of Crowd Psychology*, pp. 100–110.

34. For the relations and borrowings among these thinkers, see Robert A. Nye,

*The Anti-Democratic Sources of Elite Theory: Pareto, Mosca, Michels* (London: Sage, 1977), pp. 7–30.

35. Georges Ribemont-Dessaignes, as quoted in J. H. Matthews, *Theatre in Dada and Surrealism* (Syracuse, N.Y.: Syracuse University Press, 1974), p. 55.

36. From F. T. Marinetti, "We Abjure Our Symbolist Masters, the Last Lovers of the Moon," in R. W. Flint, *Marinetti: Selected Writings* (New York: Farrar, Straus, & Giroux, 1972), p. 68. Subsequent references are indicated parenthetically in the text.

37. Marjorie Perloff, *The Futurist Moment: Avant-Garde, Avant-Guerre, and the Language of Rupture* (Chicago: University of Chicago Press, 1986), p. 87.

38. On these aspects of futurist theater and performance art, see Michael Kirby, *Futurist Performance* (New York: Dutton, 1971), pp. 18–24, and Christiana J. Taylor, *Futurism: Politics, Painting, and Performance* (Ann Arbor, Mich.: Research Press, 1974), pp. 51–53.

39. Richard Huelsenbeck, *Memoirs of a Dada Drummer*, trans. Joachim Neugroschel (Berkeley: University of California Press, 1991), p. 68. Subsequent references are indicated parenthetically in the text.

40. As Michel Sanouillet wrote in *Dada à Paris* (Paris: Pauvert, 1965), p. 391, Dadaists "possessed an innate sense of mass psychology." See also pp. 152–72.

41. André Breton, as quoted in Matthews, *Theatre in Dada and Surrealism*, p. 95.

42. Ibid., p. 104.

43. José Ortega y Gasset, *The Revolt of the Masses* (New York: Norton, 1960), p. 75.

44. See Nye, *Origins of Crowd Psychology*, pp. 177–82; idem, *Anti-Democratic Sources of Elite Theory*, pp. 31–37; and A. James Gregor, *The Fascist Persuasion in Radical Politics* (Princeton, N.J.: Princeton University Press, 1974).

45. On this essential point, see Mosse, *Nationalization of the Masses*, esp. pp. 207–12.

BARKAN: Victorian Promiscuity

1. F. G. Stephens in *The Athenaeum; The Art Journal*. Both quotes are in Christopher Wood, *Olympian Dreamers: Victorian Classical Painters, 1860–1914* (London: Constable, 1983), p. 48.

2. See, for example, Catherine Gallagher and Thomas Laqueur, eds., *The Making of the Modern Body: Sexuality and Society in the Nineteenth Century* (Berkeley: University of California Press, 1987); Frank Mort, *Dangerous Sexualities: Medico-Moral Politics in England Since 1830* (London: Routledge & Kegan Paul, 1987); Jeffrey Weeks, *Sex, Politics, and Society: The Regulation of Sexuality Since 1800* (London: Longmans, 1981, 2nd ed. 1989); Judith Walkowitz, *Prostitution and Victorian Society: Women, Class and the State* (Cambridge: Cambridge University Press, 1980); and Sheila Jeffreys, *The Spinster and Her Enemies: Feminism and Sexuality, 1880–1930* (London: Pandora, 1985).

3. Edward Said, *Culture and Imperialism* (New York: Knopf, 1993).

4. The purity campaign and its ambivalent relations to the state, the church, and the feminist movement were a response to diverse issues ranging from the rejection of expertise about sexuality among civil servants to an emphasis on women's autonomy (sexual or nonsexual) and independence from men. Thus the loss of state medical control over sexuality, which preceded the rise of the purity campaign, was one of the factors contributing to its popularity. See Mort, *Dangerous Sexualities*, pp. 103–50.

5. Conservatives have long argued about whether censorship or education is more successful in confronting sinister sexuality (for Victorians generally, all sexuality was harmful). The issue has been and remains contentious. For example, Ellice Hopkins wrote in 1883, "it is argued that to speak on this subject is only to suggest the very evil you want to cure, and to do more harm than good. . . . Let us recognize once and for all that the modest silence . . . has landed England in child harlotry" (quoted in Mort, *Dangerous Sexualities*, p. 114).

6. Elizabeth Blackwell, *The Human Element in Sex* (1884), as quoted in Mort, *Dangerous Sexualities*, p. 116.

7. Chronology seems to transcend the disparate narratives. Others accept a similar demarcation; see, for example, Thomas Laqueur, *Making Sex* (Cambridge: Harvard University Press, 1990).

8. Michel Foucault, *The History of Sexuality, Vol. 1: An Introduction* (New York: Vintage Books, 1979, 1990), p. 10. Subsequent references are indicated parenthetically in the text.

9. Other examples are the campaign against the Contagious Diseases Act and the role of Josephine Butler, or the politics of the National Vigilance Association; see also note 2 above.

10. Havelock Ellis, *Studies in the Psychology of Sex, Vol. 1: The Evolution of Modesty, The Phenomena of Sexual Periodicity, Auto Eroticism* (1897; 3rd ed., London: 1928), p. 32.

11. Foucault sees sexology as the science of evasions: unable to address sex itself, it focuses on aberrations, perversions, exceptional oddities, pathological abatements, and morbid aggravations (*Sexuality*, p. 53). For a critique, see Weeks, *Sex, Politics, and Society*, pp. 140–56. In *Making Sex*, Thomas Laqueur also implies that "wrong" theories are not merely outdated but were "sinister" because of their contribution to patriarchy.

12. But even as sexology was becoming legitimized, the earlier, "mainline" Victorian approach remained powerful into the twentieth century, as is evident in William Graham Sumner's popular work *Folkways* (Boston: Ginn, 1906).

13. Weeks, *Sex, Politics, and Society*, p. 141. For a critique of the gender bias in this discourse, see Mort, *Dangerous Sexualities*, pp. 146–49. In the preceding generation, there had been a few "strictly medical" studies of sexuality, the best known of which was Richard von Krafft-Ebing's *Psychopathia Sexualis*. Krafft-Ebing produced

numerous editions of the widely translated work and kept up with the changing attitudes of the younger generation as he reclassified inversions and abnormalities from "a degeneration" to "a variation." Nonetheless, his style and tone privileged a clinical approach and limited his audience to physicians. See Havelock Ellis, *Sexual Inversion*, 2 vols. (Philadelphia: F. A. Davis, 1915), pp. 69–70.

14. The word *homosexuality* was introduced into English probably in 1892. See, for example, David M. Halperin, *One Hundred Years of Homosexuality and Other Essays on Greek Love* (London: Routledge, 1990), and Richard Dellamora, *Masculine Desire: The Politics of Victorian Aestheticism* (Chapel Hill: University of North Carolina Press, 1990).

15. Phyllis Grosskurth, *Havelock Ellis: A Biography* (New York: New York University Press, 1985).

16. See Halperin, *One Hundred Years of Homosexuality*, p. 154, n. 12.

17. Sigmund Freud, *Three Essays on Sexuality* (1905; rpt., New York: Basic Books, 1975), p. 15.

18. Jacobus X was the Paris-based publisher Charles Carrington; see Weeks, *Sex, Politics, and Society*, p. 156. During the nineteenth century, the British Museum accepted pornography sent by executors who found such material in private libraries and sought to deposit it in a safe place. It seems that not a little of the material came from collections acquired elsewhere in the Empire. Those who had connections in the library could use the material by requesting access to information on anthropology or "the Cult of Priapus." See Ronald Pearsall, *The Worm in the Bud: The World of Victorian Sexuality* (New York: Macmillan, 1969), pp. 369–70. Discussions of and opinions on the nature of the Private Case in the British Library appear in numerous books on the subject, all ridiculing its existence. My own favorite encounter was finding Bronislaw Malinowski's paperback reprint of *The Sexual Life of Savages* (1978) classified as obscene.

19. See note 2 above.

20. See George W. Stocking, Jr., *Victorian Anthropology* (New York: Free Press, 1987), and Adam Kuper, *The Invention of Primitive Society: Transformation of an Illusion* (London: Routledge, 1989).

21. See Stocking, *Victorian Anthropology*, pp. 197–208.

22. See Elman R. Service, *A Century of Controversy: Ethnological Issues from the 1860's to 1960* (London: Academic Press, 1985).

23. Marx and Engels never described the future communist society and left even basic arrangements undefined. If the family were the elementary economic formation on which capitalist society was built, one might anticipate the reverse in a "back to the future" scenario where the family would be abolished in preference of a promiscuous society. This enhanced the association of radicalism with alternative constructions of sexuality, but within a few short years communist regimes (regardless of early sentiments) repressed sexuality as one more area over which to exercise central control.

24. See, for example, Catherine Gallagher, "The Body Versus the Social Body in the Works of Thomas Malthus and Henry Meyhew," in Gallagher and Laqueur, *The Making of the Modern Body*, pp. 83–106, and Richard A. Soloway: *Demography and Degeneration: Eugenics and the Declining Birthrate in Twentieth-Century Britain* (Chapel Hill: University of North Carolina Press, 1990).

25. See also Elazar Barkan, "Rethinking Orientalism: Edward Westermarck and the Representations of 'Primitives' at the Turn of the Century," in the 1992 *Journal of the History of European Ideas*.

26. Edward Westermarck, *The History of Human Marriage* (New York: Macmillan, 1901), pp. 19, 22. Subsequent references are indicated parenthetically in the text.

27. Reading Westermarck's pre-publication manuscript, Alfred Wallace, Darwin's codiscoverer of evolution by natural selection, suggested that Westermarck tone down the discussion by replacing the term "sexual intercourse" with "marriage," especially in the last chapter, which was expected to be most widely read. As Edward Tylor, the first professional British anthropologist put it: "Some of the data in it are too sexual for even a special public." See Wallace's letter to Westermarck of May 14, 1891 and Tylor's to Westermarck of Nov. 20, 1890, both in K. Rob V. Wikman, *Letters from Edward B. Tylor and Alfred Russell Wallace to Edward Westermarck* (Abo, Finland: Abo Akademi, 1940).

28. Elizabeth Anne McCauley, *A. A. E. Disdéri and the Carte de Visite Portrait Photograph* (New Haven: Yale University Press, 1985), p. 106.

29. See Kenneth Clark, *The Nude: A Study in Ideal Form* (New York: Doubleday, 1953, 1959) for a "classic" statement. This view has been radically contested by feminist critics who view it as primarily erotic and exploitative. See, for example, Norma Broude and Mary D. Garrard, eds., *Feminism and Art History: Questioning the Litany* (New York: Harper and Row, 1982). But within the last decade, some feminist art historians have come to view depictions of female nudes as open to conflicting interpretations. See Broude and Garrard, eds., *The Expanding Discourse: Feminism and Art History* (New York: HarperCollins, 1992).

30. William Thackeray's response on reviewing the Royal Academy exhibit of 1845, where Etty's *Aurora and Zephyr* was shown (Aurora has been kidnapped by Zephyr and is about to be raped), was as follows: "It must be confessed that some of these pictures would not be suitable to hang up everywhere — in a young ladies' school, for instance. But how rich and superb is the colour." On another occasion, Thackeray allowed himself a more candid delight: "The luscious colours . . . are poured out for you on the liberal canvas, and warm you with the sight of the beautiful sirens that appear on it." Robert Browning described Etty's nudes as "mistresses with great smooth marbly limbs," which Jeremy Maas quotes in his *Victorian Painters* (London: Barrie and Rockliff, 1969), p. 166.

31. John Ruskin, as quoted in Maas, *Victorian Painters*, p. 164.

32. These included William Edward Frost, Frederick Richard Pickersgill, George Patten, William Gale, and Edward Armitage; see Christopher Wood, *Olympian*

*Dreamers* (London: Constable, 1983), p. 16. For instance, in his *Bathers* William Mulready depicted a group of realistic nudes with two women at the center, neither especially erotic. His biographer, F. G. Stephens, complained that Mulready had "reduced the extremities of the nudities till they were out of proportion to the rest of the figures" (as quoted in Maas, *Victorian Painters*, p. 168).

33. Maas, *Victorian Painters*, p. 164.

34. A Photographic Society complaint about the discrepancy was published in the *Art Journal* and is quoted in Aaron Scharf, *Art and Photography* (New York: Penguin Books, 1968; 2nd ed., 1979), p. 157.

35. Rejlander appears in almost all accounts of nineteenth-century photography. Especially good is Edgar Y. Jones's *Father of Art Photography: O. G. Rejlander, 1831–1875* (New York: New York Graphic Society, 1973).

36. *Photographic News* (July 30, 1886), as quoted in Jones, *Father of Art Photography*, p. 17.

37. O. G. Rejlander, at the London Photographic Society, April 1858 (a year after the Manchester Art Treasures Exhibition opened), as quoted in Jones, *Father of Art Photography*, p. 19.

38. On the complexity of the concept of realism in this context, see, for example, Raymond Williams, *Keywords* (New York: Oxford University Press, 1976).

39. From a letter to the *Photographic News*, in 1860, quoted in Scharf, *Art and Photography*, pp. 130, 345.

40. Thomas Sutton, as quoted in Jones, *Father of Art Photography*, p. 19.

41. See Eunice Lipton, *Alias Olympia: A Woman's Search for Manet's Notorious Model and Her Own Desire* (New York: Scribners, 1992). There is, unfortunately, no room here for a discussion of the protagonists' religious and moral perceptions — or of the reputations of the women involved in each case, fascinating though the comparison would be.

42. See the interview with O. G. Rejlander in the 1860 *Photographic News*, as quoted in Jones, *Father of Art Photography*, p. 26.

43. Once the censorship of the nude was broken, others were quick to follow Frederick Leighton, until it became characteristic of the leading Academicians. Albert Moore, for example, exhibited *A Venus* in 1869. The painting was criticized, but Moore was defended by Leighton and the opposition was overruled.

44. For a recent appraisal of Leighton, see Richard Jenkyns, *Dignity and Decadence: Victorian Art and the Classical Inheritance* (Cambridge: Harvard University Press, 1992), pp. 202–33.

45. There is no evidence of a physical relationship between Leighton and his male or female models, though many historians would like to have discovered one. Dorothy Dene was his favorite model. An aspiring, poor cockney actress who became a model, she was supported openly for years by Leighton, despite gossip about the President of the Royal Academy promoting a second-rate actress. Though not sexu-

ally involved, Leighton preferred such rumors to those that might have resulted from his lack of ties to any other women. But the relations between Leighton and Dene were not merely cynical, and she is said to have brought new intensity and warmth to his paintings (Wood, *Olympian Dreamers*, p. 76). Still their friendship did not quell all the rumors, especially after Leighton left England for the Continent during Wilde's trial. It was said that John Hanson Walker, one of several male models, who had artistic aspirations, might have blackmailed him, but by then Leighton was dying (Pearsall, *The Worm in the Bud*, pp. 512–14).

46. Leonée and Richard Ormand, *Lord Leighton* (New Haven: Yale University Press, 1975), p. 114.

47. An example is Leighton's *Psamanthe* (ca. 1880), a painting of a massive nude on the beach, viewed from the back and of Courbet-like proportions. In other works, such as Leighton's *Cymon and Iphigenia* (ca. 1884), the erotic atmosphere is achieved without nudity.

48. Michael Grant, *Eros in Pompeii: The Secret Rooms in the National Museum of Naples* (New York: Morrow, 1975). Earlier material was available to visitors uncensored until the beginning of the nineteenth century. As attitudes changed and the collection grew, it was opened only selectively to visitors.

49. Maas, *Victorian Painters*, p. 169.

50. See Walter Kendrick, *The Secret Museum: Pornography in Modern Culture* (New York: Penguin, 1987); Steven Marcus, *The Other Victorians* (New York: Basic Books, 1966) states what is considered "the popular view." See also Pearsall, *The Worm in the Bud*, and H. Montgomery Hyde, who has written several very readable books on the pornography of the period including (1) *The Love that Dared Not Speak its Name* (Boston: Little Brown, 1970); (2) *A History of Pornography* (New York: Dell, 1966); and (3) *The Cleveland Street Scandal* (London: W. H. Allen, 1976).

51. See Halperin, *One Hundred Years of Homosexuality*, and Elaine Showalter, *Sexual Anarchy: Gender and Anarchy at the Fin de Siècle* (New York: Viking, 1990).

52. Among such publications, *The Cremorne, The Boudoir*, and *The Pearl* are considered unequaled. See Pearsall, *The Worm in the Bud*, pp. 364–92.

53. For example, "the New Age" and "the New Review." Oscar Wilde's story "The Picture of Dorian Gray" was attacked as "the New Voluptuousness," and Wilde himself wrote of "the New Remorse"; see Holbrook Jackson, *The Eighteen Nineties* (London: J. Cape, 1931). See also Dennis Farr, *English Art, 1870–1940: The Oxford History of English Art* (New York: Oxford University Press, 1978), p. 74.

54. Max Beerbohm, *The Works of Max Beerbohm* (1896; rpt., London: W. Heineman, 1922).

55. See Showalter, *Sexual Anarchy*.

56. Farr, *English Art, 1870–1940*, p. 70.

57. For an alternative reading, see, for example, Carol Duncan, "Virility and Domination in Early Twentieth-Century Vanguard Painting," in Broude and Gar-

rard, *Feminism and Art History*, p. 293. Duncan argues strongly that the vanguard dehumanized women by representing them as mere flesh and blood, thus accentuating sexuality and diminishing individuality.

58. Peter Gay, *The Bourgeois Experience: Victoria to Freud, Vol. 1: Education of the Senses* (Oxford: Oxford University Press, 1984), pp. 206–7. One may wonder about Gay's abstract quantification as a mode of persuasion. If it refers merely to the number of "representations" of women in these lights, without accounting for the general growth of population, money, communication, literacy, etc., what is its significance? Are we to have a per capita index for misogyny?

59. Linda Zatlin, *Aubrey Beardsley and Victorian Sexual Politics* (Oxford: Oxford University Press, 1990), p. 8.

60. For a different interpretation, see Showalter, *Sexual Anarchy*, pp. 150–56.

61. For a discussion of Beardsley's drawing "The Man in the Moon," see Catherine Slessor, *The Art of Aubrey Beardsley* (Secaucus, N.J.: Quintet, 1989), p. 41. The confusion was most wonderfully demonstrated in an illustration to an advertisement by Cornell University Press in *The New York Review of Books* (May 16, 1991), where the caption had the better of the drawing: the male in the moon had his penis erased. The Press adopted the print from Gail Finney, *Women in Modern Drama: Freud, Feminism, and European Theater at the Turn of the Century* (Ithaca, N.Y.: Cornell University Press, 1989).

62. Aubrey Beardsley, *The Story of Venus and Tannhäuser or Under the Hill* (New York: St. Martin's, 1896). See Linda Dowling, *Language and Decadence* (Princeton, N.J.: Princeton University Press, 1986), pp. 144–48.

63. Stanley Weintraub, *Aubrey Beardsley: Imp of the Perverse* (Philadelphia: Pennsylvania State University, 1976), p. 199.

64. Ibid.

65. R. A. Walker, *The Best of Beardsley* (London: Spring Book, n.d.), probably published in the 1950's, does not include any of the "daring" illustrations.

66. Then again, the caption was, perhaps, a different kind of disguise. In 1918, *The Vigilante* published an attack on a production of *Salome* by the Canadian dancer Maud Allan entitled "The Cult of the Clitoris," calling her a lesbian sadist. A libel suit followed, in which a defense expert testified that Allan's cognizance of the word "clitoris" proved her guilt: no decent person should have known the Greek term. The court agreed. See Showalter, *Sexual Anarchy*, p. 162.

67. Zatlin, *Aubrey Beardsley*, p. 65.

68. The most pertinent question about the relations between European colonizers and those colonized is that of the conflicting perspectives along lines of race and gender. See Nupur Chaudhuri and Margaret Strobel, eds., *Western Women and Imperialism: Complicity and Resistance* (Bloomington: Indiana University Press, 1992). A controversial account is found in Ronald Hyam, *Empire and Sexuality: The British Experience* (Manchester: Manchester University Press, 1990).

69. These few imperial agents are, not surprisingly, the subjects of numerous

studies. But the singularity of these people is perhaps more noteworthy than the claim that their activities are a testimony to general attitudes and behavior. For example, the British disposition in India changed drastically in the second half of the nineteenth century, once English women were able to travel to the subcontinent in large numbers.

70. For a nineteenth-century perspective on the literature, see, Yrjö Hirn, *The Origins of Art* (London: Macmillan, 1900). While the vast majority of Westerners must have known that heterosexual relations (prostitution included) were prevalent within the British Empire, it is also probable that homosexual experimentations — as well as other sexual practices, including pederasty (paedophilia) — were becoming more widespread in Europe itself at the time. But, most importantly, we simply do not know what sexual practices occurred.

71. See Christraud M. Geary, *Images from Bamum: German Colonial Photography at the Court of King Njoya, Cameroon West Africa, 1902–1915* (Washington, D.C.: National Museum of African Art, 1988).

72. Complaints of British mistreatment of indigenous women were made by the Ndebele in 1896, the Zulus in 1906, and several times in India. See Hyam, *Empire and Sexuality.*

73. For example, Fijian complaints were directed against British behavior that led to their own loss of control over their women. See Hyam, *Empire and Sexuality*, p. 20, and C. Knapman, *White Women in Fiji, 1835–1930* (Sydney: Allen and Unwin, 1986), p. 173. Perhaps the status of Indian women, especially the practice of suttee, led to the most prolonged struggle between traditional oppression of women and imperial modernity. See, for example, various essays by Gayatri Spivak (e.g., in Spivak, *The Postcolonial Critic* [New York: Routledge, 1990]). A special case was Japan, viewed in the Occident as somewhere between a primitive and a civilized culture; its allure became an immediate craze in the West. Western men were eager to tap into its sexual riches because Japanese women and tradition proved exceptionally erotic from first sight. As a nation of Eves, it had no Marys (see Robert Rosenstone, *Mirror in the Shrine* [Cambridge: Harvard University Press, 1988]) but possibly many Delilahs and Salomes. Charles MacFarlane, in *Japan: An Account . . .* (Hartford: S. Andrus, 1856), raves about Japanese ladies who are the most "fascinating, elegant" anywhere, who "excited" in him "a deep and lively interest" that expanded into a general interest in Japan. See also Earl Miner, *The Japanese Tradition in British and American Literature* (Princeton, N.J.: Princeton University Press, 1958, 1966), pp. 26–28. (Beardsley's Salome, incidentally, is drawn in the Japanese style.) For a compilation of misogyny, see Bram Dijkstra, *Idols of Perversity: Fantasies of Feminine Evil in Fin-de-Siècle Culture* (Oxford: Oxford University Press, 1986). Sex with no guilt could, after all, hardly exist even in fantasy.

74. One of the best selections is in Malek Alloula, *The Colonial Harem* (Minneapolis: University of Minnesota Press, 1986). A similar impression of erotic representations as invariably exploitative may result from articles in this volume (those of

Virginia-Lee Webb, Wendy Martin, and probably my own), but this is often a result of the focus and methodology of the essay in question. The nonerotic, nonexploitative is less a subject for contemporary commentary.

75. See, for example, Carl Dammann, *Anthropologisch-Ethnographisches Album in Photographien* (Berlin: Weigardt, Hempel and Parey, 1873–76), which is perhaps the most extensive, early two-volume collection and which, at the time it was published, reflected the best scientific approach. Dammann's work often appears in other collections as individual photographs. The album is very rare; few copies survived. Photographing "primitives" was especially prone to the temptation to create the illusion of a contemporary primordial society, even when photographs were taken in studios in the West, as Dammann did in Hamburg and as Franz Boas did during the Chicago World's Fair (see Ira Jacknis, "Franz Boas and Photography," *Studies in the Anthropology of Visual Communications* 10, 1 [1984]: 2–60). For a general comparison, see Elizabeth Edwards, ed., *Anthropology and Photography, 1860–1920* (New Haven: Yale University Press, 1992). A recent issue of *African Art*, 24, 4 (1991), was devoted to imperialist photography. See also Virginia-Lee Webb's essay below.

76. Few explicitly erotic images were published, but Fig. 11 was an exception. See *African Art* 24, 4 (1991).

77. Unlike writings or artwork, "photographed images do not seem to be statements about the world so much as pieces of it, miniatures of reality that anyone can make or acquire," as Susan Sontag put it in her *Sermons on Photography* (New York: Farrar, 1977), p. 4. The statement is frequently quoted, for example, in *from site to sight* (Cambridge, Mass.: Peabody Museum Press, 1986).

78. See L. Goodrich and N. Cameroon, *The Face of China: As Seen by Photographers and Travelers, 1860–1912* (1978), and W. Franke, *China and the West* (Oxford: Blackwell, 1967), quoted in Leonard Bell, "Artists and Empire: Victorian Representations of Subject People," *Art History* 5, 1 (March 1982): 73–86.

79. For example, see C. Geary, *Images from Bamum*, p. 12, which discusses the tension between the contemporary critique and the photographic records. Regardless of the macro-imperial disparities, the Court in Bamum enjoyed and utilized photography. Geary's evidence shows this, although she is more inclined to emphasize the exploitation.

80. For other "external" motivations involved in the biological rejection of racism in science, see Elazar Barkan, *Retreat of Scientific Racism* (Cambridge: Cambridge University Press, 1992).

CRAPANZANO: The Moment of Prestidigitation

1. Emile Durkheim, *Le Suicide: Etude de sociologie* (1897; rpt., Paris: Quadrige/PUF, 1930), pp. 284–85, published in English as *Suicide: A Study in Sociology*, trans. John A. Spaulding and George Simpson (New York: Free Press, 1951); this translation is from p. 256. Subsequent references are indicated parenthetically in the text.

2. Durkheim (*Le Suicide*, p. 282; *Suicide: A Study*, pp. 255–56) uses *effervescence*, in the English translation "excitement," at the start of the paragraph from which I am quoting to describe the "*déchaînement des désirs*" and the "passions" that arrive with industrialization and the undefinable extension of the market — when the producer's client becomes the entire world. He also uses *effervescence* to describe the emotional intensity of the ritual crowd in *Les Formes élémentaires de la vie religieuse: Le système totémique en Australie* (1912; rpt., Paris: Quadrige/ PUF, 1960); published in English as *The Elementary Forms of the Religious Life*, trans. Joseph Ward Swain (New York: Free Press, 1965). Subsequent references are indicated parenthetically in the text. Unless otherwise indicated, references are to the 1960 French edition. The parallel between the excitement of the industrial age — through the market, in the crowd — and the primitive ritual experience is noteworthy. Both are, for Durkheim, at the edge of control — and order. The latter produces order by rendering society the object of its veneration; the former risks producing disorder, for the object of veneration is the object of (individual) desire.

3. Steven Lukes, *Emile Durkheim: His Life and Work, A Historical and Critical Study* (Stanford: Stanford University Press, 1985), pp. 191, 400. Subsequent references are indicated parenthetically in the text.

4. Charles Baudelaire, *Le Peintre de la vie moderne: Oeuvres complètes* (1860; rpt., Paris: Bibliothèque de la Pléiade, 1954), pp. 881–920, esp. p. 892. Subsequent references are indicated parenthetically in the text.

5. See Eugen Weber, *France: Fin de Siècle* (Cambridge, Mass.: Harvard University Press, 1986), and Robert Nye, *Crime, Madness, and Politics in Modern France: The Medical Concept of National Decline* (Princeton, N.J.: Princeton University Press, 1984). Subsequent references are indicated parenthetically in the text. The comparison could, of course, be extended to Durkheim's description of the egoistic suicide: "indolent melancholy with self-complaisance," "the skeptic's disillusioned sangfroid" (*sangfroid désabusé du sceptique*).

6. See Lukes, *Emile Durkheim*, pp. 206, 195–99. See also Stjepan G. Mestrovic, *Emile Durkheim and the Reformation of Sociology* (Totowa, N.J.: Rowman and Littlefield, 1988) for a discussion of Schopenhauer's influence on Durkheim, specifically with respect to desire and representation.

7. Compare Durkheim, *Le Suicide*, p. 424; *Suicide: A Study*, p. 370.

8. This concern with illusion is particularly striking in the early writings of the popular philosopher Jules de Gaultier, best known today for his delineation of Bovarysm. Under the influence of Nietzsche, he wrote extravagantly around 1900: "To the hypothesis ventured and then accepted by Nietzsche, according to which life has an illusion, a fiction as a prop, we shall add this corollary: knowledge tends to destroy Life." Gaultier argued that the "instinct of knowledge," which dominates in ages when life is in decline (fin-de-siècle France?), destroys the illusions that affirm life and through this destructive act creates the conditions that give rise to new life-

affirming illusions. See Jules de Gaultier, *From Kant to Nietzsche*, trans. Gerald M. Spring (1902; N.Y.: Philosophical Library, 1961), p. 3.

9. Primitive (*primitif*) had other meanings as well. It can also refer to an irreducible foundation or to a beginning, an original condition.

10. See William Rubin, "Modernist Primitivism: An Introduction," in idem, ed., *"Primitivism" in 20th Century Art: Affinity of the Tribal and the Modern*, vol. 1 (New York: The Museum of Modern Art, 1984), pp. 1–79, esp. p. 2. We should note a parallel with the premodernist and early modernist ethnographic compendia, including Mauss's study of magic. See Marcel Mauss, *Esquisse d'une théorie générale de la magie* originally published in 1902–3 in *L'Année sociologique*, vol. 5; reprinted in Mauss, *Sociologie et anthropologie* (Paris: Quadrige/PUF, 1950) — the edition cited hereafter as *Esquisse*, in text and notes alike — and published in English as *A General Theory of Magic*, trans. Robert Brain (New York: Norton, 1972).

11. See Rubin, "Modernist Primitivism," pp. 5–7, and Kirk Varnedoe, "Gauguin," in Rubin, ed., *"Primitivism,"* vol. 1, pp. 170–209, and the sources in Varnedoe's notes 6, 7, and 9.

12. Picasso's *Les Demoiselles d'Avignon* is generally taken by art historians as marking the reevaluation and incorporation of a primitive or tribal art, *l'art nègre*, within the Western aesthetic. Matisse, Derain, Vlaminck, and Picasso all seem to have "discovered" tribal art in the years 1906–7. William Rubin associates this discovery and appropriation with a shift from a perceptually to a conceptually based aesthetic. See Rubin, "Modernist Primitivism," and Varnedoe, "Gauguin," for a discussion of Gauguin's primitivism. Gauguin apparently had little interest in Polynesian art per se, and it seems to have had scant effect on his aesthetic. In the few works where he makes reference to it, it serves primarily a decorative or symbolic function.

13. See below, particularly my discussion of Durkheim's *The Elementary Forms*. See also Michele Richman, "Anthropology and Modernism in France: From Durkheim to the *Collège de sociologie*," in Marc Manganaro, ed., *Modernist Anthropology: From Fieldwork to Text* (Princeton, N.J.: Princeton University Press, 1990), pp. 183–214, esp. pp. 195–96.

14. Mauss's *Esquisse* was written in collaboration with Henri Hubert. See note 10 above.

15. Steven Collins, "Categories, Concepts, or Predicaments? Remarks on Mauss's Use of Philosophical Terminology," in Michael Carrithers, Steven Collins, and Steven Lukes, eds., *The Category of the Person: Anthropology, Philosophy, History* (Cambridge: Cambridge University Press, 1985), pp. 46–82.

16. Cf. Dominique Parodi's criticism of Durkheim and his school in D. Parodi, *La Philosophie contemporaine en France: Essai de classification des doctrines* (Paris: Félix Alcan, 1925). In his "Categories, Concepts, or Predicaments?" Collins argues convincingly that Mauss was more willing to entertain a relativist epistemology than was Durkheim.

17. The two principal neo-Kantian influences on Durkheim and Mauss were C.

Renouvier and Octave Hamelin. See Collins, "Categories, Concepts, or Predicaments?" for a discussion of this relationship.

18. Adolph Bastian, *Der Mensch in der Geschichte* (Leipzig: Wigand, 1860), and idem, *Ethnische Elementargedanken in der Lehre vom Menschen* (Berlin: Weidmannische Buchhandlungen, 1895).

19. Lucien Lévy-Bruhl, *Les Fonctions mentales dans les sociétés inférieures* (Paris: Alcan, 1910).

20. Emile Durkheim and Marcel Mauss, "De quelques formes primitives de classification; contribution à l'étude de représentations collectives," *L'Année sociologique*, vol. 6 (1901–2), Paris, 1903, pp. 1–72; published in English as *Primitive Classification*, trans. Rodney Needham (Chicago: University of Chicago Press, 1967), p. 6. Subsequent references are indicated parenthetically in the text.

21. Among the many critical discussions of Durkheim and Mauss's thesis, see N. J. Allen, "The Category of the Person: A Reading of Mauss's Last Essay," in Carrithers, Collins, and Lukes, eds., *The Category of the Person: Anthropology, Philosophy, History* (Cambridge: Cambridge University Press, 1985), pp. 26–45, and Collins "Categories, Concepts, or Predicaments?" in the same volume.

22. See Mauss, *Esquisse*, pp. 3–141, esp. p. 123. Subsequent references to the 1950 edition are indicated parenthetically in the text. Given the gross inaccuracies of Robert Brain's 1972 translation (cited in note 10 above), I refer only to the French edition, except where I make explicit reference to his English version. All translations are my own.

23. Cf. Durkheim, *The Elementary Forms*. He argues, on the one hand, that the presence of a church distinguishes religion from magic: "There is no Church of magic" (*Les Formes élémentaires*, p. 61; *The Elementary Forms*, p. 60). On the other hand, citing Hubert and Mauss, he suggests that magic is born of religion (pp. 518 and 405, respectively). Behind magical practices is "a background of religious conceptions and a whole world of forces, the idea of which has been taken by magic from religion" (*un arrière-fond de conceptions religieuses, tout un monde de forces dont la magie a emprunté l'idée à la religion*). Given Durkheim's theory of the role of religion in the genesis of categories and ideas, it would follow that the categories and ideas of magic are derived from religion.

24. Mauss, trans. Brain, *A General Theory of Magic*, p. 131.

25. Walter Benjamin, "On Some Motifs in Baudelaire," in idem, *Illuminations*, trans. Harry Zohn, ed. Hannah Arendt (1939; rpt., New York: Schocken Books, 1969), pp. 155–200, esp. p. 173.

26. For a historical discussion of the crowd, see Robert Nye, *The Origins of Crowd Psychology: Gustave LeBon and the Crisis of Mass Democracy in the Third Republic* (London: Sage, 1975); for a recent, somewhat rhetorical sociological account, see Serge Moscovici, *L'Age des foules* (Paris: Fayard, 1981).

27. Stanley J. Tambiah, *Culture, Thought, and Social Action: An Anthropological Perspective* (Cambridge, Mass.: Harvard University Press, 1985), pp. 17–59, 60–86.

28. Claude Lévi-Strauss, "Introduction à l'oeuvre de Marcel Mauss," in Mauss, *Sociologie et anthropologie*, pp. ix–lii. Subsequent references are indicated parenthetically in the text.

29. See Marcel Mauss, *The Gift: Forms and Functions of Exchange in Archaic Societies* (1923–24; rpt., New York: Norton, 1950, 1967). For comment, see Vincent Crapanzano, *Hermes' Dilemma and Hamlet's Desire: On the Epistemology of Interpretation* (Cambridge, Mass.: Harvard University Press, 1992), Introduction and chapters 4 and 5, for a discussion of metapragmatic glossing and masking. There I discuss the effect of the referentiality of metapragmatic descriptions within a linguistic ideology — the "Western" — that gives priority to the referential. It is not clear whether or not Polynesian linguistic ideology gives the same priority to reference. Given the complex "grammar" of "mana" and "*hau*," I would suspect not.

30. The risk in any exchange — the possibility of real or accidental betrayal — is exquisitely dramatized in Keith Gordon's film *A Midnight Clear*, based on a William Wharton novel.

31. Jacques Derrida, *Donner le temps, Vol. 1: La Fausse Monnaie* (Paris: Galilee, 1991).

32. Contrast Derrida's discussion of risk in his consideration of J. L. Austin in "Signature, Event, Context," in Jacques Derrida, *Marges de la philosophie* (Paris: Editions de Minuit, 1972), pp. 309–30.

33. Marcel Mauss, "Essai sur le don: Forme et raison de l'échange dans les sociétés archaïques," in idem, *Sociologie et anthropologie*, pp. 143–279, esp. p. 159. Subsequent references are indicated parenthetically in the text.

34. I use "foundational" with some caution, for it is possible that the Polynesians may not give the same stress to reference in their linguistic understanding and therefore to a (referential) ground or grounding. See note 14.

35. See Lévi-Strauss's discussion of Mauss's use of categories of indigenous understanding in his 1950 Introduction to Mauss's *Sociologie et anthropologie*. See note 28.

36. Durkheim, *Les Formes élémentaires*, p. 269. All references, unless otherwise indicated, are to the 1960 French edition (see note 2).

37. See Baldwin Spencer and F. J. Gillen, *The Native Tribes of Central Australia* (London: Macmillan, 1899), and idem, *The Northern Tribes of Central Australia* (London: Macmillan, 1904); and A. W. Howitt, *The Native Tribes of South-East Australia* (London: Macmillan, 1904). See also W. E. H. Stanner, "Reflections on Durkheim and Aboriginal Religion," in M. Freedman, ed., *Social Organization: Essays Presented to Raymond Firth* (Chicago: Aldine, 1967), pp. 217–40.

38. Durkheim, *The Elementary Forms*, p. 247, gives this translation: "When they are once come together, a sort of electricity is formed by their collecting which quickly transports them to an extraordinary degree of exaltation. Every sentiment expressed finds a place without resistance in all the minds, which are very open to outside impressions; each re-echoes the others, and is re-echoed by others. The initial

impulse that proceeds, growing as it goes, as an avalanche grows in advance. And as such active passions so free from all control could not fail to burst out, on every side one sees nothing but violent gestures, cries, veritable howls, and deafening noises of every sort, which aid in intensifying still more the state of mind which they manifest."

39. Durkheim, *The Elementary Forms*, p. 247 has: "This effervescence often reaches a point that it causes unheard-of actions. The passions released are of such an impetuosity that they can be restrained by nothing. They are so far removed from their ordinary conditions of life, and they are so thoroughly conscious of it, that they feel they must set themselves outside of and above their ordinary morals. The sexes unite contrarily to the rules governing sexual relations. Men exchange wives with each other. Sometimes even incestuous unions, which in normal times are thought abominable and are severely punished, are now contracted openly and with impunity."

40. See Lukes, *Emile Durkheim*, pp. 31, 438; and Emile Durkheim, "Lévy-Bruhl and 'The Elementary Forms,'" in Anthony Giddens, ed., *Selected Writings* (1912; rpt., Cambridge: Cambridge University Press, 1972), pp. 246–49.

41. In *The Elementary Forms*, there is a frequent association of violence with the (delimitation of the) sacred.

42. As I noted earlier, in *The Elementary Forms* Durkheim refines the argument he and Mauss advanced in *Primitive Classification*. The effervescent energy of the crowd is the prototype for the physicist's notion of force (Durkheim, *Les Formes élémentaires*, p. 292; see also his Introduction and Conclusion).

43. See Emile Durkheim, "Le Dualisme de la nature humaine et ses conditions sociales," *Scientia* 15 (1914): 206–21, and idem, "Le Problème religieux et la dualité de la nature humaine," originally published in 1913 in *Bulletin de la Société française de philosophie*, vol. 13; reprinted in Victor Karady, ed., *Textes: Religion, moral anomie*, vol. 2 (Paris: Editions de Minuit, n.d.), pp. 23–59, esp. p. 23.

44. Durkheim does not distinguish between sign and symbol.

45. See Jacques Derrida, *De la grammatologie* (Paris: Editions de Minuit, 1967).

46. Durkheim does not differentiate clearly between symbols, ideas, concepts, and categories. At some level all of them are socially — religiously — derived. He does suggest, however, that in the development of science the socially — religiously — founded *concepts* gradually free themselves from their social and religious foundations as societies differentiate and as methodological controls are elaborated (*Les Formes élémentaires*, pp. 616–27, 634). Yet it would seem that, despite their liberation, the concepts cannot fully escape their social roots. The same would be true of symbols and ideas. The categories seem to be most resistant to change. Durkheim is thus caught in the circularity of his argument, since society's effect on cognition and classification, on logic, can never be completely eliminated. He is driven to a sort of social relativism — a position with which he is not comfortable.

47. Quoted in Lukes, *Emile Durkheim*, p. 338, n. 71. Note Lukes's discussion here

of the relationship between Durkheim's thought and fascism (pp. 338–39). I am not referring to Durkheim's explicit political philosophy but to the thought—the episteme—that he shared, unwittingly and perhaps inevitably, with later fascist thinkers.

LISS: Patterns of Strangeness

For their comments on earlier drafts of this essay, I would like to thank Elazar Barkan, Vincent Crapanzano, Richard Handler, Sue Houchins, Robert Nye, Daniel Segal, Michael Meranze, and the anonymous referee for Stanford University Press.

1. Franz Boas was born in Minden, Westphalia, in 1858 and immigrated to the United States in the 1880's. After brief stints at Clark University and the Columbian Exhibition in Chicago, he settled in New York. Affiliated for a short time with the American Museum of Natural History and, for the remainder of his career, with Columbia University, Boas died in 1942. His students read like a *Who's Who* of American anthropology: Ruth Benedict, Margaret Mead, Edward Sapir, Robert Lowie, Alfred Kroeber, and Melville Herskovits, among others. No full-scale biography of Franz Boas exists, but a number of studies focus on various aspects of his achievements, the most important of which are George W. Stocking, Jr., "Anthropology as Kulturkampf: Science and Politics in the Career of Franz Boas," in Walter Goldschmidt, ed., *The Uses of Anthropology*, Special Publication of the American Anthropological Association, no. 11 (Washington, D.C.: American Anthropological Association, 1979), pp. 33–50; and idem, *Race, Culture and Evolution: Essays in the History of Anthropology* (New York: Free Press, 1968; rpt., Chicago: University of Chicago Press, 1982). See also Marshall Hyatt, *Franz Boas, Social Activist: The Dynamics of Ethnicity* (Westport, Conn.: Greenwood, 1990), and Walter Goldschmidt, ed., *The Anthropology of Franz Boas: Essays on the Centennial of His Birth*, Memoir of the American Anthropological Association, 61 (October 1959).

2. The definition of modernity as "the transitory, the fugitive, the contingent" is Baudelaire's ("The Painter of Modern Life," 1863). The English translation is from Lois Boe Hyslop and Francis E. Hyslop, *Baudelaire As a Literary Critic* (University Park: Pennsylvania State University Press, 1964), pp. 296–97; quoted in Matei Calinescu, *Faces of Modernity: Avant-Garde, Decadence, Kitsch* (Bloomington: Indiana University Press, 1977), pp. 4–5, 48. See Calinescu also for a useful discussion of the relationship of modernity and modernism. On the varieties of modernism, especially in its literary contexts, see also Malcolm Bradbury and James McFarlane, "The Name and Nature of Modernism," in idem, eds., *Modernism, 1890–1930* (Harmondsworth, England: Penguin Books, 1976), pp. 19–55, and Michael H. Levenson, *A Genealogy of Modernism: A Study of English Literary Doctrine, 1908–1922* (Cambridge: Cambridge University Press, 1984), especially his discussion of the "anthropological temper" of T. S. Eliot, pp. 194, 206–7. On modernism more broadly, as a cultural movement including anthropology, see Marc Manganaro, ed., *Modernist Anthropology: From Fieldwork to Text* (Princeton, N.J.: Princeton University Press, 1990), and

George E. Marcus and Michael M. J. Fischer, *Anthropology as Cultural Critique: An Experimental Moment in the Human Sciences* (Chicago: University of Chicago Press, 1986), esp. pp. 67–73.

3. Douglas Cole, "'The Value of a Person Lies in His *Herzensbildung*': Franz Boas' Baffin Island Letter-Diary, 1883–1884," in George W. Stocking, Jr., ed., *Observers Observed: Essays on Ethnographic Fieldwork*, History of Anthropology, vol. 1 (Madison: University of Wisconsin Press, 1983), pp. 17, 50; and George W. Stocking, Jr., "From Physics to Ethnology," in his *Race, Culture and Evolution*, pp. 135–36, 144–46, 149–51, 151–52.

4. On the "hermeneutics" of self-understanding and -transformation in anthropology, see Paul Rabinow, "'Facts are a Word of God,' An Essay Review of James Clifford, *Person and Myth: Maurice Leenhardt in the Melanesian World*," in Stocking, ed., *Observers Observed*, p. 200; Paul Rabinow, *Reflections on Fieldwork in Morocco* (Berkeley: University of California Press, 1977); and Clifford Geertz, *Works and Lives: The Anthropologist as Author* (Stanford: Stanford University Press, 1988), esp. chap. 4: "I-Witnessing: Malinowski's Children."

5. Although beyond the purview of this essay, Boas's later work for the U.S. Immigration Commission, *Changes in Bodily Forms of Descendants of Immigrants*, Senate Document No. 208, 61st Cong., 2nd sess., 1911, *Reports of the Immigration Commission*, vol. 64 (Washington, D.C.: Government Printing Office, 1911), extends his anthropological work into the realm of immigration debates. The volume argued for the plasticity of physical — and, by extension, possibly mental — types and was the only one to support keeping the doors open to new immigrants. Boas also sought to broaden the mandate of the Bureau of Ethnology to encompass African Americans and immigrants as well as Native American peoples. See, for instance, Franz Boas (hereafter FB) to Alexander Graham Bell, 8 November 1902, Boas Papers, American Philosophical Society (hereafter BP).

6. I. C. Jarvie, *Rationality and Relativism: In Search of a Philosophy and History of Anthropology* (London: Routledge & Kegan Paul, 1984), pp. 16–17.

7. Thanks to Michael Meranze for helping me clarify these relationships.

8. See, for instance, Stocking, "Franz Boas and the Culture Concept in Historical Perspective," in idem, *Race, Culture and Evolution*, pp. 195–233. On the complexities of localism and cultures, see James Clifford, "Traveling Cultures," in Lawrence Grossberg, Carey Nelson, and Paula Treichler, eds., *Cultural Studies* (New York: Routledge, 1992), pp. 96–112. Clifford argues, much like my discussion here concerning Boas's experience and anthropological vision, that ethnography has "privileged relations of dwelling over relations of travel" and analyzes instead "the ways people leave home and return, enacting differently centered worlds, interconnected cosmopolitanisms" (pp. 99, 103). Thanks to Richard Handler for directing me to this essay.

9. Boas's cosmopolitanism was essentially one of marginality, as opposed to what I call elsewhere a "cosmopolitanism of culture," which characterized the world of

certain New York elites. Whereas Boas's search for universals and connections that would overcome narrow and divisive affiliations led him to proclaim loyalty to the higher aims of professional knowledge, New York elites were motivated by a different form of cosmopolitanism. This cultural cosmopolitanism was essentially an ideology of local justification and dominance that stressed New York's role as a capital of commerce and finance which drew the world's peoples and goods through its port. In search of cultural institutions to match the city's economic importance and control its diverse population, these elites built New York's museums and created Columbia University, institutions with which Boas would be affiliated for the duration of his career. In institutionalizing his ideas, Boas alternately cooperated and battled with this ideology, but ultimately the two came into conflict. See Julia E. Liss, "The Cosmopolitan Imagination: Franz Boas and the Development of American Anthropology" (Ph.D. diss., University of California, Berkeley, 1990). On cosmopolitanism more broadly, especially as it pertains to intellectual life, see David A. Hollinger, "Ethnic Diversity, Cosmopolitanism, and the Emergence of the American Liberal Intelligentsia," in his *In the American Province: Studies in the History and Historiography of Ideas* (Bloomington: Indiana University Press, 1985), pp. 56–73, and idem, "Postethnic America," *Contention* 2 (Fall 1992): 79–96. I thank Daniel Segal for bringing this last piece to my attention.

10. The crisis of identity for post-emancipation German Jews is addressed in Solomon Liptzin, *Germany's Stepchildren* (Philadelphia: The Jewish Publication Society of America, 1944); Michael A. Meyer, *Response to Modernity: A History of the Reform Movement in Judaism* (New York: Oxford University Press, 1988); and George L. Mosse, *German Jews Beyond Judaism* (Cincinnati: Hebrew Union Press, and Bloomington: Indiana University Press, 1985), especially his discussion of Aby Warburg, Erwin Panofsky, and Ernst Cassirer on pp. 42–53. On the relationships among Boas's Jewishness, his assimilationist tendencies, and his later anthropological work, see Leonard B. Glick, "Types Distinct from Our Own: Franz Boas on Jewish Identity and Assimilation," *American Anthropologist* 84 (Sept. 1982): 545–65; Ellen Messer, "Franz Boas and Kaufmann Kohler: Anthropology and Reform Judaism," *Jewish Social Studies* 48 (Spring 1986): 127–40; and Hyatt, *Franz Boas, Social Activist*.

11. FB, "An Anthropologist's Credo," *The Nation* 147 (Aug. 27, 1938): 202, 201.

12. On the revival of geography and its preoccupation with these issues, see Richard Hartshorne, "The Concept of Geography as a Science of Space, from Kant and Humboldt to Hettner," in Fred E. Dohrs and Lawrence M. Sommers, eds., *Introduction to Geography: Selected Readings* (New York: Thomas Y. Crowell, 1967), pp. 74–90; and Margarita Bowen, *Empiricism and Geographical Thought: From Francis Bacon to Alexander von Humboldt* (Cambridge: Cambridge University Press, 1981), pp. 11–12.

13. A. L. Kroeber, "Franz Boas: The Man," *Memoirs of the American Anthropological Association* 45 (July–Sept., 1943): 7–8; John Cole, "The Reminiscences of Franziska Boas," interview, Aug. and Sept. 1972, Columbia University Oral History

Research Office, p. 11; and "Dogs Vivisected, Scientific Torture at Clark University," and "If He Be a Cur Cut Him Up . . . ," *Worcester Sunday Telegram*, Mar. 9, 1890, p. 8, Mar. 16, 1890, p. 7, respectively. Kroeber conflates a number of different incidents in his rendition. Boas's daughter, Franziska, also reported the possibility of an anti-Semitic incident but did not confirm that it had taken place.

14. It is interesting to consider how paradigmatic Boas's experience of exclusion was for anthropologists. Margaret Mead also endured a painful moment of exclusion when she was not allowed to join a sorority at De Pauw University. See her autobiography, *Blackberry Winter* (New York: Washington Square Press, 1972), pp. 97–109, in which she describes how the incident made her realize what it was to be an outsider, to experience injustice, to be an "exile." Recent revelations about Mead's bisexuality add to the reasons for her sense of marginality. See Mary Catherine Bateson, *With a Daughter's Eye: A Memoir of Margaret Mead and Gregory Bateson* (New York: Washington Square Press, 1984), pp. 140–53, and Margaret Caffrey, *Ruth Benedict: Stranger in the Land* (Austin: University of Texas Press, 1989), pp. 188–205.

15. FB to Reinhard Krüer, May 18, 1877, transl. and orig. in box of Boas Papers Miscellany, American Philosophical Society (hereafter BPmisc.). On Boas's reluctance to associate with Jewish students, see FB to Family, Apr. 21, 1877, transl. BPmisc.; FB to Mother, Apr. 30, 1877, transl. BPmisc. (I could not locate the originals of these); and FB to Parents, May 3, 1877, Boas Personal Papers, American Philosophical Society (hereafter BPP). Boas's membership also reinforces our picture of the broader experience of this generation of middle-class German intellectuals. On Max Weber's experience with the Allemannen, see Arthur Mitzman, *The Iron Cage* (New York: Alfred A. Knopf, 1969), p. 23. My understanding of German student life in this period is drawn from Konrad Jarausch, *Students, Society, and Politics in Imperial Germany: The Rise of Academic Illiberalism* (Princeton, N.J.: Princeton University Press, 1982). On dueling, see also E. J. Hobsbawm, "Mass-Producing Traditions: Europe, 1870–1914," in Eric Hobsbawm and Terence Ranger, eds., *The Invention of Tradition*, (Cambridge: Cambridge University Press, 1983), pp. 294–97, and Peter Gay, "Mensur: Cherished Scar," *Yale Review* 80 (Apr. 1992): 94–121.

16. Gay, "Mensur," pp. 94, 96–97.

17. Arctic Expedition Diary (hereafter AED), trans. by Boas's daughter, Helene Boas Yampolsky, BPP, July 18, 1883. The tension between memories and desires was heightened by the process of writing letters, which encouraged comparisons between the power of his present experience and the longing of his dreams. In this respect, his Baffin Island letter-diary — a vehicle for internal reflection and his only means of communicating with a world he had left behind — became a dialogue of contrasts. Because he addressed one of these diaries to his fiancée, Marie Krackowizer, the entries also served as love letters and their emotional pitch was greater. Although Boas's claims of frustrated love were the most visible indications of an unstable experience, they were not the only ones; they merely compounded the dynamics of the journey itself.

18. An impressionistic account of travel with some reference to the nineteenth century is Paul Fussell, *Abroad: British Literary Traveling Between the Wars* (New York: Oxford University Press, 1980). On the connections between geography, exploration, and travel, see D. R. Stoddart, *On Geography and Its History* (Oxford: Basil Blackwell, 1986); Richard A. Van Orman, *The Explorers: Nineteenth Century Expeditions in Africa and the American West* (Albuquerque: University of New Mexico Press, 1984); J. N. L. Baker, *A History of Geographical Discovery and Exploration* (Boston: Houghton Mifflin Co., [1931]); and Philip J. Pauly, "The World and All That Is In It: The National Geographic Society, 1888–1918," *American Quarterly* 31 (Fall 1979): 517–32. Boas himself later participated in a symposium entitled "Is Stanley Dead?" *North American Review* 147 (Dec. 1888): 601–15; his contribution appears on pp. 612–15.

19. AED, Dec. 23, 1883. I have changed the translation somewhat.

20. See especially AED, June 25 and 30 and July 5, 18, and 20, 1883.

21. AED, Sept. 19, 1883.

22. AED, back of the page dated Jan. 23, 1884. See also July 20, 1883 and [June] 18, 1884.

23. AED, Feb. 15, 1884.

24. AED, Dec. 16, 1883.

25. AED, July 20, 1883.

26. AED, Dec. 16, 1883.

27. AED, Dec. 23, 1883. See also Feb. 16, 1884 and Jan. 3 and 22, 1884.

28. AED, Mar. 20, 1884.

29. FB to Parents and Sisters, Dec. 24, 1884, BPP, transl. BPmisc.

30. FB to Marie [Krackowizer, his fiancée], Mar. 26, 1885, BPP, transl. BPmisc.

31. Michael Seidel, *Exile and the Narrative Imagination* (New Haven, Conn.: Yale University Press, 1986), p. ix; and Paul Tabori, *The Anatomy of Exile: A Semantic and Historical Study* (London: Harrap, 1972), p. 27; quoted in Seidel, *Exile*, p. 201.

32. FB to Parents, Jan. 14, 1885, BPP, transl. BPmisc.

33. 1886 Diary, Dec. 4, 1886, transl. BPP.

34. Boas had been nominated "from among the most distinguished American Jews" as an honorary fellow of the Jewish Academy of Arts and Sciences. He accepted the award because he was a member of "various European Academies" but requested no public ceremonies. Abraham Burstein to FB, Oct. 16, 1934, and FB to Abraham Burstein, Oct. 30, 1934, BP.

35. FB, "The Aims of Ethnology" (New York: Hermann, Bartsch, 1889); reprinted in his *Race, Language, and Culture* (New York: Free Press, 1940; rpt., Chicago: University of Chicago Press, 1982), pp. 627–28.

36. FB, "Advances in Methods of Teaching," *Science* 9 (1899); reprinted in his *Race, Language, and Culture*, p. 624. On the aims of history and general laws, see FB's review of A. F. Chamberlain's *The Child and Childhood in Folk-Thought* (New

York: Macmillan & Co., 1896), in Letters to the Editor, *Science*, 3 (May 15, 1896): 742; and FB, "The Aims of Ethnology," in his *Race, Language, and Culture*, pp. 633–37.

37. FB, "The Growth of Indian Mythologies," *Journal of American Folk-Lore* 9 (1896); reprinted in his *Race, Language, and Culture*, pp. 434–36. See also FB, "The Aims of Ethnology," reprinted in ibid., pp. 635–36, and FB, "The Limitations of the Comparative Method of Anthropology," *Science* 4 (1896); reprinted in ibid., p. 270.

38. 1886 Diary, Dec. 8, 1886, transl. BPP; 1888 Diary, July 9, 1888, transl. BPP. These continental connections were later the focus of the Jesup North Pacific Expedition (1897–1902), Boas's major expedition for the American Museum of Natural History.

39. FB, lecture, U.S. National Museum, Mar. 2, 1895, pp. 1–5, 11–12, ms., BPP.

40. FB, "Races of Man," lecture, American Museum of Natural History, 1896, pp. 1–5, ms., BPP. This appears to be a later version of an 1895 lecture at the U.S. National Museum.

41. FB, "The Aims of Ethnology," reprinted in his *Race, Language, and Culture*, p. 631.

42. FB, "The Growth of Indian Mythologies," reprinted in his *Race, Language, and Culture*, pp. 428–29. See also FB, "Dissemination of Tales among the Natives of North America," *Journal of American Folk-Lore* 4 (1891): 13–20, reprinted in ibid., pp. 438–39, 444–45.

43. FB, "The Aims of Ethnology," reprinted in his *Race, Language, and Culture*, p. 629. See also FB, "The Limitations of the Comparative Method of Anthropology," reprinted in ibid., pp. 276–77, and his review of Chamberlain's *The Child and Childhood in Folk-Thought*.

44. FB, "Some Recent Criticism of Physical Anthropology," *American Anthropologist* 1 (Jan. 1899), reprinted in his *Race, Language, and Culture*, p. 166; FB, "Notes on the Snanaimuq," *American Anthropologist* 2 (Oct. 1889): 321; and FB, "Dissemination of Tales among the Natives of North America," reprinted in his *Race, Language, and Culture*, p. 443.

45. FB, "Under the Arctic Circle," 1, orig. pub. in the *New-Yorker Staats-Zeitung*, Jan.–Mar. 2, 1885, trans. by Ernst Boas, Boas's son, with corrections by FB, BPP.

46. A good example of Boas's effort to communicate this message is a series of lectures he offered in 1896 at the American Museum of Natural History as a Columbia University extension course. The lectures were entitled "Primitive Art," "Primitive Language," "Primitive Religion," "Primitive Society," and "The Races of Man"; mss., BPP.

47. FB, "The Aims of Ethnology," reprinted in George W. Stocking, Jr., ed., *A Franz Boas Reader: The Shaping of American Anthropology, 1883–1911* (Chicago: University of Chicago Press, 1974), p. 71.

48. Ibid.

49. FB, "The History of Anthropology," *Science* 20 (Oct. 21, 1904): 517, 524.

HERBERT: Frazer, Einstein, and Free Play

1. "Perhaps no book has had so decisive an effect upon modern literature as Frazer's," declared Lionel Trilling in 1961 (Trilling, "On the Modern Element in Modern Literature," in Irving Howe, ed., *The Idea of the Modern in Literature and the Arts* [New York: Horizon, 1967], p. 69). John B. Vickery's *The Literary Impact of "The Golden Bough"* (Princeton, N.J.: Princeton University Press, 1973) provides copious evidence to support such a view and asserts that Frazer's book "came to occupy [a] . . . central . . . position in the thinking of the modern world" and in particular "came to influence literature . . . pervasively and profoundly" (p. 74). For Vickery, Frazer stands as a fountainhead of the radical, experimental tradition of Yeats, Eliot, Lawrence, and Joyce, a hero and patron of the modern literary imagination in its most liberated forms. The essays collected in Robert Fraser, ed., *Sir James Frazer and the Literary Imagination: Essays in Affinity and Influence* (New York: St. Martin's, 1990) form the latest example of this general view of Frazer.

2. References to *The Golden Bough* in this paper are to the 1922 one-volume abridged edition (*The Golden Bough: A Study in Magic and Religion* [1922; rpt., New York: Collier, 1963], hereafter "abridged *Golden Bough*"); to the two-volume first edition of 1890 (*The Golden Bough: The Roots of Religion and Folklore* [1890; rpt., New York: Avenel, 1981], hereafter "first *Golden Bough*"); and to *The Magic Art and the Evolution of Kings*, 2 vols. (1911; rpt., London: Macmillan, 1917, hereafter "*Magic Art*"), the first part of the 1911–15 twelve-volume third edition. Subsequent references are indicated parenthetically in the text.

3. René Girard, *Violence and the Sacred*, trans. Patrick Gregory (Baltimore and London: Johns Hopkins University Press, 1977), p. 318. Seen from this vantage point, modern thinking in anthropology defines itself as a repudiation of Frazer. In Mary Douglas's account (*Purity and Danger: An Analysis of Concepts of Pollution and Taboo* [London: Routledge, 1966]), Frazer is eclipsed chiefly by the developing, sociologically oriented heritage of Emile Durkheim. I. C. Jarvie, *The Revolution in Anthropology* (London: Routledge, 1964); James A. Boon, *Other Tribes, Other Scribes: Symbolic Anthropology in the Comparative Study of Cultures, Histories, Religions, and Texts* (Cambridge: Cambridge University Press, 1982); Marilyn Strathern, "Out of Context: The Persuasive Fictions of Anthropology," *Current Anthropology* 28 (1987): 251–81; and others give versions of this narrative as Oedipal drama, in which it is chiefly Frazer's student Bronislaw Malinowski, as the exponent of scientific fieldwork and functionalism, who plays the role of the inspiring sponsor of genuinely modernist anthropology — anthropology, that is, which defines itself in a concerted antagonism to Victorian received ideas. "Malinowski plotted and directed the revolution in social anthropology — aiming to overthrow the establishment of Frazer and Tylor and their ideas; but mainly it was against Frazer" (Jarvie, *Revolution in Anthropology*, p. 173).

4. Strathern, "Out of Context," p. 254.

5. Albert Einstein, *Essays in Science*, trans. Alan Harris (New York: Philosophical Library, 1934), p. 49, and idem, *Relativity: The Special and the General Theory*, trans. Robert N. Lawson (1916; rpt., New York: Crown, 1961), p. 53, respectively. Subsequent references to these and other works by Einstein cited below are indicated parenthetically in the text.

6. A. S. Eddington, *The Nature of the Physical World* (1928; rpt., Cambridge: Cambridge University Press, 1932), p. 61; see also pp. 15, 16, 21, and 113. Subsequent references are indicated parenthetically in the text.

7. Bertrand Russell, *The ABC of Relativity* (New York and London: Harper, 1925), p. 53.

8. Claude Lévi-Strauss, *Tristes tropiques*, trans. John and Doreen Weightman (Chicago: University of Chicago Press, 1969), pp. 385, 386 (subsequent references are indicated parenthetically in the text); and Boon, *Other Tribes, Other Scribes*, p. ix, respectively. Deborah Tannen extends the same principle into the field of popular sociolinguistics, asserting that characteristic misunderstandings that occur in conversations between men and women need to be related to the tendency of the two sexes to express themselves in "different *but equally valid* styles," each of which "is valid on its own terms" (*You Just Don't Understand: Women and Men in Conversation* [New York: Ballantine, 1990], pp. 15, 47). The tendentiousness of much of this book's argument shows how much easier it is to pay lip service to Einstein's principle than actually to put it into practice.

9. Douglas, *Purity and Danger*, p. 24.

10. Einstein stresses this aspect of relativity theory and of modern physics in general. See, for example, his *Essays in Science*, p. 69: "The hypotheses with which [modern theoretical science] starts become steadily more abstract and remote from experience. . . . Meanwhile the train of thought leading from the axioms to the empirical facts or verifiable consequences gets steadily longer and more subtle." Special relativity theory, according to Gerald Holton, entails nothing less than "the abandonment of the conceptions of experiential space and experiential time" (see Holton, "Mach, Einstein, and the Search for Reality," *Daedalus* 97 [1968]: 655).

11. Henry Margenau, "Einstein's Conception of Reality," in Paul Arthur Schilpp, ed., *Albert Einstein: Philosopher-Scientist* (Evanston, Ill.: Library of Living Philosophers, 1949), p. 255.

12. Bronislaw Malinowski, *A Scientific Theory of Culture and Other Essays* (Chapel Hill: University of North Carolina Press, 1944), p. 36.

13. "Among the objects of public utility which magic may be employed to secure, the most essential is an adequate supply of food," says Frazer (abridged *Golden Bough*, p. 70). Malinowski praises Frazer particularly for his "insight in linking up ritual with the practical activities of food production" (*A Scientific Theory of Culture*, p. 191).

14. René Girard amazingly accuses Frazer of participation in anthropological "concealment of the violent impulse that lurks within the rite of sacrifice" (*Violence*

*and the Sacred*, p. 317). It is true that Frazer does not speak of a craving for violence as an instinctual drive and that he avoids explaining sacrifice by invoking anything like Girard's personified mythic figure, "Violence": "Violence is frequently called irrational. It has its reasons, however, and can marshal some rather convincing ones when the need arises. . . . Violence itself will discard them if the initial object remains persistently out of reach. . . . When unappeased, violence seeks and always finds a surrogate victim" (ibid., p. 2). It may be doubted whether the introduction of this fantastic personage into would-be scientific discourse marks an advance in sophistication over Frazer, however.

15. "The consideration of human suffering is not one which enters into the calculations of primitive man" (abridged *Golden Bough*, p. 756).

16. The dominance of violence in *The Golden Bough* evokes as well that persistent factor in anthropological literature pungently identified by Claude Lévi-Strauss as "a certain taste for the obscene and the grotesque which is for the science of religion like a childhood disease" (*The Scope of Anthropology*, trans. Sherry Ortner Paul and Robert A. Paul [London: Cape, 1967], pp. 44–45).

17. Albert Einstein, "Remarks on Bertrand Russell's Theory of Knowledge," in Paul Arthur Schilpp, ed., *The Philosophy of Bertrand Russell* (Evanston and Chicago: Northwestern University Press, 1944), p. 287. Einstein's formulation echoes Kant in *The Critique of Judgment*, trans. James Creed Meredith (Oxford: Clarendon, 1952), p. 14: "Between the realm of the natural concept, as the sensible, and the realm of the concept of freedom, as the supersensible, there is a gulf fixed, so that it is not possible to pass from the former to the latter (by means of the theoretical employment of reason), just as if they were so many separate worlds, the first of which is powerless to exercise influence on the second." As we shall see, Einstein specifically identifies the realm of scientific theory as "the realm of the concept of freedom."

18. Albert Einstein, "On The Method of Theoretical Physics," in idem, *Essays in Science*, pp. 16, 15.

19. Albert Einstein, "Autobiographical Notes," in Schilpp, ed., *Albert Einstein*, pp. 7, 13.

20. Friedrich Nietzsche, "On Truth and Falsity in Their Ultramoral Sense," in idem, *Early Greek Philosophy and Other Essays*, trans. Maximilian A. Mugge (New York: Russell and Russell, 1964), p. 180.

21. Paul Feyerabend, with his credo of "theoretical anarchism" and his call for giving absolutely unrestricted scope to "the freedom of artistic creation" in science, is, of current philosophers of science, probably the one who most closely replicates Einstein's position (Feyerabend, *Against Method*, rev. ed. [London and New York: Verso, 1988], pp. 9, 38).

22. Adam Smith, "The History of Astronomy," in idem, *Essays on Philosophical Subjects*, ed. W. P. D. Wightman and J. C. Bryce (Oxford: Clarendon, 1980), pp. 66, 105.

23. Einstein, *Essays in Science*, p. 11; see also p. 114.

24. Albert Einstein, "Physics and Reality," trans. Jean Picard, *Journal of the Franklin Institute* 221 (1936): 351.

25. "As far as I am conscious of it, the immediate influence of Hume on me was greater [than that of Ernst Mach]": letter of Einstein to Michelange Besso, Jan. 8, 1948, quoted in Holton, "Mach, Einstein, and the Search for Reality," p. 648. For Frazer's thoroughgoing indebtedness to Hume, see Robert Fraser, *The Making of "The Golden Bough": The Origins and Growth of an Argument* (New York: St. Martin's, 1990), pp. 18–21.

26. David Hume, *A Treatise of Human Nature*, 2nd ed., ed. L. A. Selby-Bigge and P. H. Nidditch (Oxford: Clarendon, 1978), p. 181.

27. Fraser, *The Making of "The Golden Bough,"* p. 212.

28. "I cannot but feel that in some places I may have pushed [my theory] too far," says Frazer in the preface to the original edition of 1890: "If this should prove to have been the case, I will readily acknowledge and retract my error as soon as it is brought home to me" (first *Golden Bough*, p. ix).

29. In an essay of 1931, which Einstein specifically endorsed as corresponding exactly to his own views, Max Planck, taking as a fundamental principle of research that *"the real outer world is not directly knowable,"* could almost be quoting Frazer as he, Planck, describes science as "an incessant struggle toward a goal which will never be reached, because by its very nature it is unreachable." Conclusive knowledge, being "of a metaphysical character," is "always again and again beyond our achievement" (quoted in Holton, "Mach, Einstein, and the Search for Reality," p. 661).

30. Albert Einstein, quoted in ibid., p. 648.

31. One contemporary attitude resembling the one I here ascribe to Frazer would be the "radical empiricism" of William James, which bases its antagonism to philosophical absolutism on the principle "that a disseminated, distributed, or incompletely unified appearance is the only form that reality may yet have achieved" (James, *A Pluralistic Universe* [1909; rpt., New York: Longmans, 1916], p. 44).

32. The reference to physics here can be glossed by a text such as Einstein's 1920 lecture "Ether and the Theory of Relativity," which begins by posing, in language closely reminiscent of Frazer's, precisely the problematic discussed here as the point of departure of modern physical science. The issue for contemporary theorists, Einstein explains, has been that of trying to reconcile the explanation of physical phenomena by the principle of "immediate contact" — by the principle of contagious magic, in Frazer's terminology — with the theory of gravity stemming from Newton and resting on the supposedly unacceptable principle of "immediate action at a distance" — by action exactly analogous to that imagined in homeopathic magic, in other words ("Ether and the Theory of Relativity," in Einstein, *Sidelights on Relativity* [1922; rpt., New York: Dover, 1983], pp. 3–5).

33. R. Angus Downie, *Frazer and the Golden Bough* (London: Gollancz, 1970), p. 16.

34. That numerous anthropological writers have raised this very problem is

shown in Christopher Herbert, *Culture and Anomie: Ethnographic Imagination in the Nineteenth Century* (Chicago and London: University of Chicago Press, 1991), pp. 1–28.

35. This theory, which we might call the amnesia theory of myth, alternates uneasily in Frazer's succeeding editions of *The Golden Bough* with the euhemerist theory, which identifies myth with origins in real historical personages and events.

36. Susan Stewart, *On Longing: Narratives of the Miniature, the Gigantic, the Souvenir, the Collection* (Baltimore and London: Johns Hopkins University Press, 1984), p. ix.

37. Margaret T. Hogden, *The Doctrine of Survivals: A Chapter in the History of Scientific Method in the Study of Man* (London: Allenson, 1936), p. 177.

38. Quoted in Vickery, *Literary Impact of "The Golden Bough,"* p. 78.

39. Ruth Benedict, *Patterns of Culture* (New York: Mentor, 1946), p. 49.

40. One notable reference here is the denunciation of relativity theory as "Jewish physics" by ideologues of the Third Reich, who thus linked it directly to all the imagery of taboo filth and perversion that was the essence of Nazi anti-Semitic discourse.

41. Michel Foucault, "What Is an Author?" in Josué V. Harari, ed., *Textual Strategies: Perspectives in Post-Structuralist Criticism* (Ithaca, N.Y.: Cornell University Press, 1979), p. 159.

42. See Feyerabend, *Against Method*, pp. 40–41.

43. Downie, *Frazer and the Golden Bough*, pp. 15–16.

44. Albert Einstein, "On the Electrodynamics of Moving Bodies," in idem, *The Collected Papers of Albert Einstein*, 2 vols., trans. Anna Beck (Princeton, N.J.: Princeton University Press, 1987), 2:141.

45. Stanley Edgar Hyman, *The Tangled Bank: Darwin, Marx, Frazer and Freud as Imaginative Writers* (New York: Atheneum, 1962), pp. 264–65. See also Malinowski, *A Scientific Theory of Culture*, p. 189, where Frazer is described as "the cicerone guiding our steps on the deserts of Australia, among the tropical jungles of the Amazon or the Orinoco, on the steppes of Asia, or the highlands of Africa."

MARSH: In a Glass Darkly

1. Sheridan Le Fanu, "Carmilla," collected in idem, *In a Glass Darkly* (London: E. Nash & Grayson, 1923), p. 326. Subsequent references are indicated parenthetically in the text.

2. Bram Stoker, *Dracula* (Oxford: Oxford University Press, 1983), p. 254. Subsequent references are indicated parenthetically in the text. Stoker deleted a first chapter, "Dracula's Guest," set in "Styria," which made the indebtedness of his tale to Le Fanu's overly apparent. For commentary, see Regenia Gagnier, "Evolution and Information, or Eroticism and Everyday Life, in *Dracula* and the Late Victorian Aestheticism," and Robert Tracy, "Loving You All Ways: Vamps, Vampires, Necrophiles and Necrofilles in Nineteenth-Century Fiction," both in Regina Barreca, ed., *Sex and*

*Death in Victorian Fiction* (London: Macmillan, 1990), pp. 140–57 and 32–59; both essays have useful bibliographies.

3. George Meredith, *The Ordeal of Richard Feverel: A History of Father and Son*, ed. John Halperin (1859; rpt., Oxford: Oxford University Press, 1984), p. 3. In his 1885 *Diana of the Crossways*, introduction by Lois Josephs Fowler (New York: Norton, 1973), Meredith puts an intriguing, quasi-"modernist" linguistic spin on the idea: women become associated with the regeneration of the English language, possessed of a power of words that can be "direct, sharp as fangs and teeth" (p. 46).

4. For a broad-based discussion of Victorian ideas of savagery, at home as well as abroad, see George W. Stocking, Jr., *Victorian Anthropology* (New York: Macmillan, 1987), pp. 96–109 and 208–18. The figure of the savage black female dies hard: in the late 1930's, Orson Welles and the Harlem Troupe revived an 1890's production of *Macbeth* that featured the witch Hecate as a bare-breasted black woman cracking a whip.

5. See Tzvetan Todorov, *The Fantastic: A Structural Approach to a Literary Genre*, trans. Richard Howard (Ithaca, N.Y.: Cornell University Press, 1975).

6. Robert Louis Stevenson, *The Strange Case of Dr. Jekyll and Mr. Hyde and Other Stories*, ed. Jenni Calder (Harmondsworth, England: Penguin Books, 1979), p. 80. Subsequent references are indicated parenthetically in the text.

7. H. G. Wells, "The Time Machine," in his *Complete Short Stories* (London: Ernest Benn, 1948), p. 44. Subsequent references are indicated parenthetically in the text.

8. Rider Haggard's *She* (London: Longman, 1887), the tale of the ageless white queen of a lost tribe of African savages, set in the necropolis of an ancient civilization, brings together the modes of science fantasy and quasi-pornographic imperialist adventure.

9. Harry M. Geduld, ed., *The Definitive Dr. Jekyll and Mr. Hyde Companion* (New York: Garland, 1983) lists 67 "straight" versions or parodies of the original story to 1976; his "Select List of Movie Variants on Motifs in *Dr. Jekyll and Mr. Hyde*" runs to 136 items to 1973. David J. Skal lists over 70 *Dracula*-inspired films worldwide to 1990; see his *Hollywood Gothic: The Tangled Web of Dracula from Novel to Stage to Screen* (New York: Norton: 1990).

10. Ernst Haeckel, *The Riddle of the Universe at the Close of the Nineteenth Century*, trans. Joseph McCabe (New York: Harper and Brothers, 1900), p. 257.

11. See H. G. Wells, *The Outline of History, Being a Plain History of Life and Mankind*, written with the advice and editorial help of Ernest Baker and others, 2 vols. (London: G. Newnes, 1919–20).

12. Quoted in Don Gifford, *The Farther Shore: A Natural History of Perception, 1798–1984* (New York: Atlantic Monthly Press, 1990), p. 23.

13. Quoted in Peter Pollack, *The Picture History of Photography: From the Earliest Beginnings to the Present Day* (London: Thames and Hudson, 1977), p. 28.

14. Gus Macdonald, *Camera: Victorian Eyewitness, A History of Photography: 1826–1913* (New York: Studio Books, 1979), p. 22.

15. Photographer Samuel Bourne, quoted in Clark Worswick and Ainslie Embree, *The Last Empire: Photography in British India, 1855–1911* (New York: Aperture, 1976), p. 10.

16. Alexander Black, writing in 1887 in *The Century*, as quoted by Sarah Greenough, "The Curious Contagion of the Camera, 1880–1918," in Sarah Greenough, Joel Snyder, David Travis, and Colin Westerbeck, eds., *On the Art of Fixing a Shadow: One Hundred and Fifty Years of Photography* (Boston, Toronto, London: National Gallery of Art and Art Institute of Chicago, in association with Bullfinch Press/Little, Brown, 1989), p. 130.

17. Ibid., pp. 131, 133, and 153, note.

18. Ibid., p. 130.

19. Terry Castle, "Phantasmagoria: Spectral Technology and the Metaphorics of Modern Reverie," *Critical Inquiry* 15, 3 (Autumn 1988): 64.

20. Wells, *Complete Short Stories*, p. 90. It is worth also comparing Wells's phantom to the "ghost" images of fast-moving figures that haunted photography in the days of long exposure times, such as those C. Piazzi Smyth captured of his Arab helpers in photographs taken in 1865 inside the Great Pyramid in Egypt, by the light of successive magnesium flares (see Macdonald, *Camera: Victorian Eyewitness*, p. 144).

21. Pollack, *Picture History of Photography*, p. 55.

22. Macdonald, *Camera: Victorian Eyewitness*, p. 164.

23. For a general discussion of changes in the perception of time and space at the end of the nineteenth century, see Steven Kern, *The Culture of Time and Space, 1880–1918* (Cambridge, Mass.: Harvard University Press, 1983).

24. Greenough notes, in "Contagion of the Camera," in idem et al., eds., *Fixing a Shadow*, p. 154, that "During the 1890's many people thought photography could be used in conjunction with psychic investigations. In 'The Image Had Vanished,' *The New York Sun*, 22 December 1894, 7, it was reported that the eyes of a murder victim were being examined to see if the last image she had seen was preserved on the retina. The article quoted Alfred Stieglitz as saying that he believed it was possible — revealing his strong belief that eyes were not only a 'window on the soul,' but also functioned like a camera."

25. Quoted in ibid., p. 130.

26. Alan Thomas, *Time in a Frame: Photography and the Nineteenth-Century Mind* (New York: Schocken Books, 1977), p. 23. In fact, retouching techniques were common practice in portrait studios by the 1850's, and many of the most famous images of the American Civil War and the Paris Commune were either dramatically faked (by moving bodies, and so forth) or the product of shameless composite-negative techniques (see Macdonald, *Camera: Victorian Eyewitness*, pp. 79–90).

27. Quoted in Macdonald, *Camera: Victorian Eyewitness*, p. 38.

28. Greenough, "Contagion of the Camera," in idem et al., eds., *Fixing a Shadow*, p. 140.

29. John Forbes Watson, ed., *The People of India*, 8 vols. (London: India Museum, 1868–75).

30. Quoted in Thomas, *Time in a Frame*, p. 32.

31. Quoted in Macdonald, *Camera: Victorian Eyewitness*, p. 96.

32. "Photographs of Zulu life in many Victorian keepsake books attest to the widespread demand among the picture buying public for commercial photographs of such 'lesser breeds outside the law'" (ibid., pp. 127–28).

33. In *China and Its People* (1873), quoted in Aaron Scharf, *Pioneers of Photography* (London: British Broadcasting Corporation, 1975), p. 112, expedition photographer John Thomson remarks, recalling Le Fanu's mountebank:

As the "Fan Qui" or "Foreign Devil" who assumed human shape, . . . I . . . frequently enjoyed the reputation of being a dangerous geomancer, and my camera was held to be a dark mysterious instrument, which, combined with my naturally, or supernaturally, intensified eyesight gave me power to see through rocks and mountains, to pierce the very souls of the natives, and to produce marvelous pictures by some black art, which at the same time bereft the individual depicted of so much of the principle of life as to render his death a certainty within a very short period of years.

Accounted, for these reasons, the forerunner of death, I found portraits of children difficult to obtain, while, strange as it may seem in a land where filial piety is esteemed the highest of virtues, sons and daughters brought their aged parents to be placed before the foreigner's silent and mysterious instrument of destruction.

34. See Macdonald, *Camera: Victorian Eyewitness*, p. 99.

35. See ibid., p. 101.

36. Quoted in Greenough, "Contagion of the Camera," in idem et al., eds., *Fixing a Shadow*, p. 138.

37. Producer Merian Cooper, quoted in Orville Goldner and George E. Turner, *The Making of King Kong* (South Brunswick and New York: A. S. Barnes, 1975), p. 38, recalled the origin of *King Kong* thus: "Then the thought struck me — what would happen to this highest representative of prehistoric animal life in our materialistic, mechanistic civilization? Why not place him at the pinnacle of the tallest building, symbol in steel, stone and glass of modern man's achievement and aspiration, and pit him against modern man?" The premise of the film, that director-adventurer Denham "always bring[s] back a picture" — no matter where from or what the danger — highlights the hunting origin of the term "snapshot": instead of big game, or natives, he "bags" images. *King Kong*'s whip-and-chain cruelty, in conjunction with the "prehistoric" premise and mise-en-scène, not only recalled the classic Victorian fantasy of sadistic black natives but anticipated, perhaps, what must surely be the most extraordinary sequel ever made: *La Marquise de Sade et un Lézard nommé King Kong*.

38. David J. Skal, *Hollywood Gothic: The Tangled Web of Dracula from Novel to Stage to Screen* (New York: Norton, 1990), p. 45.

39. Stanley Kauffman, "D. W. Griffith's *Way Down East*," *Horizon* 14, 2 (Spring 1972): 52.

WEBB: Manipulated Images

Research for this paper was made possible by 1991 and 1993 Professional Travel Grants from the Metropolitan Museum of Art, with the support of Julie Jones, Curator-in-Charge, Department of the Arts of Africa, Oceania, and the Americas. I am also grateful to Thomas Frontini, Assistant Photo Archivist there, and to J. Ross Day, Assistant Museum Librarian, and Peter Blank, Librarian, of the Robert Goldwater Library. My sincere thanks to Alan Davies, Curator, Photography Collection, and Jennifer Broomhead, Copyright and Permissions Librarian, the Mitchell Library, State Library of New South Wales, Sydney, and their knowledgeable staff. Also in Sydney, Dr. Jim Specht, Liz Bonshek, Carl Bento, and staff at the Australian Museum provided helpful assistance.

1. Gaston Tissandier, *A History and Handbook of Photography*, The Literature of Photography (London: Sampson Low, 1878; rpt., New York: Arno Press, 1973), p. 158.

2. Ibid., p. 159.

3. Before the perfection of the halftone reproduction process, the way the photograph was to be used or distributed also determined, to an extent, the amount of retouching or alteration it received. As a result of these early technical limitations, photographic images that were used in books, newspapers, and journals were generally copied by a wood engraver and relief printed. For descriptions of the Heliotype, Albertype, Woodburytype, and other early photographic printing processes, see Helmut and Alison Gernsheim, *A Concise History of Photography* (New York: Grosset & Dunlap, 1965); *International Center of Photography Encyclopedia of Photography*, A Pound Press Book (New York: Crown Publishers, 1984); James M. Reilly, *Care and Identification of 19th-Century Photographic Prints*, Kodak Pub. No. G–2S (New York: Eastman Kodak Company, 1986); and Naomi Rosenblum, *A World History of Photography* (New York: Abbeville Press, 1984). Subsequent references are indicated parenthetically in the text.

4. "Documentary" is in quotation marks to acknowledge the limited ability of the photograph to record a certain type of reality. Space does not permit a detailed discussion of the theoretical issues of the documentary image here, but see Abigail Solomon-Godeau, *Photography at the Dock*, Media and Society, no. 4 (Minneapolis: University of Minnesota Press, 1991). For theoretical discussions relevant to this essay but not directly addressed, see Roland Barthes, "Rhetoric of the Image," in Robert E. Innis, ed., *Semiotics: An Introductory Anthology*, Advances in Semiotics (Bloomington: Indiana University Press, 1985); Roland Barthes, *Camera Lucida: Reflections on Photography*, trans. Richard Howard (New York: Hill & Wang, 1981); Victor Burgin, *Thinking Photography* (Atlantic Highlands, N.J.: Humanities Press, 1982); and Rosalind Krauss, "Notes on the Index: Part 1," in her *The Originality of the Avant-Garde and Other Modernist Myths* (Cambridge, Mass.: MIT Press, 1985).

5. Henry Herbert Goddard (1858–1928) offered photographs as evidence to support his conclusion that physical characteristics help identify feebleminded people

and morons. Stephen Jay Gould examined Goddard's photographs of "test" families and found that the facial expressions of the people had been altered to "produce an appearance of evil or stupidity." See Gould, *The Mismeasure of Man* (New York and London: W. W. Norton, 1981), p. 172.

6. For two important essays about retouching photographs and manipulating subject matter, see Ira Jacknis, "Franz Boas and Photography," *Studies in Visual Communication* 10, 1 (1984): 2–60, esp. 36–42, and the important early work by Joanna C. Scherer, "You Can't Believe Your Eyes: Inaccuracies in Photographs of North American Indians," *Studies in the Anthropology of Visual Communication*, 2, 2 (1975): 67–79. I am indebted to Scherer for the premise of the present essay.

7. Scholarship of the past decade has shown an increasing awareness regarding the accurate reporting, research, and use of so-called ethnographic or field photographs. In particular, see Christraud M. Geary, *Images of Bamum: German Colonial Photography at the Court of King Njoya, Cameroon, West Africa, 1902–1915* (London and Washington, D.C.: Smithsonian Institution Press, 1988); the exhibition catalogue *Burton Brothers: Fotografen in Nieuw-Zeeland, 1866–1898* (Rotterdam: Museum voor Land-en Volkenkunde, 1987); Markus Schindlbeck, *Die ethnographische Linse* (Berlin: Museum für Völkerkunde, Berlin, Veröffentlichungen des Museums für Völkerkunde Neue Folge 48, 1989); Thomas Theye, *Der geraubte Schatten* (Munich: Münchner Stadtmuseums, 1990); and V. L. Webb, *Altered Exposures: Photographs of the Maori of New Zealand* (New York: Metropolitan Museum of Art, 1988); see also their bibliographic entries. A recent study of the relationship between anthropology and photography (published since the present essay was written) also contains many relevant contributions: see Elizabeth Edwards, ed., *Anthropology and Photography, 1860–1920* (New Haven and London: Yale University Press, in association with the Royal Anthropological Institute, London, 1992).

8. All the photographers discussed in this paper are male because the profession was male-dominated in the Pacific colonies. Some widows took over their husbands' firms, but usually the stock was sold instead. Photographic representation of Pacific Island women, particularly from Polynesia, was prolific, and the way they were pictured often verged on pornography. The surviving work of the few women who were able to make a name for themselves, such as Madame S. Hoare of Tahiti, shows a much different depiction of women. For published examples of Hoare's work, see Patrick O'Reilly, *Les photographes à Tahiti et leurs oeuvres 1842–1962* (Paris: Société des Océanistes, Musée de l'Homme, 1969), pp. 24–27.

9. This division between studio and exterior photographs is not unique to the Pacific. It is also seen during this period in the United States and Africa. See J. Luskey and P. R. Fleming, *The North American Indians in Early Photographs* (New York: Harper & Row, 1986); Scherer, "You Can't Believe Your Eyes"; and V. L. Webb, "Fact and Fiction: Nineteenth-Century Photographs of the Zulu," *African Arts* 25, 1 (1992): 50–59, 98–99.

10. It is important to note here publications regarding colonialism. For a discus-

sion of demeaning policies now described as colonial mimicry, see Homi K. Bhabha, "Of Mimicry and Man: The Ambivalence of Colonial Discourse," *October* 28 (1984): 125–33. Photographic parallels are often seen, such as indigenous people dressed in European clothing and posed with colonists.

11. H. P. Robinson, *The Studio and What To Do in It*, The Literature of Photography (London: Piper & Carter, 1891; rpt., New York: Arno Press, 1973), pp. 1–11.

12. Michael King and Marti Friedlander, *Moko: Maori Tattooing in the 20th century* (Auckland: David Bateman, 1992; unpaginated). For biographical information about Robley (1840–1930) and his military career, see A. H. McLintock, ed., *An Encyclopaedia of New Zealand*, vol. 3 (Wellington, N.Z.: Government Printing Office, 1966), pp. 110–11.

13. Major-General Robley, *Moko; or Maori Tattooing* (London: Chapman and Hall, 1896; rpt., Auckland: Southern Reprints, 1987). Subsequent references are indicated parenthetically in the text.

14. William Main, *Maori in Focus* (Wellington, N.Z.: Millwood Press, 1976), p. 27.

15. A case in point is the work of Reverend William Lawes of the London Missionary Society, who worked in British New Guinea. His photographs, which I am researching, were later marketed by a commercial firm.

16. Shar Jones, *J. W. Lindt, Master Photographer* (South Yarra, Australia: C. O'Neil Ross, on behalf of the Library Council of Victoria, 1985), p. 3. Subsequent references are indicated parenthetically in the text.

17. A discussion of one of Lindt's exterior photographs of a group of unidentified Aboriginal people can be found in Jones, *J. W. Lindt*, p. 24. Jones notes the static pose: "The standing figures probably have their backs to the camera as a concession to the prudery of the time."

18. The similarity in composition between the studio portraits of Aboriginal people and those of Australian laborers is noted by Jones, *J. W. Lindt*, p. 29.

19. For a case study of this studio practice in Africa, see Webb, "Fact and Fiction."

20. The Burton Brothers, as they were professionally known in New Zealand, brought their own blankets and Maori cloaks to use as costumes when making many of their most famous photographs (*Burton Brothers*, p. 75). For examples by other photographers who used blankets and props, see the publication of images by the American Photographic Company, Auckland, in Michael King, *Maori: A Photographic and Social History* (Auckland: Heinemann, 1984), p. 8. Another photographer who used an extensive collection of objects in his work was Francis H. Dufty; see S. Hooper and J. Roth, *The Fiji Journals of Baron Anatole Von Hügel, 1875–1877* (Suva, Fiji: Fiji Museum, in association with Cambridge University Museum of Archaeology and Anthropology, 1990), p. 463. Many of Dufty's studio photographs can be seen in the photographic archive of the University Museum of Archaeology and Anthropology, Cambridge, England.

21. An example that now has several photographers' names attached to it is the image of Te Rangitahau's house at Opepe taken by Herbert Deveril (Main, *Maori in*

*Focus*, p. 16). Deveril made a group of Maori portraits for the New Zealand government display at the 1876 Philadelphia Exhibition, among them this one. Two prints are in the collection of the Metropolitan Museum of Art: one is initialed "JM" (for Josiah Martin), whereas another is signed "Wheeler & Son." For discussions of this image, see King, *Maori: A Photographic History*, p. 55, and Main, *Maori in Focus*, p. 16.

22. See William C. Darrah, *Cartes de Visite in Nineteenth-Century Photography* (Gettysburg, Penn.: W. C. Darrah, 1981), pp. 119, 150–51. For a discussion of the *carte-de-visite* and related formats like the cabinet card see pp. 4–11.

23. See the discussion of Lindt's photographs in the essays by Roslyn Poignant and Christopher Pinney in Edwards, ed., *Anthropology and Photography*.

24. For a description of the Autotype process (and the London company of the same name), which used carbon and gelatin to reproduce continuous-tone reproductions of photographs, see William Welling, *Photography in America: The Formative Years 1839–1900* (New York: Thomas Y. Crowell, 1978), pp. 189, 351. See also *Encyclopedia of Photography*, pp. 47–48.

25. See especially the plates in John W. Lindt, *Picturesque New Guinea* (London: Longmans, 1887), opposite page 108, plate XLI, and p. 38, plate XV. Subsequent references are indicated parenthetically in the text.

26. Fig. 10, the image of an unidentified Samoan woman, is one of the more well known from Kerry's firm because of its props and heavy retouching. The negatives of Charles Kerry and Henry King (1855–1923) are now in the Powerhouse Museum, Sydney. Notes included with prints in the Tyrrell Collection, in the Mitchell Library, State Library of New South Wales, Sydney, list the photographers actively working for Kerry's studio as George Ball, J. C. Cruden, Harold Bradley, and W. van der Velden. Recently, the attribution of this image to Kerry has been questioned, it being suggested that it was made instead by George Bell. (This man's name is cited differently in two places: the Tyrrell Collection notes have "George Ball," but David P. Millar, *Charles Kerry's Federation Australia* [Sydney: David Ell, 1981], p. 19 has "George Bell." "Ball" would seem to be a typographical error in the Tyrrell notes.) For a discussion of Kerry's Samoan images and their possible attributions, see Alison Devine Nordström, "Early Photography in Samoa: Marketing Stereotypes of Paradise," *History of Photography* 15, 4 (1991): 272–85. The communal publishing of images under a single firm name was very common in many countries during the nineteenth century. For an essay that provides a relevant discussion of erotic imagery in European art and photography, see Linda Nochlin, "Eroticism and Female Imagery in Nineteenth-Century Art," in her *Women, Art, and Power and Other Essays* (New York: Harper and Row, 1988), pp. 136–44.

27. This photograph (Fig. 11) is published in Frances Awdry, *In the Isles of the Sea: The Story of Fifty Years in Melanesia* (London: Bemrose & Sons, 1902), p. 34, with a credit to Montgomery. The book tells the story of the Melanesian Mission. An introduction by Bishop H. H. Montgomery notes that "ten years . . . have elapsed since I was in Melanesia." Based on Awdry, I believe Fig. 11 to be by Montgomery.

Kerry could have obtained Montgomery's negatives and marketed them under his own name. Many of Montgomery's photographs have been misattributed to other photographers who published them at a later date, such as J. Beattie of Hobart, Australia. The Mitchell Library, Sydney, holds a selection of photographs by Montgomery.

28. Millar, *Charles Kerry's Federation Australia*, p. 15. Primary information about Kerry can also be found here.

29. Patrick O'Reilly, *La Nouvelle-Calédonie vue par le photographe Allan Hughan il y a cent ans* (Paris: Nouvelles Editions Latines, 1978). The exact dates for Hughan are difficult to determine. For a discussion, see *La Nouvelle-Calédonie*, p. 66. Negatives and prints by Hughan are in the collection of the Mitchell Library, Sydney.

30. Hughan is reported to have produced several series of *cartes-de-visite* with the titles "Indigènes de la Nouvelle-Calédonie," "Indigènes des Nouvelles-Hebrides," "Indigènes des Iles Loyalty," "Indigènes de Samoa et de Tahiti," and "Indigènes du Pacifique" (O'Reilly, *La Nouvelle-Calédonie*, p. 61). The Haddon Photograph Archive, Cambridge University Museum of Archaeology and Anthropology, has several Hughan photographs in its collection.

31. O'Reilly, *La Nouvelle-Calédonie*, p. 58.

32. The photographs and manuscripts of Reverend George Brown are in the Mitchell Library, State Library of New South Wales, Sydney. His glass plate negatives are in the Australian Museum, Sydney. The prints that illustrate this essay were obtained from European archives in Cologne and London and are used with permission from all sources. See Figs. 16–19 for details.

33. R. J. Lacey, "Brown, George (1835–1917)," *Encyclopaedia of Papua New Guinea*, vol. 1 (Melbourne: Melbourne University Press, 1972), pp. 124–27, esp. p. 124. Information on Brown and other European missionaries in Papua can be found in Diane Langmore, *Missionary Lives: Papua, 1874–1914* (Honolulu: University of Hawaii Press, Pacific Islands Monograph Series, no. 6, 1989) and in Brown's writings (see notes 34–37).

34. See George Brown, *George D. D. Brown, Pioneer-Missionary and Explorer: An Autobiography* (London: Hodder and Stoughton, 1908); and idem, *Melanesians and Polynesians: Their Life Histories Described and Compared* (London: Macmillan, 1910). I am researching the corpus of photographs Brown made in the Pacific. Subsequent references are indicated parenthetically in the text.

35. George Brown Letterbooks, A1686–2, 1871–76, p. 638, George Brown Collection, the Mitchell Library, Sydney.

36. Brown, *George D. D. Brown*, p. 489. Brown describes a lantern-slide presentation he made in Port Hunter, Duke of York, in a letter dated Nov. 9, 1877: "We have a nice young fellow called Powell staying with us. . . . He owns a small magic lantern and I have a large one so we intend to give a grand scenic performance this evening to astonish the natives. We had a preliminary trial last night which was quite a suc-

cess." From George Brown Letterbooks, A1686–3, 1876–80, pp. 125–26, the Mitchell Library, Sydney.

37. Brown, *George D. D. Brown*, p. 520. See George Brown Journal, A1686–17, 1890–97, the Mitchell Library, Sydney, entry for June 30, 1897, about the "before and after" photographs he was making.

38. See Anonymous, "Scenes and Savages of the Solomon Islands," *The Town and Country Journal*, Sept. 27, 1902, pp. 31–33.

39. Brown, *George D. D. Brown*, plate facing p. 520. The "sparklet" cartridge probably refers to a brand or type of ammunition used during the time and available in Europe (Stuart Pyhrr, Arms and Armor Dept., Metropolitan Museum of Art, personal communication, Feb. 1992). It is possible that the cartridge was used by Brown's party, since ammunition was listed in supply orders in his journals and letterbooks, although no brand names are indicated.

40. Another very similar photograph appears in Brown, *George D. D. Brown*, plate facing p. 520, but cropped at the top edge to form an arch. About twenty images of this series exist. The Mitchell Library holds prints of this series made for Brown by the Crown Studios, Sydney.

41. For photographic examples that do show cultural appropriation of European or American objects as body ornamentation, see Bob Connolly and Robin Anderson, *First Contact* (New York: Viking Penguin, 1987), p. 128; included are images made by the Leahy brothers in the Papua New Guinea Highlands of a man wearing part of a "Kellogg's Whole Wheat Biscuit" package pinned into his hair and an empty tin can as a forehead ornament. Unpublished photographs by Dr. William Moss and Sidney Shurcliff, made on the 1928–29 Crane Pacific Expedition, show the incorporation of a "Heinz brand" soup-can label into a Kambot village headdress. There are many other examples as well.

42. An announcement of Brown's voyage to the Solomon Islands was published, with a photograph of the expedition members, in *The Town and Country Journal*, May 10, 1902, p. 39, with the assurance that additional news of the progress made by the missionaries would appear in the pages of this journal.

43. Woodford used his own photographs to illustrate his book about the Solomon Islands. Fig. 20 appears in Charles M. Woodford, *A Naturalist Among the Headhunters* (New York: Longmans, Green and Co., 1890), p. 152. Subsequent references are indicated parenthetically in the text. See also Lord Amherst of Hackney and Basil Thompson, *The Voyage of the Mendana to the Solomon Islands in 1568* (London: Hakluyt Society Publications, Series II, 7 & 8, 1901), p. 352; and Deborah Waite, *Art of the Solomon Islands from the Collection of the Barbier-Müller Museum* (Geneva: Musée Barbier-Müller, 1983), pp. 31, 33, and 46 for additional photographs of personal ornamentation.

44. Henry B. Guppy, *The Solomon Islands and Their Natives* (London: Swan Sonnenschein, Lowrey, 1887), p. 133.

45. Lt. Henry B. T. Somerville, "Ethnographical Notes in New Georgia, Solo-

mon Islands," *Royal Anthropological Institute of Great Britain and Ireland, Journal* 26, 4 (1897): 362. See the essay by Poignant in Edwards, ed., *Anthropology and Photography*, pp. 62–63 and plate 40, for a discussion of Somerville's use of these images in his lantern-slide lectures.

S T E I N E R : Travel Engravings

Earlier drafts of this essay benefited from thoughtful commentary and suggestions by Monni Adams, Elazar Barkan, Vincent Cheng, Christraud Geary, Margaret Hardin, Dorinne Kondo, Jerome Levi, Thomas Miller, John Ojo, Sally Price, Dan Rosenberg, Enid Schildkrout, and Kathy Skelly. Research for this project was partially funded by grants from the Life Sciences Research Fund of the Natural History Museum of Los Angeles County and from the American Council of Learned Societies.

1. Grafton Elliot Smith, *In the Beginning: The Origin of Civilization* (New York: Morrow, 1928). For an overview of this perspective, see A. L. Kroeber, "Diffusionism," in Edwin Seligman, ed., *Encyclopaedia of the Social Sciences*, vol. 5 (New York: MacMillan, 1931), pp. 139–42; and Marvin Harris, *The Rise of Anthropological Theory* (New York: Harper & Row, 1968), pp. 373–92.

2. See Klaus-Peter Koepping, *Adolf Bastian and the Psychic Unity of Mankind* (St. Lucia: University of Queensland Press, 1983).

3. The structuralist project of Claude Lévi-Strauss was, arguably, a revival, albeit in an extremely different guise, of the comparative method of nineteenth-century anthropology.

4. Although not always set off in quotation marks, the words "primitive" and "savage" are used throughout this essay as historically specific European terms that were meant to describe a range of different non-Western cultures.

5. Howard Eilberg-Schwartz, *The Savage in Judaism: An Anthropology of Israelite Religion and Ancient Judaism* (Bloomington: Indiana University Press, 1990), p. 1.

6. See Geoffroy Atkinson, *The Extraordinary Voyage in French Literature Before 1700* (New York: Columbia University Press, 1920); Margaret T. Hodgen, *Early Anthropology in the Sixteenth and Seventeenth Centuries* (Philadelphia: University of Pennsylvania Press, 1964), pp. 20–29; George B. Parks, "The Turn to the Romantic in the Travel Literature of the Eighteenth Century," *Modern Language Quarterly* 25 (1968): 22–33; and Charles L. Batten, Jr., *Pleasurable Instruction: Form and Convention in Eighteenth-Century Travel Literature* (Berkeley: University of California Press, 1978).

7. Annemarie de Waal Malefijt, "Homo Monstrosus," *Scientific American*, 219, 4 (1968): 113.

8. Barbara Maria Stafford, *Body Criticism: Imaging the Unseen in the Enlightenment Art and Medicine* (Cambridge, Mass.: MIT Press, 1991), p. 256.

9. Barbara Maria Stafford, *Voyage Into Substance: Art, Science, Nature, and the Illustrated Travel Account, 1760–1840* (Cambridge and London: MIT Press, 1984), p. 51.

10. Commenting on the frontispiece to Bronislaw Malinowski's classic Melanesian ethnography, *Argonauts of the Western Pacific* (London: G. Routledge and Sons, 1922), James Clifford notes that the photograph of the Trobriand "natives" underscores the authority of the observer by signaling to the reader, "You are there, because I was there." See James Clifford, "On Ethnographic Authority," *Representations* 1, 2 (1983): 118.

11. Rüdiger Joppien and Bernard Smith, *The Art of Captain Cook's Voyages* (Melbourne: Oxford University Press, 1985).

12. Cf. Ezio Bassani and Letizia Tedeschi, "The Image of the Hottentot in the Seventeenth and Eighteenth Centuries," *Journal of the History of Collections* 2, 2 (1990): 157–86.

13. E. H. Gombrich, *Art and Illusion: A Study in the Psychology of Pictorial Representation* (Princeton, N.J.: Princeton University Press, 1960), pp. 68–69.

14. Ibid.

15. John Northbrooke, *A Treatise Against Dauncing* (orig. pub. ca. 1577; rpt., John P. Collier, ed., London: The Shakespeare Society, 1843).

16. Quoted in Roderyk Lange, *The Nature of Dance: An Anthropological Perspective* (London: MacDonald & Evans, 1975), p. 11.

17. See, for example, Robert L. McGrath, "The Dance as Pictorial Metaphor," *Gazette des Beaux-Arts* 89 (1977): 81–92.

18. David Freedberg, *The Power of Images: Studies in the History and Theory of Response* (Chicago: University of Chicago Press, 1989), p. 378. Also, see Elise Lawton Smith, "Women and the Moral Argument of Lucas van Leyden's *Dance Around the Golden Calf*," *Art History* 15, 3 (1992): 296–316.

19. Quoted in Freedberg, *The Power of Images*, p. 379.

20. Van Leyden's painting did so along with scores of subsequent renditions of the same theme: e.g., *The Adoration of the Golden Calf* depicted in Gabriello Simeoni's illustrated Bible entitled *Figure de la Biblia* (Lyon, 1564–65), and Nicolas Poussin's painting *Dance Round the Golden Calf* (ca. 1634).

21. See Svetlana Alpers, "Bruegel's Festive Peasants," *Simiolus* 6, 3/4 (1972/73): 163–76; Keith P. F. Moxey, "Sebald Beham's Church Anniversary Holidays: Festive Peasants as Instruments of Repressive Humor," *Simiolus* 12, 2/3 (1981/82): 107–30; and Margaret D. Carroll, "Peasant Festivity and Political Identity in the Sixteenth Century," *Art History* 10, 3 (1987): 286–314.

22. See Bernadette Bucher, *Icon and Conquest: A Structural Analysis of the Illustrations of de Bry's Great Voyages*, trans. Basia Miller Gulati (Chicago: University of Chicago Press, 1981).

23. See Wilhelm Bode, *Florentine Sculptors of the Renaissance* (New York: Charles Scribner's Sons, 1909), pp. 149–64; and H. W. Janson, "The Putto with the Death's Head," *The Art Bulletin* 19 (1937): 423–49.

24. Cf. Johannes Fabian, *Time and the Other* (New York: Columbia University Press, 1983) and David Lowenthal, *The Past is a Foreign Country* (Cambridge: Cambridge University Press, 1985).

25. Cf. George W. Stocking, Jr., *Victorian Anthropology* (New York: Free Press, 1987), p. 163.

26. Loren K. Waldman, "An Unnoticed Aspect of Archibald Dalzel's *The History of Dahomey*," *Journal of African History* 6, 2 (1965): 185–86.

27. J. W. Buel, *The World's Wonders as Seen by the Great Tropical and Polar Explorers* (St. Louis, Mo.: Historical Publishing Company, 1884), p. 248.

28. Emile Durkheim, *The Elementary Forms of the Religious Life*, trans. Joseph Ward Swain (New York: Free Press, 1965), pp. 249–50. It is ironic to note in this context that Durkheim understood moments of effervescence as a kind of vibrant and collective *aide mémoire*. "Keeping alive their memory by means of celebrations," wrote Durkheim, it is in those hours of effervescence that men "regularly reproduce their fruits." If the *practice* of effervescence resulted in the recreation of beliefs, the *image* of effervescence was itself the result of recreated belief—redundancy thus playing a critical role in ritual as well as in representation.

29. Baldwin Spencer and F. J. Gillen, *The Northern Tribes of Central Australia* (London: Macmillan 1904); my emphasis.

30. Baldwin Spencer, *Across Australia*, vol. 1 (London: Macmillan, 1912), p. 236; my emphasis.

N. PERLOFF: Gauguin's French Baggage

I wish to thank Albert Boime for his careful reading of this paper and for offering an invaluable perspective, and Marjorie Perloff for stimulating many of my early ideas on Gauguin.

1. Bengt Danielsson, *Gauguin in the South Seas* (Garden City, N.Y.: Doubleday, 1966), p. 35.

2. Paul Gauguin, *Letters to His Wife and Friends*, trans. Henry J. Stenning, ed. Maurice Malingue (Cleveland: World Publishing, 1949), no. 154, to August Strindberg. Subsequent references are indicated parenthetically in the text.

3. For instance, in the catalogue for the 1988 Gauguin retrospective, Claire Frêches-Thory writes: "It is therefore not surprising that Gauguin's quest for a landscape unscathed by modern civilization took him to [Brittany], where one could still hope to see the vigor of a primitive culture." See Richard Brettell, Françoise Cachin, Claire Frêches-Thory, and Charles F. Stucky, *The Art of Paul Gauguin* (Washington, D.C.: National Gallery of Art, 1988), p. 55.

4. See Kirk Varnedoe, "Gauguin," in William Rubin, ed., *"Primitivism" in 20th-Century Art: Affinity of the Tribal and the Modern*, 2 vols. (New York: Museum of Modern Art, 1984), 1:183, 187; Jehanne Teilhet-Fisk, *Paradise Reviewed: An Interpretation of Gauguin's Polynesian Symbolism* (Ann Arbor: UMI Research Press, 1975), pp. 48, 77, 171; Wayne Andersen, *Gauguin's Paradise Lost* (New York: Viking, 1971), pp. 174, 192; and Henri Dorra, "The First Eves in Gauguin's Eden," *Gazette des Beaux-Arts* 41 (Mar. 1953): 197.

5. Abigail Solomon-Godeau, "Going Native," *Art in America* 77 (July 1989): 123.

The reference to "organic, natural imagery" appears in Vojtech Jirat-Wasiutynski, "Paul Gauguin's Self-Portraits and the Oviri: The Image of the Artist, Eve, and the Fatal Woman," *The Art Quarterly* (Spring 1979): 176.

6. See James Clifford, *The Predicament of Culture: Twentieth-Century Ethnography, Literature, and Art* (Cambridge, Mass.: Harvard University Press, 1988), "Introduction: The Pure Products Go Crazy."

7. See Albert Boime, "Entrepreneurial Patronage in Nineteenth-Century France," in Edward C. Carter II, Robert Forster, and Joseph N. Moody, eds., *Enterprise and Entrepreneurs in Nineteenth- and Twentieth-Century France* (Baltimore, Md.: Johns Hopkins University Press, 1976), p. 188.

8. For a chronology of Gauguin's early financial career and gradual shift to art, see Richard Brettell et al., *The Art of Paul Gauguin*, pp. 4–9. Pissarro's statement is cited by Boime in "Entrepreneurial Patronage in Nineteenth-Century France," p. 188.

9. For a discussion of the Opportunists, see Gordon Wright, *France in Modern Times*, 3rd ed. (New York: W. W. Norton, 1981), p. 240.

10. For information on Ferry's plans for the exhibition, see Deborah Silverman, "The 1889 Exhibition: The Crisis of Bourgeois Individualism," *Oppositions* 8 (Spring 1977): 71, 90 (footnotes 2 and 3).

11. Ibid., pp. 72, 91 (footnote 15), 73.

12. Information on the number of visitors appears in Emile Monod, *L'Exposition universelle de 1889* (Paris: Librairie de la Société des Gens de Lettres, 1890), p. 40.

13. John Rewald discusses the Volpini Exhibition in *Post-Impressionism: From Van Gogh to Gauguin*, 3rd ed. (New York: Museum of Modern Art, 1978), pp. 256 ff.

14. Albert Boime places the encyclopedic scope of the Paris Exposition in the context of previous world's fairs in "The Chocolate Venus, 'Tainted' Pork, the Wine Blight, and the Tariff: Franco-American Stew at the Fair," in Annette Blaugrund, ed., *Paris 1889: American Artists at the Universal Exposition* (Philadelphia: Pennsylvania Academy of the Fine Arts, 1989), p. 67.

15. See Silverman's detailed account of these exhibits in "The 1889 Exhibition," pp. 80, 81.

16. Cited by Dorra in "The First Eves in Gauguin's Eden," p. 193.

17. Silverman, "The 1889 Exhibition," pp. 77, 78.

18. For a discussion of state paternalism, see ibid., p. 81.

19. For a map of the Colonial Exhibit on the Esplanade des Invalides, see the plan reproduced in Caroline Mathieu, ed., *1889: La Tour Eiffel et L'Exposition Universelle* (Paris: Editions de la Réunion des Musées Nationaux, 1989), pp. 266–67.

20. Quoted by Silverman in "The 1889 Exhibition," p. 91 (footnote 47); my translation.

21. Boime discusses the notion of "progress" expressed in the fair's contrast between curios and technology in "The Chocolate Venus," p. 69. On "progress" at the fair, see also Silverman, "The 1889 Exhibition," p. 80.

22. See Danielsson's account of Gauguin's application to the Colonial Department and his new interest in Madagascar in *Gauguin in the South Seas*, p. 30.

23. Danielsson quotes these passages from Louis Henrique's *Les Colonies françaises* in *Gauguin in the South Seas*, pp. 32–33.

24. Gauguin, *Letters*, nos. 100 and 126, to Mette Gauguin. See also Gauguin's letter to J. F. Willumsen included in Daniel Guérin, ed., *Oviri: Ecrits d'un sauvage* (Paris: Editions Gallimard, 1974), pp. 67–68.

25. See Danielsson, *Gauguin in the South Seas*, p. 33, and Gauguin, *Letters*, no. 105, to Bernard.

26. Richard Brettell et al., *The Art of Paul Gauguin*, p. 50.

27. For Gauguin's views on Loti, see Daniel Guérin, ed., *The Writings of a Savage, Paul Gauguin*, trans. Eleanor Levieux (New York: Viking, 1978), pp. 138, 218. For further discussions of Pierre Loti, see Loti, *The Marriage of Loti*, trans. and with an introduction by Wright and Eleanor Frierson (Honolulu: University Press of Hawaii, 1976); F. C. Gray, *Tahiti in French Literature from Bougainville to Pierre Loti*, Ph.D. dissertation, University of Arizona, 1970; and Clive Wake, *The Novels of Pierre Loti* (The Hague and Paris: Mouton, 1974).

28. Pierre Loti, *Rarahu or The Marriage of Loti*, trans. Clara Bell (New York: W. S. Gottsberger, 1890), pp. 119, 55. Loti's descriptions of the carefree existence of his mistress — "Her business in life was very simple: to dream, to bathe — especially to bathe — to sing, and to wander through the woods" — were clearly borrowed by the compilers of the colonial handbooks. See ibid., pp. 12–13.

29. For the quotations in this paragraph, see ibid., pp. 10, 15, 20, 22, 8, 29, 43.

30. Ibid., p. 214.

31. Gauguin refers to *Certains* in an article on Huysmans and Redon written in 1889 and included in Guérin, ed., *Oviri*, p. 59. For Huysmans's praise of Redon, see his *Certains* (Paris: Tresse & Stock, 1889), pp. 21–22.

32. Théophile Gautier, "Notice," in Charles Baudelaire, *Les Fleurs du mal* (Paris: Michel Lévy Frères, 1868), édition définitive, p. 17; my translations.

33. Ibid., pp. 31, 39.

34. Quoted in Philippe Jullian, *Dreamers of Decadence: Symbolist Painters of the 1890s* (New York: Praeger, 1971), p. 37.

35. See Joris-Karl Huysmans, *A Rebours* (Paris: Fasquelle Editeur, 1961), pp. 31, 35.

36. Quotations from *A Rebours* taken from a 1959 English translation by Robin Baldick reprinted in Glenn Watkins, *Soundings: Music in the Twentieth Century* (New York: Schirmer, 1988), p. 132.

37. Translation by Robin Baldick in Watkins, *Soundings*, pp. 132, 135.

38. Huysmans, *A Rebours*, pp. 95–96, and John Rewald's translation in *Odilon Redon, Gustave Moreau, Rodolphe Bresdin* (The Museum of Modern Art, New York, in collaboration with the Art Institute of Chicago; Garden City, N.Y.: Distributed by Doubleday, 1961), p. 31. Two years before the publication of *A Rebours*, the young literary critic Emile Hennequin reviewed Redon's work and praised many of the decadent elements that Huysmans's hero Des Esseintes found so riveting. Hennequin

wrote of Redon: "He has succeeded in conquering, somewhere on the border between reality and fantasy, a desolate domain which he peopled with formidable ghosts, monsters, monads, composite beings of every possible human perversity. . . . Redon alone has managed to express by certain symbols . . . our most profound ideas about corruption, depravity, guile and on the other hand, about the grandiose and the beautiful." See Rewald, *Post-Impressionism*, pp. 161–62.

39. For information on the impetus behind Mirbeau's article on Gauguin, see Brettell et al., *The Art of Paul Gauguin*, p. 163. The excerpt from Mirbeau's article, originally published in *Echo de Paris* (Feb. 16, 1891), appears in an English translation by Rewald in *Post-Impressionism*, pp. 439–41.

40. Pissarro's critique appeared in a broadside later published in John Rewald, ed., *Camille Pissarro: Lettres à son fils Lucien* (Paris: Michel, 1950). Excerpts are quoted in Brettell et al., *The Art of Paul Gauguin*, p. 105.

41. See Françoise Cachin's discussion of the symbolism of the yellow mass in Gauguin's "Self-Portrait with Halo" (Fig. 4) in Brettell et al., *The Art of Paul Gauguin*, p. 166.

42. In a letter to Emile Bernard, Gauguin described the panel and identified himself as a "monster seizing the hand of a protesting woman, saying to her: Be amorous and you will be happy." See Gauguin, *Letters*, no. 87, to Bernard.

43. Andersen, *Gauguin's Paradise Lost*, p. 89.

44. Christopher Gray's identification of the six other women in the relief is helpful. See his *Sculpture and Ceramics of Paul Gauguin* (Baltimore, Md.: Johns Hopkins University Press, 1963), pp. 43 ff.

45. Wayne Andersen points out Gauguin's curious recasting of the Eve story in *Gauguin's Paradise Lost*, p. 89.

46. Henri Dorra provides this information on the watercolor's caption and on Jules Antoine's questioning of the inconsistency in "The First Eves in Gauguin's Eden," p. 192.

47. Richard Brettell summarizes Gauguin's contact with the Borobudur relief figures in Brettell et al., *The Art of Paul Gauguin*, pp. 154–55.

48. Loti, *The Marriage of Loti*, p. 67.

49. Delaroche's review appeared in *L'Ermitage* 5 (Jan. 1894): 36–39. Morice's article appeared in *Mercure de France* 9, 48 (Dec. 1893): 289–300. Both are quoted by Charles Stucky in Brettell et al., *The Art of Paul Gauguin*, p. 270. Stucky also mentions Morice's consultation with Gauguin.

50. Charles Stucky reports that most late twentieth-century scholars have compared Gauguin's plant to the visionary plant in Redon's lithograph. See, for example, Andersen, *Gauguin's Paradise Lost*, p. 177. Stucky also discusses interpretations of Gauguin's allusions to the peacock in Brettell et al., *The Art of Paul Gauguin*, p. 270.

51. Stucky compares the detail of Eve's head adjacent to the lizard with Redon's lithograph of the bird above the woman's head in Brettell et al., *The Art of Paul Gauguin*, p. 271.

52. Jullian, *Dreamers of Decadence*, p. 88.

53. Stucky identifies the staring fox in the relief as a prototype for the evil spirit in the painting in Brettell et al., *The Art of Paul Gauguin*, p. 268.

54. See, for example, Stucky's commentary in ibid., p. 267.

55. Paul Gauguin, *Noa Noa*. Bois dessinés et gravés d'après Paul Gauguin par Daniel de Monfreid. Edition définitive (Paris: G. Cres, 1924), pp. 92–93.

56. In *The Loss of Virginity* (1890; see Fig. 1), the ravaged girl holds a plucked flower.

57. See Stucky's commentary in Brettell et al., *The Art of Paul Gauguin*, pp. 283–84.

58. See, for example, Richard Brettell's reference to genre scenes and Charles Stucky's discussion of *Aha oe feii?* in ibid., pp. 263–64, 233.

59. See ibid., p. 236.

60. See the discussion of this Greek prototype in ibid., p. 278.

61. Loti, *The Marriage of Loti*, p. 121.

62. James Clifford, *The Predicament of Culture*, p. 9.

63. Ibid., pp. 4, 10.

NORTH: Modernism's African Mask

1. Paul Guillaume, "African Art at the Barnes Foundation," *Opportunity* 2 (May 1924): 140–41. Quoted in Chidi Ikonné, *From DuBois to Van Vechten: The Early New Negro Literature, 1903–1926* (Westport, Conn.: Greenwood Press, 1981), pp. 3–4.

2. See the catalogue of the Museum of Modern Art exhibition, William Rubin, ed., *"Primitivism" in 20th Century Art: Affinity of the Tribal and the Modern* (New York: Museum of Modern Art, 1984), in which Rubin takes issue with previous opinions like Guillaume's but also argues at length for an important but vaguely defined "affinity" between "tribal" art and the modern. The controversy surrounding this exhibition gives a good indication of current opinion about this "affinity." See, for example, James Clifford, "Histories of the Tribal and the Modern," *Art in America* (Apr. 1985): 164–77, 215; Hal Foster, "The 'Primitive' Consciousness of Modern Art," *October* 34 (Fall 1985): 45–70; and Rosalind Krauss, "Preying on 'Primitivism,'" *Art & Text* 17 (Apr. 1985): 58–62.

3. There is a good deal of dispute about the timing and significance of this discovery. For Stein's account, in which Matisse surprises Picasso with an African statue, see Gertrude Stein, *The Autobiography of Alice B. Toklas* (1933; rpt., New York: Random House/Vintage, 1960), p. 63. For the most minute investigation, see William Rubin, "Picasso," in idem, ed., *"Primitivism" in 20th Century Art*, esp. pp. 337, n. 86, and 339, n. 138.

4. Stein, *Autobiography of Alice B. Toklas*, p. 64. See the critical commentary on this and other passages in Stein's work in Aldon Lynn Nielsen, *Reading Race: White American Poets and the Racial Discourse in the Twentieth Century* (Athens: University of Georgia Press, 1988), pp. 22–24. Picasso's later dismissals of African art as an influence are considered strategic by William Rubin. See his "From Narrative to 'Iconic'

in Picasso: The Buried Allegory in *Bread and Fruitdish on a Table* and the Role of *Les Demoiselles D'Avignon*," *Art Bulletin* 65 (Dec. 1983): 645, and idem, "Picasso," p. 335, n. 52. See also Gertrude Stein, *Picasso: The Complete Writings*, ed. Edward Burns (1970; rpt., Boston: Beacon, 1985), p. 47.

5. Rubin, "Picasso," pp. 297–98.

6. Ibid., pp. 247–48. For Stein's account of her sittings for the portrait, see *Autobiography of Alice B. Toklas*, pp. 46–47, 49, and 53.

7. Stein, *Autobiography of Alice B. Toklas*, p. 54.

8. Among many accounts of the similarities between Stein's *Q.E.D.* and "Melanctha," the most interesting is still Richard Bridgman's "Melanctha," *American Literature* 33 (Nov. 1961): 350–59. See also his *Gertrude Stein in Pieces* (New York: Oxford University Press, 1970), and Jayne L. Walker, *Gertrude Stein: The Making of a Modernist* (Amherst: University of Massachusetts Press, 1984), pp. 27–38.

9. James R. Mellow, *Charmed Circle: Gertrude Stein & Company* (New York: Praeger, 1974), p. 44.

10. Cary D. Wintz, *Black Culture and the Harlem Renaissance* (Houston, Tex.: Rice University Press, 1988), pp. 45–47.

11. Ikonné, *From DuBois to Van Vechten*, pp. 27–28. It should be noted that the exact relationship between African art and African-American art and literature was discussed from a number of different points of view in Alain Locke, ed., *The New Negro* (1925; rpt., New York: Atheneum, 1968). Locke himself was at least ambivalent on the subject, as shown by his own essay, "The Legacy of the Ancestral Arts," which he significantly bracketed with Countee Cullen's poem "Heritage," which begins, "What is Africa to me?" in *The New Negro*, pp. 250–67.

12. Carl Van Vechten, *Nigger Heaven* (1926; rpt., New York: Octagon, 1980), pp. 55, 57. Van Vechten's curious preface to *Three Lives* is worth noting here, because in it he praises Stein as "so distinguished, so instinct with *race* and force and character" (original emphasis); see Gertrude Stein, *Three Lives* (1909; rpt., Norfolk, Conn.: New Directions, 1933), p. viii.

13. I. A. Richards, "Preface," in Claude McKay, *Spring in New Hampshire* (London: Richards, 1920), p. 1; Zora Neale Hurston, *The Sanctified Church* (Berkeley: Turtle Island, 1981), p. 54.

14. Rubin, "Picasso," p. 254. Rubin is particularly fond of this comparison. See his "From Narrative to 'Iconic' in Picasso," pp. 632, 634.

15. Leo Steinberg, "The Philosophical Brothel, Part 2," *Art News* 71 (Oct. 1972): 41. For Steinberg's latest thoughts on this painting, see the updated version of "The Philosophical Brothel" in *October* 44 (Spring 1988): 7–74.

16. Quoted in Steinberg, "The Philosophical Brothel," *Art News*, p. 20.

17. D. H. Kahnweiler, "Negro Art and Cubism," *Horizon* 18 (1948): 415.

18. Ibid., p. 414; Stein, *Picasso*, p. 73. See Picasso's own discussion of signs in André Malraux, *Picasso's Mask*, trans. June Guicharnaud (New York: Holt, Rinehart and Winston, 1976), p. 120.

19. For a brief discussion of British colonial language policy as it related to school-

ing, see Carol Sicherman, *Ngugi wa Thiong'o: The Making of a Rebel* (London: Hans Zell, 1990), pp. 27–28. Sicherman's notes list a number of more detailed studies.

20. Patricia Leighten, "The White Peril and *L'Art nègre*: Picasso, Primitivism, and Anticolonialism," *Art Bulletin* 72 (1990): 627.

21. Yve-Alain Bois, "Kahnweiler's Lesson," *Representations* 18 (Spring 1987): 33–68.

22. Quoted in Walker, *Gertrude Stein*, p. 1.

23. Gertrude Stein, *Three Lives* (1909; rpt., New York: Random/Vintage, 1936), pp. 94 and 92. All subsequent parenthetical page references in the text are to this edition.

24. Walker, for example, fails to follow up on the reference to Caliban in her discussion of "Melanctha," though she says at the beginning of *Gertrude Stein* that Stein's motive is "to give speech to Caliban, to a 'reality' that lies this far outside *vraisemblance*" (pp. 1–2). An example of the more recent trend is Marianne De-Koven's *Rich and Strange: Gender, History, Modernism* (Princeton, N.J.: Princeton University Press, 1991), pp. 67–85.

25. Tzvetan Todorov, *The Conquest of America*, trans. Richard Howard (New York: Harper & Row, 1984), p. 36.

26. Alfred Simson, *Travels in the Wilds of Ecuador and the Exploration of the Putumayo River* (London: Samson Low, 1886), pp. 170–71. Quoted in Michael Taussig, *Shamanism, Colonialism, and the Wild Man: A Study in Terror and Healing* (Chicago: University of Chicago Press, 1987), p. 91.

27. Sara Suleri, *The Rhetoric of English India* (Chicago: University of Chicago Press, 1992), p. 163; see also p. 31.

28. See also Etienne Balibar, "Paradoxes of Universality," in David Theo Goldberg, ed., *Anatomy of Racism* (Minneapolis: University of Minnesota Press, 1990), pp. 283–94.

29. Rubin, "Picasso," pp. 241–42.

30. The Radcliffe themes are reprinted in Rosalind S. Miller, *Gertrude Stein: Form and Intelligibility* (New York: Exposition Press, 1949); see esp. pp. 139–44.

31. Quoted in Mellow, *Charmed Circle*, p. 69; see also pp. 64 and 77.

32. Trial dust wrapper for *Three Lives*, reproduced in Robert A. Wilson, *Gertrude Stein: A Bibliography* (New York: Phoenix, 1974), p. 4.

33. Rubin, "Picasso," pp. 241–42.

34. Mellow, *Charmed Circle*, pp. 113–14.

35. Malraux, *Picasso's Mask*, pp. 10–11.

36. Gelett Burgess, "The Wild Men of Paris," *Architectural Record* 5 (May 1910): 407–14; Ezra Pound, "The New Sculpture," *The Egoist*, Feb. 16, 1914, pp. 67–68, rpt. in Harriet Zinnes, ed., *Ezra Pound and the Visual Arts* (New York: New Directions, 1980), p. 182.

37. Nathan I. Huggins, *Harlem Renaissance* (New York: Oxford University Press, 1971), p. 93.

38. The term "transcendental homelessness" is from Georg Lukács, *The Theory of the Novel*, trans. Anna Bostock (Cambridge, Mass.: MIT Press, 1971); its application to modernist primitivism is Marianna Torgovnick's. See her *Gone Primitive: Savage Intellects, Modern Lives* (Chicago: University of Chicago Press, 1990), p. 188.

39. See *The Collected Early Poems of Ezra Pound*, ed. Michael John King (New York: New Directions, 1976), p. 34, and *The Variorum Edition of the Poems of W. B. Yeats*, eds. Peter Allt and Russell K. Alspach (New York: Macmillan, 1940), p. 263. A year later, Gordon Craig signified the importance of masks in modern drama by beginning to publish *The Mask* (1908–29). See also Walter Sorell, *The Other Face: The Mask in the Arts* (Indianapolis, Ind.: Bobbs-Merrill, 1973), p. 71.

40. A similar point has been made about costume by Kaja Silverman in "White Skin, Brown Mask: The Double Mimesis, or With Lawrence in Arabia," *differences* 1 (1989): 48.

41. A. David Napier, *Masks, Transformation, and Paradox* (Berkeley: University of California Press, 1986), p. 4.

42. Joseph Conrad, *The Nigger of the "Narcissus,"* ed. Robert Kimbrough (New York: Norton, 1979), p. 11.

43. Rubin, "Picasso," pp. 263–64. Rubin believes that the figure on the far left was "unquestionably reworked after Picasso had completed the painting in its original, Iberian form" (p. 264). But he hypothesizes that there were "*two* periods of repainting," with the figure on the left being reworked before the visit to the Trocadéro and the two figures on the right repainted after the visit.

44. This is an interpretation of the evolution of the painting supported by Rubin ("Narrative to 'Iconic' in Picasso," pp. 630–32) and Steinberg ("The Philosophical Brothel," *Art News*, pp. 39–40 and 59, n. 32), though Steinberg does propose other models, including Max Jacob, and Rubin discusses a drawing of André Salmon that is in some ways similar to the original figure on the left ("Picasso," p. 285). In fact, the "thanatophobic" interpretation of the painting that Rubin and Steinberg have made current rests on the assumption that Picasso is himself implicated in the scene it portrays. Many of the studies for *Les Demoiselles d'Avignon* are reproduced and discussed in Steinberg; see esp. p. 25 for the transition discussed here. All the materials relating to this painting have been collected and discussed in the exhibition catalogue *Les Demoiselles d'Avignon* 3, 2 vols. (Paris: Musée Picasso, 1988). The sketchbook Picasso kept in March 1907, while planning *Les Demoiselles*, has been published, with a text by Brigitte Leal, as *Picasso: "Les Demoiselles d'Avignon": A Sketchbook* (London; Paris: Thames and Hudson: Editions de la Réunion des Musées Nationaux, 1988).

45. Steinberg, "The Philosophical Brothel," *Art News*, pp. 40, 26. Rubin has quite successfully demonstrated that the masks in *Les Demoiselles* could not have been based on any particular African masks available to Picasso in Paris at the time of the painting ("Picasso," pp. 262–66). However, it is clear that Picasso did handle and purchase African masks, as well as African sculpture, at this time. Inez Haynes Irwin,

who visited Picasso at his studio in April 1908, reports seeing *Les Demoiselles* and simultaneously being shown "a mask of the Congo and some totem-pole like hideosities that [Picasso] made himself" (*Les Demoiselles d'Avignon* 3, vol. 2, p. 560).

46. John Richardson, *A Life of Picasso* (New York: Random House, 1991), 1: 408.

47. Leal, *Picasso: "Les Demoiselles,"* unpaged introduction.

48. Silverman, "White Skin, Brown Mask," p. 11. See also Suleri, *Rhetoric of English India*, p. 142.

49. See Patrick Brantlinger on India as "a realm of imaginative license . . . a place where the fantastic becomes possible in ways that are carefully circumscribed at home," in his *Rule of Darkness: British Literature and Imperialism, 1830–1914* (Ithaca, N.Y.: Cornell University Press, 1988), p. 13. But this is not entirely a European mode of thought. See Taussig's discussion of the fact that "wherever you go, the great *brujos* [magicians or sorcerers] are elsewhere" (*Shamanism, Colonialism, and the Wild Man*, p. 179).

50. Henry Louis Gates, Jr., *Figures in Black: Words, Signs, and the "Racial" Self* (New York: Oxford University Press, 1987), p. 168. See also Dennis Duerden, *The Invisible Present: African Art & Literature* (New York: Harper & Row, 1975), esp. p. 117.

51. Rubin, "Picasso," pp. 255, and 335, n. 53.

52. Stein, *Picasso*, p. 52.

53. Ibid., p. 34. Note also Picasso's famous comment, quoted in Mellow (*Charmed Circle*, p. 93), among other places, that, though Stein does not now resemble her portrait, "She will."

54. Kahnweiler, "Negro Art and Cubism," p. 418.

55. For one use of the idea of the dialectical image, see Walter Benjamin, *Charles Baudelaire: A Lyric Poet in the Era of High Capitalism*, trans. Harry Zohn (London: New Left Books, 1973), p. 171. See also Theodor Adorno's attack in Ernst Bloch, Georg Lukács, et al., "Letters to Walter Benjamin," in Ronald Taylor, ed., *Aesthetics and Politics* (London: Verso, 1977), pp. 111–15, and W. J. T. Mitchell's application in his *Iconology: Image, Text, Ideology* (Chicago: University of Chicago Press, 1986), pp. 93 and 158. Most important for my discussion is Taussig's application of the idea to the popular art of South America. See his *Shamanism, Colonialism, and the Wild Man*, pp. 200–201.

56. Adam Gopnik, "'High and Low': Caricature, Primitivism, and the Cubist Portrait," *Art Journal* 43 (Winter 1983): 374.

57. Gates, *Figures in Black*, pp. 169, 171. See also the discussion of dialect and mask in Benedict R. O'G. Anderson, *Language and Power: Exploring Political Cultures in Indonesia* (Ithaca, N.Y.: Cornell University Press, 1990), pp. 129–31, 144, 149–51.

58. Gilles Deleuze and Félix Guattari, *A Thousand Plateaus: Capitalism and Schizophrenia*, trans. Brian Massumi (Minneapolis: University of Minnesota Press, 1987), p. 104. See also Deleuze and Guattari's *Kafka: Toward a Minor Literature*, trans. Dana Polan (Minneapolis: University of Minnesota Press, 1986).

59. Shirley Brice Heath, *Ways with Words: Language, Life, and Work in Communities and Classrooms* (Cambridge: Cambridge University Press, 1983).

60. George F. Whicher, quoted in Bridgman, "Melanctha," p. 356. This has been said in more recent criticism as well: "The syntactical devices Stein uses to probe the psyches of her characters, recorded in black English, are authentic"; Bettina L. Knapp, *Gertrude Stein* (New York: Continuum, 1990), p. 86. And see the lengthy, quite favorable, discussion in Sylvia Wallace Holton, *Down Home and Uptown: The Representation of Black Speech in American Fiction* (London and Toronto: Associated University Presses, 1984), pp. 96–98.

61. Mellow, *Charmed Circle*, p. 87; Stein, *Autobiography of Alice B. Toklas*, p. 68.

62. Mellow, *Charmed Circle*, p. 64.

63. A few exceptions might be found, such as the invariant *be* in Melanctha's promise to Jeff: "I be home Jeff to-night to see you" (*Three Lives*, p. 196). Yet even here the usage is incorrect, because the invariant *be* usually expresses an ongoing condition.

64. Richard Bridgman, *The Colloquial Style in America* (New York: Oxford University Press, 1966), p. 92.

65. Kenneth Burke, *A Grammar of Motives* (1945; rpt., Berkeley: University of California Press, 1969), p. 52.

66. Gertrude Stein, *Selected Writings*, ed. Carl Van Vechten (1962; rpt. New York: Random/Vintage, 1972), p. 519.

67. Gertrude Stein, *Lectures in America* (1935; rpt., Boston: Beacon Press, 1985), p. 210.

68. For another discussion of the word "certainly" in *Melanctha*, see Nathaniel Mackey, "Other: From Noun to Verb," *Representations* 39 (Summer 1992): 66.

69. Heath, *Ways with Words*, p. 141.

70. Stein, *Lectures in America*, p. 214.

71. Henry Alford, *A Plea for the Queen's English* (London: A. Strahan, 1864), p. 244.

72. Quoted in Edward Finegan, *Attitudes Toward English Usage: The History of a War of Words* (New York: Teachers College of Columbia University Press, 1980), p. 67.

73. Dennis E. Baron, *Grammar and Good Taste: Reforming the American Language* (New Haven, Conn.: Yale University Press, 1982), p. 26.

74. Hurston, *Sanctified Church*, pp. 49–55.

75. Gates, *Figures in Black*, p. 171.

76. For a useful discussion of this strategy, see Marjorie Perloff, *The Poetics of Indeterminacy: From Rimbaud to Cage* (1981; rpt., Evanston, Ill.: Northwestern University Press, 1983), pp. 67–108. Other useful discussions of such representational strategies in Stein include Randa Dubnick, *The Structure of Obscurity: Gertrude Stein, Language, and Cubism* (Urbana: University of Illinois Press, 1984), and Wendy

Steiner, *Exact Resemblance to Exact Resemblance: The Literary Portraiture of Gertrude Stein* (New Haven, Conn.: Yale University Press, 1978).

77. Richard Wright, "Gertrude Stein's Story Is Drenched in Hitler's Horrors" (review of *Wars I Have Seen*), *P.M.*, Mar. 11, 1945, p. 15. For a discussion of this and other statements by Wright in praise of *Three Lives*, see Eugene E. Miller, "Richard Wright and Gertrude Stein," *Black American Literature Forum* 16 (Fall 1982): 107–12. For other African-American writers' reactions to *Three Lives*, both favorable and unfavorable, see John Malcolm Brinnin, *The Third Rose* (Boston: Little, Brown, 1959), p. 121.

78. Rosalind Krauss, "In the Name of Picasso," in *The Originality of the Avant-Garde and Other Modernist Myths* (Cambridge, Mass.: MIT Press, 1986), pp. 23–40.

DAWIDOFF: "Alexander's Ragtime Band"

1. See Nelson George, *The Death of Rhythm & Blues* (New York: Pantheon Books, 1988), esp. pp. 3–14.

2. My account of Irving Berlin is based on Laurence Bergreen's *As Thousands Cheer: The Life of Irving Berlin* (New York: Viking Press, 1990), an invaluable source for Berlin's career. Subsequent references are indicated parenthetically in the text. Ian Whitcomb's *Irving Berlin and Ragtime America* (New York: Limelight, 1988) offers a personal and suggestive account of Berlin's accomplishments and context that is well worth reading. Alex Wilder's chapter on Berlin in James T. Maher, ed., *American Popular Song: The Great Innovators, 1900–1950* (New York: Oxford University Press, 1972), pp. 91–120, gives a wonderful account of Berlin's genius and accomplishments. Wilder makes two comments that should preface any consideration of Berlin: "I am convinced that were Irving Berlin ever to read these pages, he would be more puzzled than pleased. I think he would be pleased at the evidence that a painstaking examination has been made of his songs, but puzzled as to why it was made. . . . I'm sure he is as eager for praise as anyone, but I believe the kind of praise given his work in a study like this would appear to him to be a waste of time. If, on the other hand, I were making an attempt to determine the precise element needed to make a hit song, he would probably be interested. For I think that to Berlin, as well as to many other song writers, a good song and a *hit* song are synonymous" (pp. 91–92), and "Berlin has most clearly been one of the great contributors to this medium of music and, unlike many of the great song writers, has never deviated in his purpose of writing songs which stem from the music of the people, whether it be ragtime, swing music, country music or the work of his contemporaries. He was obviously a persistent listener. Anything which he liked he absorbed and re-created in his own uniquely singing fashion. . . . Let it be said that he is the best all-around, over-all song writer America has ever had. In this area or that I will say, and have said, that I believe so-and-so to be the master. But I can speak of only one composer as the master of the entire range of popular song — Irving Berlin" (pp. 119–20). For the history of the

American popular song, see Charles Hamm, *Yesterdays: Popular Song in America* (New York: W. W. Norton, 1979).

3. Quoted in Bergreen, *As Thousands Cheer*, p. 58.

4. Quoted in ibid., p. 46. On Foster, see William W. Austin, *"Susanna," "Jeanie," and "The Old Folks At Home": The Songs of Stephen C. Foster from His Time to Ours* (Urbana: University of Illinois Press, 1989), and Martin Greif, *The Gay Book of Days* (Secaucus, N.Y.: Lyle Stuart, 1982), p. 117.

5. Bergreen, *As Thousands Cheer*, pp. 45–46. Joan Morris and William Bolcom, perform "The Mesmerizing Mendelssohn Tune" on *Blue Skies: Songs by Irving Berlin* (Nonesuch Records 79120–4).

6. Rudy Blesh and Harriet Janis, *They All Played Ragtime* (New York: Knopf, 1958), is the standard book about ragtime; see also Gunther Schuller, *Early Jazz: Its Roots and Musical Development* (New York: Oxford University Press, 1968).

7. See Bergreen, *As Thousands Cheer*, pp. 49–61; see also Robert Dawidoff, "Some of Those Days," in *Western Humanities Review* 41 (3): 263–86.

8. There is a growing literature on this crucial subject. See George, *The Death of Rhythm & Blues*, for a clear account of the dynamics at a later period. See also Dawidoff, "Some of Those Days."

9. In 1924, Jerome Kern wrote on Berlin as a composer for Alexander Wolcott's biography of Berlin, concluding: "In short, what I really want to say, my dear Wolcott, is that Irving Berlin has *no* place in American music. HE *IS* AMERICAN MUSIC" (quoted in Bergreen, *As Thousands Cheer*, p. 223). Johnny Mercer made his remark in an interview with Maurice Levine, host of the New York 92nd St. "Y" Series of Lyrics and Lyricists, on a Book of the Month Club recording.

10. Miles Kreuger, *Show Boat: The Story of a Classic American Musical* (New York: Oxford University Press, 1977).

11. It will not do to underestimate anti-immigrant, anti-Jewish feeling in the U.S. George M. Cohan introduced Berlin as "a Jew boy that had named himself after an English actor and a German city. Irvy writes a great song. He writes a song with a good lyric, a lyric that rhymes, good music, music you don't have to dress up to listen to, but it's good music. He is a wonderful little fellow, wonderful in lots of ways. He has become famous and wealthy, without wearing a lot of jewelry and falling for funny clothes. He is uptown, but he is there with the old downtown hard sell" (quoted in Hamm, *Yesterdays*, p. 332).

12. Gilbert Vivian Seldes, *The Seven Lively Arts* (1924; rpt., New York: Sagamore Press, 1981), p. 71.

13. Carl Van Vechten, *Nigger Heaven* (1926; rpt., New York: Octagon, 1980); Blair Niles, *Strange Brother* (New York: Harris, 1949).

14. Barry Singer, *Black and Blue: The Life and Lyrics of Andy Razaf* (New York: Schirmer Books, 1992), pp. 334–37. This illuminating biography is indispensable to the study of the subject of this essay. Razaf was clear-eyed and militant about the situation of the black songwriter in the era of appropriation that Berlin apotheosized.

15. Nicholas Jenkins, ed., *By With To & From: A Lincoln Kirstein Reader* (New York: Farrar Straus Giroux, 1991), p. 32.

MARTIN: "Remembering the Jungle"

1. Phyllis Rose, *Jazz Cleopatra: Josephine Baker in Her Time* (New York: Doubleday, 1989).

2. For an astute and detailed cultural analysis of this phenomenon, see Marianna Torgovnick, *Gone Primitive: Savage Intellects, Modern Lives* (Chicago: University of Chicago Press, 1990).

3. Nella Larsen, *Quicksand* (New York: Knopf, 1929), p. 57. Subsequent references are indicated parenthetically in the text.

4. PBS documentary, *Chasing a Rainbow*, 1988.

5. e. e. cummings, *e. e. cummings: A Miscellany* (New York: October House, 1967), pp. 159–63.

6. *Literary Digest*, 1933, p. 21.

7. *Time*, 1935, p. 34.

8. Madonna is a religious variation on the trope — that is, her persona parodies sainthood, in part by employing tropes of the slut, the whore, the prostitute.

9. Henry Louis Gates, Jr., "An Interview with Josephine Baker and James Baldwin," *The Southern Review* 21 (Summer 1985): 594–602.

10. Ishmael Reed, *Shrovetide in Old New Orleans* (New York: Doubleday, 1978).

11. F. S. Fitzgerald, *The Great Gatsby* (New York: Scribner's, 1925), p. 31. The actual book referred to in this passage is Lothrop Stoddard, *The Rising Tide of Color Against White World Supremacy* (New York: Scribner's, 1920).

12. See Rose, *Jazz Cleopatra*, pp. 33–36.

13. *Life*, Dec. 1936, p. 13.

14. Gates, "Interview with Josephine Baker," p. 598.

15. This bifurcation along gender lines has its origins in ancient Greece. For a detailed discussion, see Froma L. Zeitlin, "The Dynamics of Misogyny: Myth and Mythmaking in the *Orestia*," *Arethusa* 2, 1–2 (Spring/Fall 1978): 149–81.

16. Nella Larsen, *Passing* (New York: Alfred A. Knopf, 1930), p. 96. Subsequent references are indicated parenthetically in the text.

17. To understand the extraordinary stylization of body movement in traditional Anglo-European culture, consider the seventeenth-century European engravings of Native Americans arrayed in balletic poses.

18. *Negro History Bulletin* 40 (Mar. 1977): 692–93.

SHELTON: Primitive Self

1. V. Y. Mudimbe, "Which Idea of Africa? Herskovits's Cultural Relativism," *October* 55 (Winter 1990): 93.

2. Louis Aragon, "Fragments d'une conférence," *La Révolution surréaliste*, 4 (July 15, 1925): 25.

3. Catherine Hodeir, "Une Journée à l'Exposition Coloniale," *L'Histoire*, special vol. no. 69, entitled *Le Temps des colonies* (1984): 48.

4. Michel Leiris, "Le Pays de mes rêves," *La Révolution surréaliste*, 2 (Jan. 15, 1925): 16–19.

5. Michel Leiris, *L'Afrique fantôme* (1934; rpt., Paris: Editions Gallimard, 1981), pp. 8–9; my translation, as is the case throughout this essay. Subsequent references are indicated parenthetically in the text.

6. James Clifford, *The Predicament of Culture: Twentieth-Century Ethnography, Literature, and Art* (Cambridge, Mass.: Harvard University Press, 1988), p. 168. Subsequent references are indicated parenthetically in the text.

7. See Odile Tobner, "Les Intellectuels français et l'Afrique," *Peuples Noirs/Peuples Africains*, 13 (Jan.–Feb. 1980): 19–28, and Sally Price, *Primitive Art in Civilized Places* (Chicago: University of Chicago Press, 1989).

8. Philippe Lejeune, *Le Pacte autobiographique* (Paris: Editions du Seuil, 1975), p. 264.

9. George E. Marcus and Michael M. J. Fischer, *Anthropology as Cultural Critique* (Chicago: University of Chicago Press, 1986), pp. 122–25.

10. See Edouard Glissant, "Michel Leiris Ethnographe," *Lettres nouvelles* (Nov. 1956): 609–51.

11. Jacques Darras, "Le Voyage en Afrique: Gide, Conrad, Leiris," *Esprit* 128 (July 1987): 1–12.

12. Alain-Michel Boyer, *Michel Leiris* (Paris: Editions Universitaires, 1974), p. 38.

13. See Paul Rivet and Georges-Henri Rivière, "Mission ethnographique et linguistique Dakar-Djibouti," *Le Minotaure* 1, 2 (1933): 3.

14. *L'Afrique fantôme*, p. 84. Recall that, in its most combative phase, surrealism had conferred a revolutionary and poetic value on blasphemy and sacrilege. However, despite their bold declarations or sexual fantasies, surrealists (as Tobner reminds us; see note 7) never actually desecrated altars and churches in Europe.

15. Price, *Primitive Art in Civilized Places*, pp. 73–74.

16. Trinh T. Minh-Ha, *When the Moon Waxes Red* (London: Routledge, 1991), p. 66.

17. Price, *Primitive Art in Civilized Places*, p. 37.

18. See Rivet and Rivière, "Mission ethnographique," p. 5.

19. Johannes Fabian, *Time and the Other* (New York: Columbia University Press, 1983), p. 174.

M. PERLOFF: Tolerance and Taboo

1. Marianna Torgovnick, *Gone Primitive: Savage Intellects, Modern Lives* (Chicago: University of Chicago Press, 1990), p. 21. Subsequent references are indicated

parenthetically in the text. In *The New York Times Book Review*, June 24, 1990, Arthur C. Danto pronounced *Gone Primitive* "powerful" and "provocative," "a superb book." In *Modern Philology* 89 (Feb. 1992): 437–39, Sander Gilman similarly declares, "Marianna Torgovnick has now provided us all (academic and nonacademic specialists) with a brilliant, exciting, and innovative reading of our 'modern' . . . fascination with the image of the primitive. . . . I put down this book feeling that cultural studies in this country had come a lot further than I had imagined." In "Otherness Is in the Details," *The Nation*, Nov. 5, 1990, pp. 530–36, Micaela di Leonardo, who does comment on some of the book's "key lacunas," calls Torgovnick's goal "laudable," her critique of humanism "valuable," and "her interpretations of the shifting meanings and wildly enhanced monetary value of primitive art . . . particularly acute" (ibid., p. 533).

2. James Clifford, *The Predicament of Culture: Twentieth-Century Ethnography, Literature, and Art* (Cambridge, Mass.: Harvard University Press, 1988), p. 42. Subsequent references are indicated parenthetically in the text.

3. See, for example, Torgovnick, *Gone Primitive*, pp. 17–18. Torgovnick also cites Edward Said and Christopher Miller as ignoring the gender issue. In keeping with her own assessment, Torgovnick's book has been marketed as a "corrective" to Clifford's. In her book blurb on the back jacket of *Gone Primitive*, for example, Catharine R. Stimpson calls the book "an extraordinary account of the ways in which race, gender, and a terrible romance with 'the primitive' have structured Western culture."

4. Leiris is now coming into his own in the United States. See the special number *On Leiris* of *Yale French Studies* 81 (1992), which contains an excerpt of Lydia Davis's new translation of *Fourbis* and essays by Marc Blanchard, Edouard Glissant, Francis Marmande, Jean-Christophe Bailly, Jean-Luc Nancy, Denis Hollier, Leah D. Lewitt, Michèle Richman, and J. B. Pontalis, as well as extracts from earlier essays by Emmanuel Lévinas and Maurice Blanchot. Subsequent references are indicated parenthetically in the text. For a good overview, see Richard Sieburth, "The Librettist of Self," *Times Literary Supplement*, Mar. 5, 1993, pp. 3–4.

5. I have seen all these except the Livre de Poche, for which I owe the relevant information to Philippe Lejeune's important *Lire Leiris* (Paris: Editions Klincksieck, 1975), pp. 109–110. Lejeune points out that the Livre de Poche blowup projects the idea of violence exercised on oneself (Lucrece) onto the figure of Judith, whereas the Folio cardgame image, "ne produit pas pour autant l'effet érotique du nu de Cranach."

6. Michel Leiris, *Manhood*, trans. Richard Howard (San Francisco: North Point, 1984), pp. 94–95; idem, *L'Age d'homme* (Paris: Gallimard, 1939), pp. 142–43.

7. Torgovnick, *Gone Primitive*, p. 111. For a good treatment of the complexity of Leiris's representation, see Michèle Richman, "Leiris's *L'Age d'homme*: Politics and the Sacred in Everyday Ethnography," *Yale French Studies* 81 (1992): 91–110. Richman writes, "In [Leiris's] favorite mythological pantheon, Judith and Lucretia trans-

form their horrific situations into parables of strength, offering dramas in which the victim/executioner relationship is played out with unexpected heroism" (ibid., p. 95). But "the particular mixture of sacred terror and pity [Judith and Lucretia] evoke is tinged with a sense of remorse due to [the narrator's] own cowardice as well as cruelty, which in turn promote the 'crainte superstitieuse d'un châtiment'" (p. 99).

8. Paul Gilroy warns of this ahistoricism (vis-à-vis the treatment of Black Britain) in "Cultural Studies and Ethnic Absolutism," in Lawrence Grossberg, Cary Nelson, and Paula Treichler, eds., *Cultural Studies* (New York and London: Routledge, 1992), pp. 187–98.

9. Cf. Leiris's "Civilization," one of the short pieces written for *Documents* (1929), collected in Michel Leiris, *Brisées* (1966), trans. Lydia Davis (San Francisco: North Point, 1989), p. 19: "However little taste one might have for proposing metaphors as explanations, civilization may be compared without too much inexactness to the thin greenish layer — the living magma and the odd detritus — that forms on the surface of calm water and sometimes solidifies into a crust, until an eddy comes to break it up. All our moral practices and our polite customs, that radiantly colored cloak that hides the coarseness of our dangerous instincts, all those lovely forms of culture we are so proud of — since it is thanks to them that we can call ourselves 'civilized' — are ready to disappear at the slightest turbulence, to shatter at the slightest impact (like the thin mirror on a fingernail whose polish cracks or roughens) allowing our horrifying *primitiveness* to appear in the interstices, revealed by the fissures just as hell might be revealed by earthquakes."

10. Even this assumption is unfounded, since the circumcision practices described at length in the passage Torgovnick cites are those of men, not women.

11. See James Clifford, headnote to section on "Phantom Africa," *Sulfur* 15 (1986): 42 (in "Special Section: New Translations of the Work of Michel Leiris," ed. James Clifford). For the original, see Michel Leiris, *L'Afrique fantôme* (1934; rpt., Paris: Editions Gallimard, 1981), p. 350: "Amertume. Ressentiment contre l'ethnographie, qui fait prendre cette position si inhumaine d'observateur, dans des circonstances où il faudrait s'abandonner." Excerpts from Leiris's *La Possession et ses aspects théâtraux chez les Ethiopiens de Gondar* (1958), which deals specifically with the zâr cult, may be found in Clifford, headnote to "Phantom Africa," pp. 113–17. Subsequent references are indicated parenthetically in the text.

12. John Guillory, *Cultural Capital: The Problem of Literary Canon Formation* (Chicago: The University of Chicago Press, 1993). I am citing from the manuscript, pp. 30–33.

13. Cary Nelson, *Repression and Recovery: Modern American Poetry and the Politics of Cultural Memory* (Madison: University of Wisconsin Press, 1989).

14. Velimir Khlebnikov, "My Own" (1919), cited in Ranier Crone and David Moos, *Kazimir Malevich: The Climax of Disclosure* (Chicago: University of Chicago Press, 1991), p. 137.

15. Cited by Charlotte Douglas, Introduction, *Collected Works of Velimir Khlebnikov: Volume 1, Letters and Theoretical Writings*, trans. Paul Schmidt, ed. Charlotte Douglas (Cambridge and London: Harvard University Press, 1987), p. 8.

16. Michel Leiris, "Glossary: My Glosses' Ossuary" (1925), in idem, *Brisées*, pp. 3–4.

17. Lyn Hejinian, *Oxota: A Short Russian Novel* (Great Barrington, Mass.: The Figures, 1991), p. 235.

K E R M O D E :  Modernism, Postmodernism

1. Ray Monk, *Ludwig Wittgenstein: The Duty of Genius* (New York: Penguin, 1991). Subsequent references are indicated parenthetically in the text.

2. Ludwig Wittgenstein, *Tractatus Logico-Philosophicus*, trans. G. K. Ogden (1922; rpt., London: Routledge & Kegan Paul, 1981), p. 189. Subsequent references are indicated parenthetically in the text.

3. Ludwig Wittgenstein, *Philosophical Investigations*, trans. G. E. M. Anscombe (1953; rpt., New York: Macmillan, 1968), pp. v–vi. Subsequent references are indicated parenthetically in the text.

4. Ferdinand de Saussure, *Course in General Linguistics*, trans. Wade Baskin (New York: McGraw-Hill, 1966), p. 81.

5. Sanford Schwartz, *The Matrix of Modernism: Pound, Eliot, and Early Twentieth-Century Thought* (Princeton, N.J.: Princeton University Press, 1985).

6. See Hans Richter, *Dada: Art and Anti Art* (New York: Oxford University Press, 1978), p. 51. Subsequent references are indicated parenthetically in the text.

7. Jürgen Habermas, "Modernity—an Incomplete Project," in Hal Foster, ed., *Postmodern Culture* (London: Pluto Press, 1985), rpt. in Peter Brooker, ed., *Modernism/Postmodernism* (London: Longman, 1992), pp. 125–38; see p. 128.

# Index

In this index an "f" after a number indicates a separate reference on the next page, and an "ff" indicates separate references on the next two pages. A continuous discussion over two or more pages is indicated by a span of page numbers, e.g., "pp. 57–58." *Passim* is used for a cluster of references in close but not continuous sequence. Bold numbers indicate pages with illustrations.

# Index

# Index

# Index

# Index

# Index

# Index

Library of Congress Cataloging-in-Publication Data

Prehistories of the future : the primitivist project and the culture
    of modernism / edited by Elazar Barkan and Ronald Bush.
        p.      cm. — (Cultural sitings)
    Includes bibliographical references and index.
    ISBN 0-8047-2390-7 (cloth) — ISBN 0-8047-2486-5 (pbk.)
    1. Ethnology—History.   2. Ethnology—Philosophy.   3. Primitivism.
4. Art, Primitive.   5. Modernism.   I. Barkan, Elazar.   II. Bush,
Ronald.   III. Series.
GN345.P74   1995
306—dc20                                                          94-28152
                                                                       CIP


⊗ This book is printed on acid-free, recycled paper.